The Berthier-Delagarde Collection of Crimean Jewellery in the British Museum and Related Material

Júlia Andrási
with contributions by
Aleksander Aibabin
and a sceintific report by
Susan La Niece and Michael Cowell

edited by D. Kidd and B. Ager

**This volume is dedicated to the memory of Dafydd Kidd,
Curator of Continental Early Medieval Antiquities in the
British Museum 1974–1999.**

Publishers

The British Museum
Great Russell Street
London WC1B 3DG

Editor

Josephine Turquet

Distributors

The British Museum Press
46 Bloomsbury Street
London WC1B 3QQ

*The Berthier-Delagarde Collection of Crimean Jewellery
in the British Museum and Related Material*
Júlia Andrási
with contributions by Aleksander Aibabin
and a scientific report by Susan La Niece and Michael Cowell
Edited by D. Kidd and B. Ager

ISBN-13 978-086159-166-4
ISSN 1747-3640
© The Trustees of the British Museum 2008
Front Cover: brooch decorated with cloisonné garnets and
granulation, dated to the end of 4th–first half of 5th century AD,
Catalogue number 15.

Note: the British Museum Occasional Papers series is now entitled
British Museum Research Publications. The OP series runs from
1 to 150, and the RP series, keeping the same ISBN preliminary
numbers, begins at number 151.

For a complete list of all published titles of OPs and RPs see the
series website: www/the britishmuseum.ac.uk/
researchpublications

For titles in print visit www.britishmuseum.org/shop
Trade orders to:
Oxbow Books, Park End Place
Oxford OX1 1HN, UK
Tel: (+44) (0) 1865 241249
e mail oxbow@oxbowbooks.com
website www.oxbowbooks.com
or
The David Brown Book Co
PO Box 511, Oakville
CT 06779, USA
Tel: (+1) 860 945 9329; Toll free 1 800 791 9354
e mail david.brown.bk.co@snet.net

Printed and bound in UK by Short Run Press Limited

Contents

Acknowledgements

The author of the catalogue wishes to thank Neil Phillips and his widow Sharon for generously funding her research and also the Hungarian Soros Scholarship Foundation for their sponsorship right from the start, which enabled her to begin her study of the Berthier-Delagarde Collection. She is especially indebted to D.S.W. Kidd, Assistant Keeper (since retired) in the former Department of Medieval & Later Antiquities, the British Museum, for providing the topic, for permission to work on the collection under his supervision, helping with the text and illustrations, and for bringing the work together. Thanks are due also to the following individuals: Dr L. Pekarska for her advice and for extracting important information from Ukrainian archives; Professor A.I. Aibabin, Tavrida National University, Simferopol, for his scholarly contributions to the catalogue; N. Stratford, who was Keeper of the former Department of Medieval & Later Antiquities, the British Museum, when she began work on the catalogue and gave it his approval and support; Professor I. Bóna, Loránd-Eötvös University, Budapest, for help in obtaining her scholarship and continuing support and advice on many queries relating to the objects in the catalogue; S.C. La Niece, M. Cowell, Dr P.T. Craddock, N.D. Meeks of the former Department of Scientific Research, the British Museum, for their rigorous scientific and technical analyses of the material; Dr F. Daim, Generaldirektor, Römisch-Germanisches Museum, Mainz, Dr T. Vida, Magyar Tudományos Akadémia, Budapest, and Dr É. Garam, her former tutor, and Dr. A. Kiss, both researching parallel material in the Magyar Nemzeti Múzeum, Budapest, all for their advice; Dr D.J.R. Williams, former Keeper of the Department of Greek and Roman Antiquities, the British Museum, for permission to study objects from the collection in the department and additional information; C. Haith, Research Assistant (since retired) in the former Department of Medieval & Later Antiquities, for helping Mr. Kidd to compile a Summary Catalogue of the Continental Early Medieval Collection, including an inventory of the Eastern European finds; J. Farrant, Senior Illustrator, for drawing all the illustrations of the material in the collection with careful regard to her requests and mounting the photographs prior to the introduction of scanning; and P. Stringer, Photographer, for the photography. A final debt of gratitude is owed to B.M. Ager for assistance with the text, enabling her to continue the work even when in Budapest, and to Dr J. Turquet, British Museum Research Publications, for seeing the book to press.

Note: The work on the material in this volume was completed in 1998 and does not therefore contain references to work published after that date.

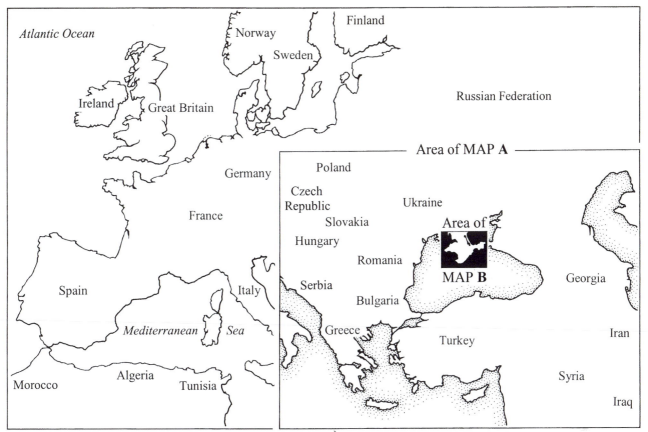

Location map of Europe to show the areas covered by Maps A and B

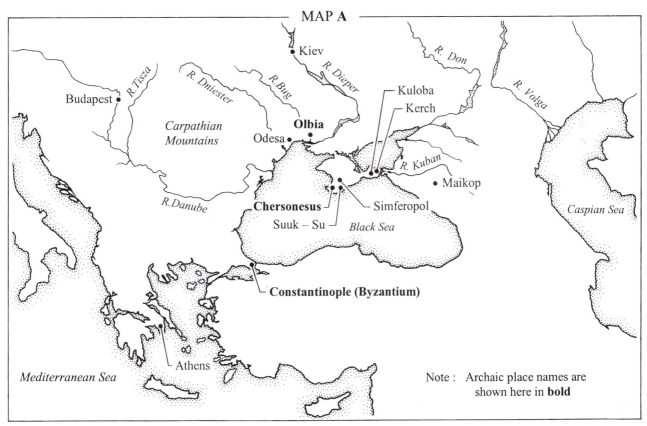

Map A The Carpathian Basin and Black Sea region

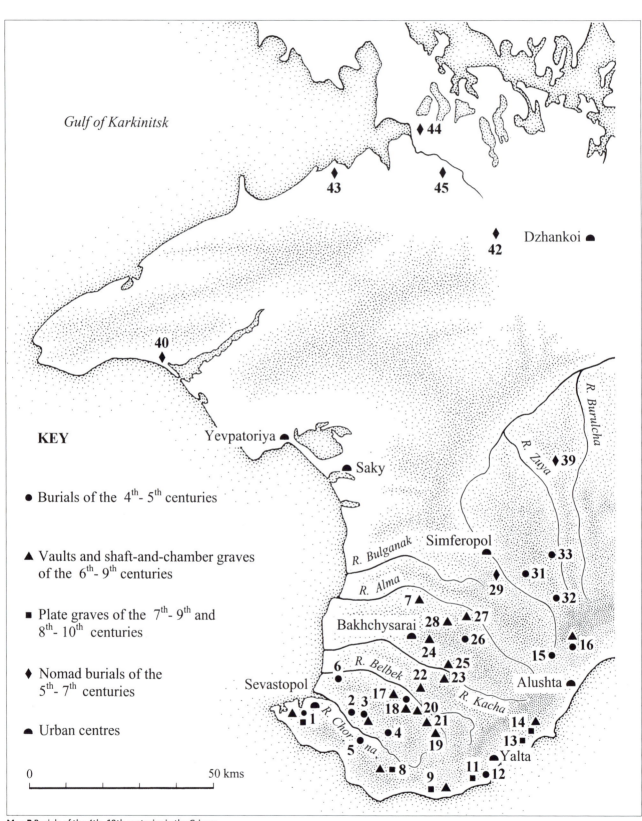

Gulf of Karkinitsk

♦ **44**

♦ **43**   ♦ **45**

♦ **42**   Dzhankoi ◖

♦ **40**

Yevpatoriya ◖

◖ Saky

R. *Burulcha*

R. *Zuya*

♦ **39**

KEY

● Burials of the 4th - 5th centuries

▲ Vaults and shaft-and-chamber graves of the 6th - 9th centuries

■ Plate graves of the 7th - 9th and 8th - 10th centuries

♦ Nomad burials of the 5th - 7th centuries

◖ Urban centres

Simferopol ◖

● **33**

● **31**

♦ **29**

● **32**

R. *Bulganak*

R. *Alma*

▲ **7**

28 ▲   ▲ **27**

Bakhchysarai ◖

● **26**

24 ▲

▲ **25**

22 ▲   ▲ **23**

● **15**   ▲
● **16**

6 ●   R. *Belbek*

Alushta ◖

Sevastopol

2 ● **3**   **17** ▲   R. *Kacha*

▲ **18** ▲   ▲ **20**

▲ **1**   R. *Chor na*   ▲ **21**

● **4**   **19** ▲

14 ● ▲

● **5**   **13** ■

Yalta ◖

▲ ■ **8**   **9**   **11** ▲
■   ▲   ● **12**

0   50 kms

Map B Burials of the 4th–10th centuries in the Crimea

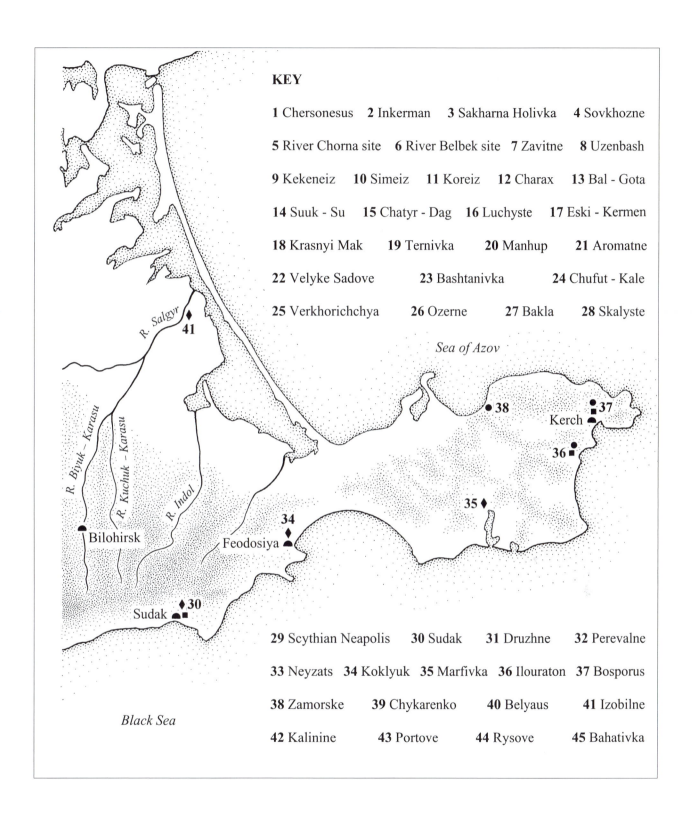

KEY

1 Chersonesus   2 Inkerman   3 Sakharna Holivka   4 Sovkhozne

5 River Chorna site   6 River Belbek site   7 Zavitne   8 Uzenbash

9 Kekeneiz   10 Simeiz   11 Koreiz   12 Charax   13 Bal - Gota

14 Suuk - Su   15 Chatyr - Dag   16 Luchyste   17 Eski - Kermen

18 Krasnyi Mak   19 Ternivka   20 Manhup   21 Aromatne

22 Velyke Sadove   23 Bashtanivka   24 Chufut - Kale

25 Verkhorichchya   26 Ozerne   27 Bakla   28 Skalyste

Sea of Azov

R. Salgyr

41

R. Biyuk – Karasu

R. Kuchuk – Karasu

R. Indol

38

37
Kerch

36

35

34

Bilohirsk

Feodosiya

♦**30**
Sudak

Black Sea

29 Scythian Neapolis   30 Sudak   31 Druzhne   32 Perevalne

33 Neyzats   34 Koklyuk   35 Marfivka   36 Ilouraton   37 Bosporus

38 Zamorske   39 Chykarenko   40 Belyaus   41 Izobilne

42 Kalinine   43 Portove   44 Rysove   45 Bahativka

Map B continued Burials of the 4th–10th centuries in the Crimea

General Background to the Collection

Aleksander Aibabin

The geographical background of the Crimea

The Crimean peninsula is situated on the northern coast of the Black Sea (Pontus), and has a total area of 26,000km². The north-eastern coast of the peninsula is washed by the Sea of Azov (Lake Maeotis) and the Sivash lowland extends in the north from the Perekop Isthmus to the Tongue of Arabat. Its dramatically indented northern shore is washed by the Sivash, a shallow lagoon which has a deep bed of silt and forms an extension of the Sea of Azov. A sandbar separates it from a number of shallow lakes. High air temperatures lead to the evaporation of the salt water in the lagoon and lakes, and the concentration of salts in the water reaches 17%. In ancient times salt was extracted from the lakes and was exported round the whole northern Black Sea shore. The north-western part of the Crimea terminates in the Tarkhankut Peninsula, and the eastern part in the Kerch Peninsula, separated from the Taman Peninsula to the east by the Strait of Kerch. The distance from Perekop in the north to Cape Sarych in the south is 195km, and from Cape Tarkhankut in the west to the Strait of Kerch is 325km. Since ancient times the shallow Sea of Azov and the bays of Karkinitska and Yevpatoriya, all warmed by the sun, have been famous for an abundance of commercial fish such as herring, khamsa (called anchovy by the ancient Greeks and Byzantines), steer, mackerel, grey mullet, beluga (white sturgeon), sturgeon and stellate sturgeon. Other sea-food included Black Sea crabs, oysters and mussels. Crab claws were used as adornments in the early-medieval period.

The Crimea consists of two topographical regions: the plain and the mountains. The plain forms part of the Black Sea coastal steppe, and is connected to it by means of the Perekop Isthmus. There are few rivers in this region: the Kacha (69km), Alma (84km), and western Bulganak (52km) rise on the north-western slopes of the mountains, cross the Alma plain and flow into the Black Sea. The longest river, the Salgyr (238km), crosses the foothills and the plain and flows into the Sivash. In summer the rivers are almost completely dry. The steppes, with their low humus blackearth and chestnut-coloured earth, are suitable for arable farming, but the hot, dry climate has prevented its development there. Beginning in the 1st millennium BC a succession of nomadic tribes arrived to pasture their cattle seasonally on the Crimean steppes, transferring their herds in the early spring when succulent fresh grass appeared. In summer the grass withered under the sun, and the nomads drove their herds to the high-water flood meadows situated on the steppes along the coasts of the northern Black Sea and the Sea of Azov.

The Crimean mountains extend for 160km along the southern and south-eastern shores, from the Heraclean Peninsula on the outskirts of Sevastopol to the village of Koktebel near Feodosiya (ancient Theodosia). They consist of three ridges: the First, or main, Ridge is the highest (1,200–

1,545m above sea level), and adjoins the narrow southern coast; the Second Ridge consists of foothills rising to 600–700m; and the Third, outer, Ridge, extending from Cape Feolent to Simferopol, rises to 250m. In the north it borders the steppe.

The mountains of the Second and Third Ridges are concentric, and consist of limestone. Their south-facing slopes are steep, and precipitous in parts, while the northern slopes are gentle, and both are covered with forest-steppe. Both ridges have numerous gentle slopes, or flat terraces, covered with blackearth soil forming highland plateaux well-suited for arable farming. The area between the First and Third Ridges contains the fertile, blackearth valleys of the rivers Chorna (Chernaya), Belbek, Kacha, Alma, and Salgyr, with their tributaries and numerous springs. To the north of Sevastopol the Chorna and Belbek rivers form extensive, fertile flood plains where they flow into the Black Sea. Soft wheat, large-grained rye and barley were grown.[1] Near the hillforts, open settlements and monasteries of the early-medieval period wild grapevines grow. Market-gardening, horticulture, viticulture and wine production developed, and in many hillforts evidence for wineries has been found.

The First Ridge consists mainly of marl, limestone, shale and, to a lesser extent, sandstone and conglomerate. The highest mountain, Roman-Kosh rises above Hurzuf (Gurzuf), reaching a height of 1,545m. The ridge declines abruptly and ends near the town of Staryi Krym. The high mountain massif of the First Ridge descends steeply into the sea. Its tops are smooth, creating flat plateaus called the 'yayla' (mountain pasture). They are covered with lush, rich meadow grass, and were used for transhumant cattle-breeding. Forests extend on the northern slopes from the spurs of Ay-Petri to Staryi Krym.

The southern coast extends from Cape Sarych to Sudak. This comprises the southern slope of the First Ridge, which has a width of 3–6km, and a narrow coastal strip of sand and pebble, some 5–60m wide. The foot of the slope is covered with bushes and low forest consisting mainly of juniper and oak trees. The coastal part of the slope is traversed to the shore line by ridges of slate and limestone with deep ravines. Only small patches of land are suitable for arable farming and there are few fresh-water springs. The arid slope to the east of Alushta, along to the coast near Feodosiya, is everywhere traversed by ridges and ravines. It should be noted that features of the modern relief along the southern coast differ from those of the early-medieval period. Due to earthquakes and landslides, which still occur today, the medieval ground surface has been covered with thick layers of soil from the upper terraces. The mountain roads and paths, which take advantage of passes through the First Ridge, unite the uplands and the southern coast into one region known as highland Crimea.

The combination of steppe and mountains, the natural connection with the Eurasian steppe to the north, and the maritime environment on three sides of the Crimea contributed both to the influx of nomadic peoples and to the impact of cultures from the Mediterranean region.

A summary of the ethnic history of the Crimea

The Classical background

The Crimea became part of the of ancient Greek sphere of interest in the 7th century BC. In the last decades of the century and at the beginning of the 6th, Greek colonists founded an emporium on the shores of the Strait of Kerch, which grew into the city of Panticapaeum (Παντιχάπης – the 'fish way'). In the 6th century BC Theodosia was founded on the east coast, Cercinitis (modern Yevpatoriya) on the west coast, and, at the end of the century, Chersonesus, later known to the Byzantines as Cherson (**Map B:1**), was established on the shore of a bay in the south-west. Very soon the Greeks colonised the Kerch Peninsula and the territory between Chersonesus and Cercinitis, founding a number of small towns and settlements and, in 480 BC, the Greek towns on the Kerch and Taman Peninsulas united to form the state of Bosporus. Its capital was at Panticapaeum and the same name was applied by ancient writers to the Kerch Peninsula, to the Strait of Kerch, and to the state itself. In the 4th century BC, however, Demosthenes used the name for the port of Panticapaeum.[2] From the 1st century AD, in the works of Roman and Byzantine writers such as Pliny the Younger, Zosimus, Stephen the Byzantine, Procopius of Caesarea, and others, the city of Panticapaeum was called Bosporus (**Map B: 37**).

During the 3rd century BC the Iranian-speaking Scythians, who led a nomadic way of life, settled in the Crimean foothills. A Scythian state developed with its capital at Scythian Neapolis (**Map B:29**), a site which has been identified with the Petrine Rocks in Simferopol.

During the 1st century AD the southern border of the Bosporan kingdom lay somewhere near Theodosia. The late-Scythian state occupied the highlands of the Third Ridge, from the outskirts of Theodosia to the fertile lower reaches of the rivers Chorna, Belbek, Kacha and Alma. The Heraclean Peninsula belonged to Chersonesus. At the very beginning of the 1st millennium AD the Iranian-speaking Sarmatians first appeared in the Crimea,[3] and, from the 2nd century, began to play an important part in Bosporus.[4] In the south-western Crimea they lived alongside the Scythians in the same hillforts, and buried their dead in the same cemeteries.[5]

Between 63 and 66 AD, at the request of the Chersonites, the Roman administration sent an army under Plautius Silvanus from Lower Moesia to the Black Sea coast. The Romans built the fortress of Charax on the southern coast (**Map B:12**) and quartered a garrison there.[6] The Bosporan kingdom became politically dependent upon the Empire[7] and, from the 2nd century AD, the Roman garrison in Chersonesus tightened its control of the coast and the adjoining part of highland Crimea. Small Roman garrisons appeared on the shores of Balaklava Bay and in the Scythian hillfort of Alma-Kermen at Zavitne (Zavetnoye), on the left bank of the River Alma (**Map B:7**).[8]

From the 1st century AD the Alans and Sarmatians (groups of Iranian-speaking, Indo-European nomads) were living between the lower reaches of the Volga and Don and in the northern and eastern Azov regions, as far as the middle reaches of the River Kuban. Cemeteries of the 1st to 2nd centuries in this region contained barrows covering a long entrance-pit (*dromos*) with a burial chamber and side-chambers.[9] The tombstone of Iraque, chief translator in Hermonassa, testifies to the fact that at the beginning of the third century, under King Sauromatus II (173/174–210/211), there were active relations between the Kingdom of Bosporus and the Alans.[10] Rostovtzev considered that it was the peaceful penetration of Bosporus by the Alans and Sarmatians in the first half of the century which led to the Iranicization of this state. Its inhabitants, including their rulers, had Iranian names, wore Sarmatian and Alanic clothing, and used the same Alanic pottery as that found on the banks of the Rivers Don and Kuban.[11]

In the first half of the 3rd century various Germanic tribes invaded the northern Black Sea coast.[12] According to Jordanes, they first settled near the northern shores of Maeotis in lands occupied by the Alans and Sarmatians.[13] A group of Alans from the Azov region joined the Germans, while the rest moved to the Crimea. According to written sources both Alans and Sarmatians participated in Gothic raids on the Danubian border provinces of the Roman Empire after 242.[14] Driven from the Azov region by the Germans, the Alans probably occupied those regions of the Crimea which were not occupied by the Scythians in the 2nd century and the first half of the 3rd. Near the slopes of the Crimean Third Ridge, Alanic cemeteries appeared in the second quarter of the 3rd century (**Map B: 31, 33**). Vaults and graves with burials in side niches have been excavated. They differ from the late-Scythian ones, but were typical of the Alans of the Azov region and Dagestan. Dark-clay pottery vessels, covered with a black burnish, have been found in them, similar to pots manufactured by the Alans of those regions.[15]

In the 240s, while attempting to reinforce the Danube frontier, the Romans changed their military policy towards the Crimea.[16] They withdrew their garrisons from highland Crimea and Bosporus, a new situation which the Germans exploited.[17] The Chronicle of John Zonaras, a 12th-century writer, records that, after pillaging in Italy, Macedonia and Greece during the reigns of Trebonianus Gallus and Volusianus (252–253), a group of 'Scythians' (Germans), had reached Bosporus and crossed the Sea of Azov, devastating several towns.[18] According to Zosimus the Germans seized the city of Bosporus in 256.[19] At that time the Germans and Alans probably moved to the south-western Crimea, where they destroyed the late-Scythian settlements and their capital at Neapolis.[20] The Germans settled the lower reaches of the River Chorna and the southern coast, and cemeteries with typically Germanic cremation burials appeared there (**Map B: 5, 12, 15**).[21] The Alans allied with the Germans and settled in the western, European, part of Bosporus and in the south-western Crimea.

The migration period

The period of the Great Migration began with the invasion of the northern Caucasus region by the Huns in 370–375.[22] Some scholars consider that they were Turkish neighbours of China who began their westward migration in 155–160,[23] although others deny any connection between the Hunnic and Turkic languages. According to Ammianus Marcellinus, during the reign of the Emperor Valens (364–378) the Huns conquered both the Tanaite Alans on the lower reaches of the Don, and the Goths under Ermanaric on the steppes of the northern Black Sea coast.[24] According to Zosimus, in the 13th year of the reign of Valens in 376, they expelled a section of the Goths and their allies, who then crossed the Danube into the Roman provinces.[25] Many Byzantine historians tell a story about the Huns hunting for a bull or fallow deer, when they saw the Bosporan Strait, crossed it, and appeared on the western, European coast; by all accounts during the reign of Valens. Probably only a small group of Huns crossed the strait on their move to the West.[26] No sign of destruction at the end of the 4th century has been revealed either at Kerch, the capital of the Bosporan state, or in smaller towns and settlements. Nor are there any Hunnic burials of this period in the Crimea.[27]

The Huns engaged in nomadic cattle-raising on the steppes they had conquered.[28] The diversity of burial rite testifies to the polyethnicity of the barbarians who had joined the Hunnic alliance, which included those Alans and Germans who had remained on the Black Sea coast. Objects decorated in the new polychrome style came into fashion among them and in the territories controlled by the Huns. These were gold adornments of solid metal, or with gold foil overlay, and inlaid with red garnets, which became widespread from the end of the 4th century until the beginning of the 6th. They included female jewellery, such as diadems, temporal pendants, and bracelets, as well as male belt- and shoe-buckles, belt-ends, sword- and dagger-mounts, and horse-harness fittings.

At the beginning of the 5th century the Huns, who were firmly established on the northern Black Sea coast, began to use the Crimean steppe for the seasonal pasturing of their cattle.[29] To these groups belong the nomad burials with polychrome goods which have been discovered in the eastern Crimea near Feodosiya on the mountain of Koklyuk (**Map B:34**), in Stepnoye at the former Kalinin kolkhoz (**Map B:42**), and at Belyaus (**Map B:40**). At the same time the Alans left the high ground of the Third Ridge bordering on the steppe and moved away to the mountains, for fear of their new neighbours. The Alanic cemeteries at Neyzats and Druzhne (Druzhnoye) (**Map B:33** and **31**) were abandoned. In the south-west of the Crimea a further group of cemeteries with vaults and graves constructed in typically Alan fashion appears at this time, e.g. Skalyste (Skalistoye) (**Map B:28**), Bakla (**Map B:27**), and Luchyste (Luchistoye) (**Map B:16**).[30] Deprived of their steppe pastures, the Alans had to master a new type of pastoral economy and radically alter their way of life. Because the mountain pastures were not very extensive they began to employ transhumance in cattle-raising, reduced the size of their herds, and changed their agricultural strategy. In the spring, summer, and warm autumn months they drove their herds to the mountain pastures, while for the rest of the year they grazed them near the settlements. Usually they raised sheep, cattle and horses, but arable farming became more significant, involving the cultivation of soft wheat, barley and large-grained rye.[31]

The Alans of the Crimea entered the sphere of political interest of Rome in the East, as the Emperors tried to strengthen their position in the region. An inscription of 370–375 from Chersonesus records the quartering of a detachment of 'ballistarii' in the city, while another of 387–388 records the presence there of an army commanded by the tribune Flavius Vitus.[32] Under Theodosius I the city walls were fortified.

Constantinople played a major part in the conversion of the local barbarians to Christianity. In 381 the ecclesiastical diocese of Cherson was in existence, spreading Christianity among the population of highland Crimea.[33] At the end of the 7th century that region still remained part of the diocese.[34] Having accepted Christianity, the Crimean Goths probably rejected cremation in the mid-5th century and adopted an Alanic burial rite more appropriate to their new religion. They abandoned their old burial grounds and began to bury their dead in the cemeteries of the Alans. The latter in their turn adopted the fashion for Gothic jewellery, such as brooches and buckles.

After the death of Attila in 453, and the defeat of the Huns at the battle on the River Nedao in Pannonia in 454, their alliance collapsed.[35] According to Jordanes many of its tribes returned to the Black Sea coast, where the Goths had lived previously. Jordanes mentions the Hunnic tribe of the Altziagiri on the steppe near Cherson.[36] According to Procopius, the steppe between Cherson and Bosporus was occupied by the Hunnic Kutrigurs.[37] The nomad burials at Chykarenko (**Map B:39**), Marfivka (Marfovka) (**Map B:35**), and Izobilne (Izobilnoye) (**Map B:41**) should be attributed to them.

Byzantines and Goths
Byzantine historians record the activities of Byzantium in the Crimea under the Emperor Justinian I (527–565). Gord, the ruler of the Bosporan Huns, was baptised in Constantinople during the very first year of Justinian's reign, and this act signified the transfer of the tribes under his control to that of the Empire. He returned to Bosporus with a detachment of Germans, who had been recruited in Spain, under the command of the tribune Delmatius, but a group of Huns who refused to accept Christianity seized the city and crushed the Byzantine garrison. The Emperor then sent two detachments of Gothic federates from Moesia to Bosporus under John, Count of the Euxine Shore, and the officers Godila and Baduria. They brought the city back under Byzantine rule[38] and Justinian ordered the fortification of the walls of Cherson and Bosporus. On the southern coast the fortresses of Aluston and Gorzubiti were built,[39] probably to protect coastal shipping.[40]

In the 6th century the way of life of the nomads who had returned to the northern Black Sea after the break-up of the Hunnic alliance is described by Jordanes: 'The Altziagiri roam from place to place over the steppe in summer, dependant on [where] forage for their cattle might be; in winter, returning to the Pontic sea, [they live] near Cherson where the greedy merchant brings his goods from Asia'.[41] It follows from this that the Altziagiri pastured their cattle to the west of the Sea of Azov on the Pontic steppe, which, according to Procopius, belonged to the Kutrigurs. Each writer probably used different names for the same nomads, and in the first half of the 6th century the descendants of the Huns were at the same stage of nomadic existence as their predecessors. In spring the Kutrigurs pastured their cattle on the Crimean steppe, where, following the spring rains, the grass grew thick and lush. The heat of summer then dried up the small rivers and the grass withered, forcing the Kutrigurs to move to new pastures on the flood-plains of the lower reaches of the Rivers Dnieper and Bug. In late autumn they returned to their winter settlements in the Crimea. The nomads sold furs and other goods in Bosporus5.[42] Burials with Kutrigur grave goods of the 6th to 7th centuries have been discovered on the Crimean steppe and in the lower reaches of the Rivers Dnieper and Bug. They were buried in pits dug into existing barrows and then covered with wood, the bodies being orientated with the head to the north-east or north-west.[43]

According to Procopius the Goths lived in the territory of Dori, situated 'on this coast', i.e. on the same shore of the Black Sea as Cherson, Bosporus and Gorzubiti.[44] He describes the territory of the Goths in three paragraphs:

> 15. The region of Dori itself is in the highlands. The soil is neither stony nor dry, but very good, and gives good fruit. 16. In this territory the Emperor did not built any towns or fortresses because the people cannot bear to be kept inside walls, liking best of all to live on the plains. 17. As it seemed their country is easy of access, having protected these passes with long walls he saved them from anxiety about the intrusion of enemies.[45]

According to the text of paragraph 16, the coast between the fortresses of Aluston and Gorzubiti should not be considered part of the territory of Dori, since we know that the Emperor did not build fortresses there. The narrow strip of coast from Hurzuf to Foros, some 2.5–3km wide, also differs from the description in paragraphs 15–17. Its steep slope, traversed by ravines and several small rivers, and with its detrital soils, could hardly be a fertile plain fit for intensive arable farming. It could not have supported the families of the three thousand warriors, which, according to Procopius, was the number of the Goths ready to muster on the Emperor's summons.[46] A single archaeological culture has been revealed belonging to the combined population of Alans and Goths on the southern coast and in highland Crimea. It was clearly this territory which was called the country of Dori, i.e. the fertile land in the regions of the Rivers Chorna, Belbek, Kacha and Alma flowing through the mountains (which are not very high), and the plateaus of the Second and Third Ridges. The plateaus themselves approximate to those described by Procopius.

In the Latin *Grammar* of Priscian, written earlier than the works of Procopius (during the reign of Anastasius 491–518), two exercises mention a town of Dori near the Pontus. In neither example does the author give the precise location of the town, which he describes in different ways. In one case it is called 'Dory ... nomen oppidi Pontici', and in the other 'hoc Dory ... nomina civitatium'.[47] It is quite obvious that both examples are borrowed from some historical or geographical treatise which mentioned the '*oppidum*', or '*civitas*', of Dori, situated in the Pontic region. The use of the same name for both the *oppidum* and the region suggests the location of the former within the latter. In more recent sources, narrating events from the beginning of the 8th century and its second half, information is given about the fortress of Dori-Doras in Gothic territory.[48] From this we may assume that the *oppidum* of Dori sprang up in the Gothic region before the end of the 5th century, and that a fortress was built in the post-Justinianic period, but before the beginning of the 7th century. Only on the fairly inaccessible plateau of Manhup (**Map B:20**) have farms been discovered which are contemporary with the Dori of

Priscian, and objects associated with a fortification of the second half of the 6th to 8th centuries.[49] This is probably the location of the *oppidum* of Dori.

In his treatise, *De Aedificiis,* Procopius names the inhabitants of the mountains, the Goths, as allies of the Romans, who, in response to the wishes of the Emperor, took part in all his military campaigns.[50] Procopius says of the inhabitants of Dori:

> Being up to 3,000 in number they are perfect in military matters, and in agriculture in which they themselves are active, and they are the most hospitable among peoples.[51]

According to Firsov, in the mid-6th century the population did not exceed 60,000.[52] Dozens of cemeteries of this period have been discovered, testifying to the large population of Dori. Such cemeteries were situated on the slopes, as at Luchyste, Suuk-Su (**Map B:14**), Kekeneiz (**Map B:9**), Koreiz (**Map B:11**), Simeiz (**Map B:10**), in the ravine of Karalez at Manhup, Chufut-Kale (**Map B:24**), near the Chernaya Rechka (**Map B:5**), on the slope of the height of Sakharna Holivka (Sakharnaya Golovka) (**Map B:3**), and in other places. Near the cemeteries at Hurzuf and other sites the associated rural settlements have been discovered.[53] In the paragraph quoted above Procopius describes the inhabitants as warriors and farmers, who cultivated the soil with their own hands, and without slave labour.[54] The grave-goods from their cemeteries show no evidence of great wealth, or social differentiation. Their status as allies of Byzantium encouraged the retention of military democracy in the rural communities of Dori.[55]

In 576 the Turks with their allies, the Utigurs, seized Bosporus,[56] and in 581 they threatened Cherson.[57] Influenced by these events, during the last years of his reign Justin II (565–578) built a wall and tower in Cherson.[58] Under the Emperor Maurice (582–602) the Duke of Cherson restored imperial authority in Bosporus in 590.[59] The material from excavations in highland Crimea testifies to the fact that, under these emperors, fortresses were erected on the plateaus of Manhup, Eski-Kermen (**Map B:17**),[60] Chufut-Kale,[61] and Bakla (**Map B:27**). From the text of the Historia Syntomas ('Breviaria') of Nikephoros we may conclude that these were the residences of the archons.[62] By the beginning of the 8th century these fortresses had probably become the centres of administrative districts, and were most likely under the jurisdiction of Cherson. Byzantium also used the fortresses as places for holding exiles. In his *Collectanea* Anastasius the Librarian gives the names of Euprepius (died 655) and Theodorus (died 667), who were exiled first to Cherson and later to the strongholds of neighbouring tribes.[63] The garrisons of such fortresses were recruited from among the Alans and the Crimean Goths, and the soldiers lived there with their families.[64] They produced moulded pottery, grew cereals, and engaged in cattle-raising and horticulture for their own needs. At Eski-Kermen and Bakla they cut dozens of pits into the rock to store grain. Beginning probably in the 7th century, the Alans acquired the skill of wine-making. Byzantine amphorae, red-slipped pottery vessels, and glass brought from Cherson in the second half of the 6th and 7th centuries, have been found during excavation of the fortresses.

The Empire attempted to strengthen the position of the Church in the south-western Crimea. It was probably to further this aim that, at the end of the 6th to 7th centuries, the

Byzantines built large basilicas in almost all the fortresses mentioned above, with the exception of Bakla. A large, three-naved basilica has been discovered in an early-medieval settlement in the upper Karalez ravine.[65] A.L. Yakobson thought that monumental buildings in the south-western Crimea were built by gangs of masons from Cherson.[66] In the 6th century churches were also built by rural communities.[67] Christian symbolism became very popular after the mid-6th century: the Alans wore buckles and finger-rings with symbols such as monograms and crosses, and amulets. There were changes in burial practice, too: from the beginning of the 7th century Christian gravestones begin to appear in the cemeteries of highland Crimea. The burial ceremony differed slightly from that of the previous period[68] and the Roman Pope Martin I, exiled to Cherson in 655, called the inhabitants of the region adjoining the city pagans.[69]

Byzantine policy stimulated the assimilation process in highland Crimea. In the 6th to 7th centuries the Alans and Goths shared the same burial rite and costume. Alan women wore contemporary Germanic fashion such as temporal pendants, brooches and wide belts fastened by eagle-headed buckles, and also a wide variety of small Byzantine buckles, or large buckles with attachment-plates decorated in repoussé with crosses, lions or tigers. Warriors were armed with daggers, narrow, single-edged broadswords, or sabres with slightly curved, single-edged blades.[70]

The steppe nomads
Around 630 Organ and Kuvrat united the nomads of the northern Black Sea coastal steppe into Great Bulgaria. Following Kuvrat's death, and due to the activities of his sons, Great Bulgaria disintegrated into five tribes between 642–668. One of his sons, Batbaian, inherited pastures with his tribe on the eastern coast of the Sea of Azov and on the northern coast of the Black Sea. Soon afterwards Batbaian and his Bulgars were subjugated by the Khazars who came from Berzilia,[71] an area located either in northern Dagestan,[72] or in the general north-west Caspian region.[73]

Oriental historians bear witness to the Turkish origins of the Khazars,[74] whose name is connected with the Ko-sa tribe of the Blue Turks.[75] From the 630s the ruler of the Khazars was called a 'khagan'.[76] In the 660s the Khazars still retained their nomadic economy, roaming the steppe all year round, and, greedy for new pastures, they seized those of the Bulgars in the steppes of the Azov and Black Sea regions.[77] Barrows over Khazar graves with niches in the side walls appeared on the lower reaches of the Dnieper and Bug, and in the Crimean steppe, in the last quarter of the 7th century. In the entrance pit was buried a horse with its harness and, in a niche with the head orientated to the north-east, a man with a weapon or a woman with her jewellery.[78] The accompanying grave-goods indicate the social status of their owners. In the graves of ordinary warriors simple copper-alloy belt-sets are found. At sites such as Portove (**Map B:43**) and Syvashivka (Sivashovka), rich warriors were buried with weapons, gold or silver belt-sets, bridled horses, and grey-ware vessels.[79] The Khazars chose the lower Dnieper region for the burial of their khagans, e.g. at Pereshchepino, and the graves of military chiefs were discovered at Hladkivka (Kelegei), Yasinovo, and Novi Sanzhary (Novyye Senzhary). At Glodosy and Voznesensk

funerary temples have been excavated similar to those built in Mongolia and Tuva at the end of the 7th and first half of the 8th centuries to commemorate Turkish khagans.[80]

The war with the Bulgars culminated in a Khazar attack on Byzantine towns on both shores of the Bosporan Strait, where archaeological excavations show evidence of destruction in the last quarter of the 7th century. At the same time several neighbouring small towns perished. The narrative of Theophanes and Nikephoros regarding the exile of Justinian II to Cherson in 695 indicates that the Khazars seized the whole of the Crimea. In 704 the exiled Emperor escaped to the Gothic fortress at Doros (Manhup), where, beyond the reach of the Byzantine administration, he took the opportunity to make contact with the khagan of Khazaria. The latter permitted him to settle in Phanagoria and gave him his sister as wife. In response to a request from the Emperor, however, the khagan ordered his provincial governor there and the archon of Bosporus to kill Justinian. But he managed to escape and regain power in Constantinople.[81] A *'ha-pakid'*, a provincial governor who ruled Bosporus for the khagan, is mentioned in a document now kept in Cambridge. In ancient Hebrew the word means 'the chief of a detachment or garrison'.[82] The walls of the citadel built by the Khazars have been excavated in the maritime area of the city.[83] They even seized Cherson, for in 711 a punitive expedition sent to the city by Justinian II captured a Khazar *'tudun'* there,[84] a senior administrator close to the khagan.[85]

Under Khazar pressure in the last quarter of the 7th century the Bulgars under Batbaian began a migration to the eastern and central parts of the Crimea. In Bosporus they settled next to the Khazar citadel in the maritime quarter. There, over the ruins of the Byzantine period, they built houses with five walls and fenced yards lacking any regular planning. The walls of the houses are laid on stone foundations in the so-called 'herring-bone' style, using clay for mortar. The Bulgars were accustomed to such masonry in the eastern-Caucasus region.[86] There were domestic buildings and hearths in the yards. It should be noted that in other districts of the city the Alan and Greek Christian population survived.

From the end of the 7th century the Bulgars, deprived of their steppe pastures, adopted a mixed arable-pastoral type of economy. They divided up the land not occupied by the Alans and Goths among their families. On the Kerch Peninsula and in the foothills settlements arose with yurt-shaped dwellings, half dug into the earth,[87] with moulded pottery characteristic of the Bulgars.[88]

On the coast of south-eastern Crimea the Byzantines founded a craft and trading settlement at Sogdaia (Sudak) (**Map B:30**), which is first mentioned in the Anonymous *Ravenna Cosmography* of the 7th century as 'Sugdabon'.[89] The earliest seal found there dates to the beginning of the 8th century and belonged to Kyriakos *'apo hyparton'*, the chief logothete of Constantinople.[90] Under the patriarch German the new diocese of Sogdaia was established and, in 740, Bishop Stephen (known as Saint Stephen of Surozh after his canonization) arrived in Sogdaia from Cappadocia.[91]

After the mid-8th century new Bulgar tribes moved into the Crimea, which was controlled by the Khazars following a crushing defeat inflicted on the khaganate by the Arabs in the Dagestan steppes.[92] Dozens of new settlements emerged in these areas of the peninsula. Their house-walls were built in herring-bone style and the yards were fenced. Cemeteries with typical Bulgar burials in pits containing wooden coffins have been found near the settlements. The Crimean economy began to grow rapidly and the Bulgars adopted farming, which became the basis of their economy.[93] Blacksmithing, spinning, weaving, and the manufacture of jewellery, pottery and glass developed. Trade developed with the territory of the Crimean Goths and large workshops with several kilns for the manufacture of amphorae and jugs were established, whose products are found in all Bulgar settlements.[94] Jewellery made by Bulgar craftsmen also came into fashion among the Alans and Goths.[95]

After the setbacks suffered by Justinian II, Byzantium became reconciled to the loss of almost all her possessions in the Crimea and maintained friendly relations with Khazaria. The Emperor Leo III (717–741) sent an embassy to the khagan and married off his own son, the future Emperor Constantine V (741–775), to the khagan's daughter.[96]

In the 8th century the Khazars permitted a Gothic diocese on their territory. Its bishop took part in the Council of Iconoclasts in 753 and the diocese is included in the Notitia Episcopatuum of 787. It comprised a see with its seat at Doros (Manhup) and dioceses were created for the spreading of Christianity to other regions of Khazaria, among them the diocese of Khotsiri, with its seat at Phullai in the eastern Crimea.[97] In 786 a confrontation between the local church authority and the Khazar administration occurred when, to judge from the text of the *Life of John the Goth*, the Khazars quartered a garrison in Doros. The population of Gothia, led by John, rose up and expelled them.[98] During the subsequent repression John was captured and sent to a Khazar prison at Phullai, and the seat and diocese of Manhup were destroyed.[99] After their victory the Khazars built fortresses on the plateaus of Kyzy-Kermen and Manhup.[100] At the same time they allowed loyal Bulgars to settle on the banks of the southern Bug and in the mountains and their settlements were established even in the neighbourhood of Cherson.[101] The Gothic, Phullaian and Sogdaian dioceses were in abeyance for several decades and not mentioned again until the reign of the patriarch Nikephoros (806–815). But Cherson and northern Klimata, i.e. highland Crimea, are named among the regions belonging to the diocese of Cherson.[102]

At the end of 830 relations between Byzantium and Khazaria improved. The successor to Theophanes reported the arrival in Constantinople of an embassy from the khagan in the year after the election of John the Grammarian as patriarch in 838.[103] They asked the Byzantines to build a fortress for them between the Rivers Volga and Don and, in the winter of 840–841, Petrona the *'spatharokandidatos'* built the fortress of Sarkel for the Khazars, on the instructions of Emperor Theophilos (829–842). He suggested to Theophilos that a theme (administrative district) be created at Cherson. The Emperor appointed him *'strategos'* of a theme founded in the summer of 841,[104] called on seals the theme of (five) Klimata (regions), to which Cherson was later added.[105] The Byzantine historians Theophanos[106] and Constantine Porphyrogenitus referred to the mountain region adjoining Cherson by that name.[107] The mountain fortresses in the neighbourhood of the city also became part of it and the other regions of the

peninsula remained under their control.[108] In 860 the Khazars unsuccessfully besieged one of the fortresses and Byzantium probably retained control over them.[109]

In 860–861 Constantine the Philosopher, who led a mission from the Imperial capital to the Khazar khagan, stayed in the Crimea. According to legend, having learned that the population of Phullai performed pagan rites, he went there to the plateau of Tepsen in the eastern Crimea and persuaded the local people to adopt Christianity.[110] In eastern Crimea and other Bulgar settlements small temples with walls built in the herring-bone style typical of the Bulgars have been discovered. It should be noted that many small temples were built in the second half of the 9th century on the foundations of Byzantine basilicas destroyed during the uprising of John the Goth.[111] The Khazars adopted Judaism in 861 at the time when the Bulgars of the eastern Crimea became Christians again.[112] Some time later the Hungarians probably expelled the Khazars from the eastern Crimea, wiping out the garrison of Bosporus.[113] Makarova thinks that the Khazar citadel of the city was burnt down in the third quarter of the 9th century.[114] A letter from the patriarch Photius to the Archbishop of Bosporus in 875 helps to date the expulsion of the Khazars from the city. It supports the archbishop's plan of baptizing all the Jews of Bosporus, an action nobody would have entertained if the city were still occupied by the Khazars.[115] In the last quarter of the 9th century the city belonged to Byzantium and, by the end of the century, the remains of the Khazar citadel had been pulled down and the whole port district was re-planned. The Magyars traded freely in the market of Bosporus.[116] In 943 the Khazars carried out their last recorded raid on Byzantine territory in the Crimea.[117]

The Magyars were expelled from the steppes of the northern Black Sea coast by the Pechenegs, Turks who had invaded the region in 889.[118] They engaged in nomadic cattle-breeding, and blocked Khazar access to the Byzantine possessions on the Kerch peninsula.[119] Constantine Porphyrogenitus located the Pechenegs as follows:

> Pachinakia … is very close to Cherson, and even closer to Bosporus. As these people of the Pachinakiti, who live near the region of Cherson, are unfriendly towards us, they may take the field against Cherson and carry out raids and ravage both Cherson itself and the Klimata.[120]

Constantine's testimony is supplemented by archaeological remains. Pecheneg graves are found only in the Sivash region, dug into earlier barrows with the head to the west, and with belt-mounts, sabres and adornments of the 10th century. In one of them there was a horse skull and parts of its legs together with the bones of a man. It is most likely that the Pechenegs moved into the Crimean steppe with their herds for only a short while in the 10th century. According to the same writer, the Pechenegs undertook missions for the rulers of Byzantium in Rus', Khazaria and Zichia. Leaving hostages in Cherson, they guarded the caravans and embassies leaving for those countries, and received money and precious gifts as commission in return. They traded with Cherson buying belts, silk, velvet, pepper, red Parthenian leather and other goods, while the townspeople purchased wax and skins from the Pechenegs and sold them to Byzantium.[121]

At the end of the 9th to 10th century the population of the Klimata gave up their old pagan traditions. They abandoned almost all their cemeteries, with the vaults, graves and burial structures associated with pagan burial rites. Temples were constructed next to many of them, and around them cemeteries appear with burials in graves of stone slabs, or in stone tombs. Judging by the few epitaphs found in highland Crimea, the population of the Klimata knew Greek, and some of them had Greek names.[122] By the end of the 10th century it is most likely that the assimilation process in the formation of the highland Crimean population was complete, absorbing Alan, Goth and Roman elements united by Christianity and Byzantine culture.[123]

On Bakla in the 10th century, and at the beginning of the 11th on Eski-Kermen, they built new town areas and temples.[124] The main temple on Eski-Kermen was rebuilt and both fortresses grew into small towns.[125] In the 10th and 11th centuries the towns and fortresses of the barbarians most probably defended the approaches to Cherson, as they had done before.

In the 1050s groups of Turkic-speaking Kipchaks – the Polovtsi as they were called in the Russian Chronicles – occupied the Don and Azov steppes, forcing many Pecheneg tribes to move to the Byzantine borders.[126] Burials with horse skulls and bones appear in the second half of the 11th century in the foothills near the Crimean territories of the Empire. In the closing decade of the century the hordes of the Polovtsi divided the steppe between them, and the Don horde began to control the Crimean steppe. The Pechenegs roaming there probably joined them, maintaining their traditions even into the 12th century.[127] The grave of a Pecheneg prince has been found on the outskirts of Simferopol dating back to the end of the 11th or beginning of the 12th century, with stirrups and gilded silver bridle-mounts decorated with foliate ornament and black niello.[128] At the end of the 11th to 12th centuries the Polovtsi actively traded with Cherson and settled there, and it was Polovtsian merchants who helped an impostor pretending to be Constantine, a son of the Emperor Romanos IV Diogenes, to escape from the city, to which he had been exiled in 1091.[129]

The Polovtsi occupied the major part of highland Crimea during the 12th century when the Arabian geographer Idrisi wrote: 'The road from Cherson to Yalita (Yalta) is in the country of the Cumans (the Polovtsi)'.[130] Cherson still controlled its neighbouring fortresses, however, as witnessed by a letter of Bishop Theodoros dating between 1222 and 1240 in which he wrote: 'Not far from Cherson the Alans live according to their own wish and that of the Chersonites, as a certain protection and guard'.[131] According to the report of William of Rubruck, who visited Sudak in 1253, the fortresses situated between Cherson and Soldaia (Sudak) paid tribute to the Polovtsi.[132] Arab historians confirm that Sudak still belonged to the Polovtsi in the 13th century, and was a major centre for their transit trade.[133] The material from archaeological excavations on the peninsula confirms the statements of medieval writers. In the 12th to 13th centuries, Polovtsian burials in timber-covered pits dug into earlier barrows spread on the steppe and foothills. In many of them, besides a coat of mail made of thick iron wire, arrow and spear-heads, sabres, buckles, and the bone parts of bows and quivers, there were skeletons of horses with stirrups and bits. Realistic sculptures of 12th-century date, carved in dense, white limestone come from the Crimean steppe. They represent a

man and a woman with braided hair, wearing a helmet, or a hat with a caftan, and holding a vessel in their hands. Their weapons and adornments are clearly visible and the tallest is around 1.65m high. Such sculptures were always put in high places, in specially prepared sanctuaries.[134] All the statues were cut from local stone and a workshop where they had been carved was found in one of the medieval quarries near Yevpatoriya.

The history of the population in the peninsula is usually derived from the reports of Late-Roman, Byzantine and Arab writers, hagiographic literature, epigraphic inscriptions, and Khazar documents. Such information is fragmentary, however, and not always reliable. Researchers in the last third of the 19th century began, therefore, to turn their attention to archaeological finds in order to reconstruct the ethnic history of the Crimea.

The history of the collection in the Ukraine

Artefacts similar to those of the Berthier-Delagarde Collection were found and recorded in Kerch from the first third of the 18th century,[135] and, on the southern coast of the Crimea, from 1889 onwards.[136] After the Crimean War of 1854–1856 similar ornaments, buckles and brooches were conveyed to the British Museum,[137] and, in the second half of the 19th century, to the museums of Stockholm and Berlin.[138] It was the arrival of such material in the West that stimulated scientific interest in the Crimea there, and these comparative collections were used together with local material to illustrate the complex interrelationships of the European 'Migration Period'.

Lieutenant-General Alexander Lvovich Berthier-Delagarde, the owner of the collection, was a military engineer and an outstanding historian, who was born in Sevastopol in 1842. From the end of the 1860s until the 1890s he built ports in Odessa, Kherson, Rostov, Sevastopol, Yalta and Feodosiya; he also constructed the mains water system and shipyards of Sevastopol and Feodosiya, and the Feodosiya railway. In 1880 he joined the Odessa Society of History and Antiquities and, in 1916, became a member of the Taurida Scientific Archives Commission. He was the author of 30 monographs and articles on the history, archaeology and numismatics of the Crimea, which appeared in the publications of these scientific societies and of the Imperial Archaeological Commission. His works show he was both a specialist with a wide range of interests and a skilful analyst. During the construction of the port at Feodosiya, he organised the first archaeological rescue excavations in the blocks of the ancient city, and in the citadel and port installations of medieval Caffa, which overlay them.

Over several decades he collected ancient and medieval artefacts and coins, which originated from Olbia and its neighbourhood, from the lower Don and Kuban regions, from Kerch, from ancient Chersonesus and from the southern Black Sea coast of the Crimea. According to N.I. Repnikov, the owner of one of the estates at Hurzuf handed over to Berthier-Delagarde in 1899, nine gold, silver and copper buckles from the area of Suuk-Su (**Map B: 14**), near Hurzuf, along with jewellery and beads.[139] Here in 1905 the general financed the excavation of an early-medieval cemetery by Repnikov.[140] The finds were made over to the Museum of the Odessa Society of History and Antiquities[141] and Berthier-Delagarde proposed the transfer of all his property and collections to the museum in a letter to the council of the society, dated 1 November 1919. He died in Yalta on 21 February 1920 and in accordance with his will, his house, library, archives and collections were to be transferred to the Taurida Scientific Archives Commission. His collection was housed in the Taurid museum, but was not registered. According to the will the collection could be sold for cash to support the society, but how his sister came to remove the collection, or a part of it, remains unknown. She appears to have commissioned Alexander Volgeninov in Paris to sell the 'Dark Age' part of the collection to the British Museum in 1923. The items are partly recorded in photographs kept among the holdings of the Museum of Crimean Republican History and Local Lore in Simferopol (file 2237, nos 62–24; for further details and analysis, see Andrási below).

Subsequently dozens of cemeteries and burial mounds, dating from the 3rd to the 13th century, have been excavated in the Crimean Peninsula from the end of the 1920s up to the present day (see Map C).

A summary of previous research
In the monographs published at the end of the 19th and in the first third of the 20th centuries the populations of early-medieval Bosporus and highland Crimea were considered to be Goths.[142] This was due to the similarity of jewellery found distributed from Kerch and Hurzuf to western Europe, including goldwork inlaid with red garnet in the polychrome style, silver and bronze buckles with attachment-plates terminating in eagles' heads, and radiate-headed brooches. Rostovtzeff thought that the polychrome style had originated among the Alans in the 3rd century AD. He systematically dated the material too early, however, because his main interest did not extend beyond the beginning of the 3rd century. Those Alans who left Bosporus to escape from the Huns, to eastern and western Europe and north Africa, took with them gold objects (or objects covered with gold sheet) with rich, garnet-inlaid polychrome decoration. These included female adornments such as diadems, temporal-pendants, bracelets, belts and footwear; and male items such as buckles, mounts for belts, swords and daggers, and horse harness-fittings.[144] This view was supported and developed by Matsulevich, who considered that the Alanic jewellers of Bosporus not only created the polychrome style, but also devised a new female jewellery set consisting of a large, eagle-headed buckle and a pair of radiate-headed brooches. The new fashion spread from Bosporus to the south-western Crimea and on to other parts of Europe.[145] Following Matsulevich many scholars regarded Bosporus as an arbiter in the European fashion for such items of personal costume and horse-harness.[146]

Minaeva and Alföldi both associated the objects with inlaid work, from Kerch and other regions with the Huns and accordingly restricted the period of polychrome decoration to the last quarter of the 4th to the mid-5th century, or 376–456.[147] Werner rejected the theory that the polychrome style was spread by fugitives from the northern Black Sea coast, associating it with the increased wealth of the Hunnic nobility at the beginning of the 5th century in the Black Sea coast and Danube regions, who were of diverse ethnic origins. The style was based on Bosporan, Sarmatian-Alan, provincial-Roman and ancient Germanic jewellery traditions and, in his view, the graves with polychrome objects at Kerch, on the steppe, and in

the Danube region, were all contemporary. He further defined Bosporus as 'a centre of Hunnic dominance' in the first half of the 5th century.[148] Zasetskaya reached the same conclusion[149] and endeavoured to establish the uniformity and contemporaneity of the above-mentioned burials in the last quarter of the 4th and first half of the 5th centuries.[150]

Ambroz divided the polychrome-decorated objects into two stylistic groups according to their technology of manufacture, ornament, and colour. His first group contained objects covered with gold sheet decorated with stamping or twisted wire and with cabochon settings with large, polished cornelian or blue glass inlays, which he compared with the decoration on belts[151] and officers' helmets,[152] made from the mid-3rd century in provincial-Roman workshops. According to him this style spread from that region to the Crimea and North Caucasus.[153] His second group contained objects decorated predominantly with small, red garnet inlays on a gold background with green pastes in the corners between the garnets. He proposed that this new polychrome style appeared in the Danube region in the first decades of the 5th century, and then spread to Bosporus and other territories conquered by the Huns.[154]

Previous studies of the chronology
The chronology of the cemeteries in Bosporus and the south-western Crimea was formulated in the late 19th and early 20th centuries, and in the 1920s. The first researchers of the cemetery at Kerch dated the periods of burial on the basis of the coins of the 2nd to 5th centuries from the excavated tombs.[155] In the cemetery at Suuk-Su the early-medieval burials were covered by a layer of earth following landslides into which flat graves were dug. Repnikov divided the burials of the lower layer into three stages according to the coins, namely those of the 3rd, 4th, and 5th to 7th centuries.[156] De Baye, who published the material from Suuk-Su in France, dated them to the 5th to 7th centuries.[157] But specialists in the typologies of Crimean radiate-headed brooches and eagle-headed buckles concluded in the early 20th century that these had been manufactured in the 6th to 7th century, contradicting the coin-based chronology of the cemeteries at Kerch and Suuk-Su.[158] Matsulevich noted that at Suuk-Su coins of the 3rd to 5th centuries were found together with objects of a later period. He divided the material from these cemeteries into four groups, dating the small, inlaid sheet brooches to the first half of the 4th century; polychrome objects inlaid with red stones to the second half of the 4th and the beginning of the 5th centuries; the Kerch radiate-headed brooches and eagle-headed buckles to the end of the 4th to 5th century; and objects of the same type from Suuk-Su to the 6th–7th century.[159] In his corpus of European radiate-headed brooches Kühn defined the Kerch brooches as the earliest group of the 5th century.[160]

The chronology for Bosporus and Suuk-Su proposed by Matsulevich was soon revised, however, by Werner, who proved that the same Kerch brooches had been modelled on patterns from the Danube region. He attributed the Danubian brooches with lozenge-shaped feet to the second half of the 5th century and the Kerch type to the 6th century or to its first half,[161] assigning the eagle-headed buckles, radiate-headed and large sheet brooches from the lower layer at Suuk-Su to the second half of the 6th and first half of the 7th centuries.[162] The dating of this layer was substantially supported by Pudovin.[163]

Ambroz further divided the grave groups with polychrome objects into three groups. The Kerch vaults containing inlaid objects were placed in the first group and dated to the first half of the 5th century, while many nomad burials from the Volga and Black Sea steppes containing objects of the same type were included in the second and third groups, dating from the second half of the 5th to the first half of the 7th century.[164] Tejral assigned the Kerch vault burials containing polychrome items to stage D1 (about 375–410 according to the Danubian chronology) and those with complexes of Untersiebenbrunn type to stage D2 (about 410–440).[165] Ambroz drew attention to the stratigraphy of the burials in Kerch vault 152/1904, with a Gepidic eagle-headed buckle of the first half of the 6th century in the lower layer and radiate-headed brooches of Aquileia type and Bosporan eagle-headed buckles in the upper one. Referring both to this and to parallels in the Ostrogothic and Gepid material from the Danube region and Italy, he identified brooches and buckles typical of the first and second halves of the 5th century, and restricted the eagle-headed buckles and radiate-headed and large sheet brooches from Bosporus and the south-western Crimea to the 6th to 7th centuries. He formulated new typologies for them, dividing the period from the 3rd to the 7th centuries in Bosporus into four stages: 1) the first half of the 3rd century; 2) the 4th century; 3) the 5th century; and 4) the 6th to 7th century. Turning to the southern coast he then divided the period from the second half of the 6th to the 9th centuries into six stages: 1) the second half of the 6th century; 2) the end of the 6th to the beginning of the 7th century; 3) the first half of the 7th century; 4) the second half of the 7th century; 5) the first half of the 8th century; and 6) the second half of the 8th to 9th century. He concluded that Bosporus in the 4th to 7th centuries was not a sufficiently large economic centre to be able to supply jewellery to the peoples of the steppe, from the Dniester to Kirgizia, and the Caucasus as well as western Europe and north Africa.[166]

The assemblages excavated from hundreds of burials of the second half of the 3rd to the 9th century during recent decades have been classified in my publications. Analysis of the correlation of similar types from each burial enabled their attribution to separate, uniform groups. The relative chronology of these groups was then substantiated by research on the burial stratigraphy of the multi-layered vaults at Kerch and Luchyste (Luchistoye) (**Map B: 16**); the absolute chronology is based on the dating of coins and imported objects. The burial stratigraphy at Luchyste corroborated Ambroz's dating of the typological development of eagle-headed buckles. The lower layers there contained buckles with their loops hinged to the attachment-plates by short, folded flaps while, the buckles in the upper layers had long, folded flaps. In such multi-layered vaults objects typical of the earlier assemblages came from the lower layers, and those typical of the later assemblages came from the upper ones. The earliest group of assemblages was attributed to the second half of the 3rd century, and the latest to the second half of the 9th century.[167]

Notes

1. Yakobson 1970, 149; Yanushevich 1976, 101
2. Latyshev 1893, 150
3. Simonenko 1993, 116
4. Rostovtsev 1918, 138
5. Vysotskaya 1972, 184
6. Rostovtsev 1916, 11–13; Rostovtsev 1920, 149
7. Tsvetaeva 1979, 160
8. Vysotskaya 1972, 54–8; Zubar, Savelya and Sarnovsky 1977, 36–8
9. Kuznetsov 1984, 20–2
10. Shkorpil 1911, 112–14
11. Rostovtzeff 1936, 90–130
12. Wolfram 1990, 55, 61
13. Jordanes 1960, 72
14. Kulakovsky 1899, 16
15. Aibabin 1996, 30-34
16. Rostovtsev 1900, 157; Rostovtsev 1907, 4; Vysotskaya 1972, 57–8
17. Tsvetaeva 1979, 20; Zonaras Ioannes 1844, *Annalium* XII, 21, 589–90; Wolfram 1990, 61
20. Vysotskaya 1972, 187; Olkhovsky and Khrapunov 1990, 111–12
21. Aibabin 1990, 65–6
22. Thompson 1948, 21–4
23. Gumilev 1960, 220; Artamonov 1962, 41–4
24. Ammianus Marcellinus 1972, XXXI, 2, 12; 3, 1
25. Zosimus 1982, IV, 20
26. Vasiliev 1936, 24–30
27. Aibabin 1993b, 209
28. Artamonov 1962, 44–5
29. Aibabin 1993b, 209
30. Aibabin 1990, 67
31. Yanushevich 1976, 101
32. Zuckerman 1991, 548–50
33. Zuckerman 1991, 548
34. Vasiliev 1936, 78
35. Thompson 1948, 123–52
36. Jordanes 1882, V, 37
37. Procopius 1928, book VIII, V, 26; Procopius, *De Bellis*, book I, XII, 9
38. Latyshev 1894, 659–60; Chichurov 1980, 51
39. Procopius 1964, *De Aedificiis*, book III, VII
40. Ambroz 1995, 64
41. Jordanes 1960, 109
42. Kulakovsky 1896, 10
43. Ambroz 1981, fig. 6
44. Procopius 1940, *Buildings*, book III, VII, 13; Sidorenko 1991, 108–9
45. Procopius 1940, *Buildings*, book III, VII, 15–17
46. Procopius 1940, *Buildings*, book III, VII, 14; Firsov, 1979, 106, 107
47. Priscian 1855, Libri XVIII, VI, 1, 195; VII, 1, 283
48. Vasiliev 1936, 91–2; Chichurov 1980, 31–2, 124, 155, 163
49. Gertzen 1990, 114
50. Procopius 1964, *De Aedificiis*, book III, VII, 13; Obolensky 1964, 57
51. Procopius 1940, *Buildings*, book III, VII, 14; Sidorenko 1991, 111
52. Firsov 1979, 109
53. Yakobson 1954, 111, 120, figs 48, 2–4; 50
54. Dombrovsky 1974, 15–16
55. Ambroz 1995, 59
56. Kulakovsky 1896, 12–14
57. Blockley 1985, fr. 19, 1, 171, 173, 179
58. Solomonik 1986, 213–14
59. Latyshev 1894, 662–72
60. Aibabin 1991, 45
61. Gertzen and Mogarichev 1992, 191
62. Chichurov 1980, 165
63. Vasiliev 1936, 78
64. I Goti 1994, 110–11
65. Sidorenko 1991, 114–15
66. Yakobson 1959, 197
67. Yacobson 1954, 111–112, fig. 50
68. Aibabin 1990, 69
69. Borodin 1991, 179, 187.
70. Veimarn and Aibabin 1993, 180–1
71. Chichurov 1980, 60–1, 110–16, 161–2
72. Artamonov 1962, 130
73. Fëdorov and Fëdorov 1970, 84
74. Artamonov 1962, 170–2; Novoseltsev 1990, 76–81
75. Golden 1980, 50–3, 58
76. Novoseltsev 1990, 89

77. Pletnëva 1982, 27
78. Aibabin 1985, 191–202; Pletnëva 1990, 49, 82, 86
79. Aibabin 1985, 102
80. Ambroz 1981, 19–20
81. Chichurov 1980, 63–5, 163–5
82. Golb and Pritsak 1982, 116–17
83. Makarova 1965, 70-6
84. Chichurov 1980, 63–4, 163–4
85. Novoseltsev 1990, 144
86. Pletnëva 1991, 104
87. Pletnëva 1982, 52
88. Gadlo 1968, 83, figs 21–2; Gadlo 1980, 133–4; Baranov 1990, 36–41
89. Ravennatis Anonymi 1860, 175
90. Shandrovskaya 1995, 120–1
91. Vasilevsky 1915
92. Pletnëva 1982, 100
93. Yakobson 1970; Baranov 1990, 69–75
94. Yakobson 1979
95. Aibabin 1977
96. Chichurov 1980, 68, 166, 183
97. Vernadsky 1941, 6
98. Vasiliev 1936, 91–2
99. Gertzen 1990, 137
100. Gertzen and Mogarichev 1992, 190–1
101. Veimarn 1963, 64-70, figs 5-10, 16; Romanchuk 1976, 9–23
102. Vasiliev 1936, 135
103. Treadgold 1988, 313
104. Constantine Porphyrogenitus 1989, 171–3; Zukerman 1997, 315–16
105. Vasiliev 1936, 117; Obolensky 1966, 492; Nesbitt and Oikonomides 1991, 182
106. Chichurov 1980, 60, 63–4, 106
107. Constantine Porphyrogenitus 1989, 36–7, 52–3, 156–7, 170–1, 174–5, 283
108. Aibabin 1991, 48
109. Vasiliev 1936, 113
110. Ahrweiler 1971, 58–62
111. Romanchuk 1976, 9-23, 140, fig. 4; Baranov 1990, 133–9, figs 52–3
112. Zuckerman 1995, 269; Gadlo 1968, 64
113. Zuckerman 1997b
114. Makarova 1982, 99
115. Photius Patriarch 1983, 132
116. Khvolson 1869, 27
117. Mosin 1931, 323
118. Artamonov 1962, 340, 350
119. Pletnëva 1982, 24
120. Constantine Porphyrogenitus 1989, 37, 157
121. Constantine Porphyrogenitus 1989, 43, 274
122. Solomonik 1986, 215–17; Solomonik 1991, 172–8
123. Aibabin 1993b, 130
124. Rudakov 1981, 73–83
125. Aibabin 1991, 49
126. Pletnëva 1981, 214
127. Pletnëva 1990, 39–40, 114–15
128. Kirpichnikov 1973, table XI, 29
129. Anna Comnena 1965, 266
130. Garkavi 1891, 244
131. Kulakovsky 1898, 17
132. William of Rubruck [Rubruk Gil'om] 1957, 104–5
133. Brun 1880, 133; Tizingauzen 1884, 26
134. Pletnëva 1974, 54, 73
135. Bich 1959, fig.2:3; Ashik 1849, 72 no. 209
136. Kharuzin 1890, 5; Repnikov 1906
137. Macpherson 1857
138. Martin 1894; Götze 1907
139. Repnikov 1906a, 106–7
140. Repnikov 1907, 102, pls XII–XVI
141. Repnikov 1907, 102
142. Dalton 1924a, b
143. de Baye 1888, 2–3; de Baye 1892, 1–16; de Baye 1908, 3–43; Shtern 1897, 1–15; Salin 1904, 123, 193, 204; Repnikov 1907, 19.2; Götze 1907, 1–35
144. Rostovtzeff 1922, 124–218; Rostovtzeff 1923a, 145–61
145. Matsulevich 1926, 41–51
146. Tatić-Burić 1956/7, 164–8; Rusu 1959, 485–523; Yakobson 1964, 14–15; Kühn 1965, 92–100; Vinski 1968; Bóna 1976, 56–7; Zasetskaya 1982, 25
147. Minaeva 1927, 112–13, 123; Alföldi 1932, 12, 36–7
148. Werner 1956, 86, 90–1
149. Zasetskaya 1968, 60–2; Zasetskaya 1993, 38
150. Zasetskaya 1978, 54, 69
151. Martin 1991, 55 fig. 22:1
152. Klumbach 1973, pls 1–9, 11–21
153. Ambroz 1989, 23–7; Ambroz 1992, 8–10
154. Ambroz 1971, 102; Ambroz 1981, 21–2; Ambroz 1985, 300–2; Ambroz 1992, 48–50
155. Kulakovsky 1881, 20–2; Shkorpil 1907, 1–2
156. Repnikov 1906a, 109–10
157. de Baye 1908, 22
158. Salin 1904, 32, 124, 129; Götze 1907, 33; Åberg 1919, 73, 94, 118
159. Matsulevich 1926, 41–51
160. Kühn 1940, 94, 99, 100
161. Werner 1950, 161; Werner 1961b, 29–32
162. Werner 1950, 164
163. Pudovin 1961, 177–85
164. Ambroz 1971, 102; Ambroz 1981, 21–2; Ambroz 1985, 300–2; Ambroz 1992, 48–50
165. Tejral 1973, 21–9, 57–61; Tejral 1987, 36; Tejral 1988, 295
166. Ambroz 1971, 115–23; Ambroz 1992, 67–87
167. Aibabin 1979; Aibabin 1984; Aibabin 1987; Aibabin 1990; Aibabin 1993b; Aibabin 1995

The Collection
Júlia Andrási

The history of the collection in the West (Archive Plates 1–10)

Alexander Berthier-Delagarde (1842–1920)

Lieutenant-General Alexander Lvovich Berthier-Delagarde was born in Sevastopol in 1842. He became a military engineer and, after his retirement in 1887, took part in excavations, either directing them or financing them himself. He also built up an outstanding personal collection of archaeological jewellery and coins. According to Markevich the collection still belonged to him in 1919, but it was not mentioned in his will made on 5 January 1920.[1] After his death in February 1920 the Hellenistic, Roman and early-medieval objects in his collection were taken to France, where members of his family emigrated. But the documentation was bequeathed to the Taurida Scientific Archives Commission (Simferopol), and is at present kept in the Crimean Regional Museum, Simferopol. (For Berthier-Delagarde's biographical details, see Kropotkin and Shelov.[2])

The purchase

The British Museum purchased part of the jewellery on the 7th of July 1923. Much of the transaction can be traced through letters kept in the museum's archives (**Archive Pls 11–13**), but a number of questions still remain unanswered.

In March 1923 Professor M.I. Rostovtsev (Rostovtzeff) suggested to O.M. Dalton, the Keeper of the (then) Department of British and Medieval Antiquities, that he look at the Berthier-Delagarde Collection with a view to its purchase. The collection was then 'in the hands of' A. Volgeninov in Paris who had been entrusted by Berthier-Delagarde's sister, Mme Beliawsky to effect the disposal of the whole group while she remained in Menton, where she was ill. Dalton contacted Volgeninov, who sent eight photographs (or 'screens' as he called them) and also informed him that there had originally been 18 illustrating about 400 objects. But he only had the eight, showing 183 objects, which the department retained (**Archive Pls 1, 2a, 3a, 5, 6, 7, 8a, 9**). The museum considered the sum of money asked for the whole collection (£3,500) too expensive, and therefore negotiated to purchase only a part of it. The Berthier-Delagarde family had not intended to divide the collection, but made an exception for the museum's sake, and also because they were short of money. On 5 June 1923 Reginald Smith, Deputy Keeper of the department, was entrusted to go to Paris to see the collection. After negotiations over the price and some of the objects, the authorities, the museum and Volgeninov reached an agreement. Since the Greek and Roman Department did not require the Greek part, the museum bought less than half of the collection offered by Volgeninov, the so-called 'non-Greek, barbaric' objects. They also agreed a price, £1,500, less than half of the original sum demanded, part of which was paid from the departmental grant. The remainder was requested from the National Art Collections Fund and from the Trustees of the British Museum, on the basis of the national and international significance of the collection. The report to the Trustees on 8 June 1923 stressed that the garnet-inlaid jewellery of the Black Sea coast

> was learned from the Sarmatians (...) by the Goths and transmitted by them to their neighbours. It thus passed from tribe to tribe and was adopted both by the Franks and the Anglo-Saxons. (...) The art of the Sarmatians was the first link in a long chain which ended in Kent. This link is hardly if at all represented in the Great European Museums, including the British.

The Trustees agreed to the purchase on 7 July 1923.

The purchased part of the collection

The museum bought 150 pieces, 71 of which appear on the photographs sent by Volgeninov. According to Volgeninov

> the collection was gathered during several tens of years. Prof. Minns has seen this collection in Russia and he knew personally Mr Berthier Delagarde. The authenticity of the objects can be guaranteed.'

He also noted that 'there was nothing sold from his collection, nor was anything added to it after the death of Mr Berthier-Delagarde.'

Rostovtsev saw the collection itself and remarked that 'the Sarmatian and Gothic part of the collection is a real beauty. (It) appears to be quite unique, not comparable to any collection of which I know.' He assured Dalton that the museum should at least buy 'the Sarmatian and Gothic sets.' He also drew attention to a Sarmatian necklace with a stone engraved with the figure of Sauromatos II, King of Bosporus. But, according to his letter, Smith did not pay it special attention since it was mounted on a screen with classical objects and was therefore not, apparently, included in the purchase, unlike two gold earrings (presumably identifiable with **cat. nos 84–85**) and gold fibulae (**cat. nos 100–103**) which were specially pointed out by Smith as being 'among the classical jewellery, where they were distinctly out of place.' Apart from two screens (**Archive Pls. 5–6**), where three of these fibulae appear, the museum purchased the entire contents of each screen, but we can only presume this is the case with the remaining 57 pieces, the contents of two or three screens for which we do not have photographs, on the basis of the conclusions below. As Volgeninov mentioned in his letter to Smith on 17 June: '(Barbaric) things you found among classical gold work (that golden earrings + fibules – barbaric style) I have marked and included in the purchasing part of the collection.' This implies that the purchase had to conform with the screens Volgeninov provided and that he was prepared to make only a few exceptions at Smith's special request, which is supported by the fact that the enamelled brooches of provincial-Roman origin appearing amongst later pieces were also purchased (**cat. nos 93–99**), but were transferred to the Greek and Roman Department straight afterwards (**Archive Pls 3a, 4**).

Archival information

The photographs from the Simferopol archives (Pls 2b, 3b, 4, 8b, 10)

The British Museum holds five further photographs received from the Taurida Scientific Archives Commission, Simferopol.[3] They are similar in style to the screens supplied by Volgeninov and three especially (**Archive Pls 2b, 3b and 8b**) bear strong resemblance to the ones retained by the department (**Archive Pls 2a, 3a, 8a**). There are, however, slight differences between the two sets of screens. The layout of the jewellery on each 'pair' of photographs is similar, but differs in the exact position of each item. A further difference is that, under the kolt on **Archive Pl. 2a**, is the silver cicada brooch (**cat. no. 16**), which is, on the other hand, missing from the screen of the Taurida Archives (**Archive Pl. 2b**) and is replaced by a gold earring. This earring appears, however, on Volgeninov's fifth screen. The British Museum purchased neither the earring nor the whole contents of this screen, apart from two of the gold fibulae already mentioned above. Alterations were made in the case of screen no. 3 as well, which originally contained 16 carefully arranged objects (**Archive Pl. 3b**), but was later supplemented with four Roman brooches and two earrings.

The implication is that the photographs in the Taurida Archives had been taken first, possibly for Berthier-Delagarde's own purposes, or, alternatively, shortly after his death, when his documentation was bequeathed to the Commission. The screens the British Museum received from Volgeninov were possibly photographed before the collection left Russia, to serve as documents for the family or for a future sale. The fact that the majority of the objects are numbered supports this idea, since one of Volgeninov's letters records that the numbers had fallen off after the collection had left Russia. By the time of the second photograph the earring had been replaced by the cicada brooch and got mounted onto screen no. 5. That would also explain why aesthetic considerations were disregarded in the second set of photographs. The British Museum retained one further photograph of a screen (**Archive Pl. 1**) containing 28 pieces, each of which was included in the purchase of 1923, but not illustrated on any of the Taurida Archives' photographs. There is, however, a photograph of a screen among the latter (**Archive Pl. 4**), the whole contents of which (23 pieces) were also purchased by the museum. Although it was not included among the eight photographs in Volgeninov's possession (**Archive Pls. 1, 2a, 3a, 5, 6, 7, 8a, 9**), the screen was certainly taken to Paris, as it appears on the photograph. Slight changes, however, similar to those described above (the position of the pieces, or the addition of a few objects), may also have occurred.

The same cannot be said about photograph no. 10, which also appears only in the Archives of Simferopol. It illustrates a number of earrings, a row of beads and a filigree cross, of which only the last was bought by the British Museum. This screen may have been altered before the sale, since there is no mention of the cross being specifically requested in the correspondence between Volgeninov and Smith.

Difficulties with the documentation of the 1923 purchase

The only written documents relating to the purchased part of the collection that survive are the correspondence concerning the purchase, and a list of objects with catalogue numbers, descriptions and provenances in the departmental archive. The latter is typed, with hand-written corrections and additions, and was presumably prepared by Smith in Paris in the course of the purchase, and later completed by him in London. He noted on it that the original catalogue numbers of the objects were missing in 70 cases. Dalton wrote to Volgeninov asking for the original catalogue to be sent to London in order to complete the list. The catalogue had been 'drawn up by Mr Berthier-Delagarde himself with all his notes' according to Volgeninov, who sent it to Smith with the purchased objects marked in red and a note that 'there were originally numbers on every object, but they were lost during the long journey from Russia.' The catalogue was returned on 17 August 1923 by registered post, but there is no further mention of it, its contents or location in the archives, or in later specialist research. Smith's subsequent departmental registration presumably made use of it in conjunction with the corrected version of his preliminary list. He made many corrections to this list, but one is especially significant: the typed version had originally recorded the wheel-brooch (**cat. no. 15**) with the incorrect catalogue number '211,' which was later emended with a hand-written note to the correct number, i.e. 271. One of the photographs sent by Volgeninov, however (**Archive Pl. 1**), shows the brooch with the number 271 clearly visible and legible on its front. Smith presumably looked at each object when making the list and could only have made such mistakes because some of the numbers of the objects had been lost or damaged during the journey from Russia (as mentioned by Volgeninov in his letter). This implies that this set of screens was photographed at a time when the objects still had their numbers, i.e. before the collection left Russia.

All the information about the objects given in the register corresponds with what is written in the list, except for the old catalogue number 311 (**cat. nos 63–69**) where the note referring to it in the list as 'horse harness' is missing from the register. Since this made use of Berthier-Delagarde's own notes, the detail is crucial for the interpretation of a whole series of objects as the fittings of possibly a single horse-harness, for it suggests the association of the set of mounts (**cat. nos 31–43**), buckles (**cat. nos 44–56**), and strap-attachments (**cat. nos 60–62**) with the above strips (see **cat. nos 63–69**).

The information given in the list also leaves a number of unanswered questions. It is a puzzle, for instance, how Smith managed to identify the catalogue numbers in about 40 of the originally missing 70 cases, when only 30 objects in the register lack the old catalogue numbers. This may imply that the pieces were illustrated in the catalogue and could thus be identified with their numbers. It is also puzzling that some of the objects have the same catalogue number (e.g. **cat. nos 22, 88, 89 and 112–115**); as noted by Volgeninov himself: 'there are 320 numbers in the catalogue, but in reality there are more objects, as some of the objects bear the same number.' There are three objects with the same old catalogue number '287', but only one of them, the finger-ring fragment (**cat. no. 135**), is annotated 'Kerch 1900'; the two armlets (**cat. nos 17 and 18**) have no further information. It is either a simple mistake in copying the relevant data from Berthier-Delagarde's catalogue, or else should be added to the unsolved questions concerning his cataloguing system.

One of the most fundamental difficulties is that it is uncertain what is really meant by the 'provenance' of the objects. In his letter of June 1923 Rostovtsev stated that the collection was unique, partly 'because the provenance of all objects is well known,' but did not give the source of his information. He was probably referring to the details in Berthier-Delagarde's catalogue, as had also been used by Smith to complete his list. In both the list and the register are given the location (Kerch, Caucasus, Olbia, Hurzuf [Gurzuf], Kuban, Cherson, 'Eltine' [probably Eltigen], or Maikop) and date (the earliest 1893 and the latest 1912) for 115 of the total 157 catalogue numbers. The register suggests that these are the provenances of the objects, although Smith's preliminary list does not indicate the nature of the information.

We know from contemporary Russian sources that in some cases provenance does *not* mean the findspot of the object, but might rather indicate the place and date of purchase. Seventy-two items are annotated 'Kerch,' with dates between 1893 and 1909, but the findspots for only an insignificant number of them can be independently derived from contemporary sources. They are as follows, beginning with the buckle (**cat. no. 82**) published by Repnikov as found at Suuk-Su in 1899, and given to Berthier-Delagarde.[4] Repnikov's published photograph is kept in the archives of the St Petersburg Institute of History.[5] The register's 'Kerch 1900' cannot possibly, therefore, refer to the findspot. The kolt (**cat. no. 87**) is published by Kondakov as found in the Kuban area[6] so the registration details 'Kerch 1893' again appear to refer to something other than the findspot: possibly the place and date of acquisition. The 11 settings (**cat. no. 29**) are all under one old catalogue number (153), and the information in both the preliminary list and the register reads: 'Kerch 1894 (different excavations).' Since it is highly unlikely that Berthier-Delagarde collected them from different excavations in Kerch in the same year, it may be that he purchased them in Kerch in 1894 and that they derive from several sites. A shield-shaped mount in the Museum of Warsaw is identical with **cat. no. 92**, and is published by Fettich as found in the Dnieper region.[7] It possibly belongs to the same set as the two Berthier-Delagarde pieces, but these are annotated 'Kerch 1893.' The most likely explanation for the discrepancy is that Berthier-Delagarde bought two mounts from the same set, recording the place and date of purchase, while Fettich gives the actual findspot for the third piece.

In a few cases, however, we find that the additional information in the register does correspond with the true findspot of the object. The filigree cross (**cat. no. 129**) is published by Kondakov as found in Cherson, and the note in the register reads: 'Hersonès 1895.'[8] This may indicate that some of the other locations given in the register, such as 'Tertre Coul Obas' (Kuloba Mound), Caucasus, An-Kache, 'Eltine' (probably Eltigen) and Hurzuf (Gurzuf), are more likely to refer to the findspots than to the places of purchase. The reason for this inconsistency may lie in the circumstances of either the finds, or the purchase of individual pieces; or it may even be that the full details were unknown. The lack of documentation concerning the collection therefore still leaves a number of unanswered questions, particularly the provenance of the bulk of the material. Did Berthier-Delagarde know, and did he have any other documentation, as the previous mention of his 'notes' may imply? What kind of information did his 'catalogue'

contain, and what criteria, if any, guided his collecting? There are about 20 objects which have a 'provenance' outside the Crimea, such as Olbia, Kuban, Maikop and Caucasus, but which of these are findspots, and which the places of purchase?

A further puzzle is the significance of Smith's handwritten note at the bottom of his list saying '? 34 bronze + bead 6th–7th AD. Kerch 1893.' It also adds that this item is 'not marked in the cat.,' which certainly means that Volgeninov did not mark it in red in Berthier-Delagarde's catalogue when he sent it to Smith to revise his list. There is no further reference to this object(s); nor does it appear in the departmental register.

The outstanding pair of mounts (**cat. no. 23**) is not mentioned in the list, but does appear in the register (1923,7-16,110 and 111), annotated 'not in catalogue,' and is illustrated on both screens **2a and 2b**, too. It is curious that Berthier-Delagarde omitted it from his catalogue. Then against the last 16 pieces in the register (1923,7-16,135–150) Smith noted that 'these (are) not identified in catalogue,' which may mean that even Berthier-Delagarde himself did not have any information about them, especially as they do not appear on the preliminary list and do not have old catalogue numbers attached to them.

The earliest published photograph of the collection is the one in the *Illustrated London News* for February 1924 and in volume 4 of the *Antiquaries Journal*, in the same year.[9] It illustrates only a small part of the collection (21 pieces), but importantly shows the gilt-silver buckle (**cat. no. 74**) with what appears to be its original tongue. The present location of the tongue is unknown and the buckle is now associated with a non-matching one of brass (**cat. no. 79**).

The gold figure of a hare (**cat. no. 127**; no. 1 in both the preliminary list and the register) unfortunately remains untraced.

The original composition of the collection

Pieces not in the British Museum

As already stated above the British Museum bought less than half of the collection as offered by Volgeninov, acquiring the full contents of only three of the eight screens illustrated on the photographs provided during the sale (**Archive Pls 1, 2a, 3a**), together with the full contents of one of the five photographs kept in the Simferopol Archives (**Archive Pl. 4**) and a further four pieces (two on **Archive Pl. 5**, one on **Archive Pl. 6** and one on **Archive Pl. 10**). This leaves a total residue of 122 objects illustrated on photographs (**Archive Pls 1–10**) about which nothing is known of either their later history, or present location. The majority of these pieces formed the Late-Antique, 'Greek part' of the collection mentioned in Volgeninov's letters, but nevertheless included important pieces highly relevant to the purchased half, since the division of the contents of the screens by date or culture was sometimes flawed.

The most significant is a sword-pommel of great historical value (**Archive Pl. 7 bottom**), which Rostovtsev noted was on sale in Paris in 1923.[10] He further remarked that it was beautifully decorated with a gold foil overlay, jade and coloured stones similar to one in the Hermitage. The pair of earrings on screen no. 7 (mid-section, one at either side) is an important parallel to the earring (**cat. no. 4**) and to the pendants of the necklace (**cat. no. 9**), both of which were in the purchase of 1923. It is also noteworthy that on the top of screen no. 9 is a pair of earrings very similar to **cat. no. 109**. One of the photographs in the Taurida Scientific Archives Commission (**Archive Pl. 10**) illustrates 34 beads published by Kondakov, said to be of gold and found in Cherson.[11] Among the objects on sale in Paris there was also a Sarmatian necklace with a stone engraved with the figure of Sauromatos II, as noted by Rostovtsev in one of his letters to the British Museum. This necklace was also not included in the purchase and it is hard to tell whether it is illustrated on any of the screens for which we have photographs. According to Volgeninov there were 18 screens altogether in Paris, 8 of which are preserved on the archive photographs, and 2 further screens are possibly illustrated on the archival photographs in Simferopol.

It is not known what the other eight screens held, as no photographs of them survive. According to the figures above, however, they displayed nearly 200 pieces, so quite a large collection of jewellery remains to be located.

In his 1908 address to the French Archaeological Society, Baron de Baye referred to an important group of jewellery from Suuk-Su, which he had seen in the collection of Berthier-Delagarde:

> (...) une série de bijoux très remarquables fut remise à M. Berthier de la Garde. ... Avant me rendre à Gourzouf et à Sououk-Sou, je m'étais arrêté à Yalta pour étudier la belle collection archéologique de l'ingénieur Berthier de la Garde. Naturellement, les objets provenant de Sououk-Sou avaient plus particulièrement fixé mon attention, et leur possesseur a bien voulu m'en donner des photographies, que je suis hereux de soumettre à la Société.[12]

The cemetery of Suuk-Su, near Hurzuf (Gurzuf) in the south of the Crimea, is one of the most important Early-Medieval sites in the peninsula. But only one piece in the British Museum is given the provenance of Suuk-Su in the register: the polyhedral-bead earring (**cat. no. 8**). One of the buckles (**cat. no. 82**) is supposed to have been found there, too, as already mentioned above, and the annotation 'Kerch 1900' may record only the place and date of purchase. Berthier-Delagarde may have bought this piece together with a whole group of other objects at the same time. The same annotation is given to a further 16 items, including some unique pieces of jewellery (**cat. nos 7, 10, 11, 14, 16, 72, 73, 78, 80, 86, 103, 105, 109 and 135;** inventory nos 1923,7–16,52–66 and 72), all of which may therefore also come from Suuk-Su. But the question arises whether the group referred to was really from Suuk-Su, or whether de Baye misinterpreted the source of his information, since Berthier-Delagarde's archaeological material is constantly described as objects of 'Suuk-Su type' by Cherepanova.[13] The inverted commas may indicate that he was quoting from the collector's own documentation, in which case Berthier-Delagarde may have designated a large part of his collection as Suuk-Su type and showed it to de Baye as such. Alternatively, if indeed such a group of jewellery was from Suuk-Su, did it remain among the objects which the British Museum purchased some 15 years later? The group may have been sold before the majority of the collection travelled to France. It is clear that individual items from the collection were disposed of, as is shown by the present location of two eagle-headed buckles, originally published by Repnikov in 1907.[14] This photograph is also kept in the St Petersburg Institute of History.[15] One of the buckles is recorded in the museum of

Breslau (now Wrocław, Poland) in 1912,[16] the other was in Berlin in 1913.[17]

Some objects said to belong to Berthier-Delagarde's collection were published in contemporary literature, but there is no further information about them. Among them are a gold bead from Kuban and a gold earring from Kerch, both of which were published by Kondakov.[18] Also a list of objects all found at Suuk-Su in 1899, which were given to Berthier-Delagarde by the landowner, Berezin, was published by Repnikov.[19] These comprise gold polyhedral-bead earrings , penannular silver bracelets, buckles, blue glass and rock-crystal beads, and a pottery mug. We cannot be certain whether any of them were included in the British Museum purchase, apart from one buckle (**cat. no. 82**). Unfortunately, only five of the objects are published in photographs, including this buckle, the two eagle-headed buckles mentioned above as being sold a few years later; a small silver armlet[20] and a copper-alloy buckle.[21] The further history of the last two items is unknown.

It would be very interesting to know whether there are any other pieces kept in other museums or collections. They might either have been acquired from Berthier-Delagarde himself before his death in 1920, or come from France (after the British Museum purchase of 1923) and be associated with the names of Volgeninov or Beliawsky. Volgeninov remarked that Mme Beliawsky (Berthier-Delagarde's sister) living in Menton, France, was 80 years old and quite ill. He did not mention any other member of the family by name, so the question arises once more regarding the fate of the part of the collection not bought by the British Museum. It could have been auctioned after the death of Mme Beliawsky, or sold as a whole, or piece by piece. But where are the objects now? The sale catalogues of the 1920s and 30s available in London unfortunately do not record any details of them, but the French auctions of the time were not so systematically catalogued and published that the documents available today can be relied upon.

Notes

1. Markevich 1928, 145
2. Kropotkin and Shelov 1971, 140–2
3. These photographs were given to the British Museum by Professor Aleksandr Aibabin
4. Repnikov 1907, 141, pl. XIV:4
5. St Petersburg Institute of History Photo Archives (Fotoarkhiv Instituta Istorii Material'noi Kul'tury Rossiyskoi Akademii Nauk), no. 6779 – I owe this information to Dr Ludmilla Pekarska.
6. Kondakov 1896, 199–200, ill. 113
7. Fettich 1953, 85, pl. XXXI:9
8. Kondakov 1896, 56–7, ill. 31
9. Dalton 1924a pl. XXXVII, reproduced from Dalton 1924b
10. Rostovtsev 1923, 36
11. Kondakov 1896, 56, ill. 30
12. de Baye 1908, 89
13. Cherepanova 1966, 81; 1968, 211
14. Repnikov 1907, 140–1, pl.II:2,3
15. Fotoarchiv Instituta Istorii Material'noi Kul'tury Rossijskoi Akademii Nauk – Photoarchives of the Institute of History of the Russian Academy of Sciences, St Petersburg, photo no. 6779 – information from Dr L. Pekarska.
16. Seger 1912, pl. I:1
17. Amtliche Berichte XXXV 1913–14, 126–7, ill. 65
18. Kondakov 1896, 57 ill. 32 and 197–8, ill. 109
19. Repnikov 1906, 102
20. Repnikov 1907, 142, pl. XVI:13
21. Repnikov 1907, pl. XVI:14

Archive Plate 1 – supplied by Volgeninov

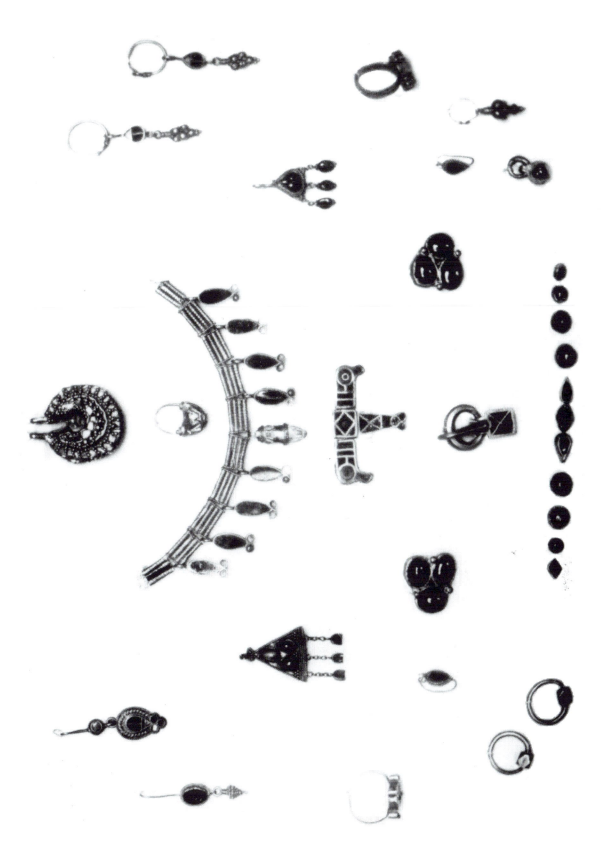

Archive Plate 2b – from Simferopol. Taurid Scientific Archives Commission

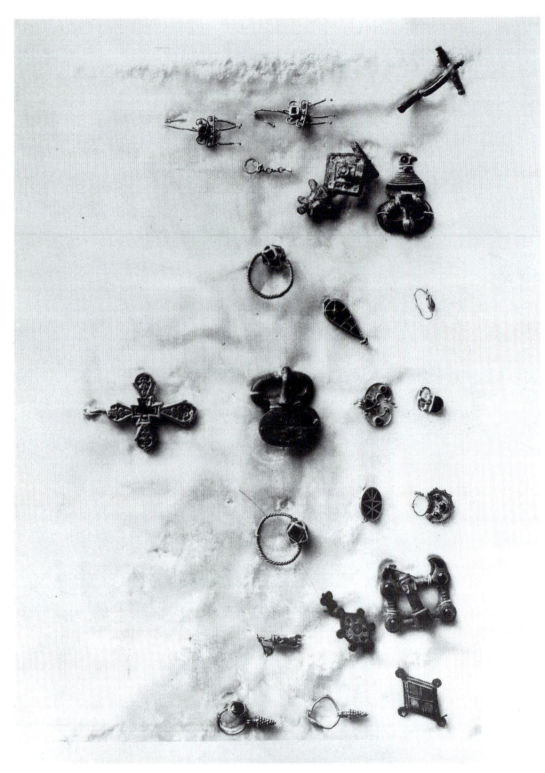

Archive Plate 3b – from Simferopol. Taurid Scientific Archives Commission

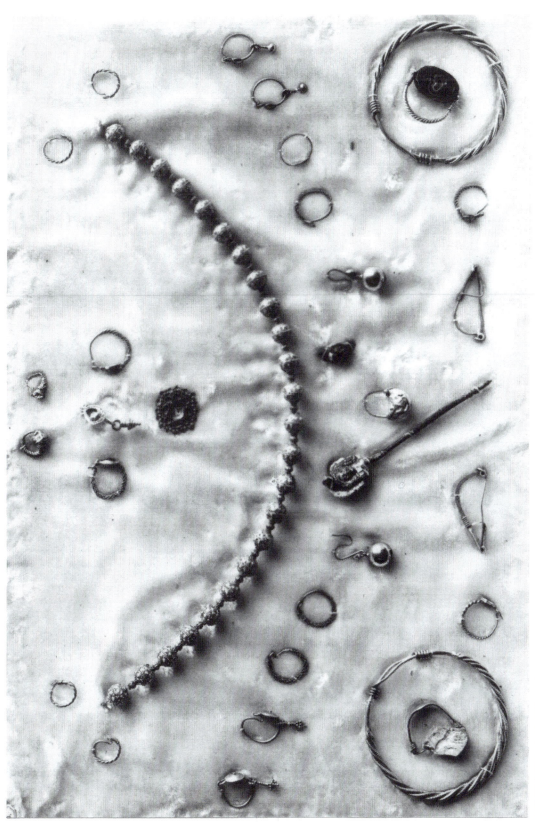

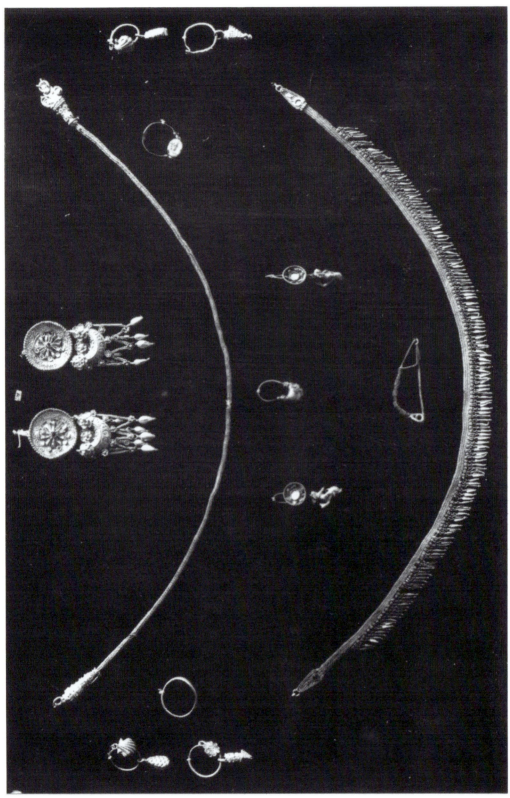

Archive Plate 6 – supplied by Volgeninov

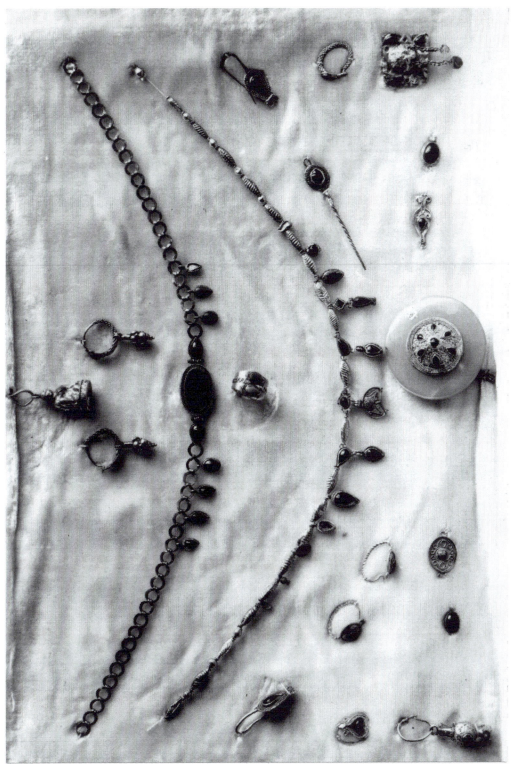

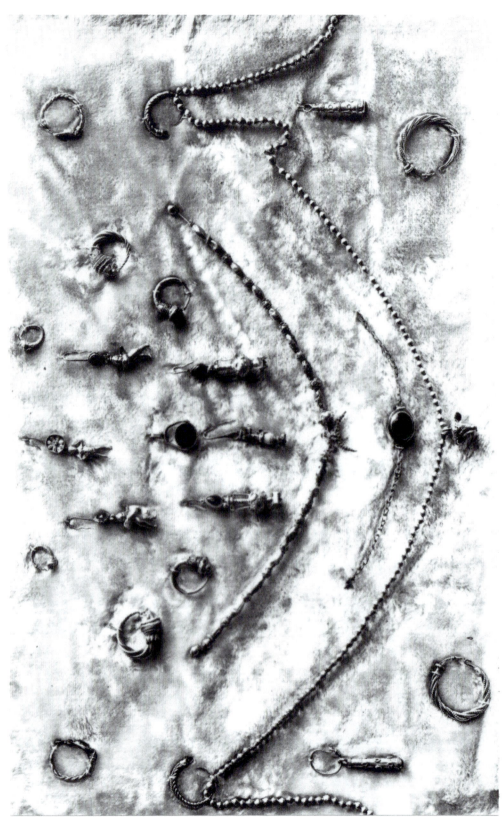

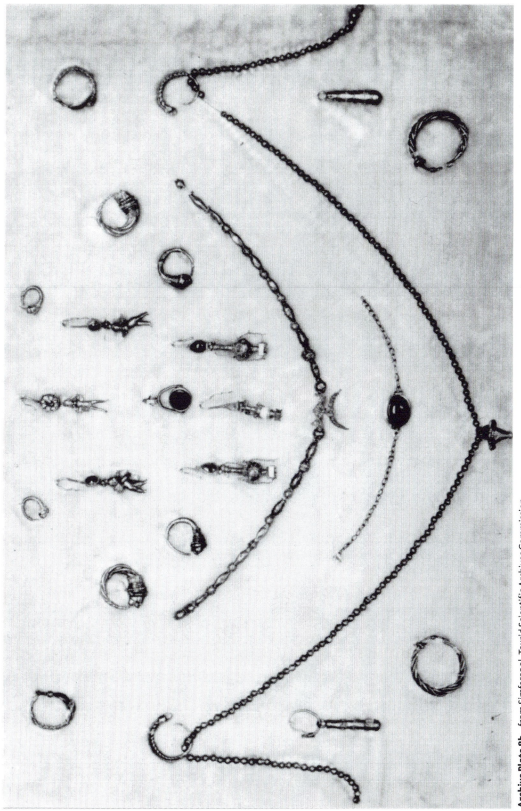

Archive Plate 8b – from Simferopol. Taurid Scientific Archives Commission

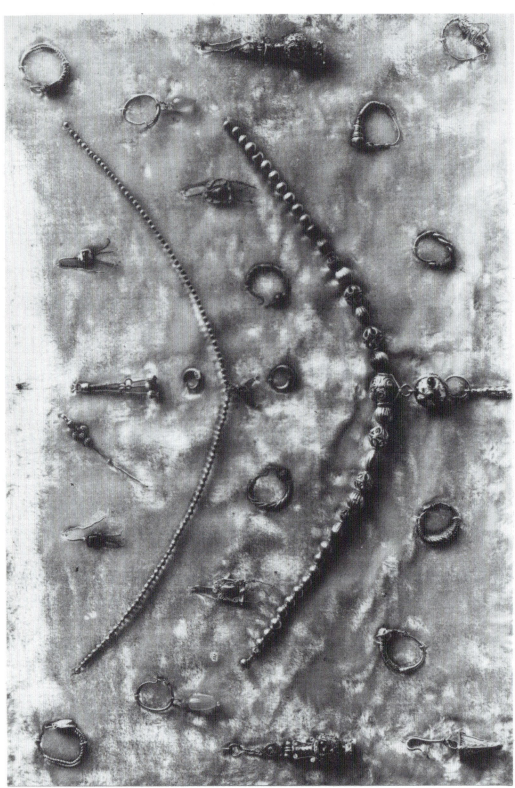

Archive Plate 9 – supplied by Volgeninov

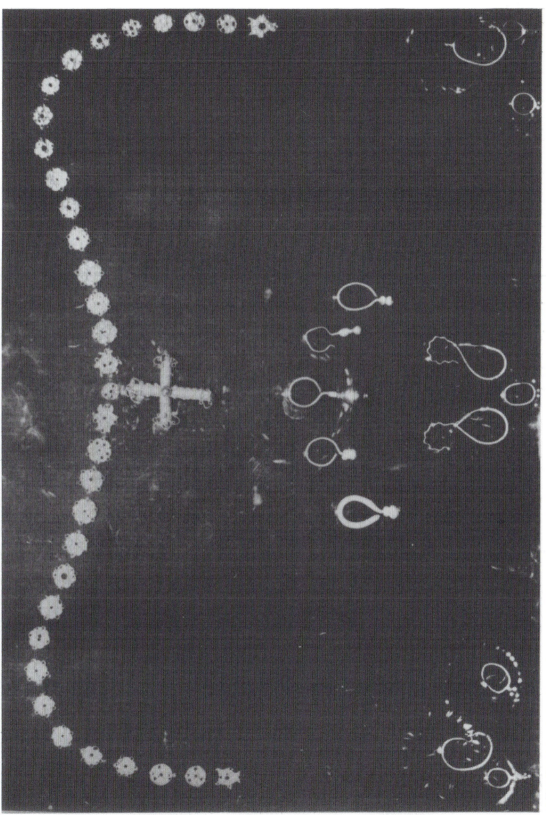

Archive Plate 10 – from Simferopol. Taurid Scientific Archives Commission

Archive **Plate 11** M.I. Rostovtsov's letter to O.M. Dalton describing the importance of the collections. See Transcription p. 31

Archive

Rostovtzeff.

the 26 of May 1923.

Dear Mr Dalton

Thank you very much for your kind letter. The Gothic and Saracenian things do not form the majority of the objects in the collection of Berthier Delagarde. But this sincerity is the best part of the collection not only from the historical but also from the artistic point of view. The Greek and Roman jewels all of little value with few exceptions. If sold separately they will not bring a very much money. I repeat that my impression is that the Saracenian and Gothic part of the collection is a real beauty. The first good collection of such thing which I have seen. My opinion is that half of the price is for the whole collection is rather too little there too much for the Saracenian and Gothic part. But the question of the

price is the affair of Volgrei-uff. He may decide it as he likes. However it is evident to me that without the Saracenian and Gothic things the collection loses its importance both artistic and scientific.

Thank you very much for the Phenoid photos which you had the kindness to send me. I will soon fall use of these.

Yours sincerely
M Rostovtzeff.

Archive Plate 12 M.I. Rostovtsov's letter to O.M. Dalton on the collections. See Transcription p. 31

May 30th 1923.

Dear Sir,

I have referred your letter to the Director of
the Museum. Though the amount suggested by you for the
non-Greek part of the Bertier Delegard Collection, viz.,
£1650, may prove more than we shall be able to give, he
thinks it very desirable that the things should be examined.
My colleague Mr.Reginald Smith, whose work here is concerned
with Barbaric art, will therefore be prepared to come to
Paris without delay, and I should be much obliged if you
could mention a day and hour when he could visit you and make
notes of the collection. He would be able to call on you
next Monday, June 4th or on either of the two following days,
Tuesday 5th, or Wednesday 6th. It is important that we
should know as soon as possible which day you choose, and at
what hour in the morning Mr.Smith could come; it would no
doubt take him a considerable time to make the notes which
we should require.

Awaiting your early reply,

M.A.Volgeninoff,   Yours faithfully.

July 11th 1923.

Dear Sir,

You will be pleased to hear that Mr.
Reginald Smith arrived safely with the collection,
which has now been listed as you desired, but the numbers
are missing in no less than 70 cases. Most of the others
are legible, and I should be glad to have at your early
convenience corresponding extracts from your Catalogue.
As so many cannot be identified, I venture to suggest that
you should send your Catalogue here by registered post
to enable us to make an extract of the part that concerns
us, and I would guarantee to send it back in a fortnight.
This would save you a deal of trouble, and enable us to
identify most of the items without numbers.

The Trustees meet on Saturday, and I anticipate
that they will authorize the purchase, in which case the
amount would be forwarded with as little delay as possible
but please let me know at once whether it is to be made
payable to yourself or to Madame Beliawsky.

I am,

Archive Plate 13a O.M. Dalton's letter M.A Volgeninov on R. Smith's visit to Paris in order to view the objects
Archive Plate 13b O.M. Dalton's letter M.A Volgeninov mentioning the missing numbers and the 'Catalogue'

Transcript of M.I. Rostovtsev's letter to O.M. Dalton describing the importance of the collection (See Archive Pl. 11)

Dear Mr Dalton

I have seen the collection of Berthier-Delagarde. My impression taken from photos was right. As far as I see there is no one fake in the collection. My second impression was also correct. I mean the fact that the Greek, Hellenistic and Roman part contains common things (some of them though unusually beautiful) but the Sarmatian and Gothic part appears to be quite unique not comparable to any collection of which I know. The collection is unique 1) because there are no things of a late date in this collection, everything being of the IIId and the IVth cent.; 2) because there are lots of fine specimens in gold and precious stones, real objects of art 3) because the provenience of all the objects is well known. My advise [sic] to you is to come and to see the collection. The photos give no idea of the value of this set of things. And my second advise [sic] is to buy at least the Sarmatian and Gothic sets. Among the Sarmatian set there is e.g. one find: a necklace (chain) with an engraved stone showing the figure of Sauromates II, King of Bosporus. Among the Gothic – a wonderful cross with an inscription ΦΩC ZΩH. Among the Christian a necklace and cross of the XIIth cent. I do not see why you should not buy the whole collection: the difference in price would be of no great importance and there are some fine things among the Greek jewels. I enclose a card with the address of an Antiquarian who has bought another important collection of S. Russian antiquities, that of Mossono [?]. There are some Sarmatian things of importance, but there are also some fakes. No Gothic things of importance. I am leaving to-morrow for Italy.

Yours sincerely
M. Rostovtseff.

Transcript of M.I. Rostovtsev's letter to O.M. Dalton on the collection (See Archive Pl. 12)

the 26 of May 1923

Dear Mr Dalton

Thank you very much for your kind letter. The Gothic and Sarmatian things do not form the majority of the objects of the collection of Berthier Delagarde. But this minority is the best part of the collection not only from the historical but also from the artistic point of view. The Greek and Roman jewels are of little value with few exceptions. If sold separately they will not bring in very much money. I repeat that my impression is that the Sarmatian and Gothic part of the collection is a real beauty. The first good collection of such thing [sic] which I have seen. My opinion is that half of the price for the whole collection is rather too little than too much for the Sarmatian and Gothic part. But the question of the price is the affair of Volgeninoff. He may decide it as he likes. However it is evident to me that without the Sarmatian and Gothic things the collection loses its importance both artistic and scientific.

Thank you very much for the splendid photos which you had the kindness to send me. I will make full use of them.

Yours sincerely
M. Rostovtseff.

The Catalogue
Júlia Andrási

Artefacts of the 4th–7th centuries AD

Jewellery

1 Earring pendant (Pl. 1, Colour Pl. 2)

Single piece of composite construction.
Triangular gold sheet with one green glass and two garnet cabochons, enriched with filigree, beaded wire and granulation. Three hollow U-shaped pendants are suspended from the base.
4th century Pontic Sarmatian
Gold, garnet, green glass
Prov.: Kerch, Krym (Crimea), Ukraine – 1893
Inv. no: 1923,7-16,11   Old cat. no. 145
Percentage of gold: 75
Size: W: 25.2mm   L: 46mm   Weight: 5.19g
Unpublished

The suspension loop of the pendant is fastened to the apex of the base-plate. It is a 0.7mm wide gold band with a median engraved line. The two ends of the loop are flattened where they are soldered. (W of loop: 1.8mm; D: 4mm).

The base-plate of the pendant is a single sheet in the form of an equilateral triangle, with a wedge-shaped projection at the top to support the decoration. In the middle are three tear-shaped cabochons in gold settings with the edges of the collets bent over to secure the inlays. They are arranged in a triangle with the two garnets side by side beneath the green glass setting. (The base-plate: H: 26mm, sides: 27.2mm, base: 25.1mm; inlays: L: 8mm; W: 5.1mm; collet H: 1mm).

In the field between the two garnets are three granules in a trefoil pattern. There is a beaded-wire border around each collet, which fills the space between the settings. In each corner of the base is a group of six granules arranged in a triangle. Across the base of the triangle runs a 'false-plait' pattern of two pairs of twisted wires. These are flanked by a beaded wire above and below. The pendant has on two sides a similar beaded-wire border, which also frames two granules at the apex. (D of granules: 1mm; W of beaded wire: 0.7mm; W of bordering wire around the pendant: 1mm; W of herring-bone patterned wire: 2 x 1mm; W of beaded wires above and below them: 1mm).

Three loops of circular-section wire with flattened ends are soldered to the back of the base-plate. From each is suspended a loop-in-loop chain of two links, each of circular section wire forming a twisted figure-of-eight. Each chain supports a hollow inverted U-shaped pendant, attached by a loop of circular-section wire soldered to the top. Each pendant consists of two U-shaped sheets attached by a strip soldered round the curved edge and is open at the end. (Size of loops: D: 0.8mm; distance between loops: 1st loop from the angle: 3.1mm; 2nd from the 1st: 7.8mm; 3rd from the 2nd: 8.7mm 3rd from the angle: 5.5mm; chain D: 0.6mm; pendants W: 5mm; L: 5mm; thickness: 2.5mm).

Originally the pendant was probably part of an earring. It may have been connected to the hoop by means of a smaller intermediate plaque connected by a hinge to the top of the triangle (see Coche de la Ferté).

There is a very close parallel from Kerch in the Louvre. It is of similar shape and construction and is dated to the 4th century by Coche de la Ferté.[1] A similar pair of earrings from Kerch-Glinishche in the Diergardt Collection, Cologne, is dated to the 4th century by Damm.[2] Two broadly similar earrings were found in Armenia in 1909–10.[3] Both are of gold and triangular with gold pendants attached to the base, but with a single, central, tear-shaped cabochon. A pair of earrings from Olbia (Mikolayiv, Ukraine) in the Metropolitan Museum of Art, New York, can be related (in shape and construction) to the Crimean ones. It is considered to be Alanic of the first half of the 5th century by Brown,[4] but is in fact of Near-Eastern origin of the 2nd–3rd century (Damm, pers. comm.). The piece in the Berthier-Delagarde Collection is of a later type of this long-lived form. According to Aibabin this type of earring was worn by the Sarmatians in the second half of the 3rd/first half of the 4th century.[5]

Comparative Bibliography
1   Coche de la Ferté 1962, pl. IX
2   Damm 1988, 126–7, ill. 75–7
3   OIAK 1913, 218, ill. 249
4   GHA 1987 (K. Brown), 115, ill. I,21
5   Aibabin below

2 Earring (Pl. 1, Colour Pl. 2)

Single piece of composite construction.
Tear-shaped garnet plate in a gold collet with a double beaded-wire border and plain wire hoop.
Gold, garnet
Prov.: Kerch, Krym (Crimea), Ukraine – 1905
Inv. no. GR 1981,9-5.12 – transferred to Greek and Roman Department in 1981; original Inv. no. 1923,7-16,69   Old cat. no. 266
Percentage of gold: base-plate: 91   hoop: 91
Size: W: 19mm   L: 13mm   Weight: 1.24g

The hoop of the earring and its eye attachment are of circular-section plain wires. They are soldered onto the back of the base-sheet.

The base-plate of the main component is not exactly tear-shaped as the end is not pointed, but stepped and squared off. There are two beaded wires soldered around the collet of the garnet, each end of which is turned back to form a small loop. There is no foil beneath the garnet. (Thickness of garnet: c. 1.5mm). The beaded wire is very uneven and many of the beads are conical rather than spherical. This occurs when the beading tool is held at an angle and pressure is applied irregularly. It is probably done with a single-bladed tool.

The base-plate contains slightly more copper than silver, which is unusual for ancient silver and may be due to contamination from the solder. There is no evidence that this component has been added recently.

There is a similar gold and garnet earring-pair of unknown provenance published by Damm as 4th-century Bosporan.[1] A similar piece from Kerch-Glinishche (Ukraine) serves as the upper part (i.e. a decorated loop) for a triangular earring similar to the one in the Berthier-Delagarde Collection (see **cat. no. 1**).[2] It is also said to be 4th-century Bosporan by Damm.[3] The parallel suggests the possibility that this 'earring' served as a suspension loop for an earring pendant like **cat. no. 1** above.

A pair of earrings of this type from Kerch is dated to the 1st–2nd century by Ondřejová.[4] Further earrings from 'south-Russia' are dated to the 3rd–4th century by Greifenhagen.[5]

Comparative Bibliography
1   Damm 1987, 127–8, ill. 78–9
2   *Op. cit.*, 126–7, ill. 75–7
3   *Op. cit.*
4   Ondřejová 1975, 48–50, pls III:4a,b, IX:4
5   Greifenhagen 1975, I, 45, pl. 22:15–17

3 Earring (Pl. 1, Colour Pl. 3)

A pair, each of composite construction.
Tear-shaped garnet plate in a gold collet with a double twisted wire border and twisted wire hoop.
3rd–4th century?   Late Hellenistic or Roman
Gold, garnet
Prov.: Kerch, Krym (Crimea), Ukraine – 1897

Inv. no. GR 1981,9-5.4 and 5 – transferred to Greek and Roman Department in 1981; original Inv. no. 1923,7-16,48 and 49
Old cat. no. 182
Percentage of gold: no. 1981,9-5.5: 88
Size: no. 4: W: 9mm   Weight: 1.37g:
            no. 5: L: 18mm   Weight: 1.34g:

Similar in shape and decoration to **cat. no. 2** above. The hoop is formed of a twisted wire with one end flattened and soldered onto the back of the base-sheet, the other end plain and bent to form an S-shaped hook. Soldered onto the back of the base-sheet is a circular loop of twisted wire, with both ends flattened. The two wires together form a hook-and-eye fastening. They are of block-twisted type.

The main component has a base-plate in the form of a tear-shaped gold sheet containing a tear-shaped garnet plate at the centre. There is no foil beneath the garnet. The collet of the garnet consists of a single strip of rectangular section, soldered onto the base and bent to form a tear-shape, with a butt-joint at the point. The border of the base-plate is decorated with two concentric lengths of twisted wire (block-twisted type), one soldered around the collet, the other along the edge of the base-plate. The ends of both meet at the point of the tear-shape. (Thickness of garnet plate: c. 1.5mm).

No. 1981,9-5.5 has had its garnet replaced. It is glued onto a pad of fibres.

This type of earring is rather difficult to date, but from similarities to the earring **cat. no. 2** above it is datable probably to the 3rd–4th century as well.

Many earrings from 'south Russia' are published by Greifenhagen[1] as late Hellenistic, of the 3rd–4th century.[1] An earring of unknown provenance in the Museum of Art, Rhode Island, is dated to the 1st century BC–2nd century AD.[2]

Comparative Bibliography
1   Greifenhagen 1975, I, 45, pl. 22:15–24; II, 53, 66, pls 42:7, 52:1–2
2   Rhode Island 1976, 100 no. 40

4   Earring (Pl. 2, Colour Pl. 3)
In two pieces, each of composite construction.
Gold hoop and a tear-shaped pendant with cloisonné garnet inlays, filigree and beaded wire.
End of 4th/first half of the 5th century.   Hunnic period. Pontic.
Gold, garnet
Prov.: Kerch, Krym (Crimea), Ukraine – 1893
Inv. no. 1923,7-16, 6   Old cat. no. 141
Percentage of gold: 93
Size: L: 49mm overall   L of loop-part: 25mm   L of pendant: 27mm
W: 15mm   Weight: 5.87g
Unpublished

The elongated hoop is of circular-section wire and narrows towards the upper end, which is in the form of a long hook for suspension from the ear. The other end is formed into a round loop which secures the pendant. It is flattened where a thin gold disc is soldered above the loop to serve as a base-plate for a garnet disc set in a cylindrical collet. It is bordered with beaded wire made with a multiple-bladed tool. There is a plain gold foil underlay beneath the garnet. (Thickness of hoop: 1mm; L: 17mm; thickness of loop: 1.7mm; D of garnet disc: 4mm; collet H: 2mm).

The pendant is attached to the earring hoop by a loop of circular-section wire, flattened at the ends which are soldered to the base-plate.

The base-plate of the pendant is a single tear-shaped sheet with a trefoil terminal. In the centre is soldered a gold strip to form a tear-shaped collet. It is sub-divided into three cells by an inverted T-shaped setting formed of two strips, each containing a cloisonné garnet inlay. The setting and the pendant itself are each bordered with the same type of beaded wire, made with a multiple tool (as the beaded wire above). In the field between these two wires is a broad corrugated band of gold. At the trefoil terminal of the base-plate there are three identical garnet discs, each in an individual collet. Beneath each of the garnets there is a plain gold foil. (Collet H: 2mm; thickness: 1mm; W of broad wire: 2mm).

One triangular and one circular garnet plate are missing. The other garnet settings are damaged and scratched.

A similar pattern of cloisonné garnet inlay can be seen on the earring pair **cat. no. 5** below.

This appears to be a rather popular type of earring coming mostly from the Black Sea region. It occurs with either two or three circular

settings at the point of the tear-shape.

There is a similar piece in the British Museum from the collection of Alessandro Castellani with an unknown, possibly Italian, provenance, dated by Marshall to the 2nd–3rd century.[1] There is a pair of similar earrings from Taman (south Russia) in the Diergardt Collection, dated to the last quarter of the 4th/first half of the 5th century by Damm,[2] and three similar pairs from Kerch excavated in 1904. One of them has a similar tear-shaped setting divided into three cells by a T-shape. Another has the same arrangement of a central tear-shape and three circular settings at the point. They are dated to the end of the 4th/first half of the 5th century by Zasetskaya[3] and Spitsin,[4] but according to Aibabin[5] they are not earlier than the 5th century. He regards these earrings as typically Hunnic of the 5th century. A similar earring from Kerch in the Louvre is dated to the 3rd–4th century by Coche de la Ferté,[6] and a similar pair from Olbia (Mikolayiv, Ukraine) in Kassel is dated to the 3rd–4th century by Stefanelli and Pettinau.[7] Two similar pairs of earrings were auctioned in Paris in June 1924, and are said to be from the Crimea.[8]

According to a drawing published by Goldina and Vodolago,[9] there are three similar pendants from the Ural region. But on account of the lack of detail in the illustration they may belong to a different, later type; they are inlaid, made of silver and bronze, and possibly date to the 6th–7th century. The other objects from the same grave tend to support the later dating of what might be an example of a long-lived form.

Comparative Bibliography
1   Marshall 1911, 280 no. 2372, pl. 51
2   Damm 1988, 125–6, ills 73, 74
3   Zasetskaya 1979, 16, pl. 2:10 (grave no. 54), 40, 41 (graves excavated 24 June 1904); Zasetskaya 1993, 53, 77, pls 22:84 with glass inlays, 24:85 (with garnets), 50:243 (central amber, circular garnets)
4   Spitsin 1905, 115; 123, ill. 29; 30
5   Aibabin below
6   Coche de la Ferté 1962, pl. IX
7   Stefanelli and Pettinau 1992, 159, ill. 167
8   Sale Cat. Paris 1924, 10. no. 138, pl. IV:138
9   Goldina and Vodolago 1990, 26, 43, 60, 78; pl. XXII:26 (from Verkh-Sainska, Bartimska and Nevolino)

5   Earrings (Pl. 2, Colour Pl. 2)
A pair, each of composite construction.
Gold hoop with tear-shaped pendant decorated with cloisonné garnet inlays and with a gold 'bunch-of-grapes' pendant suspended from its base.
End of 4th/first half of 5th century.   Bosporan.
Gold, garnet
Prov.: Kerch, Krym (Crimea), Ukraine – 1893
Inv. no. 1923,7-16, 9 and 10   Old cat. no. 144
Percentage of gold: cell wall: 91   granulation area: 90
Size: L: 61mm overall   Weight: no.9: 5.11g   no.10: 5.03g
Unpublished

The hoop is made of a twisted gold wire with one end turned back forming a hook, and the other end bent to form a loop then twisted cylindrically around itself in a return. The two ends together form a hook-and-eye fastening. (D of hoop: 18mm; D of wire: 1.5mm; 0.5mm at the hook; D of the loop: 5.5mm).

The pendant has a tear-shaped base-plate. Upon its edge is soldered a 1mm thick gold strip to form a collet which is joined at the point. The tear-shape is divided into three cells by a T-shaped arrangement of two strips. Each cell contains a flat garnet: a triangular one at the point and two triangles with curved outer sides below. The top edges of the cell walls are burred over to hold in the garnets. The garnets have well-finished edges, tapering towards the lower surface. There are plain gold foils beneath the garnet plates, but there is no evidence of backing paste. (Size of tear-shape: 8 x 11mm; H: 2mm; collet thickness: 0.5mm; size of the cells: sides of the triangle: 5mm; 4mm; 4mm; sides of the curved triangles: 2.5mm; 5.5mm; curved side: c. 8mm; thickness of garnets: 1.5mm).

The tear-shaped pendant is suspended by means of a loop hammered to shape and flattened at the end where it is soldered to the back of the base-plate. (D of loop: 6mm; thickness of wire: 1.3mm). At the other end is a similar but smaller loop also soldered to the base-plate. From it is suspended a 'bunch-of-grapes' pendant (D of loop:

4mm; thickness of loop: 1mm; size of the pendant: 22 x 8.5mm).

This is made of seven hollow gold spheres soldered together with small granules in between. Four of the latter form a terminal at the point. Each sphere is made of two hemispheres soldered together. The pendant is suspended by a loop made of a gold strip with a rib along each edge. The loop is soldered to a ribbed strip which has been folded to form a cylinder on top of the pendant and is bordered by beaded wire at the base. (D of spheres: 4mm; D of granules: 1.5mm; D of suspension loop: 4mm, W: 2mm, thickness: 0.8mm; D of cylinder at the top: 2.5mm, L: 3.5mm; thickness of beaded wire: 0.8mm).

The lower suspension loops of the tear-shaped pendants have worn thin, suggesting use over a long period of time.

The 'bunch-of-grapes' pendant and the hoop may not originally have belonged to the tear-shaped pendant (see below).

The triangular garnet plates of both earrings are missing.

The earring **cat. no. 4** above has a similar arrangement of garnets, i.e. in a tear-shaped collet divided into two bow-sided triangles and one triangular cell.

This pair of earrings is constructed with a rather unusual combination of two different types of pendant.

The garnet-inlaid part is very similar to the central pattern of cloisonné garnets that can be seen on the earring **cat. no. 4**. above and also on a pair of earrings from Kerch (excavated 24 June 1904).[1] This part therefore could be dated to the end of the 4th–first half of the 5th century.

But on the other hand, the loop and the 'bunch-of-grapes' pendant are very similar to those of the earring (**cat. no. 106**) below also in the Berthier-Delagarde Collection, and now in the collection of the Greek and Roman Department in the British Museum. There is also a Late-Antique 3rd-century necklace with a similar 'bunch-of-grapes'.[2] Accordingly the lower pendant of the earring – and maybe the hoop as well – seems to be earlier than the garnet-inlaid part.

Comparative Bibliography
1   Spitsin 1905, 119, ill. 29
     Zasetskaya 1979, 7, ill. 2:41; 1993, 53, pl. 24:85
2   Stefanelli and Pettinau 189, no. 226, ill. 226

6   Earrings (Pl. 3, Colour Pl. 1)
A pair.
Small plain hoop and cast polyhedral bead terminal.
End of 4th–5th century – or later (see below).   North Pontic.
Gold
Prov.: Kerch, Krym (Crimea), Ukraine – 1893
Inv. no. 1923,7-16,30 and 31   Old cat. no. 152
Percentage of gold: 78
Size: no. 30: 21 x 20mm   Weight: 5.96g
      no. 31: 20.5 x 20mm   Weight: 6.07g
Published: GHA 1987, (Kidd) 97,110, ill. I,16.h.

The hoop is of thick, circular-section rod bent to form an open ring and hammered to its final shape. At one end it is joined to the bead either by casting or by solder; the other end is free and is slightly thinner, with a cut-off end. (D of hoop: 20mm; D of the hoop-wire at bead: 2.5mm; at the free end: 1.8mm).

Each polyhedral bead is cast with four hexagonal, eight triangular and two octagonal faces. There are indistinct traces of a diamond-shaped depression with concave sides on the hexagonal faces. The decoration is clearest on the front of no. 1923,7-16, 31. (Size of bead: no. 30: 6.5 x 6mm; no. 1: 6 x 7mm).

Both are in good condition. Some of the triangular faces are irregularly formed.

There is a basic disagreement over the origin of polyhedral earrings (see also **cat. no. 7** below). According to one theory (e.g. Vágó and Bóna,[1] Bierbrauer,[2] Damm[3]) this type of earring was popular in the Danubian provinces of the late Roman Empire, and appears in East Germanic graves from the late 4th century up to the mid-6th century. But according to another theory (e.g. Salamon and Barkóczi,[4] Horedt,[5] von Freeden[6]) they derive from the Black Sea/Caspian region, and were spread by Germanic tribes from the 4th century. According to von Freeden they were in use in Central Europe until the 7th century.

The silver and bronze variants of the same type are imitations of the gold ones, which appear in the richer graves. I have surveyed only the gold earrings with solid polyhedral beads. There is an earring from Kerch, found on 24 June, 1904, dated to the end of 4th/first half of 5th century by Zasetskaya.[7] Aibabin dates this type from the 5th to the first

half of the 7th century on the basis of the dating of the other finds from the same grave.[8] The earring from Intercisa (Dunaújváros, Hungary) is dated to the late 4th century.[9] A pair from Maikop (south Russia) is dated to the 4th–5th century by Damm[10] and the earring from Phanagoria (Taman, south Russia) is dated to the same period by Werner.[11] The earring pair from Regöly (Hungary) and its type are dated to the 5th century.[12] A pair of earrings from Sigişoara (Segesvár, Romania) is considered to be a characteristic piece of Gepid fashion of the Hunnic period by Bóna.[13] They are dated to the period between 472–568 by Csallány,[14] while according to Bierbrauer the East Germanic variants of this late-Roman (late 4th-century) type of earring can be dated to the 5th–6th century.[15] There is one from Aquileia (Italy)[16] and another with no provenance, but probably from southern Italy.[17] There is a pair from a woman's grave at Hochfelden (France)[18] found together with late 4th/early 5th-century jewellery, and a smaller and a slightly bigger earring of this type come from Saône-et-Loire, Burgundy.[19] They were found together with objects of fashionable Danubian East Germanic type. There is a pair of unknown provenance in the Museum für Kunst und Gewerbe, Hamburg.[20]

The earring-pair of the Berthier-Delagarde Collection can be considered as early examples of the type, and therefore may be dated to the end of the 4th–5th century.

Comparative Bibliography
1   Vágó and Bóna 1976, 196
2   Bierbrauer 1975, 163–5
3   Damm 1988, 121
4   Salamon and Barkóczi 1971, 74
5   Horedt 1979, 246
6   Von Freeden 1979, 277–287
7   Zasetskaya 1979, ill. 2:39; 1993, 53, pl. 22:86; *I Goti* 1994, (A. I. Aibabin) 116–17, pl. II.7.i
8   Aibabin 1990, 58, pl. 2:60
9   R. Alföldi, Barkóczi *et al.* 1957, 431, 432, ill. 93
10   Damm 1988, 121–2, ill. 63
11   Werner 1956, pl. 48:5
12   Bóna 1991, 160 ill. 100, 288; 1993, 143, ill. 100; 258
13   Bóna 1986a, pl. 26:7;8
14   Csallány 1961, 198, pl. CCXIII:9;10
15   Biebrauer 1975, . 163–5
16   Bierbrauer 1975, 163–4, pl. I:4
17   Bierbrauer 1975, pl. LV:4
18   Hatt 1965, 250
19   Marin 1990, 72
20   Hoffmann and von Claer 1968, 130–131, ill. 85a

7   Earrings (Pl. 3, Colour Pl. 1)
A pair, each of composite construction.
Twisted wire hoop and polyhedral bead with garnet inlays.
5th/early 6th century. North-Pontic.   East Germanic – Alanic?
Gold, garnet, gypsum (core)
Prov.: Kerch, Krym (Crimea), Ukraine – 1900
Inv. no. 1923,7-16, 64 and 65   Old cat. no. 231
Percentage of gold: no. 64: 93   no. 65: 62
Size: no. 64: L: 33mm   W: 31mm: Weight: 8.36g
      no. 65: L: 32mm   W: 30.5mm   Weight: 7.6g   Total: 15.96g
Published: Dalton 1924a, 262, pl. XXXVII:15 and 16 reproduced from Dalton 1924b; Tait 1976, 130 no. 192d, pl. 192; GHA 1987, (Kidd) 113, ill. I,18.a.

The hoop is made of a pair of wires twisted together. They show no evidence of manufacture by twisting or drawing, and may have been hammered. One end of the hoop is fastened into the perforation in one of the square faces of the gold frame. The other end is free and thinner (about half of its thickness: from 2mm to 1mm). (Hoop D: 31mm).

Each polyhedral bead consists of an openwork frame of gold strip filled with eight identical triangular and four identical square garnet inlays. There are no foils visible beneath the garnet plates. The bead has a white core of gypsum. Surface examination under magnification gives no additional information on the construction method. (Size of openwork frame: W: 11.3mm; L: 14mm; thickness: 2mm. Size of garnet inlays: sides of triangles: 4mm; sides of squares: 5mm).

The two opposed square faces have not been cut out but are solid, with a central perforation for attachment of the hoop. Each perforation is bordered by a beaded-wire ring. Between the two holes is an internal cylindrical collar of gold sheet which passes right through the centre of the bead. One of its ends is folded over the beaded wire for reception of the pointed end of the wire hoop. (Perforations D: 2mm).

The gold frame of earring no. 1923,7-16, 65 has been restored. It was made in two halves and soldered together. The garnets were replaced with lighter-coloured, slightly smaller (*c.* 1mm) garnet plates which are not set in the gold as precisely as on no. 1923,7-16, 64; their edges project from the frame.

The hoop of no. 1923,7-16,65 is broken; the inlays are possibly later replacements.

There is a wide variety of garnet-inlaid polyhedral earrings. The closest parallels are as follows. There is a pair of earrings from Mahlberg, grave 1 (Germany) dated to the end of the 5th/beginning of the 6th century by von Freeden.[1] According to her theory this type of earring was spread from the East-Roman provinces of the Black Sea/ Caspian region and Pannonia by the Gothic migration. It disappeared with the fall of the Ostrogothic Kingdom in Italy and was unknown to the Langobards.[2] Salamon and Barkóczi,[3] and Horedt[4] also presume a Caucasian origin, whence this type of earring was spread by Germanic or Alanic tribes. The pair of earrings from Beograd-Čukarica (former Yugoslavia) is dated to the 5th–6th century by Bierbrauer.[5] He regards it as an Ostrogothic-Italian type of an originally provincial-Roman form which appeared among various Germanic groups (Ostrogoths, Gepids and Burgundians) in the 5th–6th century. Bóna and Vágó[6] also assume the late-Roman origin of the form. There is a very similar pair from Olbia (Mikolayiv, Ukraine)[7] and one from Kerch (Crimea).[8] According to Aibabin these earrings were imported to Kerch.[9]

There is a recent brief survey of the bibliography of the type by Quast.[10]

On polyhedral earrings see also **cat. no. 6.**

Comparative Bibliography

1   Von Freeden 1979, pl. 62:2
2   Von Freeden 1979, 253, 260
3   Salamon and Barkóczi 1971, 74
4   Horedt 1979, 246
5   Bierbrauer 1975, 165; pl. LXXVIII:6,7
6   Vágó and Bóna 1976, 196
7   OIAK 1906, 149; ill. 290; it might be the same earring as in Ross 1965, 117; pl. LXXXII:166
8   Fettich 1953, pl. XX:4
9   Aibabin below
10 Quast 1993, 75–7

8   Earring (Pl. 3, Colour Pl. 1)

Single piece of composite construction.
Large hoop with composite polyhedral sheet bead and glass inlays in high collets.
Second half of 6th/beginning of 7th century. East Germanic. Gothic
Gold, glass
Prov.: near Hurzuf ('Gourzouff,' Register), Krym (Crimea), Ukraine – 1900 (more precisely: Suuk-Su; see de Baye below)
Inv. no. 1923,7-16,92   Old cat. no. 234
Percentage of gold: 86
Size: L: 52mm   W: 52mm   Weight: 14.57g
Published: de Baye 1908, 101–3, fig. 11; Dalton 1924a, 262, pl. XXXVII:9 reproduced from Dalton 1924b; Tenishcheva 1930, 102, pl. XXXIX:150; GHA 1987, (Kidd) 113, ill. I,17.

The large hoop is an oval of circular-section wire with one end fastened inside the bead to another wire inside the hole. The other end is free. The small internal wire is flattened where it is soldered to both the hoop and bead; the other end emerges from the hole at the opposite side of the bead. It is possibly the fragment of a clasp, or else may secure the hoop, or give strength to the bead. (Size of hoop: 51.5 x 40mm; thickness: 1.8mm).

The body of the polyhedral bead is made from a single sheet which covers a solid core. The bead is effectively a tube with the ends folded in, and the structure is supported by its core of paste (sulphur). It has four lozenge-shaped and eight triangular faces, with two diamond-shaped ends. In the centre of each of the lozenge-shaped faces is a setting in a high collet. Each collet is formed by a strip bent to shape with the edges folded over to secure a flat, diamond-shaped, red glass inlay imitating garnet. There are no foils visible beneath the inlays. Each collet is bordered by small granules soldered onto the base sheet and each of the eight triangular faces has a central triangle of granulation. Some of the granules – at the points of the triangles or at

the corners of the diamond-shaped settings – are slightly larger than the others. (Size of bead: 21.5 x 19mm; sides of lozenge-shaped faces: 9mm; sides of triangular faces: 7.7mm; sides of garnet-plates: 6mm, size of collets: H: 4mm; D of granules: 0.7mm; some larger ones: D: 1mm).

Each end of the bead has a central perforation through which the hoop passes. Two concentric rings of wire, beaded on one side only, surround the perforation: the inner one lies directly around it and there is a space of about 2mm between the wires. Radial lines observable between the wires are the traces of the folding of the sheet. (D of perforation: 4mm; W of beaded-wire: 1mm).

The beaded wire is of a distinctive type, similar to that on the spacers of necklace (**cat. no. 9**) and on the studs (**cat. no. 29 I–K**).

The gold sheet and collets are damaged and the granulation is imperfect.

This type of earring is very typical in the Crimea, especially at Suuk-Su. Repnikov dated those from Artek and Suuk-Su to the 5th–7th century.[1] There is a pair from Luchyste (Luchistoye) found together with an eagle-headed buckle and radiate-headed brooches of 'Kerch type' in the same chamber.[2] According to Aibabin the earrings are typical south Crimean objects of the second half of the 6th/first half of the 7th century.[3] A very similar earring with a pendant attached to its bead was found in Kuban.[4]

Widespread variants of the type, but with smaller hoops and more faces containing garnet inlays; appear in East Germanic contexts in Italy, Romania (more precisely Transylvania), Austria and the Danube region (e.g. from Laa a.d. Thaya, of the 5th century, from Desana, of the end of 5th/beginning of 6th century, and from Mikelaka, of the 5th century and Gepidic).[5]

Comparative Bibliography

1   Repnikov 1906, 43–4; pl. I:13;17–19; 70 ill. 32,36–8; 72 ill. 52
2   *I Goti* 1994, (A.I. Aibabin) 132–4, pl. II.49; Aibabin and Chajredinova 1995, 191, 193, ills 73, 78 – recently excavated gold earrings with red glass inlays from Luchyste (Luchistoye).
3   Aibabin below
4   de Baye 1891, 468 ill. 420
5   Beninger 1929; GHA 1987, (P. Stadler) 345, 327 pl. 53 ill. VII,37d Bierbrauer 1975, 204–7, pls VI:3,4; IX:4 Bóna 1986a, pl. 26:1,3

9   Necklace (Pls 4–5, Colour Pl. 1)

Eight composite gold pendants with garnet inlays, alternating with 10 composite gold sheet spacers and one blue faience pendant.
End of 4th/first half of the 5th century.   Hunnic period. Bosporan.
Gold, gilt-silver, garnet, blue faience, blue glass
Prov.: Kerch, Krym (Crimea), Ukraine – 1893
Inv. no. 1923,7-16,8   Old cat. no. 143
Percentage of gold: collet of faience pendant 79
                               spacers (all three types) 85
Size: L overall: 160mm   W: 29mm   Weight: 28.5g
Published: Smith 1923, 170; Tait 1976, 130 no. 192a, pl. 192; Tait 1986, 103, 247, ill. 226g; GHA 1987, (Kidd) 110, 111, ill. I,16.a

A Eight gold spacers are of the same type, consisting of four cylinders formed from two ribbed sheets. Each sheet is rolled into a pair of cylinders having a closed S-shaped section. Each spacer was then formed by soldering two pairs of cylinders side by side. Each spacer has a ribbed wire border, imitating beaded wire, but with indentations on one side only. (Spacers: 15.2 x 13.8mm; cylinders D: 2mm). **See Pl. 5**

B Two of the spacers were differently made, comprising only three cylinders: one consists of a pair of cylinders of closed S-shaped section, with a single cylinder soldered alongside. The other spacer consists of a central single cylinder soldered in the middle of a ribbed gold sheet which has its edges rolled inwards to form two outer cylinders. The sheets used have slightly different ribbing. These two spacers have no border wires around their ends. (Spacers: 13 x 8mm; cylinders D: 2; 2.5mm). **See Pl. 5.**

C Each of the eight pendants has a tear-shaped gold sheet base-plate with lobed ends. The collet round each pendant consists of a single gold strip bent outwards at each end to form a cylinder. Each collet contains a flat tear-shaped garnet with two circular cabochons beneath. The other tear-shape is not flat, but a cabochon garnet. There is a gilt-silver foil beneath each garnet plate (the black fragments preserved in the collets of the missing cabochons might be the remains of such foils). The suspension loop of each pendant is made of a circular-section gold wire, bent to form an open ring. It is attached by soldering to either side of a small projection from the top of the back-plate and to the corresponding part of the collet. The spacers and pendants are now strung by threads going through the cylinders of the spacers and the loops of the pendants. (Pendants: 24.5 x 7.5mm; tear-shapes L: 15.4mm; collet H: 3.8mm, thickness of collet: 0.5mm; circular cabochons D: 4mm; thickness of the loop: 1.4mm; D: 6mm). **See Pl. 5.**

D The blue faience pendant is biconical and decorated with longitudinal ribs. It is held in a sheet gold collet which has a soldered seam and is crimped around the girth of the pendant and over a sheet gold disc at the top. A pair of block-twisted gold wires are soldered around both the top and bottom edges. Three tear-shaped settings of blue glass decorate the upper part of the collet, each in a gold strip collet. The loop of the pendant is a cast, circular gold band with ribbed decoration, which is soldered to the top disc. (Pendant: 27 x 12mm; stone L: 9.5mm, upper D: 7.8mm; W of each wire: 0.5mm; size of small tear-shapes: 4.5 x 3.1mm; collet H: 1.3mm; D of the loop: 0.8mm; thickness of the band: 5.6mm).

The fourth pendant from the left was possibly mended later because its loop is fastened to a projection of the side strip.

Thirteen of the circular cabochon garnets are missing. Traces of two of them are visible in their settings. The fastener of the necklace is also missing.

The beaded wires on eight of the spacers are of a distinctive type, beaded on one side only, similar to that on the studs (**cat. nos 29 I–K**) and on the earring (**cat. no. 8**).

The original photograph (**Archive Pl. 2a, 2b**) shows that, at the time it was taken, all the spacers and pendants were associated together. It is possible that they were contemporary, but some of the pieces may have been added in modern times: two of the spacers were made in a different technique, and the faience pendant is very different from the others. Since there is no positive evidence that they were originally associated the new photograph omits one of the spacers and the faience pendant.

There are similar tear-shaped pendants from south Russia in the Diergardt Collection. One single pendant and four pendants as parts of a necklace were found at Maikop; another pendant comes from Taman, and all are dated to the 5th century by Damm.[1] A necklace with similar pendants of bronze and glass was found at Shipovo on the Derkul (Ukraine) and is dated to the 5th century by Werner.[2] A gold hair-pin from Normandy has a terminal of a similar shape to the necklace pendants, although constructed differently, and may be compared with them. Kazanski dates it to the end of the 4th/beginning of the 5th century.[3] A pair of similarly-shaped earrings formerly belonged to the Berthier-Delagarde Collection, but is now only recorded in an archival photograph (**Arch Pl. 7**).[4]

Necklaces from the Terlecki Collection (Kerch) and from the Massoneau Collection (south Russia) contain similar components to the spacers of the Berthier-Delagarde necklace and are dated to the 1st–2nd century by Greifenhagen.[5] One of these necklaces also contains a pendant very similar to the mount (**no. 26**) in the collection[6] and another has a pendant in the shape of a clenched fist, like **no. 104**.[7] It is therefore possible that the spacers were made earlier than the garnet-inlaid pendants, and were parts of a separate necklace (they differ also in their gold composition).

Gold objects similar to the spacers of our necklace have been found at Kerch, grave nos 154 and 175, and are considered to be Bosporan of the end of 4th/first half of the 5th century.[8]

According to Aibabin this type of necklace belongs to the 5th-century Hunnic period.[9]

Comparative Bibliography
1   Damm 1988, 132–3 ills 91, 92; 137–138 ills 101–3
2   Werner 1956, pl. 7.1; Zasetskaya 1994, 189, pl. 40:8
3   Kazanski 1989, 61 ill. 1/3
4   Volgeninov's photograph; see Archive Pl. 7
5   Greifenhagen 1975, 22–5, pls 13:6,7; 14; 16:4,6,7
6   Greifenhagen *op. cit.*, pl. 14:3
7   Greifenhagen *op. cit.*, pl. 14:6
8   Zasetskaya 1993, 74, pl.47:220 (four, same size as the Berthier-Delagarde ones), 87, pl. 57:324; *I Goti* 1994, (A.I. Aibabin) 125–6, pl. II.27.b
9   Aibabin below

10   Pendant (Pl. 6, Colour Pl. 3)

Single piece of composite construction.
Gold pendant in the form of two conjoined birds' heads, decorated with beaded wire, granulation and garnet inlays in collets.
5th century. Pontic. East Germanic.
Gold, garnet.
Prov.: Kerch, Krym (Crimea), Ukraine – 1900
Inv. no. 1923,7-16,54   Old cat. no. 216
Percentage of gold: 90
Size: L: 26mm   W: 21mm   Weight: 3.7g
The object is in good condition.
Published: Tait 1986, 103, 247, ill.226b; GHA 1987, (Kidd) 97, 110, ill. I,16.b; Kargopol'tsev and Bazhan 1993, pl. 2:14

The suspension loop consists of a triple-ribbed strip bent to form a cylinder. It is fastened to the back of the base-plate where it is flattened for soldering, but the front edge is free. (Size of loop: D: 4mm; W: 4mm).

The base-plate of the pendant consists of a lunate gold sheet. The outline has been transformed by placing a cylindrical collet containing a garnet disc on each side to represent the eyes of a bird. In the centre directly below the loop is a triangular collet with a flat garnet inlay. Each of the three collets has been formed by bending a single gold strip, and is bordered with a beaded wire. The garnets are roughly shaped and there is no foil visible beneath them. The pendant has a precisely-formed, beaded-wire border made from three separate sections soldered onto the edge of the sheet: a single wire runs along the outside curve, passing within the loop, and the other two lie along the inner curves. There are five granules in a V-formation flanking the beaded-wire border of the central triangular setting. A similar large granule is soldered onto both birds' beaks at the points of the base-plate. (Size of garnet disc: D: 4.5mm; collet H: 2.3mm; thickness: 0.5mm; W of beaded wire: 1mm; D of granules: 1.5mm).

Kargopol'tsev and Bazhan give a brief survey of the different types of lunate pendant from the 3rd to the 6th century.[1] They date the Berthier-Delagarde and similar pendants to the end of the 4th–5th century regarding this variant as a combination of Sarmatian, Alanic, Sassanian, provincial-Roman and possibly Hunnic components.

The early types of lunate pendant from the Siret and Dniester area were surveyed by Werner.[2] It is possible that they gave rise to the later forms of garnet-inlaid pendants, some of which incorporate two opposed birds' heads in their decoration. Lunate pendants, both of stamped sheet and cast, with bird-headed terminals, are known from Scandinavia in the 5th century.[3] The closest parallel to the Berthier-Delagarde example is the pendant from a Gepid grave at Oradea (Nagyvárad, Romania), dated by Bóna to the end of the 5th/beginning of the 6th century.[4] A similar pendant from Gáva (Hungary) is dated to the first half of the 5th century by Alföldi,[5] but to the second half by Annibaldi and Werner.[6] There is a similar pendant from Laa an der Thaya (Austria) in Berlin (Museum für Vor- und Frühgeschichte).[7] The pendant from Strachotín (Bohemia) is considered to be Herulian, of the second half of the 5th century by Tejral.[8] Two pendants of this form from Verkhnyaya Rutka (Ossetia) are dated to the end of the 4th–5th century by Kargopol'tsev and Bazhan.[9] According to Aibabin this type of pendant was imported to the Crimea from the Gepid or Ostrogothic regions.[10]

Comparative Bibliography
1   Kargopol'tsev and Bazhan 1993, 113–22
2   Werner 1988, 241–86
3   Kargopol'tsev and Bazhan *op. cit.*, 116–18
4   Bóna 1986, 153 pl. 29.2
5   Alföldi 1932, 58 ill. 19; GHA 1987, (P. Németh) pl. 19:V,9.a; 222 as 'early Gepid' (4th/early 5th century).
6   Annibaldi and Werner 1963, 371
7   Kühn 1935a, 456 no. 10
8   GHA 1987, (J. Tejral) 376; pl. 58.VIII,18.b
9   Kargopol'tsev and Bazhan *op. cit.*, 116
10 Aibabin below

11   Pendant (Pl. 6, Colour Pl. 3)

Single piece of composite construction.
Tear-shaped gold pendant decorated with all-over garnets, green glass and a central cabochon, with beaded wire and granulation.
5th century.   Pontic. East Germanic.
Gold, garnet, green glass.

Prov.: Kerch, Krym (Crimea), Ukraine – 1900
Inv. no. 1923,7-16,55   Old cat. no. 217
Percentage of gold: 90
Platinum group inclusions are present in the gold, suggesting an alluvial source.
Size: L: 37mm   W: 14mm   Weight: 5.08g
Published: Dalton 1924a, 262, pl. XXXVII:1 reproduced from Dalton 1924b; Moss 1935, xiv, pl. III B lower right; Tait 1976, 130 no. 192c, pl. 192; Tait 1986, 103, 247, ill. 226e; GHA 1987, (Kidd) 110, 111, ill. I, 16.c.

The suspension loop is a triple-ribbed strip bent to form a cylinder and is flattened where soldered to the base-plate (D: 3mm; thickness: 0.6mm). The loop is similar to that of **cat. no. 10** above.

The base-plate consists of a tear-shaped gold sheet with a squared end. By means of an overlapping joint a trefoil of gold sheet has been soldered to the end to create a point.

At the centre of the pendant is a tear-shaped cabochon garnet. Round it are seven symmetrically-placed cloisons each containing a flat garnet, with another of triangular green glass directly below the suspension loop. The garnets are roughly cut. The cell walls are burred over at the top to secure the inlays. This obscures the joins in the cells and nothing can be said about how the strips forming them were assembled. There is no foil visible beneath the garnets. A single beaded-wire border passes within the loop. (Size of central cabochon: L: 7.2mm; W: 4mm; H: 0.8mm; W of the collet of the inlays: 0.8-1mm; W of beaded wire: 0.6mm).

The terminal is formed by a trefoil gold sheet soldered to the end of the base-plate and is decorated with four soldered-on granules (D: 2mm).

(Size of each setting from the point: circumference of the triangle: 2 x 6mm+4mm; of each rectangle above: 1.8mm+4.7mm+4.2mm+3mm; of rectangles above: 3mm; 5mm; 5.5mm; 2.7mm; rectangles at the top: 2.7mm+6.5mm+4mm+4.2mm; of the green glass triangle: 2 x 4.2mm+6.9mm).

The gold collet is damaged at the point of the tear-shape.

No exact parallels to this pendant could be found in the literature but there are some similarities in technique to the pendant above (**cat. no. 10**).

According to Aibabin this type of object is a unique find in the Crimea.[1] It was imported from the Gepid or Ostrogothic regions, and is evidence of connections between Crimean Gothia, the Danube region and Italy.

Comparative Bibliography
1   Aibabin below

12   Finger-ring (Pl. 7)

Single piece of composite construction.
The circular gold bezel is decorated with cloisonné garnets and cabochon glass inlays in cylindrical settings. The hoop is formed by a strip of triangular section.
Second half of the 5th century.   East Germanic.
Gold, garnet, glass
Prov.: Kerch, Krym (Crimea), Ukraine – 1893
Inv. no. 1923,7-16,14   Old cat. no. 148
Percentage of gold:83
Size: W of the bezel at the hoop: 20mm   W across: 19mm   H: 24.5mm
Weight: 5.18g
Published: GHA 1987, (Kidd) 110, ill. I,16.i.

The base-plate of the bezel consists of a single circular sheet with four pairs of projecting lobes in a cruciform arrangement to support eight cylindrical collets. The wall of the bezel is formed by a single strip soldered to the base-plate. Each of the eight cylinders is independently soldered to the base-plate, to the wall of the bezel and to its pair. Not all of the collets have soldered seams.

At the centre of the bezel is a cabochon glass inlay in a circular cell. The bezel is further divided into four quadrants, each cell containing a cloisonné garnet which is roughly cut. There is a plain gold foil beneath each of the garnet plates. The cell walls do not extend to the full depth of the bezel. The junctions of the central cell walls are soldered and the tops are burred over to secure the stones. (Size of cells: sides: 3.2mm; thickness of the sides differs: 0.2mm-0.9mm; D of central glass: 3.6mm; H: 1.9mm).

There are four pairs of cabochon settings in the cylindrical collets. The original inlays were all possibly garnets, but are now pink and yellow glass. Several of the stones, including the central cabochon and two of the cloisonné garnets, are held by wax (probably beeswax) which, together with gypsum, fills the cavity. (Stones: D: 2.6mm; cylinder H: 4mm; each pair of cylinders W: 6mm; collet thickness: 0.2mm).

The hoop consists of a strip, triangular in section and slightly oval in plan. The ends are lap-jointed where they are flattened and soldered off-centre beneath the base-plate of the bezel. The axis of the hoop to the bezel deviates slightly from a right angle. (Size of hoop: 32.5 x 18.5mm; thickness: 1mm; hoop W: 3mm).

One of the four garnet plates in the bezel is missing. The other inlays are damaged and some of them are possibly not original. The base-plate is damaged and one of the cabochons is missing.

A very similar ring, probably from the same workshop, was found in a Germanic aristocratic grave at Dunapataj-Bödpuszta ('Bakodpuszta,' Hungary).[1] According to Kiss it was made in one of the Late-Antique workshops of the Black Sea area, and such rings were worn by members of the Scirian ruling family in the second third of the 5th century.[2] Bierbrauer dated it to the mid to second half of that century.[3] There is a similar ring from the Kuban region (south Russia) with a circular bezel and peripheral cylindrical collets.[4] Another, broadly similar ring in the British Museum (P&E AF 493) with a garnet-inlaid circular bezel enriched with granulation, is dated to the 6th century and said to be Ostrogothic.[5] According to Bóna these rings appear from the second half of the 5th century.[6] Aibabin[7] considers this type of ring as a unique find in the Crimea. They are Germanic objects of the second half of the 5th century and were imported to the Crimea.

Comparative Bibliography
1   Fettich 1951, pl. XVIII:3,3a
     Bóna 1968, 125 (who considers it as Scirian)
2   Kiss 1983, 95–131; Garam and Kiss 1992, 12; ills 31, 34
3   Bierbrauer 1975, 168
4   Kondakov et al. 1891, 475; ill. 430
5   Museum register
6   Bóna 1991, 291; 1993, 260
7   Aibabin below

13   Finger-ring (Pl. 7)

Single piece of composite construction.
The square gold bezel is decorated with cloisonné garnets, white inlay and cabochon glass inlays. The hoop is enriched with beaded wire and filigree.
Second half of the 5th century.   East Germanic.
Gold, garnet, glass, cristobalite white inlay, wax
Prov.: Kerch, Krym (Crimea), Ukraine – 1893
Inv. no. 1923,7-16,15   Old cat. no. 149
Percentage of gold: 85: side of bezel
84: hoop
Size: W (bezel): 20.6mm   H: 26mm   Weight: 7.67g
Published: GHA 1987, (Kidd) 110, 111, ill. I,16.j.

The base-plate of the bezel consists of a single square sheet with four pairs of projecting lobes at the corners to support eight cylindrical collets. The walls of the bezel and of the eight cylinders are all formed from a single strip, made by complex folding, and soldered to the base-plate. This construction differs from that of **cat. no. 12** above.

At the centre of the bezel is a small yellow glass cabochon, secured with black wax, probably beeswax. The bezel is further divided into a square in the centre, which is filled with a white inlay (cristobalite, SiO_2) and into eight isosceles-triangular garnet settings. Four of the triangles are arranged around a central square and are enclosed by the other four, the cell walls thus forming a square within a square within a square. The garnets are roughly cut. It cannot be ascertained whether there are foils beneath them. All the internal cell walls are joined with solder and the tops are burred over to secure the stones. (Sides of bezel: 11mm; sides of squares: 11mm; 7.5mm; 6mm; collet thickness: 0.2–0.7mm; D of central cabochon: 1.4mm).

A pair of cylindrical collets projects from each corner. One of the pairs is filled with light red glass cabochons and two collets contain cream-coloured ones. Three of the inlays are missing. The collets contain a white paste (gypsum), which may be the remains of the original supporting paste (cylinder H: 4mm).

The base-plate is decorated with double granulations directly above the hoop (D of granules: 1.8mm).

The hoop consists of a bent strip, slightly oval in plan, and its ends are butt-jointed under the centre of the bezel. It is decorated with a 'false-plait' pattern of two pairs of twisted wires along the centre, and a beaded-wire border along both edges. The beaded wires are soldered to the edges of the hoop. The axis of the hoop to the bezel deviates slightly from a right angle (as on **cat. no. 12** above). (Size of hoop: D: 20.5mm; 19mm; 5mm wide and 1.2mm thick).

Four cabochon inlays are missing and the glass ones are possibly replacements.

The material of the central white inlay (cristobalite) is unusual; most inlays of this type are of shell, bone/ivory or magnesite ($MgCO_3$).[1]

This ring is a variant of the same basic type as **cat. no. 12** above. Similar rings with a square bezel and peripheral circular inlays have been found in Taman (south Russia),[2] Olbia (Mikolayiv, Ukraine),[3] Dunapataj-Bödpuszta ('Bakodpuszta,' Hungary),[4] Cluj-Someşeni (Kolozsvár-Szamosfalva, Romania),[5] Ficarolo (Italy)[6] and Lörrach (Germany).[7] There are also three pieces of unknown provenance, one in the Hungarian National Museum (Inv. no. N.465),[8] and two in a German private collection.[9] Also five pendants of the same form have been found at Cluj-Someseni [10] They are considered to belong to the second half of the 5th century. The ring from Taman is in the Diergardt Collection and is dated to the 5th century by Damm.[11] The one from Lörrach was found together with Aquileia-type radiate-headed brooches and is dated to the first half of the 6th century by Werner[12] and Bierbrauer.[13] The ring from Ficarolo is early 6th century, Gepid, Ostrogothic or Alamannic according to Bierbrauer,[14] and related to the similar Danubian East Germanic rings of the mid/second half of the 5th century. The one from 'Bakodpuszta' is considered to be Scirian of the second third of the 5th century by Kiss.[15] According to Bóna these rings appear from the second half of the 5th century.[16] Aibabin regards this type of ring, like the comparable example above (**cat. no. 12**), as a unique find in the Crimea.[17]

Comparative Bibliography

1   La Niece 1988, 238–40
2   Götze 1915, 12 no. 5 ('4th–5th century')
3   Ross 1965, 117–118; pl. LXXXI:D (Gothic, late 4th/early 5th century)
4   Fettich 1951, pl. XVIII:2,2a,2b
5   Horedt and Protase 1970, 96; pls 24:1–3; 23.19–24
6   Bierbrauer et al. 1993, ills 2; 4; 4:2
7   Werner 1961a, 68–75; pl. 6:4a,b
8   Bierbrauer 1975, 168; Kiss 1983, 111
9   Catalogued by Dr. A.B. Chadour, Coll. no. 38,34; 38,35; Chadour 1994, 151, nos 505, 506
10 Horedt and Protase op. cit., pl. 23:19–24
11 Damm 1988, 155
12 Werner 1961a, 75
13 Bierbrauer 1975, 168
14 Bierbrauer et al. 1993, 324–8; I Goti 1994, (V. Bierbrauer) 186–7, pl. III.61.d
15 Kiss 1983, 95–131; Garam and Kiss 1992, p. 12; ills 31–4
16 Bóna 1991, 291; 1993, 260
17 Aibabin below

14   Brooch (Pl. 8, Colour Pl. 4)

Single piece of composite construction.
Flat, oval gold brooch with all-over cloisonné garnet inlays.
End of 4th–5th century.   North Pontic.
Gold, garnet.
Prov.: Kerch, Krym (Crimea), Ukraine – 1900
Inv. no. 1923,7-16,59 Old cat. no. 224
Percentage of gold: 64
Size: 15.5 x 19.5mm   H: 13.5mm   Weight: 4.4g
Published: Dalton 1924a, 262, pl. XXXVII:8 reprinted from Dalton 1924b; Tait 1986, 103,247, ill. 226c; GHA 1987, (Kidd) 110,111, ill. I,16.e.

The brooch has an oval base-plate of gold sheet. Around its edge is soldered a 2.5mm high and 1mm thick gold strip forming a collet. Inside, and dividing it in half, is a median strip,. on either side of which are five triangular cells, each with a flat garnet inlay. The shape and arrangement of the triangles is, apparently, deliberately asymmetrical. The garnets are roughly cut to shape and are of different sizes. There is no means of access to examine foils or backing paste, but both are probably present. The internal cell walls were made individually (except for the median longitudinal one ?) and their top edges are heavily burred over to secure the garnets. No joins are visible in the cell walls. (Size of garnets: sides from the equilateral triangle on the bottom: 5.3mm; 6.1mm; 5.7mm; 3mm; 5.2mm; 6.1mm; 5.8mm;

6mm; 3.5mm; collet thickness: 1mm).

The spring-holder and pin-catch are soldered to the base-plate. Both were made of a single gold strip folded double and soldered to the base-plate by being bent at a right angle at each end. The spring-holder is perforated to secure the pin-spring axis. (Size of spring-holder and pin-catch: thickness: 0.8mm; W of pin-catch: 6.2mm; W of spring-holder: 4mm; H of both of them: 5mm; D of perforation through the spring-holder: 1.5mm).

The pin is missing.

This brooch is unique in the Berthier-Delagarde Collection, and hard to parallel elsewhere. The closest parallel is to be seen in the asymmetrical garnet cloisonné of the gold disc brooches in the second Szilágysomlyó-treasure (Şimleul Silvaniei, Romania),[1] or the gold strap-ends from Szeged-Nagyszéksós (Hungary),[2] since they are all decorated with different-sized triangular garnet inlays. There is a gold brooch from Novae (near Svishtov, Bulgaria)[3] with all-over cloisonné cell walls possibly for garnet inlays, but it is square with a circular setting at each corner resembling the finger-ring **cat. no. 13** in the collection).

The Berthier-Delagarde brooch may therefore be dated to the end of the 4th/first half of the 5th century.

Comparative Bibliography

1   Fettich 1932, 18–19, pls IV:1, V
2   Alföldi 1932, pl. XV:61, 71–2; Fettich 1953, pl. II:2–4
3   Chichikova 1980, 66, ill. 15

15   Brooch (Pls 8–9, Colour Pl. 1)

Single piece of composite construction.
The brooch is in the form of an openwork wheel with wedge-shaped projections. It is decorated with cloisonné garnets and granulation.
End of 4th–first half of 5th century ?
Gilt-silver, silver, garnet
Prov.: Olbia (Mikolayiv), Ukraine – 1909
Inv. no. 1923,7-16,73   Old cat. no. 271
Percentage of silver: 68
Size: D: 55mm   Weight: 21.66g
Published: Dalton 1924a, 262, pl. XXXVII:13 reproduced from Dalton 1924b; Rupp 1937, 82, pl. 24:10; Werner 1961b, 37 no. 172 note (who sheds doubt on findspot and attribution, and gives a false provenance of Kerch to this piece)

The silver base-plate of the brooch is cast in one piece. It consists of a ring of flat rectangular section containing four arms in a cruciform shape, and has seven trapezoidal plates projecting from the outer edge. The base-plate is overlaid with a gilt-silver plate which consists of a ring of similar section containing an identical internal cross. Its diameter is slightly less than that of the base-plate. Around the outer edge is a border of granulation. It does not have any projection cast around the edge, but instead, seven wedge-shaped gilt-silver collets are individually attached to the base-plate. (D of ring: 42mm; W: 7mm; distance between the trapezoids: 15mm; sides of the trapezoids: 7.3mm; 2 x 5.5mm; thickness of the double plate: 2mm).

The upper ring contains twenty-four equilateral triangular openings, each containing a flat garnet inlay. Each projecting wedge is also inlaid with a flat garnet plate. Each arm of the openwork cross contains a pair of stepped garnet inlays. The centre of the cross is an octagon with four concave sides. Each of these contains a garnet strip inlay in the form of an arc of a quarter circle cut to match each other. From the centre protrudes a circular gilt-silver collet containing a garnet disc and secured with a rivet. There is a rectangular area containing four fragments of flat garnet around the rivet-shank. It is impossible to determine whether this is in its original state, was caused by drilling for the central collet, or has occurred after manufacture. Each garnet plate is 1mm away from the edge and most of them well-cut edges, but the step-shapes are not of the finest workmanship. There are no foils or backing pastes in evidence now. The garnets are held in place by slight burring of the top edges of the gilded front plate. (Sides of the triangles: 4mm; 2mm between each triangle; size of the stepped garnets: 3.5 x 5.5mm; steps: 1mm, garnet strips: 1 x 8mm, sides of central garnet: 5mm, central garnet disc: D: 4mm; H: 2mm).

The pin-holder and pin-catch are soldered onto the back of the base-plate. The catch consists of a single strip of silver, folded double and bent at a right angle to form a hook. The fragment of the pin-holder is a single strip.

See **Pl. 9** for construction.

The brooch has suffered heavy restoration, making the surface appearance difficult to interpret.

Many of the garnets are now cracked. One of the peripheral trapezoid garnet plates is missing.

There is a disc brooch in the Diergardt Collection, said to be 7th-century Merovingian by Werner, who cites this piece as a parallel.[1] There are two other related brooches of unknown provenance, one in the Hungarian National Museum,[2] the other published by Rupp.[3]

There is no evidence for the exact dating of the type, although they might be related to late-Roman wheel-shaped disc brooches.

According to Aibabin this type of brooch is a unique find in the Black Sea region.[4]

Comparative Bibliography

1 Werner 1961b, 37, pl. 37:172
2 Hungarian National Museum, Inv. no. 61.118.2
3 Rupp 1937, pl. XXIV:7. It is in the Wallraf-Richartz Museum, Cologne, and possibly from the northern Rhineland (Inv. no. 4620)
4 Aibabin below

16 Cicada brooch (Pl. 10)

Single piece of composite construction.
Silver brooch in the form of a winged insect, or perhaps of a plant.
Late 4th–5th century.   Hunnic period. (Sarmatian ? Alanic ?)
Silver, copper-alloy
Prov.: Kerch, Krym (Crimea), Ukraine – 1900
Inv. no. 1923,7-16,57
Old cat. no. 221
Percentage of silver: 87
Size: L: 38mm   W: 29mm   Weight: 6.39g
Published: Kühn 1935b, 90 no. 55; pl. 24:51; Brentjes 1954, 902 note 14; GHA 1987, (Kidd) 110, 111, ill. I,16.d.

Silver brooch with the features cast in relief on the front. It has a hemispherical terminal of plano-convex section with two moulded ribs beneath. This forms the base for two outer wings (or leaves), which splay out either side of the central body (or bud). The wings have a roof-shaped cross-section and their edges are slightly curved. (D of terminal: 7mm; H of plate: 2.5mm; W of each wing: 7mm; ribs: 1.2 x 7mm).

The back of the brooch is flat.

The pin-catch and the spring-holder are cast. The spring-holder is a semicircular lug, perforated to secure a copper-alloy pin-spring axis. Fragments of the copper-alloy spring are preserved. The pin-catch is a single strip bent over to secure the pin. A fragment of the copper-alloy pin is preserved. (Spring-holder: W: 7mm; H: 6mm; thickness: 1mm; spring-holder bar: D: 2mm; L: 10.5mm; spring: W: 2mm; thickness: 0.4mm; pin-catch: 8.5mm; H: 6mm; thickness: 1mm; pin: D: 1.4mm).

The left wing is broken; the tip is glued on.

There is a wide range of different types of cicada brooch, but the Berthier-Delagarde piece must be distinguished from the east Asiatic and Roman types. The closest parallels are brooches with wings and body of the same size, their edges slightly curved and with a hemispherical 'head,' which occur in the area extending from the Crimea as far as Serbia and Slovakia.[1] There are a few of this kind from Kerch and Cherson (Crimea),[2] Šarovce (Slovakia),[3] Dubravica[4] and Novi Banovci[5] (former Yugoslavia).

Pieta dates the Slovakian brooch to the 5th century.[6] The brooches from the region of the former Yugoslavia are dated to the 5th century by Kovačevič.[7] According to Bóna the cicadas from the Crimea and the Caucasus represent a 'non-Germanic fashion.'[8] They were worn by Greek-Sarmatian-Alanic women in the Black Sea region, from where they were spread by the Huns after 375. Kühn surveyed a great number of cicada brooches, but did not distinguish those of the Hunnic period as representatives of a separate type.[9] Vinski published a few Yugoslavian cicada brooches as pieces of the 'Migration Period' type.[10] Fitz published a few Roman and 'Migration Period' examples from an Austrian private collection and also outlined the history of their research.[11] According to Aibabin they were worn in the Crimea and in the Danube region from the 5th until the beginning of the 7th century.[12]

Comparative Bibliography

1 Kühn 1935b, pl. 24:52, 56; Aibabin 1990, 26–7; pl. 10:13; Roth 1979, pl. 25a; same in: Martin 1894, 18–19
2 Yakobson 1959, ill. 134.6; same in: Aibabin 1990, pl. 10:7; Aibabin 1979, pl. 5:9
3 Novotný 1976, 154, ill. 20 B3, pl. XXI:2; GHA 1987, (K. Pieta) 401,

414, ill. IX.23
4 Kovačevič 1960, pl. V:19
5 Kovačevič 1960, pl. XIV:59
6 GHA 1987, (K. Pieta) 414
7 Kovačevič 1960, p.20
8 Bóna 1991, 196–7, 231–2, 91 ill. 34; 1993, 181–2, 210, 85 ill. 34 is a distribution map
9 Kühn 1935, 85–106
10 Vinski 1957, 136–60
11 Fitz 1985–86, 24–76
12 Aibabin 1990, 26–7

17 Armlet (Pl. 10)

Single piece.
Silver penannular armlet.
Second half of 4th–5th century.
Silver
Inv. no. 1923,7-16,119   Old cat. no. 287
Percentage of silver: 84
Size: 72 x 60mm   Weight: 44.58g
Published: GHA 1987, (Kidd) 113, ill. I.18.e

The armlet is D-shaped. It has an oval section, expanding to trumpet-shaped terminals with flat, sharply cut-off ends. There are four engraved transverse grooves on each terminal which do not go right round; the internal faces are plain.

(Size of central section: 4 x 5mm; at the ends: 10 x 8.5mm; distance between the two ends: 9.5mm; thickness of ribs: 1-2mm).

No. 923, 7-16, 20 is similar, but with slight differences.

Silver armlets with engraved decoration on both ends are frequent finds, such as: Oradea (Nagyvárad, Romania),[1] Tiszafüred, grave no. 1 (Hungary),[2] Suuk-Su (with an eagle-headed buckle),[3] Domolospuszta (Hungary) (with a large buckle with a pentagonal attachment-plate),[4] Laa an der Thaya[5] and Atzgersdorf (Austria),[6] Luchyste (Luchistoye), grave no. 42 (Crimea) (with an eagle-headed buckle),[7] Keszthely-Fenékpuszta, burial no. 5 (with polyhedral bead earring)[8] and Miszla (Hungary) (with polyhedral earrings and brooches with chip-carved decoration).[9]

Comparative Bibliography

1 Bóna 1986, pl. 28:4 – Gepid
2 Csallány 1961, 217, pl. CXCVI:8; CXCV:2 – 520–68 Gepid
3 Seger 1912, 47–9, pl. I:3 – Ostrogothic
4 Annibaldi and Werner 1963, pl. 45 – second half of the 5th century – Ostrogothic
5 Beninger 1929, 143–55
6 Werner 1956, 109, pl. 6:A:3 – first half of the 5th century
7 Aibabin 1990, 33, pl. IX – beginning of the 7th century
8 Erdélyi 1982, 66, ill. 3 – 5th century
9 I Goti 1994, (A. Kiss) 168–169, pl. III.6.f – second half of the 5th century

18 Armlet (Pl. 10)

Single piece.
Silver penannular armlet.
Second half of the 4th–5th century
Silver
Inv. no. 1923,7-16,120   Old cat. no. ?
Percentage of silver: 93
Size: 70 x 51mm   Weight: 16.27g
Prov.: unknown
Unpublished

The armlet is oval. It has a flat oval section, very thin at the centre and expanding to faceted, trumpet-shaped terminals with flattish ends. (Size of central section: 4 x 2mm; at both ends: 5 x 6mm; distance between the two ends: 11mm).

No. 17 above is similar, but has transversely ribbed ends. It is also D-shaped in section, heavier and thicker. Trumpet-shaped solid silver armlets with ribbed or plain ends are simply variants of the same type.

There are many similar armlets of gold, silver, or copper alloy from barbarian Europe. They appear from the 3rd century with Central-Asiatic and Caucasian roots and became popular during the Hunnic era, representing an 'international fashion' which lasted into the 7th century. The silver and copper-alloy armlets are simpler variants of the gold ones. Silver ones have been found, e.g. in Skalyste (Skalistoye), grave no. 288,[1] at Artek (Ukraine)[2] and Valea Strîmbă (Tekero" patak;

Romania),[3] Ficarolo, grave 4 (Italy),[4] Kapolcs, grave 1[5] and Soponya (Hungary).[6]

There is a wide range in the dating of these armlets due to different theories concerning the associated grave goods. They appear for instance with eagle-headed buckles (Skalyste, copper-alloy armlet, grave 420),[7] with large buckles with pentagonal attachment-plates (Skalyste, grave 288), and with earrings with polyhedral beads (Kapolcs, grave 1).

According to Werner the gold ones were in use for 300 years from the beginning of the 3rd century till the end of the 5th century in the Germanic world.[8] They were symbolic of high rank and were worn on the right wrist.

Comparative Bibliography

1   Veimarn and Ambroz 1980, 248 ill. 1:14; 15 – dated to mid-7th century; Veimarn and Aibabin 1993, 57–8, ill. 37:4, 5
2   Repnikov 1906, pl. XI:9
3   Bóna 1986, pl. 24:2 – dates it to the 4th century – Visigothic
4   Bierbrauer et.al. 1993, 320, ill. 4:1 – second half of the 5th/mid-6th century – Frankish, Alamannic with 5th-century East Germanic roots
5   Cs. Dax 1980, 98, 102, ill. 6:33;34; 11:1;2 – Gepid, Ostrogothic or Alanic type
6   Bóna 1971, 230, ill.9 – 5th century Suevic
7   Veimarn 1979, 34, 37; ill. 2:5 – dates it to the second half of the 6th century; Veimarn and Aibabin 1993, 98–101, ill. 72, 73, dating: 187
8   Werner 1980, 4–7, 23

19   Brooches (Pl. 11)

A pair, each of composite construction.
Gilt-silver 'Aquileian-type' radiate-headed brooches with five moulded knobs. Decoration of cabochon garnets and relief scrollwork.
End of 5th–6th century.   East Germanic (Ostrogothic?)
Gilded base silver, garnet, brass
Prov.: Kerch, Krym (Crimea), Ukraine – 1893

Inv. no. 1923,7-16,39 and 40	Old cat. no. 161
Percentage of silver: no. 39: 69	no. 40: 61
Size: no. 39: 106 x 55mm:	Weight: 27.19g
no. 40: 107 x 55mm:	Weight: 28.15g

Published: Dalton 1924a, p.262, pl. XXXVII:19 reproduced from Dalton 1924b; Kühn 1940, 97 no. 2, pl. 63:4, 2; Kühn 1974, vol.2, 617 pl. 244:4,42; GHA 1987, (Kidd) 111,110, ill. I,16.f.

Each brooch is gilded base silver (mercury-gilded), cast in one piece.

The semicircular head-plate is decorated with a semicircular zone of relief scrollwork and has a plain semicircular zone in the centre with an incised border. There are five moulded knobs cast round the edge of the head-plate, the central one and the two outer ones in the shape of two conjoined discs; each knob has a cabochon garnet inlay on its lower part in a cast cylindrical collet. The garnets are secured simply by pressure from the collet and there must be backing paste beneath them, but no access is available for analysis. The other two knobs are in the shape of a rectangle with a rounded end. Each is decorated with three engraved crosswise grooves (two of the lines are arranged next to each other near to the top of the knob, the third is near to the base). (D of head-plate: 33.5mm; size of moulded knobs: 11 x 6.5mm; 8mm between each; collet D: 4mm; H: 3.5mm).

The bow of each brooch has a high-arched section. Each has two wide longitudinal grooves with two engraved horizontal lines below and one above. (Size of bow: 19 x 6.5mm; W of grooves: 4mm).

The foot-plate is sub-lozenge-shaped with a cabochon garnet at the two lateral corners, each in a cast cylindrical collet (the dimensions and method of setting are the same as above). Between them is a longitudinal panel of two opposed relief scrolls, each of which consists of a spiral and a conjoined 'S' below which diminishes towards the terminal. The foot-plate widens out below the scrollwork to form a trapezoidal shape with one horizontal and two vertical engraved lines underneath it in the middle of the plate. Two holes have been cast one below the other on each side. There are two cabochon garnets, each in a cast cylindrical collet (dimensions as above) at the two lower corners, forming an elaborate animal-mask terminal. The trapeziums may be the ears of the head with the two cabochons as the eyes. The foot-plate narrows to an oval shape below the cabochon garnets and is decorated with two carved ovals next to each other which might represent the animal's nostrils. The end of the foot-plate is formed by a semicircular plate with a line engraved round its edge (the animal's mouth?). The

brooch no. 1923,7-16, 39 has two engraved points inside the semicircle. (Size of foot-plate: 19 x 20mm; sides of trapezoid below the scrollwork; 21mm; 12mm; 12mm; 14.5mm; L of engraved lines: 7mm; D of holes: 2mm; size of carved ovals on terminal: 5 x 3mm).

The back of each brooch is flat and ungilded. The pin-catch and spring-holder are cast. The spring-holder consists of a pair of semicircular lugs perforated to secure the pin-spring axis. The pin-catch is a single strip bent over to secure the pin. Both brooches preserve fragments of the springs, and no. 1923,7-16, 39 has the fragment of a brass pin in its catch.

One of the cabochon garnets of no. 1923,7-16, 40 is missing.

This type of radiate-headed brooch is known as the Aquileian type. Its main characteristic is the widened foot-plate with projections forming originally two opposed birds or bird-heads. Variants of this type preserve only the schematic figure of birds as lappets with one or two perforations and circular garnet inlays (representing the bird's eyes in some cases). The Crimean and south Russian brooches show characteristic features in terms of decorative technique.

There are contradictory theories about the dating of Aquileian-type brooches. Kühn surveyed a number of this type from south Russia, central and western Europe, and dated all of them between 450–550.[1] Brooches from northern Italy and southern Germany are dated to the end of the 5th–6th century by Bierbrauer.[2] Pokrovsky[3] and Rybakov[4] dated the south Russian pieces to the 5th–6th century; Werner to the first half of the 6th century;[5] Pudovin to the 6th century[6] and Zasetskaya to the second half of the 6th–beginning of the 7th century.[7] According to Ambroz[8] and Aibabin[9] this type of brooch was made in south Russia after the 5th–6th century with Danubian and Italian prototypes.[10] Ambroz dates them to the second half of the 6th–7th century.[11] As Aibabin pointed out, brooches like the Berthier-Delagarde ones represent a distinctive type of Aquileian brooch which he calls the 'Kerch variant'.[12] Brooches of this kind have been found in the Kuban region (Pashkovska),[13] and at Kerch (in grave 78 with an eagle-headed buckle)[14] and Nikopol (Ukraine).[15] Aibabin dates them to the end of the 6th and to the 7th centuries.[16] There is a pair of unknown provenance in the Metropolitan Museum, new York.[17]

Comparative Bibliography

1   Kühn 1974 II, 613–17, pl. 241–4 (no. 4, 28 is also in: Tackenberg 1928/29, p. 266 ill. 132 'in Museum of Sofia,' nos 4, 23–4, 25 are also in: Tackenberg 1928, 267, ill. 133a–c; no. 4, 18 is said to be from Torriano by Bierbrauer 1975, pl. XLII:1; 2; no. 4, 43 is said to be from Artek by Repnikov 1906, 36;62;77, pl. VI.2
2   Bierbrauer 1975, 102–14; pls I:1;2; XLII:1;2; XLVI:1; LXXIV:7
3   Pokrovsky 1936, 159–69
4   Rybakov 1953, 57
5   Werner 1961b, 29–30
6   Pudovin 1962, 146
7   Zasetskaya 1990, pl. 2:35, 36; 1993, pl. 4:21, 22
8   Aibabin 1990, 21 mentions Ambroz's 1974 doctoral dissertation, 182–4; 213; 214
9   Aibabin 1990, 21–2
10 Apart from the pieces in the above-mentioned publications there are Danubian-type brooches from Sirmia in: GHA 1987,206, ill. V,23a; Kovačevič 1960, pl. VII:26
11 Ambroz as no. 8 above
12 Aibabin 1990, 21
13 Pokrovsky 1936, ill. 3
14 Rybakov 1953, ill. 8:1, the same in Matsulevich 1933, ill. 1c; Aibabin 1990, pl. 15:5;6
15 Kühn 1974, pl. 244:4, 40, the same in: Werner 1961b, 29–30, pl. 26:109a–b
16 Aibabin 1990, 22
17 Inv. no. 17.192.149–50

20   Brooches (Pl. 12)

A pair, each of composite construction.
Gilt-silver radiate-headed brooches with five moulded knobs.
Decoration of cabochon garnets and relief scrollwork.
End of 5th–mid-6th century ?   Ostrogothic.
Gilded base silver, garnet, brass
Prov.: Kerch, Krym (Crimea), Ukraine – 1893

Inv. no. 1923,7-16,41 and 42	Old cat. no. 162
Percentage of silver: no. 41: 58	no. 42: 56
Size: no. 41: 96 x 51mm	Weight: 23.2g
no. 42: 95.5 x 51.5mm	Weight: 22.34g

Published: Dalton 1924a, p. 262, pl. XXXVII:17 reproduced from Dalton 1924b; Kühn 1974, vol. 2, 759, pl. 264: 67,5

Each brooch is gilded base silver (mercury-gilded), cast in one piece.

The semicircular head-plate is decorated with a semicircular zone of relief scrollwork consisting of two confronted S-shapes. The top spiral of each pair is bigger and they meet at the centre of the head-plate. The rest of the space in the semicircular zone is filled with three relief triangles between the scrolls. The head-plate has an engraved line round the curved edge and five moulded knobs cast round it, each in the shape of two conjoined discs with the lower part containing a cabochon garnet in a cast cylindrical collet. The garnets are secured simply by pressure from the collet and must have backing paste beneath them, but no access is available for analysis. (D of head-plate: 30mm; size of moulded knobs: 13 x 7mm; 7mm between each; collet: D: 5mm; H: 4mm).

The bow of each brooch has a high-arched section. Each has two wide longitudinal grooves, with two horizontal engraved lines below and one above. (size of bow: 11 x 15mm; W of grooves: 2.5mm).

The foot-plate is lozenge-shaped, with two opposed longitudinal relief scrolls in the centre, each of which consists of a spiral with a conjoined 'S' below, diminishing towards the terminal. Each lateral corner of the lozenge has a projecting cabochon garnet in a cast cylindrical collet (dimensions and method of setting are the same as above). Similar garnets project from the edges right above the terminal and might belong to the animal-mask terminal of the foot-plate as they possibly suggest the eyes of an animal. (Sides of foot-plate: 2.24mm). The foot-plate narrows to a tear-shaped terminal below the garnets, representing the animal's nose. It has two engraved tear-shapes with an engraved line in the middle of each, representing the nostrils. (Size of tear-shapes: 3 x 7mm).

The back of each brooch is flat and ungilded. The pin-catch and spring-holder are cast. The spring-holder consists of a pair of semicircular lugs perforated to secure the pin-spring axis. The catch is a single strip bent over to secure the pin (as no. 19 above). Both brooches preserve fragments of the brass spring.

Both pins are missing.

The foot-plate of no. 1923,7-16, 42 has a modern repair.

This type of brooch is characterised by a semicircular head-plate and a lozenge-shaped foot-plate, both of which are decorated with scrollwork. The foot in most cases is enriched with circular garnet inlays (one or two pairs, seldom three) in cylindrical collets. The Crimean and south Russian brooches show characteristic features in terms of their decorative technique (like the brooches **cat. no. 19** above and **cat. no. 21** below).

According to Kühn's typology these brooches belong to the Krainburg type, although there are also parallels among his Taman type.[1] Both developed from the Kerch type and can be dated to the period between 500 and 550, as also by Werner.[2] The Italian and Danubian parallels are dated to the end of the 5th/first half of the 6th century by Bierbrauer.[3] Similar pieces from Bosporus (Crimea), Suuk-Su and Knazhaya Gora are dated to the second half of the 5th/first half of the 6th century by Pudovin.[4] Zasetskaya gives a similar dating.[5] According to Aibabin[6] and Ambroz[6] the Crimean pieces were made after the Danubian prototypes of the second half of the 5th/first half of the 6th century. Ambroz dates them to the period between the first half of the 6th/second half of the 7th century. According to Aibabin's typology they belong to the Kerch type.[7] The Bosporan and Crimean pieces can be dated from the second half of the 6th century to the second half of the 7th, since they were found together with red-painted bowls and eagle-headed buckles.

A pair of similar brooches was found in Ascoli Piceno (Italy)[8] and there is another brooch of this type in the Ashmolean Museum.[9]

Comparative Bibliography

1   Kühn 1974, 718–19; 758–79, pls 264–6
2   Werner 1961b, 30; 31
3   Bierbrauer 1975, 108–14, pls XXXVII:1;2; LXX:4
4   Pudovin 1962, 148, ills 1:3; 2:9;10
5   Zasetskaya 1993, pl. 4:16
6   Aibabin 1990, 21, pl. 15:3;11; also mentions Ambroz's 1974 doctoral dissertation,. 174–7
7   Aibabin 1990, 21
8   Götze 1913, ill. 4
9   Inv. no. 1909.799

21   Brooches (Pl. 13)

A pair, each of composite construction.
Gilt-silver radiate-headed brooches with three moulded knobs. Decoration of cabochon garnets, relief scrollwork and concentric lozenges.
End of 5th–6th century? Ostrogothic.
Gilded base silver, garnet, brass
Prov.: Kerch, Krym (Crimea), Ukraine – 1893
Inv. no. 1923,7-16,43 and 44   Old cat. no. 163
Percentage of silver: no. 43: 53; 57   no. 44: 58
Size: 76 x 38mm   Weight no. 43: 11.29g;   no. 44: 10.87g
Published: Kühn 1974, vol. 2, 738 no. 50, pl. 262:64,50

Each brooch is gilded base silver (mercury-gilded), cast in one piece.

The semicircular head-plate has cast decoration of two opposed relief spirals with a triangle between them. There are three moulded knobs cast round the edge of the head-plate, each in the shape of an elongated disc with double-grooved ribbing across the base. (D of head-plate: 21mm, size of knobs: 7 x 9mm).

The bow is of hollow V-section. (size of bow: 18 x 8mm).

The foot-plate is lozenge-shaped with cast decoration of concentric grooves forming a border around a deep lozenge. Each lateral corner of the lozenge has a projecting, cast, cylindrical collet containing a cabochon garnet which is secured simply by pressure from the collet. There must be backing paste beneath them, but no access is available for analysis. The foot-plate terminates in a rib above a double knob. There is a similar rib separating the two knobs of the terminal. (Sides of foot-plate: 9.5; 21mm, sides of deep lozenges: no. 3: 4.5mm; 10.5mm; no. 4: 6mm; 10.3mm, collets: H: no. 4: 4mm; no. 3: 2mm; D: 4.5mm, terminal of no. 3: 15 x 8mm; no. 4: 16.5 x 8mm).

The back of each brooch is flat and ungilded. The pin-catch and spring-holder are cast. The spring-holder is a semicircular lug, perforated to secure the pin-spring axis (different from nos 19 and 20 with a pair of spring-holding lugs). The catch is a single strip, bent over to secure the pin. Both brooches preserve fragments of the brass spring.

Both pins are missing and both of the brooches are broken.

This type of brooch is characterised by the two opposed relief or chip-carved spirals on the head-plate and concentric engraved lozenges on the foot-plate. The head-plate is enriched with three or five moulded knobs, while the foot has either a pair of circular settings at its corners containing garnet inlays, or a pair of plain circular projections. It has an animal mask or knob at the terminal. Brooches of this type appear in the Crimea, the Dnieper area and also in the Danube region and Italy. The Crimean pieces show characteristic features in terms of their shape and decorative technique.

Kühn calls them the Gurzuf type, coming mainly from south Russia but also from Central Europe and the Baltic (although he includes some brooches of different shape and decoration), and which he dates between 500 and 550.[1] South Russian brooches of this type in the Diergardt Collection are from the first half of the 6th century according to Werner.[2] Kovačevič dated a similar brooch from Zmajevo (former Yugoslavia) to the 5th century[3] and others of the type from Cherson were made in the 5th/first half of the 6th century according to Yakobson,[4] and Zubar and Ryzhov.[5] Rybakov dated a piece from the Middle Dnieper region to the same period.[6] According to Aibabin there is a unique brooch of this type from Cherson showing Danubian features in its technique of chip-carving, which date it to the second half of the 5th century.[7] He considers it to be either an import from the Danube region, or the work of a Danubian craftsman transferred to the Crimea. The earliest local products in the Crimea, however, were made in the first half of the 6th century, while later variants with cast or shallow, carved decoration are of the 7th century.[8] Mashov dates a similar brooch from Harlec (Bulgaria) to the 6th–7th century[9] and, according to the theory of Salin10 and Ambroz,[11] the Crimean brooches were made in the 6th–7th century copying 5th–6th century Danubian prototypes, although this was opposed by. Matsulevich.[12] The brooch from Spas Pereksha (Upper Dnieper region) suggested to Ambroz that there were cultural connections between the Upper Dnieper region and the Crimea in the 6th–7th century.[13]

A similar garnet-inlaid silver brooch is published by Repnikov[14] and there is a pair of brooches of this type from Kerch in the Ashmolean Museum, each with five knobs round the head-plate and cabochon garnet inlays on the foot.[15] A similar brooch but decorated with three circular blue enamel inlays was auctioned in Vienna in 1996.[16]

Comparative Bibliography
1 Kühn 1974, 729–38, pls 261–2
2 Werner 1961b, 31–2, pls 31; 32:122,123; 33:124–6
3 Kovačevič 1960, 40, pl. XIX:90
4 Yakobson 1959, 267 ill. 137:2; 271 ill. 137:5
5 Zubar and Ryzhov 1976, 328
6 Rybakov 1953, 57 ill. 8:2
7 Aibabin 1979, 22–34; 1990, 20–1, pls 2:72; 14:8, 10–13
8 Aibabin 1990, pl. 14:8 (Danubian brooch from Cherson), pl. 14:11 (earliest local product), pl. 14:10; 12; 13 (later pieces)
9 Mashov 1976, 35–9, ill. 3
10 Salin 1904, 123; 193; 197; 207, ill. 38
11 Ambroz 1970, 70–4
12 Matsulevich 1933, 593–6
13 Ambroz 1970, 74, ill. 2:6
14 Repnikov 1907, 101–48, ill. 132
15 Inv. nos 1909.800 and 1909.801. They were acquired by Sir John Evans, and presented to the Ashmolean by Sir Arthur Evans in 1909.
16 Dorotheum 1996, no. 233.

22   Brooch (Pl. 13)
Single piece.
Radiate-headed brooch with five moulded knobs and geometric decoration.
Second half of 5th century
Copper alloy (brass)
Prov.: Olbia (Mikolayiv), Ukraine – 1909
Inv. no. 1923,7-16,87   Old cat. no. 320
Size: 40 x 22mm   Weight: 4g
Published: Kühn 1974, vol.2, 745 no. 8, pl. 263:65,8

The head-plate is semicircular and decorated with fan-like, cast, linear decoration. Five moulded knobs project from the edge. (D of head-plate: 14mm; thickness: 2mm; size of knobs: 5.5 x 3.5mm).

The bow is of semicircular section.

The foot-plate is lozenge-shaped and decorated with a lozenge-shaped pattern (cast ?) and circular lappets on the two lateral corners. (L of foot-plate: 17mm; thickness: 2mm; D of lappets: 5.5mm).

The back is flat with remains of the cast pin-catch and spring-holder.

The terminal of the foot-plate is broken off and some of the knobs are fragmentary. It has been repaired after being broken in two. It appears to have been conserved in the past with a caustic cleaning agent.

Brooches of this type have similar fan-like ornament on the head-plate and a concentric lozenge-pattern on the foot. They have been found mainly in south Russia,[1] the Czech Republic,[2] Hungary,[3] Germany[4] and Italy.[5] A similar pair of gilt-silver brooches was found in one of the 'Bakodpuszta' graves (Dunapataj-Bödpuszta, Hungary).[6] A piece from Kerch is dated to the second half of the 5th century by Aibabin[7] and a pair of gilt-silver brooches from south Russia is dated to the same period by Werner, who named them the south Russian type.[8]

In Kühn's classification this kind of brooch is listed under his Sisak type, which also includes pieces with slightly different decoration on the foot-plate.[9] He considers them to be Ostrogothic and dates them to the period between 500 and 550. A brooch from Tortona (Italy) is said to be from an Ostrogothic woman's grave by Bierbrauer.[10]

Comparative Bibliography
1 Werner 1961b, pl. 25:107a; 107b
    Kühn 1974, pl. 262:65,4; possibly the same in: Aibabin 1990, pl. 14:9
2 Kühn 1974, pl. 263:65, 9–12 – no. 5, 9 and 65, 10 are also listed under the Gurzuf type: pl. 261:64, 28; 64, 29
3 Fettich 1951, pl. XIX:4; 4a; 5; 5a
4 Kühn 1974, pl. 262:65, 1 – Mainz Zahlbach, pl. 263:65, 14 – Garlitz
5 Bierbrauer 1975, pl. XLIV:5
6 Fettich 1951, 24, pl. XIX:4; 4a; 5; 5a – Different theories on dating and ethnic affiliation are discussed by Kiss 1983, 95–131
7 Aibabin below
8 Werner 1961b, 29
9 Kühn 1974, 742–7; pls 262–3
10 Bierbrauer 1975, 324–7, pl. 44:5

Mounts

23   Mounts (Pl. 14, Colour Pl. 1)
A pair, each of composite construction.
Trefoil gold mounts, each with a box-section body containing three cabochon garnets. There are peripheral attachment-rivets in cylindrical collars.
End of 4th– first half of 5th century.   Pontic. Hunnic era. (Probably Hunnic-Alanic)
Gold, garnet, silver
Prov.: unknown
Inv. no. 1923,7-16,110 and 111   Old cat. no. unknown (These are the only pieces which appear on the archival photograph, but are not listed on R. Smith's list of the objects purchased in 1923.)
Percentage of gold: 99
Size: no. 110: 28 x 25mm   Weight: 14.36g
    no. 111: 26.5 x 23mm   Weight: 12.44g:
Published: Dalton 1924a, 262, pl. XXXVII:7 and 10 reproduced from Dalton 1924b; Tait 1976, 130 192e pl. 192; Tait 1986, 103, 247, ill. 226h

The base-plate consists of a trefoil sheet to which three individual collets are soldered, with their walls soldered to each other where they touch. The settings are oval and arranged in a trefoil. Two of the cells are conjoined along their length, with the third one lying across the two shorter ends at the top. The upper edges of the collets are folded in around the settings, which are oval cabochon garnets of semicircular section. A plain silver foil survives beneath one of them, but no backing paste survives. (Size of settings: W: 9mm; L: 13mm; one of no. 1923,7-16, 111 is smaller: L: 11mm; H: 8-10mm; collet H: 4mm; thickness: 1mm).

There is a circular perforation in the base-plate, directly at the centre of each setting, beneath the stone. The base-plate of no. 1923,7-16, 110 has two small perforations at its centre, between the conjoined collets, while no. 1923,7-16, 111 has only one. The edges of each hole show that it was perforated from the upper surface of the plate (i.e. from inside the mount). (Perforations at the centre: D: 0.7mm).

There are three cylindrical collars soldered to the walls of the oval collets where they join. Each contains a gold attachment-rivet with a hemispherical head. The rivets extend c. 2mm beyond the depth of the collar, and the end of each is flattened and slightly bent. (Size of rivet collars: H: 4.5-5.5mm; thickness: 0.8mm; D: 2.5mm; D of rivet-heads: 3mm; L of rivets: 9mm).

The holes through the base-plate behind the stones were made for pushing the cabochons up to the tops of the settings, after the tops of the collets had been hammered over to secure the inlays. This idea is supported by the fact that the silver foil underlay also bears traces of perforation.

A similar mount has been found at Kerch, but there is no information regarding its use.[1] There are three buckles from Kerch with trefoil arrangements of oval cabochons on the attachment-plates which have attachment-rivets similar to those of the mounts in the Berthier-Delagarde Collection.[2] It is conceivable that the latter might have formed the counter-plates of similar buckles. Fettich calls this technique of stone-setting 'Persian style' and considers that these objects represent Hunnic-Alanic craftmanship.[3] There is also a buckle, but with only one oval cabochon on the attachment-plate and three similar dome-headed rivets from Normandy.[4] There is a gold buckle from Beja (Portugal) in the Museu Nacional de Arqueologia e Etnologia, Lisbon, with a similar oval cabochon garnet on its plate and three peripheral dome-headed in cylindrical collars.[5] Its inlaid loop and tongue and the method of attachment are comparable with the buckles from Regöly (Hungary)[6] and Kerch (Ukraine; found 24 June 1904).[7] Both buckles are dated to the Hunnic era. There is a bronze buckle in the British Museum from Er Rastan (Syria) also decorated with a large oval cabochon (glass) and peripheral cylinders for the attachment-rivets.[8] These parallels suggest that the Berthier-Delagarde 'mounts' belonged to a similar type of buckle, which also shows the characteristic loop and tongue of the buckles worn by the military aristocracy associated with the Hunnic empire (see also **cat. no. 70**).

Mounts of much smaller size and with flat base-plates containing garnet-disc inlays in a trefoil arrangement also occur on sword or dagger handles, and a pair of this kind was found at Taman (south Russia).[9] A similar mount was found at Pécsüszög (Hungary),[10] six at Szeged-Nagyszéksós (Hungary) (two of them with four circular inlays),[11] two at Gültlingen (Germany)[12] and two at Landriano (Italy).[13]

All the parallels above – except Landriano – are dated to the Hunnic period, that is, to the end of the 4th–5th century. Landriano is considered to be Ostrogothic by Bierbrauer.[14]

Comparative Bibliography

1 Fettich 1953, pl. XX:2
2 Fettich 1953, pls XXI:5; 6 ; XX:1; also in: Salin 1904, p.115 ill. 302 and Aibabin 1990, pl. 22:20
3 Fettich op. cit. 77–8
4 Salin 1904, 112, ill. 295
5 Schlunk and Hauschild 1978, 158, pl. 51b
6 Mészáros 1970, 74–75, ills 10–11; Bóna 1993, 242, ill. 13
7 Zasetskaya 1979, ill. 3:61
8 Inv. no. P&E 1926,10–14,1
9 Damm 1988, 192, ills 210–11
10 Alföldi 1932, 76, pls IV:13 and VII:7
11 Fettich 1953, pl. II:11–14, 16, 17
12 Quast 1993, 90, 92; pls 12:35, 36; 26:35, 36
13 Bierbrauer 1975, 285–6, pl. XXV:4, 4a, 5, 5a
14 Bierbrauer op. cit.

24 Mounts (Pls 14–16, Colour Pl. 4)

Three single pieces of composite construction.
Three flat gold mounts with all-over cloisonné garnet inlays, two of which are in the form of a bird's head in profile and one square.
Late 4th/5th century.   Bosporan.
Gold, silver, garnet
Prov.: Kerch, Krym (Crimea), Ukraine – 1893
Inv. No: 1923,7-16,12   Old cat. no. 146
Percentage of gold: 86 strips
Size: right-facing bird   L: 19.5mm;   W: 14mm   Weight: 2.43g
      left-facing bird: L: 20.4mm;   W: 11.5mm   Weight: 2.76g
      rectangle: L: 13mm;   W: 11.2mm   Weight: 1.75g
Published: Dalton 1924a, p. 262, pl. XXXVII:3 reproduced from Dalton 1924b; Moss 1935, p. xiv, pl. III B upper; Tait 1986, 103, 247, ill. 226a; GHA 1987, (Kidd) 97, 112, pl. I,16.l.

The two bird-headed mounts are almost identical in form, one facing left (**A**), the other, which is slightly smaller, to the right (**B**). Both are decorated with all-over garnet inlays. The heads are formed of single garnet discs, each within a silver ring. An inner circle representing an eye has been ground out of each garnet and inlaid with a gold ring. The necks are formed by T-shaped settings, each containing a pair of settings beneath which are two rectangular cells one above the other. (Sides of rectangles directly below the circle: 4.7mm; 3.3mm; 2.2mm; 4mm; sides of the two other rectangles: 6.8mm; 2.5mm; the left bird-mount's: 2.8mm; D of eye and head: 3mm; 8mm).

The rectangular mount (**C**) contains a central square with its corners to the centres of the sides of the frame, creating a triangle in each corner of the rectangle. The frame of the mount and the collet of the central inlay are each made of single strips. There is a ground ring in the middle of the garnet plate of the rectangular mount, very likely for the same kind of gold ring-inlay as on mounts A and B. (Sides of inner square: 6.5mm; W of gold frame: 1mm).

The bird-headed and rectangular mounts were made in the same technique: the outer wall and those of the cells are of silver with a thin strip of gold soldered to the top (W c. 0.5mm). The garnets are roughly edged and probably all had a silver backing, since there are the remains of a grid-patterned silver foil behind the head of one of the bird-headed mounts. There is a white backing paste surviving beneath the foils and garnets (calcite, $CaCO_3$).

See **Pl. 14, and Pls 15–16** for construction.

Two gold ring-inlays are missing: one from the middle of the square (**C**), the other from one of the birds' eyes. The left-facing bird's eye (**A**) is reshaped from a straight-sided stone.

On the original photograph they are fastened to a modern cloth together with the sub-triangular mount (**cat. no. 25** below), although the latter may not belong with the other three mounts and is perhaps a strap-end (see **cat. no. 25** below).

There are no signs of attachment-fittings on either the bird-headed or square mounts. The gold sheet overlay extends regularly beyond the edges of the outer wall, suggesting that there was originally an outer frame which has not survived. Iron corrosion products cover the backs of these mounts, suggesting that they were buried close to an iron object such as, perhaps, a purse-fastening, or possibly sword-mounts.

There are comparable examples of purse-mounts or sword mounts of broadly similar construction with two opposed birds' heads, including a very similar sword-sheath mount from Kerch, grave no. 163.[1] It has an iron base and gold frame containing garnet and red glass inlays and the bird's eyes are formed in the same way as on the Berthier-Delagarde mounts. A buckle from Kerch also has the same arrangement of rectangular and bird-headed mounts attached to an iron base and both the sword-sheath mount and the buckle date to the late 4th/first half of the 5th century.[2] A purse from Basel-Kleinhüningen, grave 212 (Switzerland), from a Merovingian context of the first half of the 6th century, has mounts fixed onto an iron base with gold cell walls containing almandine and glass plate inlays with patterned gold foils beneath them.[3] Between the two birds' heads is a rectangular cell containing a green glass inlay. A similar arrangement of two bird-headed mounts with a rectangular one on a purse was found at Flonheim (Germany).[4] They are considered as Frankish, still preserving Hunnic characteristics, by Fettich. A bronze bird-headed mount of similar shape was found near Lake Borovoe (Kazakhstan), but the inlays are not preserved and there is a perforation behind the eye for an attachment-rivet. It is dated to the Hunnic period by Zasetskaya,[5] but to the end of the 5th/beginning of the 6th century by Bóna,[6] and to the 7th century by Ambroz.[7] There are similar bird-headed decorations on the head-plates of a pair of brooches found at Desana (Italy), which are considered to be Ostrogothic, of the beginning of the 6th century, by Bierbrauer.[8] A pair of gold disc brooches, each with six projecting birds' heads, from Imola (Italy) are dated to the first half of the 6th century and are also considered to be Ostrogothic.[9] Their base-plates are each made of a single sheet with flat emerald, ivory and garnet inlays. The eyes are formed by disc settings in gold strip collets. There are two buckles and two belt-mounts in the Dumbarton Oaks collection, which are said to have been found in Germany.[10] Each is decorated with a central, stepped, red glass inlay with a circle ground out and inlaid with a central gold ring. According to Ross these objects were purchased with the expertise of Otto von Falke, who stated that this type of jewellery was made in Constantinople during the 5th century, often as official gifts for Germanic princes.[11] Ross, however, observed that it originated in south Russia and spread across Europe to North Africa.[12]

Comparative Bibliography

1 Zasetskaya 1993, 80, pl. 52:269; *I Goti* 1994, (A. I. Aibabin) 128–30, pl. II.40.a
2 Zasetskaya 1993, 81, pl. 52:271
3 Moosbrugger-Leu 1971, Band A, 169–76; Band B, pl. 43; Giesler-Müller 1992, 186, pl. 45:7a-f; 82:1a
4 Ament 1970, 68–70, pl. 12:3; 28; 30:7; Fettich 1953, 53–4, pl. XXXII:9–11
5 Zasetskaya 1975, 43 no. 14; Zasetskaya 1994, 124–5, ills 26:9, 28
6 Bóna 1986b, 102–3
7 Ambroz 1971, 119–20
8 Bierbrauer 1975, pl. VI:1,2
9 *Imola dall'Età …* 1979, 23; 24; 86 ,pl. IX:1; 3
10 Ross 1965, 119–120 no. 167, pl. LXXXIII

25 Mount (Pl. 17, Colour Pl. 4)

Single piece of composite construction.
Sub-triangular, box-shaped mount (probably a strap-end) with all-over cloisonné garnet inlays. Two silver attachment-rivets on the back.
Late 4th/5th century.   Bosporan
Gold, silver, garnet
Prov.: Kerch, Krym (Crimea), Ukraine – 1893
Inv. no. 1923,7-16,12   Old cat. no. 146
Percentage of gold: 87
Size: L: 22mm   W: 10mm   Weight: 3.45g
Published (together with mounts no. 24 above): Dalton 1924a, p.262, pl. XXXVII:3 reproduced from Dalton 1924b; Moss 1935, p.xiv, pl. III B upper; Tait 1986, 103, 247, ill. 226a; GHA 1987, (Kidd) 97, 112, pl. I,16.l.

The base-plate is a sub-triangular gold sheet with a double-lobed end. The outer wall and possibly the cell walls are soldered onto it. The wall is possibly formed of a single strip by complex folding. It is decorated with all-over cloisonné garnet inlays: one sub-rectangular divided by a saltire into four triangles and a sub-trapezoid above that. There are plain gold foils beneath the garnets. Two silver attachment-rivets project through the base-plate with their heads in the interior of the mount. The ends of the rivets are missing. (Sides of the sub-rectangular cell: 9.7mm; 9.7mm; 10.1mm; 6mm; sides of the triangles: 6mm; sides of sub-trapezoid: 2 x 6mm; 4.1mm and a curved side; collet thickness: 0.5–1mm).

See **Pl. 17** for construction.

Although this mount has always been associated with the mounts (no. 24) above, it differs from them in its method of construction, the rivets on the back and the different thickness (this one is much deeper: 3.9mm, the others: 2.3mm). Therefore it may not belong with them and is perhaps a strap-end.

The garnet inlays are damaged.

On the original photograph it is fastened to a modern cloth together with the mounts (**cat. no. 24**) above.

Its shape has parallels in the Hunnic treasure of Szeged-Nagyszéksós (Hungary).[1]

Comparative Bibliography
1   Fettich 1953, pl. II:2–4; GHA 1987, (B. Kürti) pl. 4; 5

26   Strap-attachment (Pl. 18, Colour Pl. 1)
Single piece of composite construction.
Drum-shaped gold attachment plate with gilt-silver suspension ring.
End of 4th/first half of 5th century.   Hunnic – Alanic
Gold, gilt-silver, silver.
Inv. no. 1923,7-16,108a   Old cat. no. 154
Percentage of gold: 79
Size: 21 x 10.5mm   Weight: 3.63g
South Russia – 1894
Published: Tait 1986, 103, 247, ill. 226f

The gold attachment-plate is circular and of composite construction. The top forms a frame for a kidney-shaped inlay, with a plain gold foil set in it as a backing for the garnet (?) now lost. There is no access to any backing material behind the foil. Beneath is a kidney-shaped base-plate which is attached to the top by a 2mm wide strip soldered between them around the edges. (Size of attachment plate: D: 10mm; thickness: 0.8mm).

The top and back-plate of the attachment-plate are made from the same sheet, linked at the base by a short strip folded to form a loop securing the ring. (D of loop: 3mm; D of ring: 7mm).

The base- and back-plates are linked together by a central silver rivet, which is secured behind the base-plate so that its head lies inside the composite plate.

The ring is made of a circular-section gilt-silver rod which narrows (from 3mm to 2mm) to each end, where it is soldered to form a closed ring.

See **Pl. 18** for construction.

The original inlay is missing.

The original photograph shows a heart-shaped garnet set in a collet (**cat. no. 28**) fixed with wax over the empty kidney-shaped setting in modern times.

This type of strap-attachment has been found in the Crimea, in the Danube region and as far west as France. They are dated to the Hunnic period, i.e. to the end of the 4th – mid-5th century. Two buckles with very similar composite plates containing kidney-shaped inlays were found in Kerch on 24 June 1904,[1] and there is another identical one, also from Kerch, in the Ashmolean Museum.[2] A similar buckle, from the Béhague collection, was auctioned by Sotheby's in Monaco in December 1987.[3] A gold strap-attachment with a circular opening was also found near Kerch.[4] There is a strap-attachment with a kidney-shaped opening and another with a beaded-wire border and circular stone inlay from Szeged-Nagyszéksós (Hungary).[5] A strap-attachment with a circular red stone inlay and three peripheral rivets was found in Lébény (Hungary),[6] while the piece from Untersiebenbrunn (Austria) has a circular garnet inlay.[7] Another from Pouan (France) is very similar, but has a beaded-wire border.[8] According to Damm a garnet inlaid gold strap-attachment with a gold foil beneath the garnet and beaded-wire decoration in the Römisch-Germanisches Museum, Cologne, has a Danubian origin.[9] Bóna shows the distribution of this type of gold and silver strap-attachment alongside that of some similar buckles.[10]

Comparative Bibliography
1   Zasetskaya 1979, ill. 3:55, 56 (one is gilt-silver with garnet, the other silver with gold setting and glass inlay); 1993, 57–8, pl. 26:106б, 107
2   Inv. no. 1909.798
3   Sale Cat. Monaco 1987, 29, no. 44
4   Werner 1956, pl. 59:28; OIAK za 1900 (1902), ill. 220
5   Alföldi 1932, 57; ill. 15; Fettich 1953, 117; pl. I:7, 7a, 8, 8a
6   Pusztai 1966, 108, pl. 6:3
7   Keller 1967, 111–113; ill. 1:11; GHA 1987, (P. Stadler) 344; pl. 48:VII,33; Kubitschek 1911, 42; pl. I,3
8   Salin and France-Lanord 1956, 72; ill. 17; Keller 1967, 113, ill. 1:3
9   Damm 1988, 102, footnote 1
10   Bóna 1991, 106 ill. 41; 255 no. 41 ; 1993, 94 ill. 41; 230 no. 41 – List of provenances and literature; 1991, ill. 39 ; 1993, ill. 39 – map

27   Mount (Pl. 19)
Single piece of composite construction.
Circular gilt-copper-alloy mount decorated with a cruciform pattern of green glass, with oval red glass inlays in between. There is a central attachment shank on the back.
End of 4th–5th century.   Bosporan.
Gilt-copper-alloy, copper-alloy, green glass, red glass, decayed glass
Prov.: Kuban area – 1912
Inv. no. 1923,7-16,98   Old cat. no. 289
Size: D: 31mm   H: 6.5mm   Weight: 10.3g
Unpublished

The base-plate is a disc of copper alloy with a collet of gilt-copper-alloy strip soldered onto it slightly in from the edge. The internal cell walls consist of four conjoined open rings of copper-alloy strip with their ends joining the frame of the mount. The surface is decorated with four oval glass inlays, two of which contain red glass. Two of them have decayed to a yellowish colour. The spaces between them are filled with green glass plates: one rectangular in the centre and four triangular around the edge, forming an equal-armed cross with expanded ends. (D of top: 30mm; D of base: 31mm; thickness: 0.5mm; size of inlays: oval: 12 x 9.5mm; rectangular: 5 x 6mm; triangles: 6mm; 2 x 4.5mm; thickness of collets: 1mm).

There is an attachment-shank of circular section in the centre of the base. Its end has been filed down from two sides giving it a sharp median edge. (D: 2.5mm; H: 2mm).

The base-plate is damaged.

From a horse-harness or belt?

Two mounts from Kerch are decorated with a similar arrangement of green glass and kidney-shaped garnet plates.[1] They are considered to be Hunnic and are dated to the end of the 4th/first half of the 5th century by Zasetskaya,[2] but to the 5th century by Damm[3] and Aibabin.[4] A similar mount from the same period with three oval amber inlays has been found at Muslyumovo (Russia).[5]

According to these parallels the mount could be dated to the 5th century, but, in view of its green glass-inlaid cross-pattern, it may possibly be related to some 6th–7th-century Byzantine material. There are more general parallels from Bône (now Annaba, Algeria) in this volume 00 below.

Comparative Bibliography
1   Spitsin 1905, p. 118, ill. 17; Damm 1988, 190–1, ill. 204; 205 – in the Diergardt Collection; Zasetskaya 1979, 10, pl. 5:18; 1993, 63 – in the Hermitage
2   Zasetskaya 1979, 5–17
3   Damm 1988, 191
4   Aibabin below
5   Zasetskaya 1975, p. 57 no. 3; 1994, 191, pl. 43:5

28   Garnet in setting (Pl. 19)
Single piece of composite construction.
Heart-shaped, three-dimensional garnet in a setting, enriched with granulation.
Antique? Bosporan?
Gold, garnet
Inv. no. 1923,7-16,108b   Old cat. no. 154
Percentage of gold: 81
Size: 8.5 x 8.5mm   Weight: 0.43g
Published: as the strap-attachment (**no. 26**) above.

The base-plate of the setting consists of a thin, heart-shaped sheet of gold. The collet is soldered onto the base-plate and is formed of a single strip of sheet gold folded round the garnet, with a small slice cut out to allow a close fit round the top. The garnet is heart-shaped and three-dimensional with two lobes and a central ridge projecting between them. It may represent two eyes and a beak. The setting is bordered by granulation soldered to the base-plate and collet. (L: 7mm; W: 6mm;

H: 2.5mm).

This setting has always been published together with the strap-attachment (**cat. no. 26**) to which it was formerly attached in modern times.

There is no access to any foil or backing paste beneath the garnet.

The earring (**cat. no. 111**) below is also decorated with a similar three-dimensional garnet inlay.

A similarly-shaped red glass inlay was found in Kerch (on 24 June 1904) and is dated to the second half of the 4th/beginning of the 5th century by Zasetskaya.[1] A necklace from Kerch in Berlin with two similar heart-shaped pendants, each with a granulated border, is dated to the 1st–2nd century by Stefanelli and Pettinau.[2] A heart-shaped gold setting containing a garnet inlay similar to the Berthier-Delagarde one, but without a granulated border, was found in Olbia (Mikolayiv, Ukraine), forming the head of a butterfly-shaped pendant.[3] A diadem from the Artyukhov kurgan in the Hermitage has pendants with similar settings, but also lacks bordering granules.[4] Both of the above-mentioned pieces are dated to the 2nd century BC by Maksimova[5] and to the 3rd–2nd century BC by Hoffmann and Davidson.[6] There is also a necklace from the Artyukhov kurgan with its ends attached to a similar three-dimensional setting.[7] A pair of earrings from Syria in the British Museum[8] and another pair from Palaiokastro (Greece) in the Museum of Hamburg[9] are both decorated with similar garnet inlays. The latter is dated to the 3rd–2nd century BC by Hoffmann and von Claer.[10] The Herakles-knot diadem from Thessaly (Greece) in the Benaki Museum (USA) has pendants with three-dimensional garnet inlays of this type.[11] It is dated to the 2nd century BC by Bromberg.[12]

Comparative Bibliography

1 Zasetskaya 1993, 66, pl. 35:157ж
2 Stefanelli and Pettinau 157, no. 164, cat. no. 118; 158; ill. 164
3 Hoffmann and Davidson 1965, 142, 143 ill. 51 – in the collection of Mr and Mrs. E. Kofler-Truninger, Inv. no. 728A
4 Maksimova 1979, 25 ill. 1, 44–8, ill. 6 ; Hoffmann and Davidson 1965, 55, ill. 1.f, Inv. no. Art I
5 Maksimova *op. cit.*
6 Hoffmann and Davidson *op. cit.*
7 Maksimova 1979, 29, ill. 6
8 Marshall 1911, 279–80, nos 2370, 2371
9 Hoffmann and von Claer 1968, 106–8, no. 68
10 Hoffmann and von Claer *op. cit.*
11 Bromberg 1991, 52, pl. 29
12 Bromberg *op. cit.*

29   Studs or appliqués (Pls 19–20, Colour Pl. 3)

Eleven, each of composite construction
Seven circular, two lozenge- and two tear-shaped stones, each set in a gold or gilt-silver collet with an attachment-rivet through the base-plate.
End of 4th–6th century.
Gold, gilt-silver, garnet, glass, carnelian
Prov.: Kerch, Krym (Crimea), Ukraine – 1894
From a buckle, dagger-sheath, cloth, leather, etc.?
Inv. no. 1923,7-16,32   Old cat. no. 153

A: Flat garnet in a tear-shaped collet.
Percentage of gold: 86
Size: 12 x 5.8mm;   H: 2.5mm;   collet thickness: 0.5mm
      Weight: 0.75g
The base-plate consists of a tear-shaped gold sheet.

The collet is formed by a gold strip with the ends soldered together at the point. There is a plain gold foil beneath the garnet which has a bevelled edge.

There is a copper attachment-rivet in the centre of the base-plate which is attached from behind the upper surface of the latter, so that its head is in the interior. The end of the rivet has been chiselled down.

B: Flat garnet in a tear-shaped collet with beaded-wire border. The base-plate consists of a tear-shaped gold sheet and the collet of a gold strip soldered to the base-plate. There is no access by which to examine whether there is any foil beneath the garnet. The beaded wire is soldered onto the base-plate all around the edge.

There are two silver (?) attachment-rivets in the base-plate which are attached from behind the upper surface of the latter, so that their heads are in the interior. The rivet-ends have been chiselled down.

The garnet plate is damaged.
Percentage of gold: 74

Size : 14 x 8.5mm;   H: 2.5mm;   Garnet: 9.5 x 4.5mm;   collet thickness: 0.3mm;   W of beaded wire: 1mm   Weight: 0.9g

C: Flat garnet in a lozenge-shaped collet.

The base-plate is a lozenge-shaped gold sheet.

The collet is formed by a thin gold strip soldered to the base-plate. There is no access by which to examine whether there is any foil beneath the garnet, which has a bevelled edge.

There is a gold (?) attachment-rivet in the centre of the base-plate which is attached from behind the upper surface of the latter, so that the its head is in the interior. The end of the rivet has been chiselled down.

The collet is damaged.
Percentage of gold: 78
Size: 9 x 6mm; sides: 6mm; H: 3mm   Weight: 0.52g

D: Flat garnet in a lozenge-shaped collet with beaded-wire border. The base-plate consists of a lozenge-shaped gold sheet and the collet of a gold strip soldered to the base-plate. The garnet has a bevelled edge and a plain gold foil underneath.

A beaded-wire border is soldered onto the base-plate all around the edge.

There are two silver attachment-rivets in the base-plate. They are attached from behind the upper surface of the latter, so that their heads are in the interior. The rivet-ends have been chiselled down.

The garnet plate is damaged.
Percentage of gold: 89
Size: 13 x 9mm; H: 2.5mm;   Garnet: 10 x 5.5mm; sides: 5.5mm; W of beaded wire: 1mm   Weight: 1.26g

E: Cabochon garnet in an oval collet.

The base-plate consists of an oval gold sheet and the collet of a gold strip soldered to the base-plate. The edge of the collet is folded in around the garnet which has is a plain gold foil beneath it.

There is a silver (?) rivet in the centre of the base-plate which is attached from behind the upper surface of the latter, so that its head is in the interior. The end of the rivet has been chiselled down.
Percentage of gold: 79
Size: 7 x 8mm; H: 4mm;   collet H: 2mm   Weight: 0.77g

F: Cabochon garnet in a circular collet.

The base-plate is circular. The collet is formed by a bent gold strip soldered to the base-plate. The edge of the collet is folded in around the stone. There is no access by which to examine whether there is any foil beneath the garnet.

There is a silver (?) rivet in the centre of the base-plate. It is attached from behind the upper surface of the latter, so that its head is in the interior. The end of the rivet has been chiselled down.
Percentage of gold: 78
Size: D: 7mm; H: 4mm;   H of collet: 2mm   Weight: 0.6g

G: Cabochon garnet in a circular collet, with granulated border. The base-plate consists of a gilt-silver circular sheet and the collet of a bent gold strip soldered to the base-plate. There is no access by which to examine whether there is any foil beneath the garnet. The granulated border is made of individual granules soldered onto the base-plate all around the edge.

There are two silver (?) attachment-rivets in the base-plate which are attached from behind the upper surface of the latter, so that their heads are in the interior. The rivet-ends have been chiselled down.
Percentage of gold: 71
Size: D: 11mm; H: 5mm; D of garnet: 7.5mm; H of collet: 2mm; D of granules: 0.8mm   Weight: 1.26g

H: Green glass cabochon in an oval collet with granulated border.

The base-plate consists of an oval gold sheet. The collet is formed by a gold strip soldered to the base-plate and its edge is folded in around the stone. The granulation consists of individual granules soldered onto the base-plate all around the edge. There are traces of hard solder on the back of the base-plate.
Percentage of gold: 40 (gilt-silver or traces of solder ?)
Percentage of silver: 51
Size: 6.5 x 8.5mm;   H: 3mm; collet H: 1mm   Weight: 0.36g

I: Brownish-red carnelian cabochon in a circular collet, with beaded-wire border.

The base-plate consists of a circular gold sheet and the collet of the cabochon of a gold strip soldered to the base-plate. A beaded-wire border is soldered onto the base-plate all around the edge. The wire is beaded on one side only (as on J and K).

There is a silver (?) rivet in the centre of the base-plate. It is attached from behind the upper surface of the latter, so that its head is in the interior. The end of the rivet has been chiselled down.

Percentage of gold: 95

Size: D: 11mm; H: 4.5mm;   D of glass: 8mm;   H of collet: 2mm; W of beaded wire: 1mm   Weight: 0.85g

J: Brownish-red carnelian cabochon in a circular collet, with beaded-wire border.

The base-plate consists of a circular gold sheet and the collet of the cabochon of a gold strip soldered to the base-plate. A beaded-wire border is soldered onto the base-plate all around the edge. The wire is beaded on one side only (as on I and K).

There is a copper rivet in the centre of the base-plate which is attached from behind the upper surface of the latter, so that its head is in the interior. The end of the rivet has been chiselled down.

Stud 'J' has the letters like 'керч' written directly on the back (Cyrillic for Kerch, but without the soft sign at the end of the word).

Percentage of gold: 94

Size: D: 11mm; H: 5.2mm;   D of glass: 9mm;   H of collet: 2.5mm; W of beaded wire: 0.5mm   Weight: 1g

K: Brownish-red carnelian cabochon in a circular collet, with beaded-wire border.

The base-plate consists of a circular gold sheet and the collet of the cabochon of a gold strip soldered to the base-plate. A beaded-wire border is soldered onto the base-plate all around the edge. The wire is beaded on one side only (as on I and J above).

There is a copper rivet in the centre of the base-plate. It is attached from behind the upper surface of the latter, so that its head is in the interior. The end of the rivet has been chiselled down.

Percentage of gold: 96

Size: D: 10.5mm; H: 6mm;   D of glass: 8mm;   H of collet: 2.3mm; W of beaded wire: 1mm   Weight: 0.9g

The beaded wire of I, J and K is of a distinctive type, beaded on one side only, similar to that on the spacers of necklace (**cat. no. 9**) and on the earring (**cat. no. 8**).

It was possible in only a few cases to analyse the metal of the rivet without also encountering significant interference from the surrounding gold backing of the stud.

The original photograph shows all of the studs fastened to the same piece of modern cloth. They are almost certainly not of the same period and origin (G and F form one group; I, J and K may form another).

Appliqués like these were used for decorating various kinds of object. H is possibly a later type, while the rest may be dated to the Hunnic period or to the post-Attila era; a selection of similar appliqués follows: The Hunnic find of Szeged-Nagyszéksós (Hungary) contains gold studs like B, but with bluish-grey cabochon inlays.[1] A Germanic buckle from Zmajevo (former Yugoslavia) is decorated with four tear-shaped studs like A, but with a cabochon inlay in each setting and a central circular inlay similar to F and G.[2] A similar silver buckle from Laa an der Thaya (Austria) is decorated with tear-shaped and circular garnet cabochons, each with a beaded-wire border around the setting, similar to I, J and K.[3] Two gold studs with sard inlays from Cherson are also similar.[4] Appliqués from Kerch with beaded-wire borders and two silver attachment-rivets are similar to C and E, but have red glass inlays.[5] There are gold appliqués of various shapes in the Diergardt Collection which have garnet inlays and chiselled-down rivet-ends.[6] They are dated to the first half of the 5th century by Damm.[7] The mounts below (**cat. no. 92**) have similar inlays to H. The rich early-Avar graves of Bócsa[8] and Kunbábony[9] also contain similar appliqués. They are dated to the first half of the 7th century.

Comparative Bibliography

1   Alföldi 1932, 70, pl. XVI:35, 36, good colour photographs in: GHA 1987, (B. Kürti) pl. 6.III,38
2   Dimitrijevič et al. 1962, 64–5
3   GHA 1987, (P. Stadler) 52.VII, 37.b
4   Zasetskaya 1975, 64 no. 64
5   Zasetskaya 1993, 65–6, pl. 35:157ж
6   Damm 1988, 98
7   op. cit.
8   Fettich 1951, pl. LI:8, 9
9   Tóth and Horváth 1992, 41–2, pl. XIV:5

30   Studs (Pl. 20)

Two, each is of composite construction.

Circular brown glass cabochon in a cylindrical gilt-copper-alloy collet. End of 4th–6th century.

Gilt-copper-alloy (brass), copper-alloy, brown glass.

Inv. no. 1923,7-16,99 and 100   Old cat. no. 289

Size: D: 13mm   Weight no. 923,7-16,99: 2.67g;   no. 923,7-16,100: 1.72g

Unpublished.

Each stud has a circular copper-alloy base-plate to which is soldered a collet of a gilt-copper-alloy (brass) strip containing a circular cabochon of brown glass. An attachment-shank with a flattened end has been soldered onto the back of each base-plate. (D of cabochons: 11mm; H: 6mm; collet H: 5mm; L of attachment-shanks: 8mm; D: 2mm).

No. 923,7-16,100 is in poor condition. The base-plate is damaged and the attachment-shank has been broken off.

Horse harness fittings

31   Pendant-mount (Pls 21, 22)

One piece, composite.

Circular pendant, constructed of a copper base with a gilt-silver sheet overlay and silver back-plate. It is decorated with blue glass cabochons and repoussé ornaments.

4th century.

Gilt-silver, silver, impure copper, copper-alloy, blue glass

Prov.: probably Kerch, Krym (Crimea), Ukraine – 1894

Inv. no. 1923,7-16,16   Old cat. no. 150

Percentage of silver: back-plate: 81

Size: 54 x 65.2mm   Weight: 11.17g

Published: GHA 1987, (Kidd) p.112, ill. I.16.k

The pendant is circular with a rectangular tongue projecting from the top for suspension. (D: 51mm; tongue: 17 x 14mm).

It is constructed in the following way: a repoussé-decorated gilt-silver (mercury-gilded) sheet is pressed onto a patterned base of impure copper. The edge of the sheet overlay is wrapped around that of the base. The circular part has a plain silver back-plate. There is a strip of impure copper behind the top of the tongue where two rivets are attached.

The pendant is decorated with five blue glass cabochons in collets: a circular one at the centre and four tear-shaped ones in a cruciform pattern around it. The collet of each is created by turning up the patterned copper base and its gilt-silver sheet overlay around the stone with the inner edge of the sheet bent in. The pendant is further decorated with a repoussé pattern of pseudo-filigree wire in a border along the edge and around the collet of each inlay. The pendant is bordered by a zigzag line of linked V-shapes with a repoussé pseudo-granule at the base of each alternate V. By the border of each tear-shaped collet there are two similar granules linked by a semicircle. There are triangles of pseudo-granulation between the tear-shaped cabochons. The projecting rectangular tongue is decorated with a central pseudo-granule within a circle. (Size of cabochons: H: 5mm, D of circular one: 11mm, tear-shaped ones: 9.5 x 5mm, W of beaded wire: 1.5mm, D of granules: 0.9mm, D of circle at the top: 2.5mm).

There are copper-alloy attachment-rivets in three of the fields between the tear-shaped cabochons, but there is no trace that a fourth one existed, as might be expected from the symmetry of their arrangement. The rivet-ends are burred over securing the silver back-plate. There are two similar rivets at the top of the tongue-shaped projection, except their ends are not burred over. There are traces of a washer at the end of one of them. They were possibly for attachment to the strap from which the pendant was suspended. All five rivet-heads are covered with gilt-silver foil. (D of rivet- heads: 4mm, L of rivets at the top: 4.8mm)

The object is in poor condition and is heavily restored. Two of the glass inlays and pieces of the back-plate are missing. The flat tear-shaped stone is not original (museum replacement). The object is heavily corroded behind the silver back-plate.

From a horse-harness ?

This mount and those below (**nos 32–43**) possibly belong to the same horse-harness, except for **no. 40** which is slightly different and is therefore probably from another set, though from the same cultural circle.

The closest parallels are the mounts from a grave at Kishpek (north Caucasus) which have copper-alloy base-plates with stamped gold sheet overlays. They are all decorated with glass and/or sard inlays, and have copper-alloy, dome-headed attachment-rivets with gold sheet overlays on the heads. There were two pairs of variants of this type of mount in the grave: one is similar to our **cat. no. 31**, the other to **cat. nos 41–43**. The grave is considered to be Hunnic by both Betrozov[1] and Bóna.[2] According to Betrozov the mounts can be dated to the 4th–5th century, while Bóna dates them to the beginning of the 5th century. The gold mounts of the horse-harness found near the town of Azov[3] are considered to be the 1st-century antecedents of the Kishpek type by Aibabin[4] although they are slightly different in shape and construction. According to his theory the mounts from Kishpek such as the Berthier-Delagarde pieces are Sarmatian from the end of the 3rd/beginning of the 4th century. A similar rectangular mount in the Museum of Saint-Germain-en-Laye may also be considered an earlier prototype of the mounts in the British Museum.[5] It has a similar pattern of decoration, but this is achieved by applied granules and wires. A whole set of rectangular gold harness-mounts inlaid with carnelian, and a similar oval box-shaped one, were found at Kerch-Glinishche and dated to the 3rd–4th century by Rostovtsev,[6] and by Kondakov, Tolstoi and Reinach.[7] There is a gold harness-set (stone-inlaid mounts, buckles, strap-distributor and plain strip-mounts) from the Adzimushkaya catacomb in the Black Sea region published by Shkorpil,[8] who refers to another similar set kept in Kerch Museum. There are a buckle and a harness-mount in the Diergardt Collection, each with a copper-alloy base with a gilt-silver plate on the top and an oval carnelian inlay, which are dated to the 4th century by Damm.[9] A very similar buckle of copper alloy with a repoussé-decorated gold foil overlay was found at Timoshevskaya-Stanitsa in the Kuban region, and according to Pósta the decorative technique is 3rd–4th-century barbarian work.[10] A polychrome bracelet and a buckle-plate from Chernaya Rechka (Crimea) are considered to be of the 3rd century by Babenchikov.[11] A circular silver pendant-fragment from Cherson with thin gold sheet overlay, a rectangular sard inlay and punched decoration was published in 1903.[12]

There are helmets of the Late-Roman period decorated in the same technique, having an iron base overlaid with gilt-silver or silver foil, decorated with repoussé patterns and coloured glass or semi-precious stone inlays. In most cases the foil overlay has a very similar repoussé pattern to that of the mounts in the Berthier-Delagarde Collection, and it is also fixed to the base by dome-headed attachment-rivets. According to Hampel the technique of an iron base overlaid with gilt-silver or silver sheet, the use of glass inlays and geometric repoussé decoration are all characteristics of barbarian technique and design in the Late-Roman period.[13] Therefore the helmets from Budapest, Pferrsee (near Augsburg, Germany – two helmets) and from south Russia were worn by barbarian auxiliary troops in the 2nd–3rd century. Klumbach dated the Budapest helmet to the 3rd–4th century and a similar helmet from Berkasovo (former Yugoslavia) to the 4th–5th century.[14] It is worth mentioning that mounts of this type were often found together with buckles, strap-attachments and mounts like **cat. nos 44–49** and **60–67** in the Berthier-Delagarde Collection. They are made of silver or copper alloy and have dome-headed attachment-rivets, often with gold or silver sheet overlay on the heads (e.g. Kerch-Glinishche and Kishpek). It is therefore possible that all of these mounts from the collection are part of the same horse-harness set, or at least belong to the same cultural circle (possibly the buckle-loops **cat. nos 50–59** as well).

Comparative Bibliography

1   Betrozov 1980, 113–22, ill. 3:1, 1a, 3
2   Bóna 1991, 264–5 no. 70; 1993, 238 no. 70.
3   Bespalyi 1992, 177 ill. 2; 179 ill. 4; 181 ill. 5;6
4   Aibabin below
5   Musée des Antiquités Nationales, Saint-Germain-en-Laye, Inv. no. 4000; said to have been bought in Paris – I wish to thank Niamh Whitfield for the information and photographs.
6   Rostovtsev 1923a, p.24
7   Kondakov et al. 1891, 313–14
8   Shkorpil 1910b, 33, ills 13–15
9   Damm 1988, 156–7, ills 145–6; 176–7 ills 179–82
10 Pósta 1905 383–5, ill. 224: 6
11 Babenchikov 1963, 94, pl. VI:5; 100, pl. XIII:1
12 OIAK 1903, 47 ill. 93
13 Hampel 1900, 361–74
14 Klumbach 1973, 15–51, pls 1–5, 12–18

32   Mount (Pls 21, 22)

One piece, composite.
Circular mount, constructed of a copper base with a gilt-silver overlay. It is decorated with a carnelian cabochon and repoussé ornaments.
4th century?
Gilt-silver, silver, copper, carnelian,
Prov.: probably Kerch, Krym (Crimea), Ukraine – 1894
Inv. no. 1923,7-16,20   Old cat. no. 150
Size: D: 44mm   H: 4mm (without rivets)   Weight: 7.85g
Unpublished

The mount is circular.
It is constructed as follows: a repoussé-decorated gilt-silver (mercury-gilded) sheet is pressed onto a patterned copper base. There is a plain copper sheet beneath the latter. The edge of the gilt-silver overlay is wrapped around the second layer of copper.
The mount is decorated with a central circular carnelian cabochon. The collet of the inlay is created by turning up the edge of the patterned copper-alloy base and its gilt-silver overlay around the stone with the inner edge of the overlay bent in. The mount is further decorated with a border and central cruciform pattern of repoussé pseudo-beaded wire. Each arm of the cross is formed by two pseudo-beaded wires 6.5mm apart flanking three X's. Between the arms of the cross the front plate is decorated with a ring-and-dot motif. (Size of cabochon: D: 10mm, H: 5mm, H of collet: 1.5mm, W of beaded wire border: 2.2mm, W of beaded wire creating the cruciform pattern: 1.9mm, size of X's: 3mm, D of ring-and-dot: 2mm, 0.8mm).
There are four silver dome-headed attachment-rivets in a rectangular arrangement on the front, each covering the outermost of the three repoussé X's. The shanks of the rivets are hammered to a rectangular section and the ends are bent over. (D of rivet-heads: 4mm, thickness of shank: 2mm, distance between the base-plate and the bent-over rivet-ends: c. 2.5mm).

By comparing the peculiarities of the three similar mounts (**cat. nos 32–34**), such as the details of the pseudo-beaded wires or the small characteristics like the single 'bead' beside one of the ring-and-dots (features which appear on all of them), it is possible to find out the technique of decoration. The broken back-plate of **cat. no. 32** shows that the copper base has the same pattern as the gilt-silver overlay. Therefore it is to be presumed that the bases of all three mounts were pressed on the same mould and then a plain gilt-silver sheet overlay was pressed onto each of them.
The base-plate is missing and the stone is possibly not original.
From a horse-harness? The distance between the back-plate and the bent-over rivet-ends shows the possible thickness of the leather they were attached to (2.5mm comparable in thickness with the width of the slots of the mounts **cat. nos 41–43** below).

33   Mount (Pls 21, 22)

One piece, composite.
Similar to **cat. no. 32** above, but with central blue glass cabochon.
4th century?
Gilt-silver (mercury-gilded), silver, copper, blue glass
Prov.: probably Kerch, Krym (Crimea), Ukraine – 1894
Inv. no. 1923,7-16,21   Old cat. no. 150
Percentage of silver: 97 showing through base-plate
Size: D: 44mm   H: 6mm (without rivets)   Weight: 9.02g
Published: GHA 1987, (Kidd) 112, ill. I,16.k

The construction, shape and decoration are the same as for **cat. no. 32** above, except that it has a blue glass cabochon in the centre (H: 4mm) which is irregularly shaped and much smaller (8 x 10mm) than the collet (D: 13mm) round it. It is possibly a secondary inlay. For the size, construction and decoration see the description of **cat. no. 32** above.
Fragmentary base-plate. Blue glass cabochon possibly not original. From horse-harness?

34   Mount (Pls 21, 22)

One piece, composite.
Similar to **cat. no. 33** above.
4th century?
Gilt-silver (mercury-gilded), silver, copper, blue glass
Prov.: probably Kerch, Krym (Crimea), Ukraine – 1894

Inv. no. 1923,7-16,22   Old cat. no. 150
Percentage of silver: 97 rear of gilded front
Size: D: 43.5mm   H: 7mm (without rivets)   Weight: 9.45g
Unpublished

The construction, shape and decoration are the same as for **cat. nos 32 and 33** above. It has a central blue glass cabochon, as on **cat. no. 33**, which is possibly also a secondary inlay (D of collet: 11mm; H of the glass: 6mm; D of glass: 9mm). For the size, construction and decoration, see **cat. no. 32** above. It is in poor condition. The blue glass is possibly not original and two of the X's along one arm of the cross have possibly been damaged.
From a horse-harness ?

35   Mount (Pls 21, 23)
One piece, composite.
Rectangular mount, constructed in the same way as **cat. nos 32–34** above. It is decorated with a carnelian cabochon and repoussé ornaments.
4th century?
Gilt-silver, silver, copper, carnelian
Prov: probably Kerch, Krym (Crimea), Ukraine – 1894
Inv. no. 1923,7-16,23   Old cat. no. 150
Percentage of silver: base-plate: 54   inner layer: 98
Size: 28 x 38.5mm   H: 5.5mm (without rivets)   Weight: 5.58g
Published: GHA 1987, (Kidd) 112, ill. I.16.k

The mount is rectangular. It is constructed as follows: a repoussé-decorated gilt-silver sheet is pressed onto a patterned copper base. There is plain copper sheet beneath the latter. The edge of the gilt-silver overlay is wrapped around the second layer of copper.

The mount is decorated with a central, rectangular, faceted carnelian cabochon set in the same way as **cat. nos 31–34** above. The mount is further decorated with a repoussé pseudo-beaded wire border and a line of repoussé X's along the longer sides of the rectangle. Along each shorter side are two repoussé arcs with dots at the ends. There are two opposed pairs of half ring-and-dot patterns along the shorter sides of the central collet. (Size of inlay: 9.5 x 11.5mm, H: 5.2mm, H of collet: 2mm, W of beaded wire: 2.5mm, X's: 3mmm, D of arcs: 3mm, dots: 0.8mm, semicircles: 3mm).

There are four silver dome-headed attachment-rivets: one on each corner of the front plate covering parts of its decoration. The shanks of the rivets are hammered to a rectangular section and the ends are bent over. (D of rivet-heads: 4mm, thickness of shank: 2mm, distance between the base-plate and the bent-over rivet-ends: c. 2.5mm).

By comparing the peculiarities of the three similar mounts (**cat. nos 35–37**), such as the details of the pseudo-beaded wire or the characteristic small line beside one of the X's (features which appear on both of them), it is possible to tell that the technique of decoration (of **cat. no. 37** as well) is the same as for the circular mounts (**cat. nos 32–34** above), i.e. the copper base of each was pressed on the same mould.

The similarities to the mounts (**cat. nos 32–34**) in terms of the pseudo-beaded wire and the X-pattern suggest that a similar tool might have been used for the decoration of the mould.

It is in poor condition: the base-plate is missing and also a piece of the front plate.
From a horse-harness?

36   Mount (Pls 21, 23)
One piece, composite.
Similar to **no. 35** above.
4th century?
Gilt-silver, silver, copper, carnelian
Prov.: probably Kerch, Krym (Crimea), Ukraine – 1894
Inv. no. 1923,7-16,24   Old cat. no. 150
Size: 36 x 27mm   H: 5.5mm (without rivets)   Weight: 3.11g
Unpublished

The construction, shape and decoration are the same as for **cat. no. 35** above, except that the central rectangular carnelian is slightly smaller (10 x 10mm; H: 3.5mm). For details, see the description of **cat. no. 35** above.
Very fragmentary.
From a horse-harness?

37   Mount (Pls 21, 23)
One piece, composite.
Similar to **cat. nos 35 and 36** above.
Gilt-silver, silver, copper
Prov.: probably Kerch, Krym (Crimea), Ukraine – 1894
Inv. no. 1923,7-16,25   Old cat. no. 150
Size: 35 x 28mm   H: 2mm   Weight:3.34g with supplementary material
Stone: 16 x 11.5mm   H: 5mm   Weight: 1.37g
Unpublished

The construction and decoration are like that of mounts (**cat. nos 35 and 36**) above, but this one is more damaged. For details of construction and decoration, see **cat. no. 35** above.

There is a faceted oval carnelian in the collection under the same inventory number (1923,7-16,25) which possibly belongs to this mount, but may not be the original inlay. The latter was possibly rectangular. It is very fragmentary.

38   Mount (Pl. 21)
One piece, composite.
Gilt-silver rectangular mount, decorated with an oval, milky quartz cabochon and repoussé ornaments.
Gilt-silver, copper alloy, milky quartz
Prov.: probably Kerch, Krym (Crimea), Ukraine – 1894
Inv. no. 1923,7-16,27   Old cat. no. 150
Percentage of silver: 95
Size: 27.5 x 23.5mm   H: 4mm   Weight: 2.29g
Unpublished

The mount is rectangular. The fragments of copper alloy behind the gilt-silver sheet suggest that it was made in the same way as the mounts (**cat. nos 32–37**) above: the gilt-silver overlay (now present) was pressed onto a patterned copper-alloy base, and the edge was wrapped around a second layer of copper alloy.

The mount is decorated with a central, oval, milky quartz cabochon which is possibly a re-used intaglio depicting a seated female. The method of setting is the same as **cat. nos 31–37** above. The mount is further decorated with a repoussé, pseudo-beaded wire border and a line of repoussé pseudo-granulation around the collet. (Size of cabochon: 17 x 12mm, H: 4mm, collet H: 1mm, W of beaded wire: 2mm, D of granules: 1mm).

There are four perforations for attachment-rivets; one at each corner of the rectangle. (D of perforations: 1.8mm).

By comparing the peculiarities of the two similar mounts (**cat. nos 38 and 39**), such as the details of the pseudo-beaded wire or the number of granules (features which correspond on both of them), it is possible to tell that the technique of decoration is the same as for the mounts (**cat. nos 32–37**) above, i.e. each copper-alloy base was made with the same mould.

The back-plate and rivets are missing. The milky quartz inlay is possibly not original. The thickness of the stone shows that it was set in after the mount had lost its copper-alloy base and the back-plate.

39   Mount (Pls 21, 24)
One piece, composite.
Similar to **cat. no. 38** above, but with central amethyst cabochon.
Gilt-silver alloy, copper alloy, amethyst
Prov.: probably Kerch, Krym (Crimea), Ukraine – 1894
Inv. no. 1923,7-16,28   Old cat. no. 150
Percentage of silver: 71
Size: 27 x 24mm   H: 5.5mm   Weight: 2.35g
Unpublished

Construction, decoration and technique are the same as for **cat. no. 38** above, but the central oval amethyst cabochon is smaller. The latter is translucent pink. (Size of cabochon: 11.5 x 13.5mm; H: 5.5mm). For details, see the description of **cat. no. 38** above.

Only small fragments of the base survive; the back-plate and rivets are missing. The stone is possibly secondary as the present irregular shape of the collet may suggest that it previously had a differently shaped oval inlay. But it can also indicate that the die used for making the patterned copper-alloy base was of a standard size, i.e. designed for larger inlays.

40 Mount (Pls 21, 24)

One piece, composite.
Rectangular mount, constructed of a copper-alloy base with a gilt-silver overlay and a base silver back-plate. It is decorated with a blue glass cabochon and repoussé ornaments.
Gilt-silver, base silver, copper alloy, blue glass
Prov.: probably Kerch, Krym (Crimea), Ukraine – 1894
Inv. no. 1923,7-16,26   Old cat. no. 150
Percentage of silver: 73
Size: 42 x 25mm   H: 5.5mm (without rivets)   Weight: 6.54g
Unpublished

The mount is rectangular. It is constructed as follows: a repoussé-decorated gilt-silver sheet is pressed onto a copper-alloy base. It is impossible to tell if it had a double (i.e. a patterned and a plain) copper-alloy layer behind the overlay as in the case of the mounts above. The edge of the sheet overlay is wrapped around the base, behind which is another copper-alloy plate with a thin base silver back-plate. The edges of the latter are turned up to create the sides of the mount. (Size of gilt-silver overlay: 24 x 42mm, thickness of all layers: 3.5mm).

The mount is decorated with a central, oval, blue glass cabochon set in the same way as **cat. nos 31–39** above and **cat. nos 41–43** below. The mount is further decorated with a repoussé pseudo-beaded wire border and repoussé pseudo-granulation forming two pairs of opposed triangles on the shorter sides. The groups of granules are framed by repoussé lines. (Size of cabochon: 12 x 15mm, H: 5mm, collet H: 2.5mm, W of beaded wire: 1.5mm, D of granules: 1mm, L of lines framing them: 10mm).

There are four circular-section silver attachment-rivets in the corners of the rectangle with mushroom-shaped heads, waisted beneath, each with a collar above the point where it meets the front plate. The ends are flattened and burred over and two have traces of a washer or other attachment surviving. (The rivets are very different from those of the mounts **cat. nos 32–37** above.) (D of rivet-heads: 2.3mm, D of shanks: 1.3mm, D of collar: 2mm, L of rivets: 9mm, distance between the silver back-sheet and washer (i.e. possible thickness of the leather: 2–3mm)).

It is in poor condition and part of the back-plate is missing.

From a horse-harness? The distance between the silver back-sheet and the rivet washer indicates the possible thickness of the leather.

The slight differences in terms of construction, decoration and rivets suggest that this mount may not belong to the same group of horse-harness fittings as the mounts above.

41 Mount (Pls 21, 25)

One piece, composite.
The mount is in the shape of an oval box with two pairs of rectangular slots in the sides. It is decorated with a carnelian cabochon and repoussé ornaments.
4th century?
Gilt-silver alloy (mercury-gilded), silver, copper alloy, carnelian
Prov: probably Kerch, Krym (Crimea), Ukraine – 1894
Inv. no. 1923,7-16,18   Old cat. no. 150
Percentage of silver: 72 (remains of back-plate)
Size: 40 x 36.5mm   H: 13mm   Weight: 14.9g
Unpublished

The mount is in the form of an oval box. It is constructed similarly to **cat. no. 42** below, but with two pairs of opposed rectangular slots. (W of side strip: 9mm, 1mm is turned in over the front plate – the difference from **cat. no. 42** is due to the different pattern of decoration; slots: 17 x 2.5mm).

The mount is decorated with a central, oval, carnelian cabochon set in the same way as **cat. nos 31–40** above. It is further decorated with a border of a repoussé, undulating line and a very broad, repoussé, pseudo-twisted wire encircling a broad groove. (Size of cabochon: 13 x 12mm, H: 4mm, H of collet:1mm, W of undulating line: 2mm, W of pseudo-twisted wire: 5.5mm, W of broad groove around the inlay: 3mm).

The side of the mount is damaged.

Cat. nos 42 and 43 below are very similar, as is the decorative technique of **cat. nos 31–43**.

From a horse-harness? The difference from **cat. no. 42** in terms of decoration, number and size of slots in the side may be due to the different position of these mounts on the harness with **cat. no. 41** at the crossing of wider straps, though of the same thickness.

42 Mount (Pls 21, 25)

One piece, composite.
Similar to **cat. no. 41** above, but with only one pair of rectangular slots in the sides and different pattern of decoration.
4th century
Gilt-silver alloy, silver, copper alloy, carnelian
Prov: probably Kerch, Krym (Crimea), Ukraine – 1894
Inv. no. 1923,7-16,17   Old cat. no. 150
Percentage of silver: 61 (remains of back-plate)
Size: 39 x 35mm   H: 15mm   Weight: 21.05g
Published: Dalton 1924a, 262, pl. XXXVII:6 reproduced from Dalton 1924b

The mount is in the form of an oval box. It is constructed as follows: a repoussé-decorated gilt-silver-alloy (mercury-gilded) sheet is pressed onto a patterned copper-alloy base behind which is another, plain copper-alloy base-plate. The side of the mount is a copper-alloy strip soldered along the edge with a gilt-silver-alloy sheet overlay. The two ends are soldered together and overlap where a large blob of solder is visible. The upper edge of the overlay is turned in over the front plate. There are two rectangular slots in the sides, one at each end. The edges of the gilt-silver-alloy sheet overlay along these cuts are tucked into the slots.

There are remains of a silver sheet back-plate soldered to the bottom of the side strip with its edge folded over the gilt-silver overlay. (W of side-strip: 9mm, 1.5mm is turned in over the front plate; size of slots: 2.5 x 12mm; 2mm of the silver back-plate is folded over the gilt-silver overlay).

The mount is decorated with a central, oval, carnelian cabochon set in the same way as **cat. nos 31–41** above. The mount is further decorated with a border of repoussé pseudo-beaded wire round a line of conjoined X's framing the collet of the cabochon. (Size of cabochon: 20 x 15mm, H: 6mm, H of collet: 2.5mm, W of beaded wire: 2mm; X's: 2mm).

From a horse-harness?

For comparative material and bibliography see the description of **cat. no. 31** above.

43 Mount (Pls 21, 26)

One piece, composite.
Similar to the box-shaped mount (**cat. no. 42**) above, but with a different pattern of decoration.
4th century?
Gilt-silver alloy, silver, impure copper, carnelian
Prov.: probably Kerch, Krym (Crimea), Ukraine – 1894
Inv. no. 1923,7-16,19   Old cat. no. 150
Percentage of silver: 54 (gilded side strip) 81 (remains of back-plate)
Size: 44 x 37mm   H: 17mm   Weight: 11.77g
Unpublished

The mount is in the form of an oval box with two slots in the sides. It is constructed in the same way as **cat. nos 41 and 42** above. (W of side strip: 9mm, 1.5mm is turned over the front plate, size of slots: 14 x 2.5mm, 1.5mm of the silver back-plate is folded over the gilt-silver (mercury-gilded) overlay)

The mount is decorated with a central, oval, carnelian cabochon set in the same way as **cat. nos 31–42** above. It is further decorated with a border of repoussé pseudo-beaded wire round a line of repoussé pseudo-granules. (Size of cabochon: 15.5 x 18mm, H: 6.5mm, W of beaded wire: 3mm, D of garnules: 1mm).

The object is in poor condition.

From a horse-harness. Its slots are of the same width as, but of different length from, those of mounts **cat. nos 41 and 42** above, which may show the different width of the same kind of strap that they were decorating.

44 Buckle (Pls 21, 26)

In three pieces, one of which is composite.
Base silver buckle with a semicircular attachment-plate with a flanged edge. Oval, faceted loop and faceted tongue.
End of 4th/first half of 5th century
Base silver
Prov.: unknown
Inv. no. 1923,7-16,123   Old cat. no. unknown
Percentage of silver: 90 (rivets)   75 (loop)
Size: 28 x 26mm   H: 7mm   Weight: 10.2g

Published: GHA 1987, (Kidd) 113, ill. I,18.d.

The semicircular attachment-plate is base silver. The front plate has a flanged edge projecting from the back. The flange is deeper at the centre and narrows towards the loop.

The front and back-plates are linked by the folded flap attachment and made from the same sheet. The folded flap attachment is rectangular with a slot cut into the centre to accommodate the buckle-tongue.

The back-plate is formed by hammering and cutting to the same size and shape as the front. (Thickness of the plate: 1mm; H: 2.5mm; D: 22.5mm; W: 13.5mm; H of flange: 2-3mm; D of folded flap attachment: 5mm; thickness of back-plate: 0.5mm)..

There are three silver dome-headed attachment-rivets on the front, the ends of which are flattened to fasten the back-plate, thereby gripping the leather (D of rivet-heads: 5mm, rivet-ends: 2mm).

The loop is oval with a faceted, octagonal section. It narrows from the centre towards the ends, where it is secured by the folded flap attachment. (Size of loop: 25 x 18.5mm; thickness: 4.5 to 3mm).

The tongue is faceted and has a trapezoidal section. Its pointed end bends over the loop and there is a plain rectangle at the base, where it is attached by folding its base around the loop. (Size of tongue; L: 19mm; W: 4.5mm; H: 2mm).

The back-plate is imperfect.

The original photograph of the collection does not show this object. From a horse-harness, or shoe?

The buckles (**cat. nos 45–47**) in the Berthier-Delagarde Collection belong to the same basic type, although they differ slightly from each other. The main characteristics are the semicircular attachment-plate, dome-headed rivets with sheet overlay in some cases, and oval loops. Small buckles with dome-headed rivets, but with oval attachment-plates, are very typical of the Late-Roman period. It is possible that the Berthier-Delagarde buckles represent a special variant within the same main type.

Similar buckles with oval attachment-plates have been found in the Kishpek chamber graves (North Caucasus), and are considered by Aibabin to be Sarmatian of the end of the 3rd/beginning of the 4th century.[1] Betrozov[2] and Bóna[3] regard them as Hunnic, Betrozov dating them to the 4th–5th century and Bóna to the beginning of the 5th. Similar buckles of copper alloy and silver have been found in the Turaevo cemetery (Kama region) and are dated to the end of the 4th–5th century by Gening,[4] as are those from the Ural region (Brodovsk) by Goldina and Vodolago.[5] Quast gives a similar dating and regards them as shoe-buckles.[6] Silver buckles of this type from a disturbed grave at Timoshevskaya-Stanitsa (Kuban region) are dated to the 3rd–4th century by Pósta on the basis of an associated, repoussé-decorated buckle.[7] Similar silver buckles from the Black Sea region are published as part of a horse-harness set by Shkorpil, who refers to another similar set in the Museum of Kerch.[8]

The above-mentioned buckles from Kishpek and the Black Sea region form parts of horse-harness sets with similar mounts to **cat. nos 31–43**; the buckle from the Kuban region can also be related to this cultural circle. It is therefore possible that our buckles belong to a similar horse-harness set, or to be more precise, to the mounts (**cat. nos 31–43**) in the collection. Further, the strap-distributor (**cat. no. 60**) and the mounts (**cat. nos 63–67**) could also be parts of the same set, since there are some similarities in their techniques of manufacture. The similarities with the strap-distributor and mounts from the horse-harness set published by Shkorpil also make this possible.

Comparative Bibliography

1   Aibabin below
2   Betrozov 1980, 113–22, pl. 3:6
3   Bóna 1991, 182–3, ill. 70, 264 no. 70; 1993, 156–7, ill. 70, 238 no. 70.
4   Gening 1976, 77, ills 27 and 32; Gening 1979, 96–106
5   Goldina and Vodolago 1990, 10–13; 20; pls XXV:13;15; LXV:1;8;16;25
6   Quast 1993, 83–4, 86; ill. 48a-c
7   Pósta 1905, 383–4, ill. 224:3
8   Shkorpil 1910b, 33, ill. 15

45   Buckle (Pls 21, 26, 27)

In three pieces, one of which is composite.
Silver buckle with a semicircular attachment-plate with a flanged edge. Oval, faceted loop.
4th–5th century.

Gold, silver, copper alloy
Inv. no. 1923,7-16,125   Old cat. no. unknown
Percentage of gold: sheet overlay on rivet-heads: 61.1
Percentage of silver: rivets: 37   loop: 91
Size: 22 x 25mm   Weight: 4.28g
Unpublished

The front plate is silver, semicircular with a flanged edge projecting from the back. The folded flap attachment is made from the same piece as the front plate and is rectangular with a slot cut into the centre to accommodate the buckle-tongue.

There are two copper-alloy dome-headed attachment-rivets with gold sheet overlays folded around the heads.

The loop is oval with a faceted, octagonal section. It narrows from the centre towards the ends where it is secured by the folded flap attachment.

The attachment-hook of the tongue survives folded around the loop.

Size of plate: L: 20mm; W: 11mm; thickness: 0.3mm; H of flange: 2mm; loop: 22 x 14mm; thickness: 2.8-3.1mm; D of rivet-heads: 4mm; H: 1.5mm.

The back-plate is missing, the tongue is fragmentary and the folded flap attachment is broken.

The original photograph of the collection does not show this object.

Cat. nos 44 and 46 are similar, but with slightly different rivets (silver or with silver sheet overlay on the head).

Shoe-buckle, or from a horse-harness?

46   Buckle (Pls 21, 28)

In two pieces, one of which is composite.
Silver buckle with a semicircular attachment-plate with a flanged edge. Oval, faceted loop.
4th–5th century
Silver, copper alloy
Inv. no. 1923,7-16,126   Old cat. no. unknown
Percentage of silver: rivets: 96   loop: 91
Size: 19 x 22.5mm   Weight: 3.61g
Unpublished

The front plate is silver, semicircular with a flanged edge projecting from the back. The folded flap attachment is made from the same piece as the front plate and is rectangular with a slot cut into the centre to accommodate the buckle-tongue.

There are two copper-alloy dome-headed attachment-rivets with silver sheet overlay on the heads.

The loop is oval with a faceted, octagonal section. It narrows from the centre towards the ends where it is secured by the folded flap attachment.

Size of plate: L: 19mm; W: 9mm; thickness: 0.2mm; H of flange: 2.2mm; loop: 19 x 13mm; thickness: 2-4mm; D of rivet-heads: 5mm; H: 2mm.

The back-plate and tongue are missing and the folded flap attachment is imperfect.

The original photograph of the collection does not show this object.

cat. no. 44 is similar, but has three dome-headed attachment-rivets.

cat. no. 45 is also similar, but the two rivet-heads have gold sheet overlays.

Shoe-buckle, or from a horse-harness?

47   Buckle (Pls 21, 28)

In three pieces, one of which is composite.
Copper buckle, with semicircular attachment-plate with a flanged edge. Oval loop and semicircular-section tongue.
4th–5th century.
Silver, copper.
Inv. no. 1923,7-16,124   Old cat. no. unknown
Size: 28 x 23mm   Weight: 7.11g
Unpublished

The semicircular attachment-plate is of copper. The front plate has a flanged edge projecting from the back. The front and back-plates are linked by a folded flap attachment and were made from the same sheet. The folded flap attachment is rectangular with a slot cut into the sheet to accommodate the buckle-tongue.

The back-plate is cut to the same size and shape as the front.

There are three copper dome-headed attachment-rivets on the front plate, each with a silver sheet overlay on the head. The ends of the rivets are flattened to fasten the back-plate and grip the leather. The loop is oval with a circular section. It narrows from the centre towards the ends, where it is secured by the folded flap attachment.

The tongue is semicircular in section with a pointed end bent over the loop and a plain base. It is attached by folding the base around the loop.

Size of plate: L: 21mm; W: 11mm; thickness: 0.2mm; H of flange: 2.8mm; D of folded flap attachment: 0.4mm; D of rivet-heads: 4mm; H: 2mm; size of loop: 23 x 16mm; thickness: 2.5–4.5mm; tongue: L: 21mm; W: 4mm.

The back-plate is imperfect.

The original photograph of the collection does not show this object.

Cat. nos 44–46 are similar buckles, but made of silver and with loops of octagonal section.

Shoe-buckle, or from a horse-harness?

48   Buckle-loop (Pls 21, 28)
In two pieces.
Silver, oval, faceted loop with faceted tongue decorated with incised, geometric pattern on its basal cube.
4th–5th century.
Silver.
Inv. no. 1923,7-16,131   Old cat. no. unknown
Percentage of silver: tongue: 94   loop: 89
Size: 31 x 21mm   Weight: 9.2g
Unpublished

The loop is oval with a faceted, octagonal section. It narrows from the centre towards the ends where it is circular in section. The tongue is faceted and has a trapezoid section. Its pointed end is bent over the loop and the base is plain with an incised 'X' on top. The tongue is attached by folding the base around the loop.

Size of loop: 31 x 21mm; thickness: 3-5mm; tongue: L: 22mm; W:4mm; H: 2mm.

The plate is missing.

A buckle from Kishpek has a similar pattern incised on its tongue and a similarly shaped loop.[1] The attachment-plate is the type of **cat. nos 44 and 47** in the Berthier-Delagarde Collection. It is therefore possible that this loop and tongue also belonged to a horse-harness, possibly to the same set as the mounts (**cat. nos 31–43**) above.

Comparative Bibliography
1   Betrozov 1980, 118 ill. 3:6, 7; Bóna 1991, 183 ill. 70b, 264 no. 70; 1993, 157 ill. 70b, 238 no. 70

49   Buckle (Pls 21, 28)
In three pieces, one of which is composite.
Miniature copper-alloy buckle with rectangular plate, oval loop and tongue.
4th–5th century?
Copper alloy (brass).
Inv. no. 1923,7-16,130   Old cat. no. unknown
Size: 25 x 16mm   Weight: 3.05g
Unpublished.

The attachment-plate is rectangular. The front and back-plates and the folded flap attachment are made from the same thin, rectangular strip folded in the middle. The front and back-plates are therefore of the same size. They are secured by a dome-headed attachment-rivet. The end of the rivet is burred over.

The folded flap attachment has a rectangular slot cut in the centre to accommodate the buckle-tongue.

The tongue is plain with the pointed end bent over the loop. It is attached by folding the base around the loop.

The loop is oval in shape and made from an oval-section rod. It narrows from the centre towards the ends.

Size of plate: 16 x 9mm; loop: 12 x 16mm; thickness: 2-3mm; tongue: L: 12mm; W: 2.5mm; D of rivet-head: 5mm; H: 2mm.

Shoe-buckle, or from a horse-harness?

Similar buckles were found attached to a horse-harness from Kerch[1] and also amongst the mounts in the Kishpek chamber grave (Kabardino-Balkaria, south Russia).[2] It is therefore possible that this buckle was part of the same horse-harness set as **cat. nos 31–43** above.

Buckles of this type were also found in a Sarmatian kurgan in the North Azov region (Ukraine),[3] dated to the second half of the 2nd/early 3rd century, and in the 4th–5th century burials at Brodovsk (Ural region).[4]

Comparative Bibliography
1   Kondakov, Tolstoi and Reinach 1891, ill. 279; Rostovtsev 1923a, ill. 13
2   Bóna 1991, 183 ill. 70b. 264 no. 70; 1993, 157 ill. 70b, 238 no. 70
3   Shepko 1987, 160, ill. 2:13, 15
4   Goldina and Vodolago 1990, 13, pl. XXIV:12, 17

50   Buckle-loops (Pls 21, 29)
Two.
4th–5th century?
Silver.
Prov.: unknown
Inv. no. 1923,7-16,138 and 139 Old cat. no. unknown
Percentage of silver: no. 138: 78   no. 139: 93
Size: no. 138: 21 x 30.5mm   Weight: 7.08g
       no. 139: L: 30mm   Weight: 5.58g:
Unpublished

Oval, faceted loops of octagonal section. Thickness: 3 to 5.5mm. Both are imperfect.

51   Buckle-loops (Pls 21, 29)
Two.
4th–5th century?
Silver.
Prov.: unknown
Inv. no. 1923,7-16,143 and 144   Old cat. no. unknown
Percentage of silver: no. 143: 93   no. 144: 94
Size: each: 12.5 x 10mm   Weight: no. 143: 1.1g no. 144: 1g
Unpublished

Oval, faceted loops of octagonal section. Thickness: 1.5–3mm.

52   Buckle-loop (Pls 21, 29)
Single piece.
4th–5th century?
Silver.
Prov.: unknown
Inv. no. 1923,7-16,142   Old cat. no. unknown
Percentage of silver: 95
Size: 16 x 12mm   Weight: 1.32g
Unpublished

Oval, faceted loop of octagonal section. Thickness: 3 to 2mm. Imperfect.

53   Buckle-loops (Pls 21, 29)
Two.
4th–5th century?
Silver.
Prov.: unknown
Inv. no. 1923,7-16,140 and 141   Old cat. no. unknown
Percentage of silver: no. 140: 93   no. 141: 90   folded flap attachment: 93
Size: each: 13 x 22mm   Weight: no. 140: 2.18g   no. 141: 2.08g
Unpublished

Oval, faceted loops of octagonal section. No. 923,7-16,141 has fragments of a folded flap attachment. Thickness: 1.5–3mm.

54   Buckle-loop (Pls 21, 29)
In two pieces.
Copper-alloy, oval, faceted loop with a semicircular-section tongue.
4th–5th century
Copper alloy (bronze).
Inv. no. 1923,7-16,133   Old cat. no. unknown
Size: 23 x 30mm   Weight: 6.8g
Unpublished

The loop is oval with a faceted octagonal section and narrows from the centre towards the ends. The tongue is of semicircular section with a plain base. Its pointed end bends over the loop. It is attached by folding the base around the loop. Size of loop: 22 x 30mm; thickness: 3–4.5mm; tongue: L: 23mm; W: 4mm; H: 1.5mm.

The plate is missing.

Cat no. 55 below is the same type.

55 Buckle-loop (Pls 21, 29)

In two pieces.
Copper-alloy, oval, faceted loop with a faceted tongue.
4th–5th century.
Copper alloy (bronze).
Inv. no. 1923,7-16,132   Old cat. no. unknown
Size: 35 x 25mm   Weight: 14.11g
Unpublished

The loop is oval with a faceted octagonal section and narrows from the centre towards the ends. The tongue is faceted with a plain base. Its pointed end bends over the loop. It is attached by folding the base around the loop. Size of loop: 22 x 35mm; thickness: 3–5.5mm; tongue: L: 25mm; W: 5.5mm; H: 3mm

The plate is missing.
cat. no. 54 above is similar.

56 Buckle-loop (Pls 21, 29)

Single piece.
4th–5th century?
Copper alloy
Prov.: unknown
Inv. no. 1923,7-16,136   Old cat. no. unknown
Size: 36 x 27mm   Weight: 7.55g
Unpublished

Oval, faceted loop of octagonal section. Thickness: 2 to 4mm. Type as **cat. nos 54 and 55** above.

57 Buckle-loop (Pls 21, 29)

In two pieces.
Copper, oval, faceted loop with a club-shaped tongue.
4th–5th century?
Copper
Inv. no. 1923,7-16,134   Old cat. no. unknown
Size: 37.5 x 23mm   Weight: 11.12g
Unpublished.

The loop is oval with a faceted octagonal section and narrows from the centre towards the ends. The tongue is club-shaped with a plain base. Its pointed end bends over the loop. It is attached by folding the base around the loop. (Size of loop: 21 x 37.5mm; thickness: 3–4.5mm; tongue: L: 24mm; W: 3–5mm).

The plate is missing.
cat. no. 58 below is similar.

58 Buckle-loop (Pls 21, 29)

In two pieces.
Copper, oval, faceted loop with a club-shaped tongue.
4th–5th century?
Copper
Inv. no. 1923,7-16,135   Old cat. no. unknown
Size: 37 x 24mm   Weight: 11.05g
Unpublished.

The loop is oval with a faceted octagonal section and narrows from the centre towards the ends. The tongue is club-shaped with a plain base. Its pointed end bends over the loop. It is attached by folding the base around the loop. (Size of loop: 37 x 21mm; thickness: 2–5mm; tongue: L: 24mm; W: 2.5–5mm; H: 3mm).

The plate is missing.
Type as **cat. no. 57** above.

59 Buckle-loop (Pls 21, 29)

Single piece.
4th–5th century?
Copper alloy (bronze).
Prov.: unknown
Inv. no. 1923,7-16,137   Old cat. no. unknown
Size: 35 x 20mm   Weight: 6.93g
Unpublished

Oval loop of oval secton. Section: 4 x 2mm. Type as **cat. nos 57 and 58** above.
Damaged.

60 Strap-distributor with two attachment-fittings (Pls 21, 30)

Copper-alloy distributor ring with two silver strap-attachments.
End of 4th/first half of 5th century.
Gilt-silver, silver, copper alloy
Inv. nos 1923,7-16,122 (the copper-alloy ring and one of the attachment-fittings) and 1923,7-16,127 (the other attachment-fitting)
Percentage of silver: no. 122 attachment: 91   no. 127: 83
Size: Ring: 54 x 44mm   Weight: Ring: 45.77g
    Strap-attachments: no. 122: 24 x 16mm   Weight: 5.46g
                        no. 127: 23 x 15mm   Weight: 5.47g
Unpublished

The copper-alloy (gunmetal) ring is slightly oval and made from a rod of solid circular section. (D: 7mm).

Each of the two strap-attachments is made from a single, thick strip of rectangular-sectioned silver. It is in the shape of two discs of equal size linked by a long strip. This is bent to form a loop linking the front and back-plates. They are attached by their loops to the copper-alloy (gunmetal) ring. (D of front and back-plates: 15mm; thickness of them: 0.8mm; D of loop: 12mm; 13.5mm; thickness of loop: 2mm).

The front and back-plates are connected by two silver, dome-headed attachment-rivets, each with a gilt-silver sheet overlay folded around the head. The end of each rivet is burred over to secure the back-plate. (D of rivet-heads: 4mm; D of their ends: 2mm).

The copper-alloy ring is broken and distorted; it was originally closed. One or two other attachment-fittings are probably missing.
From a horse-harness?
The original photograph of the collection does not show this object.

A silver horse-harness set found in the Crimea contained a similar strap-distributor, but with three attachment fittings.[1] This grave also contained a decorated mount like **cat. nos 35–37**, buckles like **cat. nos 44–47** and mounts similar to **cat. nos 63–67**. The question is whether they can possibly be related to each other (see further **cat. nos 31 and 44** above). Aibabin dates them to the second half of the 3rd century.[2]

Snaffles with similar fittings of bronze and iron, but with only one central attachment-rivet, have been found in a grave at Kislovodsk (north Caucasus), which Ruchin considers it to be a chieftain's burial of the end of the 4th/beginning of the 5th century.[3]

Comparative bibliography
1   Shkorpil 1910b, 33; ills 13–15. He also refers to another similar set in the Museum of Kerch – see footnote 3
2   Aibabin below
3   Ruchin 1976, 265; ill. 4:3–5

61 Strap-attachment (Pls 21, 30)

Single piece of composite construction.
Copper-alloy, oval loop with flat, rectangular, overlapping ends.
4th–5th century?
Silver, copper alloy.
Inv. no. 1923,7-16,129   Old cat. no. unknown
Size: 19 x 23mm   Weight: 3.06g
Unpublished.

The piece was made from a single copper-alloy strip. The loop is oval, and has a rectangular section. Both of its ends are flattened into triangular shapes which overlap each other. The top one has two of its edges turned down (c. 1mm of it) at a right angle. The ends were originally secured by three silver dome-headed rivets, one at each corner of the triangle, but only one now remains. The end of the rivet is burred over on the back.

D of loop: 16mm, 19mm, thickness of strip: 3mm, sides of triangular overlapping ends: 10mm, distance between the ends: 3mm, D of rivet-head: 4mm, D of shank: 1.5mm, L of rivet: 7mm.

Two of the rivets are missing and the overlapping ends are imperfect.
cat. no. 62 below is similar, but the overlapping ends are triangular and there are three rivets of silver.
From a horse-harness?

62 Strap-attachment (Pls 21, 30)

Single piece of composite construction.
Copper-alloy, oval loop with flat overlapping ends.
4th–5th century?
Copper alloy (brass).
Inv. no. 1923,7-16,128   Old cat. no. unknown
Size: 25 x 17mm   Weight: 3.33g

Unpublished.

The piece was made from a single copper-alloy strip. The loop is oval, and has an oval section. It is flattened to a tear-shape at both ends, which overlap each other. They are secured by a dome-headed rivet. The end of the rivet is burred over on the back. There is a gap of 2mm between the two overlapping ends indicating the thickness of the material to which it was attached.

Size of loop: 13 x 17mm; thickness: 3mm; flat ends: 12 x 12mm; D of rivet-head: 5mm.

cat. no. 61 above is similar, but with three silver rivets.

From a horse-harness?

63 Mount, or strap-end (Pls 21, 31)

One piece composite.

A silver strip sheet with folded loop.

4th–5th century?

Silver

Prov.: 'An-Kache (Sourcil Blanc)' in the register (i.e. 'White Brow'); see above, Krym (Crimea), Ukraine

Inv. no. 1923,7-16,105   Old cat. no. 311 ?

Percentage of silver: 91

Size: 49 x 10mm   Weight: 3.78g

Unpublished

A strip of silver sheet folded at the centre to form a prominent loop end. There are two dome-headed attachment-rivets with flattened ends along the centre. (Thickness of strip: 0.5mm, distance between front and back-plate: 2mm; D of loop: 4mm; D of rivet-heads: 4mm; distance between the rivets: 32mm).

Imperfect.

cat. no. 65 below is similar; **no. 64** is similar, but thinner and narrower.

64 Mount, or strap-end (Pls 21, 31)

One piece composite.

Similar to **cat. no. 63** above, but slightly thinner and narrower.

4th–5th century?

Silver

Prov.: 'An-Kache (Sourcil Blanc)' in the register (i.e. 'White Brow'); see above, Krym (Crimea), Ukraine

Inv. no. 1923,7-16,106   Old cat. no. 311 ?

Percentage of silver: 91

Size: 34 x 8mm   Weight: 1.33g

Unpublished

A strip of silver sheet folded at the centre to form a loop end. There are two dome-headed attachment-rivets with flattened ends along the centre. (Thickness of strip: 0.2mm, distance between front and back-plate: 2.5mm – slightly larger than at **cat. no. 63** above; D of rivet-heads: 4mm; distance between the rivets: 15mm).

Imperfect.

Cat. nos 63–65 are similar, but wider and thicker.

65 Mount, or strap-end (Pls 21, 31)

One piece composite.

Similar to **cat. no. 63** above.

4th–5th century?

Silver

Prov.: 'An-Kache (Sourcil Blanc)' in the register (i.e. 'White Brow'); see above, Krym (Crimea), Ukraine

Inv. no. 1923,7-16,107   Old cat. no. 311 ?

Percentage of silver: 88

Size: 31 x 10mm   Weight: 1.75g

Unpublished

Type as **cat. no. 63** above, but shorter and with only one rivet.

Thickness of strip: 0.5mm, distance between front and back-plate: 2mm, D of loop: 4mm, D of rivet- heads: 4mm

Imperfect.

66 Mount (Pls 21, 31)

Single piece of composite construction.

A strip sheet of base silver with an applied gilt-silver strip.

4th–5th century (?)

Gilt-silver, base silver

Prov.: 'An-Kache (Sourcil Blanc)' in the register (i.e. 'White Brow'); see above, Krym (Crimea), Ukraine

Inv. no. 1923,7-16,103   Old cat. no. 311 ?

Percentage of silver: 61

Size: 115 x 13mm   Weight: 3.66g

Unpublished

A strip of base silver sheet with a gilt-silver strip attached to its top by bending each longitudinal edge of the latter around the edge of the sheet beneath (2mm is bent in).

Along the centre are six circular perforations for attachment. There are three dome-headed attachment-rivets with flattened ends. (L of rivets: 7mm; D of rivet-heads: 4mm; distance between the rivets: 15 to 28mm).

Imperfect. The rivets are missing from three of the rivet-holes.

cat. no. 67 below is similar.

From a horse-harness?

67 Mount (Pls 21, 32)

Single piece of composite construction.

A silver strip sheet with an applied gilt-silver strip.

4th–5th century?.

Gilt-silver, silver

Prov.: 'An-Kache (Sourcil Blanc)' in the register (i.e. 'White Brow'); see above, Krym (Crimea), Ukraine

Inv. no. 1923,7-16,104   Old cat. no. 311 ?

Percentage of silver: 96

Size: 40 x 13mm   Weight: 4.6g

Unpublished

A strip of silver sheet with a gilt-silver strip attached to its top by bending each longitudinal edge of the latter around the edge of the sheet below (similar to no. 923,7-16,103 above). (Approx. 1.5mm is bent in).

A fragment of a silver sheet strip which acted as a backing is attached by the central rivet, its width virtually the same as that of the composite strip above. (Distance between strips i.e. thickness of original strap: 3.5–4mm).

There are three dome-headed attachment-rivets with flattened ends along the centre. (L of rivets: 7mm; D of rivet-heads: 4mm, distance between the rivets: 13mm; 16mm).

Fragmentary.

cat. no. 66 above is similar, but with no back-sheet.

68 Mount (Pls 21, 32)

Single piece.

A strip sheet of copper-silver-alloy with two perforations.

4th–5th century?

Copper-silver-alloy.

Prov.: 'An-Kache (Sourcil Blanc)' in the register (i.e. 'White Brow'); see above, Krym (Crimea), Ukraine

Inv. no. 1923,7-16,102   Old cat. no. 311 ?

Percentage of silver: 49

Size: 84 x 20mm   Weight: 2.18g

Unpublished

A strip of thin copper-silver-alloy sheet with two holes for attachment-rivets. Both ends are (?) cut straight. (One hole is 2.5mm from the end of the strip, the other is 30mm from the other end. D of holes: 4–5mm; 40mm between two holes.)

Fragmentary. It is damaged above one of the perforations (a small part of the strip is missing here).

cat. no. 69 below is very similar.

Similar foils made of gold, and found in the Don region are considered as funerary horse-harness fittings by Guguev and Bezuglov[1].

Comparative Bibliography

1   Guguev and Bezuglov 1990, 172, 173, ill. 4

69 Mount (Pls 21, 32)

Single piece.

A strip sheet of copper-silver-alloy, perforated in the centre.

4th–5th century?

Copper-silver alloy

Prov.: 'An-Kache Sourcil Blanc' in the register (i.e. 'White Brow'); Krym (Crimea), Ukraine

Inv. no. 1923,7-16,101   Old cat. no. 311?

Percentage of silver: 44

Size: 19 x 76mm   Weight: 2.36g

Unpublished

A strip of thin copper-silver-alloy sheet with a hole for an attachment-rivet in the centre. There are traces of another perforation at the broken end. The other end is (?) cut straight.

Distance between the two perforations: 36mm, D of perforation: 4.5mm

Imperfect.

cat. no. 68 above is similar.

From a horse-harness?

Comments see **cat. no. 68** above.

Buckles

70   Buckle (Pl. 33, Colour Pl. 4)

In three pieces, one of which is composite.

The gold buckle has a rectangular plate with all-over cloisonné garnet inlays, an oval loop and faceted tongue.

End of 4th/first half of 5th century.   Hunnic

Gold, garnet

Prov.: Kerch, Krym (Crimea), Ukraine – 1894

Inv. no. 1923,7-16,29   Old cat. no. 151

Percentage of gold: loop: 89 side of cell: 88

Size: L: 38.7mm W: 21.1mm   Weight: 24.14g

Published: Dalton 1924a, 262, pl. XXXVII:5 reproduced from Dalton 1924b; Moss 1935, xiv, pl. III B lower left; Tait 1986, 103,247, ill. 226i; GHA 1987, (Kidd) 112, ill. I,16.n.

The attachment-plate is rectangular and composite, with four levels of construction. Its top is the same size as the base-plate and they are joined round the edges by a 1mm wide, rectangular gold strip soldered between them. The top consists of a frame divided by a saltire into four triangular cells. The frame is recessed into the triangular garnet inlay at the point where the tongue is hinged to the plate. There are plain gold foils beneath the garnets, which are moderately well cut, but chipped. The tops of the cell walls are burred over to secure the garnets, which has obscured any joins. (Size of attachment-plate: 14 x 12.4mm; thickness: 2.7mm; size of cells: bases of triangle: 10mm; 9.2mm which are the sides of the rectangle as well; sides of the triangles: c. 7mm; collet thickness: 1.3mm; between the triangles: 0.5mm).

The top and the back-plate are linked by the folded flap attachment and were made from the same gold sheet. There is a 2mm wide slot in the centre of the folded flap attachment to accommodate the buckle-tongue.

The back-plate of the buckle is rectangular, the same size as the top. It is fastened to the base-plate with rivets which are secured behind the base-plate, so that each rivet-head lies inside the composite unit. (Thickness of top and flap attachment: 1mm; thickness of back-plate: 0.7mm; D of rivet-heads: 0.8mm; distance between them: 11.2mm).

The loop is oval of solid gold and octagonal in section. It is thickest at the centre and narrows towards the ends where it is secured by the folded flap attachment. It is not possible to tell from surface examination to what extent the loop was cast to shape. It has a butt joint concealed by the tongue, so it could have been entirely worked. (Size of loop: W: 18.7mm; L: 21mm; D from 5.5mm to 3mm).

The tongue is club-shaped, heptagonal in section and faceted. Its end is sharply hooked about 4mm over the loop. The base is cut off where the attachment-hook of the tongue is connected; there are two engraved lines here. This hook is in the form of a rectangular-section strip narrowing towards the end and is formed from the same piece as the tongue. The tongue gives no surface indication of its techniques of manufacture. (Size of tongue: L: 25.5mm; point D: 2.5mm; base D: 6mm; thickness: from 2mm to 1.3mm).

See **Pl. 33** for construction.

It is in good condition.

Shoe-, sword-, or belt-buckle.

Many similar buckles have been found in the region of the Hunnic empire. According to Bóna they were worn during a single generation in the second third of the 5th century (425–455) in Pannonia and its neighbourhood by the military aristocracy associated with the Hunnic empire.[1] They functioned as belt-, sword- or shoe-buckles. There is a wide range of buckles of this type varying in the exact shape of the attachment-plate, garnet inlays, loop and tongue, number of attachment-rivets, etc. The closest parallels are the gold examples with rectangular buckle-plates and flat garnet inlays such as that from Novogrigorevka (Ukraine) in the Hermitage.[2] Its tongue is missing. There are buckles from Kerch (find of 24 June 1904) with a similar feature of the frame recessed into the garnet inlay where the tongue is hinged to the plate. Zasetskaya[3] and Kovalevskaya[4] dated these buckles to the end of the 4th/first half of the 5th century. But in Aibabin's opinion, according to the comparative pieces from Kerch, the buckle from the Berthier-Delagarde Collection cannot be dated earlier than the 5th century.[5] There is a buckle with a flat, rectangular garnet inlay from Kerch in the Massoneau Collection, Cologne, dated to the first half of the 5th century by Damm.[6] The buckle from Jędrzychowice (Höckricht, Poland)[7] has triangular settings, while the one from Wolfsheim (Germany)[8] is decorated with a different sort of rectangular inlay. A buckle in the Magyar Nemzeti Múzeum (Budapest) has four square settings.[9]

In most cases similar buckles with rectangular attachment-plates belonged to women according to Bóna.[10]

Comparative Bibliography

1   Bóna 1991, 100–1, 252–4; ill.39 has a distribution map of the Pannonian pieces
2   Minaeva 1927 91–123; 1993, 90–1, 228–9, ill. 39; Alföldi 1932, 62, 78; pl. XXII:20
3   Spitsin 1905, 118, ills 12, 16 (silver with gold settings); Zasetskaya 1979, 5–17; pls 3:62, 63, 6; 1993, 56–7, pl. 26:103; 1994, 165, pl. 5:10
4   Kovalevskaya 1979, 16; pl. II:3
5   Aibabin below
6   Damm 1988, 101; ills 31–2
7   Werner 1956, pl. 27:3, 64:9
8   Werner 1956, 124; pl. 4:7a-b
9   Inv. no. 5.1886.2; Alföldi 1932, 85–8; pl. XXXIV:12; Bóna 1991, 100–1 ill. 39, 253 no. 14; 1993, 90–1 ill. 39, 228 no. 4
10 Bóna 1991, 291; 1993, 261

71   Buckle-tongue (Pl. 34)

Single piece, of composite construction.

Cast, gold, club-shaped tongue.

End of 4th/first half of 5th century.   Hunnic

Gold

Prov.: Kerch, Krym (Crimea), Ukraine – 1894

Inv. no. 1923,7-16,4   Old cat. no. 81

Percentage of gold: 92

Iridium, osmium and ruthenium inclusions in the metal indicate the use of alluvial gold.

Size: L: 22.5mm; with hook: 25mm   Weight: 6.55g

Unpublished

The tongue is cast with some working, and is of circular section, narrowing towards the end where it is bent at a sharp angle to fit over the loop. Its terminal is obliquely cut off, and is decorated with three oblique engraved lines on each side meeting at the centre in a V-shape. At its base the tongue is flattened to a semicircular-section where the attachment-hook is soldered on. The base is decorated across the top with a line of seven small, faceted triangles which interlock between two pairs of semicircular moulded ribs. The decoration was cast in but has been accentuated with an abrading tool. (D of base: 5.1mm; end: 3.5mm).

The attachment-hook is a U-shaped strip with a rectangular section. It has been shaped by hammering and has a deliberately cut end. (W of attachment-hook: 2mm).

The loop is missing.

The original photographs of the collection do not show this object.

This tongue belongs to a Hunnic type of gold buckle, typical of the first half of the 5th century, which functioned as belt-, sword- or shoe-buckles. The main characteristics of this type are: a garnet-inlaid attachment-plate; a loop which is slightly oval or circular, with a faceted or circular section; and a tongue which is club-shaped with a circular or faceted section and with its end bent over the loop at a sharp angle. The tongue is often decorated at its end or at its base with various engraved or faceted ornaments like the present piece.

According to Zasetskaya similar buckles from Kerch can be dated from the end of the 4th to the beginning of the 5th century.[1] Kovalevskaya gives a similar dating.[2] But according to Aibabin the Kerch graves must be dated from the beginning of the 5th century.[3] In Bóna's opinion, in Pannonia and in its neighbourhood, such buckles were worn during a single generation (425–455) by the military aristocracy associated with the Hunnic empire.[4] Damm dates the parallels in the Diergardt

Collection to the first half of the 5th century.[5] Buckles of this type from different findspots are also published by Alföldi,[6] Werner[7] and Bakay.[8]

Comparative Bibliography

1 Zasetskaya 1979, 5–17
2 Kovalevskaya 1979, 15–16, pls I:6–9, II:2; 3
3 Aibabin below
4 Bóna 1991, 100–101, 252–4, ill. 39 gives a distribution map of Pannonian examples; Bóna 1993, 90–1, 228–9, ill. 39
5 Damm 1988, 100–101 ills 29–32; 158–65 ills 149–64
6 Alföldi 1932, 61–2, 78–9, 85–8; pls XXII:19–22, XXVI:2–5, XXXIV:1–12
7 Werner 1956, 124, pls 4:1a, b; 7a, b; 27:3; 64:9
8 Bakay 1978, 149–72, ills 3:2–4, 4:2–4

72   Buckle (Pls 34–35, Colour Pl. 1)

In three pieces, one of which is composite.
Miniature gold buckle has a semicircular plate decorated with a flat garnet, an oval loop and tongue.
Second half of 5th/beginning of 6th century.   Pontic. East Germanic.
Gold, garnet.
Prov.: Kerch, Krym (Crimea), Ukraine – 1900
Inv. no. 1923,7-16,58   Old cat. no. 223
Percentage of gold: 84
Size: L: 16mm   W: 15mm   Weight: 2.64g
Published: Tait 1986, 103, 247, ill. 226d; GHA 1987, (Kidd) 112, ill. I,16.0; Kazanski 1994, 144, pl. 5:9

The attachment-plate is semicircular and of composite construction. A single strip forming a semicircular collet is soldered onto the top of the base-plate and contains a flat garnet filling the surface area of the plate. The top of the collet is folded inwards to secure the garnet. There is no foil visible beneath the garnet. (Size of garnet plate: H: 10.4mm; W: 6.8mm; collet H: 2.7mm; thickness: 0.7mm).

The base-plate and the back-plate are linked by the folded flap attachment and were made from the same gold sheet. The folded flap attachment is 9mm wide with a 2.2mm slot cut in the centre to accommodate the attachment-hook of the buckle-tongue.

The back-plate is almost rectangular in shape with the end rounded off to match the end of the base-plate. The base-plate and the back-plate are held together by a central attachment-rivet. The rivet is secured behind the base-plate, so that the head lies inside the composite unit. (Size of back-plate: L: 8mm; W: 6mm; thickness: 0.2mm).

The loop is oval in shape and made from a circular-section wire. It is stepped at each end to fit within the folded flap attachment (L: 15mm; W: 7mm; thickness: 1.7mm).

The tongue is of gold strip with a flattened D-shaped section which becomes narrower inside the flap attachment. The point of the tongue is bent over the loop. The other end is bent to form an attachment-hook underneath. Its base is grooved crosswise. (Size of tongue: L: 9mm; W: 2.5mm).

It is in good condition.
Purse-, sword- or shoe-buckle.

There is a small buckle with its plate forming a kidney-shaped setting and with a slightly differently shaped loop and tongue in the Magyar Nemzeti Múzeum, Budapest.[1] Buckles like this were possibly the Hunnic antecedents of the type in the Berthier-Delagarde Collection.

There is a similar miniature buckle from Flonheim (Germany), but with a kidney-shaped plate and setting.[2] According to Ament this is a component part of a purse-mount with two opposed birds' heads, which also very much resembles the garnet-inlaid mounts (**no. 24 A-C**). The buckle from Flonheim is said to be Frankish still preserving Hunnic characteristics by Fettich.[3] A similar purse-fitting from Schwarzrheindorf (Germany) has similar birds' heads and a semicircular inlay above the buckle.[4] It is therefore possible that the Berthier-Delagarde buckle also belonged to a purse, decorated with inlaid mounts similar to **cat. no. 24 A-C**. Ament dates this type of inlaid purse-mount to the early Merovingian period (first half of the 6th century).[5]

There is also a miniature buckle with a semicircular plate and setting from Kudnietov (Bylym, south Russia, Black Sea region), but with a rectangular loop. It is dated to the Hunnic period by Fettich.[6] Aibabin also dates this type of buckle to the 5th century.[7]

Comparative Bibliography

1   Alföldi 1932, 88, pl. XXXIV:15; Diner 1890 – Catalog 9, no. 12, pl.

II:7; Bóna 1993, 256 no. 3, pl. XXVI:3
2   Ament 1970, 68–79, pls 12:1; 28; 30:7
3   Fettich 1953, 53–4, pl. XXXII:5
4   Ament op. cit., 69, ill. 6
5   Ament op. cit., 69
6   Fettich 1953, 45, 72, pl. XXXVIII:8
7   Aibabin below

73   Buckle (Pl. 36)

In three pieces, one of which is composite.
The gilt-silver buckle has a heart-shaped plate with a bird's head terminal in profile. The loop is kidney-shaped. The tongue has a basal cube and animal-head terminal.
Late 5th–6th century.   North Pontic. Byzantine – East Germanic.
Gilt-silver, silver, carnelian.
Prov.: Kerch, Krym (Crimea), Ukraine – 1900
Inv. no. 1923,7-16,52   Old cat. no. 213
Percentage of silver: 93: back
Size (overall): L: 47mm   Weight: (total): 18.57g
W: 33mm   Loop and tongue: 14.32g   Plate: 4.25g
Published: Dalton 1924a, 262, pl. XXXVII:2 reproduced from Dalton 1924b

The attachment-plate is gilt-silver, cast, flat and heart-shaped, with a bird's head terminal in profile. The neck of the bird is formed by multiple moulded ribs. The eye is represented by a perforation containing an orange carnelian cabochon secured by a silver strip around it, visible only from the back. There are small incisions in the metal which radiate from the inlay. There is a perforation directly below the bird's head, perhaps for an attachment-rivet.

The folded flap attachment is made from the same sheet as the attachment-plate. Fragments of the folded flap attachment are fastened to the loop. (Size of attachment-plate: 24 x 23mm; thickness: 2.5mm; D of inlay: 3mm; D of perforation for rivet: 2mm; remains of folded flap attachment: two 2mm wide and 0.5mm thick strips).

The loop is kidney-shaped with a plain tongue-rest and is gilded all over, including the back. The ends of the loop are stepped and joined by a thick rod to secure the folded flap attachment. (Tongue-rest: 32 x 23.5mm; rod: from 9 to 7mm; under the folded flap attachment: 3mm).

The tongue has a solid cast cube at the base, then a triangular section, and ends in an animal-head terminal which bends over the loop. The attachment-hook of the tongue, cast in one with it, is of rectangular section and hammered to shape. (Tongue: L: 22.5mm; W: 7.5mm; thickness: 5mm; attachment-hook: W: 2.5mm).

The folded flap attachment is broken and incomplete, and the back-plate is missing.

On the original photograph the folded flap attachment is still connected to the attachment-plate.

This type of buckle shows Byzantine and Germanic influences. The loop is of Byzantine type, while the plate and tongue show Germanic characteristics. Similar buckles have been found in the Crimea, mostly in Kerch.[1] A loop and tongue with similar features were found in Cherson, but there is no evidence for the shape of the attachment-plate. In Zasetskaya's chronological system it is grouped amongst the buckles of the late 5th/early 6th century.[2] A silver buckle with a similar bird-head terminal was found in south Russia and is now in the collection of F.L. von Gans, in Berlin.[3] According to the typology of Kovalevskaya they were made in the 5th–6th centuries.[4] Aibabin dates them to the first half of the 6th century,[5] but according to Ambroz's chronology these buckles belong to the 6th–7th century.[6]

Comparative Bibliography

1   Aibabin 1990, 37; 218 ill. 39:5 (Kerch 1907, grave 78); same in: Shkorpil 1910a, p.33 ill. 20; Aibabin 1982, 177; Kovalevskaya 1979, 43, pl. XX:18 (Kerch); Ambroz 1970, 70–4; 72 ill. 2:1, 3 (1 said to be from Simferopol, but possibly from Kerch; 3 from Kerch)
2   Zasetskaya 1990, 97–106 ill. 1:40
3   Greifenhagen 1975, 116 pl. 79:11
4   Kovalevskaya op. cit., pl. 5
5   Aibabin 1990, 37, 218, pl. 39:2
6   Ambroz op.cit., 71

74   Buckle (Pl. 36)

In two pieces.
The gilded base silver buckle has an oval attachment-plate with chip-carved scrollwork, and an oval loop with ribbed decoration.

End of 5th/beginning of 6th century. North Pontic. East Germanic.
Gilded base silver, copper alloy
Prov.: Kerch, Krym (Crimea), Ukraine – 1895
Inv. no. 1923,7-16,47   Old cat. no. 166
Percentage of silver: back-plate:45   folded flap attachment: 54
Size: 46 x 45mm   Weight: 22.45g
Published: Dalton 1924a, 262, pl. XXXVII:21 reproduced from Dalton
1924b; Aibabin 1979, 31, fig. 2:11; Aibabin 1990, 37, pl. 37:2; Kazanski
1994, 164–5, pl. 22:1

The cast, oval front plate is of gilded base silver. It has a rebated,
kidney-shaped panel decorated with chip-carved scrollwork within a
grooved border. The scrollwork consists of two groups of four
confronted spirals in a cruciform pattern, symmetrically arranged,
one in either lobe of the kidney. The two groups are separated by a
chip-carved rectangle in the centre of the plate. There is a double-
grooved line which is transversely notched to resemble beaded wire
forming a rib all around the edge of the kidney-shape. (Size of top
plate: 40 x 23mm).

There is a flange, 3.5mm high and 2mm wide, projecting all around
the edge at the back, which is otherwise flat.

The front and the back-plate are linked by the folded flap
attachment and made out of the same piece of metal. The folded flap
attachment is a 20mm wide strip with a 4.5mm wide slot to
accommodate the buckle-tongue.

The back-plate has an irregular shape with the end of the broken
end of a copper-alloy (?) rivet going through the centre of the front
plate. (Size of back-plate: 12 x 21mm; 1.8mm thick)

Three peripheral attachment-lugs are cast on the edge of the plate.
One retains a copper-alloy attachment-rivet. (D: 3.2mm; H of lugs the
same as the flange of the plate).

The loop is gilded base silver and cast in one piece. It is oval in shape
with a flattened rectangular section. The tongue-rest is plain and of
rectangular section and on either side of it is a sunken panel extending
around the loop, which is decorated with a double-grooved rib running
along it. The ribs are transversely notched in a dense pattern matching
those bordering the attachment-plate. Each panel has a high border all
round it, with forming a rectangular shoulder at each end. The ends
are stepped down to a circular-section hinge-bar through the folded
flap attachment. The bar is slightly thicker in the centre, where the
tongue was attached. (Size of loop: 39 x 19mm; W at sunken panels:
6.5mm; H: 3mm; tongue-rest: 7 x 4.5; H: 2mm; rod: L: 21mm; D: 2mm;
D in the centre: 3mm).

There are traces of heavy wear on the inside edge of the loop,
particularly on one side.

One of the attachment-lugs is broken; the loop is damaged and the
tongue is missing. Only the rebated panels preserve the gilding now,
and it is probable that the whole buckle was originally gilded. The
attachment-rivet through the centre of the front plate may be
secondary.

An early 20th-century photograph from the Simferopol Archives
(Dalton 1924a, 262 pl. XXXVII:21) and the register show the buckle
associated with a tongue presumably of gilt-silver with two
rectangular inlays (possibly garnets) on the cube at its base. The
present location of this tongue is unknown. However the buckle is now
associated with a non-matching tongue which is of copper alloy (now
no. 79; former Inv. no. 1923,7-16, 47b; new Inv. no. OA 10695).

According to Ambroz similar buckles were made by Germanic tribes of
the Danube region and further west in the late 5th/first half of the 6th
century who adopted the technique of chip-carving from the Late-
Roman provinces.[1] A buckle with a very similar attachment-plate from
Grocka (Serbia) is dated to the end of the 5th/beginning of the 6th
century and said to be Ostrogothic by Mrkobrad.[2] A silver buckle from
Hessen (Germany)[3] and a gilt-silver one from Gültlingen (Germany)[4]
have similar chip-carved scrollwork on their rectangular attachment-
plates. A buckle from Demidovka (Dnieper region)[5] decorated with
scrollwork is considered to have been made by a local craftsman in a
technique adopted from the Danube area. The loops of these buckles
differ from that of the Berthier-Delagarde one, and the similarities
extend only to the decoration of the attachment-plate. There is a buckle
with a very similar plate, but a geometric pattern, from Borkovskaya
(Russia).[6]

According to Aibabin this type of buckle is a unique find in the
Crimea.[7]

Comparative Bibliography
1   Ambroz 1970, 70–4
2   Mrkobrad 1980, p. 151, pl. XXV:3
3   Salin 1904, 113 ill. 300
4   Quast 1993, 84, pls 14:20, 26:20
5   Ambroz *op. cit.*, 72 ills 1.1, 1.2, 1.7
6   Pósta 1905 II, 579 ill. 331; same in Ambroz 1970, 72 ill. 1:3
7   Aibabin 1990, 37; Aibabin below

75   Buckle (Pl. 37)

In three pieces, one of which is composite.
Gilt-silver buckle has a triangular attachment-plate decorated with
ribs and a central glass insert. The loop is oval, in the form of two
confronted animal heads. The tongue is decorated with an animal-
head terminal.
Mid-5th - early 6th century? North Pontic. ? Late Antique, Byzantine
Gilt-silver, silver, clear glass
Prov.: Kerch, Krym (Crimea), Ukraine – 1895
Inv. no. 1923,7-16,46   Old cat. no. 165
Percentage of silver: loop: 84   back-plate: 85   tongue: 78
Size: 65 x 39mm   H: 12mm   Weight: 34.44g
Published: Dalton 1924a, p. 262, pl. XXXVII:18 reproduced from Dalton
1924b

The front plate is of gilt-silver, cast in the shape of an isosceles triangle.
It has a central triangular collet containing an inlay of clear glass with
three blue blobs which appears to be a modern replacement (see note
below). A gold-coloured foil can be seen through the glass. The high
central collet is bordered by double ribbing which is transversely
notched. There is a lobe at each corner decorated with a transversely
notched, circular rib around it. The terminal lobe has traces of a central
attachment-rivet. The other two lobes are not drilled through and each
has a pseudo-attachment-rivet cast in the centre. (Sides of plate: 2 x
45mm; 35mm; sides of central frame: 2 x 23mm; 13mm; H of plate:
2.5mm; D of lobes: 9mm; D of circular ribbings: 5.5mm; W of rib: 1mm).

The front and back-plates are linked by the folded flap attachment
and were made from the same silver sheet. There is a 4mm wide slot cut
in the centre of the folded flap attachment to accommodate the buckle-
tongue. The sheet has been hammered to obtain a thin back-plate
which is ungilded and cut to the shape of the front plate. (W of folded
flap attachment: 16mm; thickness of back-plate: 0.5mm).

The cast loop is oval and has a flat, rectangular section. There is a
tongue-rest in the middle which has an offset edge stepped for part of
its length. It is decorated with a heavily moulded, anthropomorphic
head at each end. (Size of loop: 39 x 20mm; W: 5-6mm, wider at the
anthropomorphic heads: 8mm; H: 4mm; W of margin: 1.5mm; H: 3mm;
size of tongue-rest: L: 6.5mm; W: 4mm; H: 3mm).

The tongue has a semicircular section and a heavily moulded,
animal-head terminal. It has cast relief features (one transversely
notched, longitudinal rib with a horizontal rib above; the eyes are
suggested by two carved wedges at the point). The base has a
semicircular zone decorated with three moulded ribs, the central one
of which is transversely notched. The tongue is attached to the plate by
a hook cast on its base. (Size of tongue: L: 20mm; H: 5mm; D: 5-9mm;
W of ribs on base: 0.8mm).

The triangular glass insert appears from its curvature to be reused
from a vessel. This type of glass is of Late-Roman date, but the edges
have been cut surprisingly well, which may indicate that it was added
recently. A cement was used to secure the insert; the pinkish colour is
due to red lead (minium) in the cement.

The back-plate is slightly damaged, but apart from that the buckle is
in good condition.

The insert may be secondary.

Two buckles with similar attachment-plates have been found in the
Crimea, and are dated to the 6th–7th century by Aibabin.[1] One of them
could possibly be identical with the Berthier-Delagarde buckle, since
there is no further information about it in the publication. The
construction of the loop as two confronted animal-heads shows
Germanic characteristics and resembles that of a gold buckle from
Szeged made in the Hunnic period.[2] There is a gilt-copper-alloy buckle
from Kerch in the Ashmolean Museum with a similarly shaped plate,
but of different construction and undecorated.[3]

This buckle seems to be a unique piece in the collection and is hard
to parallel elsewhere, in view of the unusual decoration of the loop and
tongue, combined with the lobed attachment-plate. The features of the

loop suggest that it is a later development of a certain type of gold and garnet buckle of the Hunnic era, and can therefore be dated to the mid-5th–early 6th century.

Comparative bibliography
1   Aibabin 1990, ill. 38:22; 23
2   Bóna 1993, 262–3, pl. XXX
3   Inv. no. 1909.803

76   Buckle (Pl. 38)
Consists of two pieces.
Gilt-copper-alloy buckle has a circular plate decorated with chip-carved, punched and incised, geometric ornament. D-shaped loop.
Mid-4th to mid-5th century.   Late-Roman.
Gilt copper alloy, leaded gunmetal, traces of iron
Inv. no. 1923,7-16,112   Old cat. no. 272
Size: 74 x 52.5mm   Weight: 62.77g
Unpublished

The attachment-plate is gilt copper-al oy (mercury-gilded) and circular. The front plate consists of a cast disc decorated in the centre with a chip-carved, six-petalled flower-motif, each petal with five or six punched dots in the middle. There are stamped triangles between each petal with all-over ribbing inside them. The central motif is surrounded by concentric lines of decoration forming a broad zone around it. The flower-motif is surrounded by six of the same kind of petal-pattern. This motif can also be seen as six conjoined triangles in a hexagonal arrangement with the petals as the sides of each triangle. There are similar ribbed triangles around this outer petal-pattern, which are surrounded by stamped ring-and-dots. Around it is a line of punched double-triangles which is surrounded by another row of ring-and-dots (the same as the one above). The decoration is framed by an incised line all around the edge. (Size of front plate: D: 46mm; thickness: 2mm; size of petals: 8 x 3mm; sides of stamped triangles: 2mm; D of stamped rings: 1.7mm).

The front and back-plates are linked by the folded flap attachment and were made from the same sheet. The folded flap attachment is rectangular with a slot cut in the centre to accommodate the buckle-tongue, and folded over. It is decorated with punched dots. (Size of folded flap attachment: W: 19mm; slot W: 6.5mm; D:8mm).

The back-plate is made by hammering and cutting to shape, thereby obtaining a thin sheet of the same size and shape as the buckle-plate.

Both the front and back-plates are perforated for attachment-rivets through the centre, and at three points around the edge in a triangular arrangement. A copper-alloy attachment-rivet survives in one of the four holes. (D of perforations: 1.5mm; rivet D: 1mm; L: 6mm).

The buckle-loop is D-shaped and made from a solid copper-alloy rod which is a leaded gunmetal. There are iron fragments on its surface in the slot of the folded flap attachment which represent the remains of an iron tongue. (Size of loop: 52 x 29mm; D of rod: 6mm).

There are traces of corrosion on the back-plate. The tongue is missing. The gilding is imperfect.

Most of the attachment-rivets are missing.

This general type of buckle, and mounts with a similar stamped pattern, occur in an area extending from the Rhine region to the Black Sea coast, including central and northern Europe, and central and south-west Poland. They are products of provincial Roman workshops of the mid-4th to mid-5th century and were possibly made to the order of the upper social strata of Germanic tribes.

Madyda-Legutko surveyed most of this type of belt-fitting and gives a chronological and typological classification.[1]

A buckle of this type from Yalta (Crimea) is published by Baranov.[2] Buckle-plates from Schinna and Sahlenburg (Germany) are also decorated with similar stamped ornament.[3]

The aspects of this cultural circle are further discussed by Bóna,[4] Tejral[5] and Aibabin.[6]

Comparative bibliography
1   Madyda-Legutko 1978, 3-16 – with list of related literature
2   Baranov 1975, 272 , ill. 1A; B
3   Böhme 1974, 77; 250; 251, pls 41:1; 40:1-6
4   Bóna 1971, 228, ill. 3; Bóna 1991, 172–3 ill. 66, 261–2; 1993, 150–1 ill. 66, 235–6
5   Tejral 1985, 308–97, pl. 2; 26
6   Aibabin 1990, 28–9, pls 2:45; 6:10

77   Buckle (Pl. 39)
Two composite pieces.
Gilt-copper-alloy buckle has a rectangular loop ribbed and moulded as two confronted birds' heads with garnet inlays. The tongue has a garnet-inlaid basal cube and animal-head terminal.
5th–6th century.   Pontic – Byzantine
Gold, gilt copper alloy, garnet
Prov.: Kerch, Krym (Crimea), Ukraine – 1894
Inv. no. 1923,7-16,45   Old cat. no. 164
Size: 39 x 43mm   Weight: 38.03g
Published: Dalton 1924a, 262, pl. XXXVII:11 reproduced from Dalton 1924b; Werner 1974a, 652, Abb. 3: 2; Aibabin 1990, pl. 22:29

The cast loop is rectangular and of D-shaped section, the back being flat. There is a cabochon garnet inlay in a heavy cast circular collet in each corner, and cast ribbed decoration across the two shorter sides. From each of the two collets at the front projects a cast lunate setting containing a flat garnet, so forming two confronted birds' heads. There is a gold foil beneath these garnets. (Size of loop: 38.5 x 43mm; D of cabochon settings: 10mm; D of garnets: 7mm; W of ribs: 1mm. Size of garnet plates: L: 6mm; W: 4mm).

The tongue has a cast basal cube inlaid with a flat, rectangular garnet and a tip cast in the form of an animal head. The animal's ears are formed by two lentoid hollows, originally inlaid with traces of a gold foil, which remains in one of them. The eyes were originally represented by two cylindrical holes set with cabochon garnets, but these are now missing. The nose is emphasised by a finely engraved V-shape on the end. (Size of tongue: L: 35mm; W: 10mm; sides of basal cube: 7mm; 8.5mm; 8.5mm; rectangular garnet: 5.5 x 6.5mm; lentoid settings: 3.5 x 7mm; D of cylindrical settings: 2.7mm).

The attachment-hook is cast in one with the tongue and is situated beneath the basal cube. (L: 12mm; thickness: 4mm).

The tongue is imperfect, the garnets of the terminal are missing and the gilding is imperfect. One side of the loop is broken.

The two cabochon eyes of the animal-headed terminal, which appear on the original photograph of the museum, are now missing.

According to Werner this is an early Byzantine type of buckle of the first half of the 6th century.[1] A buckle from Wachendorf (Germany) is also made of copper alloy and has traces of gilding, but the inlays are all missing).[2] There is a similar buckle from Syria in the Kofler-Truniger Collection, Lucerne (Switzerland), which is also made of copper-alloy and has inlays with gilt-bronze foils beneath them.[3] There is a similar copper-alloy buckle from Kalna (Slovakia)[4] and another from an unknown provenance with a Christian symbol on its plate in the Kunsthistorisches Museum, Vienna.[5] A gilt-copper-alloy buckle-tongue of the same type was found in Pilismarót (Hungary).[6] A similar buckle, but with a circular base to its tongue, was found in a chamber grave at Kerch on 24 June, 1904. It is dated to the end of the 4th/first half of the 5th century by Zasetskaya.[7] In 1991 a very similar buckle was found by chance near the river Kuban in Krasnodar (south Russia).[8] It is of copper alloy and decorated with red inlays (possibly garnets). It is of particular importance as its attachment-plate survives, which is cross-shaped with a folded flap attachment at one end. The arms of the cross are ribbed and there is a central, rectangular inlay at the crossing. The attachment-plate is further decorated with three kidney-shaped settings, one at the end of each arm of the cross. The buckle is dated to the second half of the 5th century by Pyankov.[9] There are two similar copper-alloy buckles with traces of gilding and garnet plate inlays in private collections in New York: one in the Ariadne Galleries[10] and the other in the Phillips Family Collection.[11] According to Bálint this type of bird-headed decoration is of Byzantine origin.[12] The motif of two opposed birds' heads appears also on the upper part of some Late-Avar belt-fittings and is rooted in the Late-Antique art of the 5th–6th century. Iron buckles with the same features from the Alamannic region at Mengen (Germany)[13] and Basel-Kleinhüningen, grave 199 (Switzerland)[14] are local imitations of the original early Byzantine ones according to Werner.[15]

Comparative Bibliography
1   Werner 1974a, 654, 656–7, with references to the parallel pieces
2   Werner *op. cit.*, ill. 2:1
3   Werner *op. cit.* ills 2:3, 3:1
4   Werner *op. cit.* ills 2:4
5   Werner *op. cit.*, ill. 3:3
6   Werner *op. cit.*, ill. 3:4
7   Zasetskaya 1979, pl. 3:64; 1990, 97–106; ill. 1:27; 1993, 58–9, pl.

26:110
8   Pyankov 1997, 57–60, ill. 1
9   Pyankov *op. cit.*, 59
10 Demirjian 1991, 69 ill. 119
11 The Phillips Family Collection
12 Bálint 1992, 347, 467; pl. 31:16; 1995, 77–9, pl. 318
13 Werner *op. cit.*, ill. 3:5
14 Giesler-Müller 1992, 178; pls 43; 6; 57:2
15 Werner *op. cit.*, 654

5   Afanas'ev 1979, 181–2; 1980, 143; 150
6   Minaeva 1956, 249, 261; ill. 8:8
7   Voronov and Yushin 1973, 182; 191; ill. 11:4
8   Quast 1993, 85–6
9   Preda 1980, pls XXVI:M47; LXVI:M47.1.
10 Preda *op. cit.*, 41, 89
11 Opaiţ 1991, ill. 19:39, no. 42407
12 Inv. no. 77,9-3,1 – Bought at Florence, presented by Rev. G. Chester
13 Kazanski 1994, 151, pl. 11:13–16

78   Buckle (Pl. 40)

In three pieces, one of which is composite.
Copper-alloy buckle has an oval plate with red and green glass inlays and punched decoration. The loop is oval and the tongue club-shaped.
6th-7th century. Provincial Byzantine.
Copper alloy (brass), copper, red glass, green glass.
Prov.: Kerch, Krym (Crimea), Ukraine – 1900
Inv. no. 1923,7-16,60   Old cat. no. 225
Size: 45 x 38.5mm   Weight: 38.37g
Published: Aibabin 1979, 31, fig. 2:13; Aibabin 1990, 37, pl. 37:17; Kazanski 1994, p.155, pl. 15:4

The attachment-plate is oval. It has a cast top plate of brass with a deep flange projecting around the edge and a soldered-on, copper base-plate of the same size to create a box-like form. The plate is filled with a material identified by XRD as a wax, probably beeswax. The top plate has a large, cross-shaped opening in the centre. Each arm of the cross expands to its end, which is concave and filled with a red glass plate cut to shape. At the centre there is a green glass disc in a crudely shaped, cylindrical copper collet. A smaller green glass disc is inlaid between each pair of arms of the cross. There is a punched, pointillé border around the cross and between each of the arms, forming an undulating line which is completed with dots above and below. There are three attachment-rivets inside the edge of the front plate in a triangular arrangement. Each passes through a perforated lug projecting on the inside of the flanged edge.

The top plate is cast together with the folded flap attachment, which narrows to a squared-off end on the back. (Size of plate: 32 x 22mm; H of side: 6mm; size of green glass inlays: two shorter ones: W: 2–5.5mm; L: 5.5mm; two longer ones: W: 13mm; L: 4–6mm; D of central green glass disc: 3.5mm; D of smaller discs: 2mm).

The loop is of brass, cast, oval, and with a circular section. It has well-defined shoulders where it narrows inside the folded flap attachment. (Size of loop: 20 x 38.5mm; D of section: 6mm-2mm).

The tongue is of brass, club-shaped, triangular in section with an attachment-hook cast on the base. (L of tongue: 23mm; W at the end: 6mm; at the base: 9mm; H: 4mm; thickness: 2mm; D: 6mm).

The buckle has been chemically stripped at some time in its history, leaving the surface clean of any plating or corrosion products.

The inlays and back-plate are damaged.

Very similar buckles with oval plates and glass inlays in cruciform patterns have been found in south Russia.[1] They are products of provincial Byzantine workshops. Aibabin dates them to the 6th/first half of the 7th century,[2] Voronov to the second half of the 6th/first half of the 7th century,[3] and Ambroz to the 7th century.[4] According to Afanas'ev the broadly similar buckle from Mokraya Balka (Caucasus) can be dated to the second half of the 5th/first half of the 6th century.[5]

There are similar buckles from the Caucasus region: one from Baital-Chapkan, grave 20, is considered to be Alanic and dated to the 5th century by Minaeva,[6] the other from Cebelda (Georgia) is dated to the beginning of the 7th century by Voronov and Yushin,[7] but to the 5th century by Quast.[8] A buckle from Callatis (Mangalia, Romania, Black Sea region) with a rectangular attachment-plate is decorated with a central cruciform pattern, but formed of the metal of the buckle, i.e. the inlays lie between the arms of the cross.[9] Preda dates it to the 5th century.[10] There is a similar buckle-plate from Ibiza (Romania)[11] and another of unknown provenance in the British Museum, purchased in Florence.[12] Kazanski dates this type to the 6th century.[13]

Comparative bibliography

1   Ambroz 1971, ill. 6:4; Kovalevskaya 1979, 19; pl. IV:4; 1993, 112; pl. 1:21; Voronov 1975, 78 ill. 21:3; Afanas'ev 1979, 180 ill. 10:3; 1980, ill. 1:25; Greifenhagen 1975, pl. 79:7 – Collection of F.L. von Gans
2   Aibabin 1979, 31 ; 1990, 37
3   Voronov 1975, 78–9
4   Ambroz 1971, 110

79   Buckle-tongue (Pl. 40)

Single piece of composite construction
Brass buckle-tongue with a garnet inlay.
5th–6th century?
Copper alloy (brass), garnet.
Prov.: unknown, unless the original association with cat. no. 74 is accepted.
Inv. no. 1923,7-16,47b   Old cat. no. 166
New Inv. no. OA 10695
Size: 22 x 10mm   Weight: 2.86g
Published: as buckle no. 923,7-16,47a

The tongue is of plano-convex section narrowing slightly to a bent-over end. It is cast together with a basal cube which is set with a flat, rectangular garnet inlay. The back of the tongue is flat with a small perforation beneath the base to secure an attachment-hook, now lost. (W of tongue at the base: 6mm, at the end: 4mm; L: 16mm; base: 5 x 10mm; H: 4mm).

The garnet inlay is broken and the gilding is imperfect.

The piece has usually been associated with the buckle, **cat. no. 74**. It differs in being of copper alloy rather than silver, and has no chip-carved decoration. See **cat. no. 74** above.

80   Buckle (Pl. 41)

In three pieces, two of which are composite.
The gilt-silver buckle has a rectangular plate with a bird's head terminal in profile, scrollwork decoration and green glass inlays. The loop is oval, the tongue is hollow and has an animal-head terminal.
2nd half of 6th/beginning of 7th century. Ostrogothic.
Gilt-silver, brass, glass
Prov.: Kerch, Krym (Crimea), Ukraine 1900
Inv. no. 1923,7-16,53   Old cat. no. 214
Percentage of silver: main part (front), gilding: 48   main part (back): 64
Size: overall: 125 x 60mm   Weight: 59.75g
Unpublished

The attachment-plate is gilt-silver (mercury-gilded), cast rectangular in shape and decorated with concentric zones forming a frame around the centre. There is a cast, cylindrical collet in each of the four corners containing a circular, pale green glass cabochon inlay. They are connected by a grooved border rib around a rectangular zone of foliate tendril ornament cast in low relief. Along the inside edge is a double-ribbed border, which frames the central panel. This contains two inward spiralling scrolls linked at the base in a heart-shape and developing into a pair of confronted, outward-spiralling scrolls. There is a cast, cylindrical collet containing a millefiori glass inlay in the centre. There is a dome-headed copper-alloy (brass) attachment-rivet at each corner of the scrollwork frame. The plate has a profiled bird's head terminal cast on the end, which has a trapezoid neck, decorated with ribbing along two edges, and a zone of parallel zigzags in between. The eye is formed by a glass cabochon in a collet without a base or foil. A hole is drilled through the plate below the eye, perhaps for a rivet attachment. (Size of attachment-plate: 42 x 49mm; collets: D: 4mm; H: 3mm; central collet: D: 6mm; H: 3mm; attachment-rivets: D: 3.7mm; eye: D: 3.5mm; perforation below the eye: D: 3mm).

The back is flat with a 3mm high, flanged edge which is 2mm wide. It projects around three of its sides and 4mm from the corner of the side where the loop is connected. There are traces of a copper-silver-alloy plate or foil beneath one of the collets and a small perforation through the scrollwork frame (casting flaw).

There are fragments of an attachment of two folded-over strips fastened to the loop.

The oval loop consists of a flat, angled strip, stepped at each end to a thin, circular-section rod for attachment to the plate. The rod is cast together with the loop and has remains of the folded flap attachment around it. The tongue-rest is plain, 11.5mm wide, with a rectangular-section shoulder on either side of it. The loop is decorated with a pattern of cast, longitudinal ribbing with a line of S-scrolls beneath it. Two cylindrical collets, possibly for glass inlays, are cast on each end of the loop. (Size of loop: 60 x 42mm; 10mm thick; 5mm high; rod L: 28mm; D: 2.8mm; remains of attachment to the plate: 0.3mm thick; 6mm and 4mm wide silver strips).

The tongue is cast, with a hollow V-shaped section, and multiple ribbing at the base. It has moulded features at the terminal representing a stylised animal-head. (Tongue, L: 48; W: 9.5mm).

The folded flap attachment is broken, three of the glass inlays are missing and the tongue is damaged.

The original photograph of the collection does not show this object.

There is a wide range of eagle-headed buckles from the Crimea and the Danube region, which may be divided into three different groups:
1) the Danubian type made by Gepid workshops. They have a square plate with a large inlay in the centre surrounded by smaller settings; the neck of the bird-shaped terminal is semicircular and the folded flap attachment is very small;
2) the south Crimean type. They are usually quite large with a large folded flap attachment and neck section. Aibabin and Ambroz distinguish further variants within this type according to the length of the folded flap attachment, those with the shortest and widest attachment being the earliest variants;[1]
3) the Bosporan type. This type is smaller than the south Crimean variants, and the loop has only a single row of decoration. The Berthier-Delagarde buckle belongs to the third group, examples of which have been found in Kerch,[2] Eski-Kermen[3] and Hurzuf (Gurzuf).[4] Another from Iatrus (Krivina, Bulgaria) probably also belongs to this group[5] and there is a buckle of the type in the Ashmolean Museum from Kerch.[6] Salin published an unprovenanced example from the Crimea.[7]

The earliest literature does not distinguish between the different types: Shkorpil dated them to the 3rd–4th century.[8] But according to Götze's typology the buckles from Kerch and Suuk-Su (south Crimea) belong to the same group and should be dated to the end of the 6th/beginning of the 7th century.[9]

There is a basic disagreement now over the chronology of the eagle-headed buckles. According to one theory they were manufactured and used from the mid-5th century. Bóna dates the Crimean pieces between the mid-5th and the early 7th century, but mainly to the second half of the 6th.[10] Only a few Crimean-type buckles are found outside of the Crimea (Fundătura [Kisjenő], Romania;[11] and Kovin[12] and Sirmia,[13] former Yugoslavia). They served as a model for the Gepid workshops during the Ostrogothic era. According to a second theory, the Crimean pieces copied Danubian prototypes. Its proponents, Aibabin[14] and Ambroz,[15] date both Crimean types to the end of the 6th–7th century and the south Crimean ones from the mid-6th up to the end of the 7th. According to Pudovin the buckles from Kerch should be dated earlier, to the end of the 5th/beginning of the 6th century, while the south Crimean ones should be later, in the second half of the 6th/first half of the 7th century.[16] Matsulevich's chronology is very similar: he considers the pieces from Kerch as 5th-century products based on Greco-Sarmatian, Scythian tradition, and used as prototypes for the 6th–7th-century south Crimean variants.[17] According to M. Rusu most of the eagle-headed buckles were made in Kerch from the beginning of the 6th century.[18] Therefore the buckles found in Kerch would be the earliest pieces.

A large number of eagle-headed buckles are published by Repnikov.[19]

Comparative bibliography

1   Aibabin 1990, 33–4, also mentions Ambroz's Doct. Diss. 1974, 225, 226, 265, 269, 270.
2   Götze 1913, pl. IX; Matsulevich 1933, pl. II; Aibabin 1990, 214, pl. 35:4
3   Aibabin 1990, 214, pl. 35:1,2
4   Hurzuf?, Götze 1907, pl. X:1,2
5   Gomolka 1966, no. 7, 300, 340; pl. X:72 – according to his theory the buckle from Iatrus was made by a Bosporan workshop. Goryunov and Kazanski 1983, 199; ill. 1:18 – they consider it as Gepid type, made before the end of the 6th century.
6   Inv. no. 1909.790 – Kerch 1886. Sir John Evans Collection, presented to the Ashmolean by Sir Arthur Evans in 1909
7   Salin 1904, 197; ill. 477

8   Shkorpil 1907, 1–2
9   Götze 1913, 33; pls VIII–XI
10   Bóna 1974, 50-51; pls 13-15
11   Rusu 1959, 491, ill. 5; Roth 1979, ill. 53b
12   Rusu 1959, 38; ill. 12
13   Rusu 1959, 495; ill. 7:1
14   Aibabin 1990, 32–5; pls 29–35 (on pl. 29:2, 4, two Gepid-type buckles from Kerch.) Aibabin and Chajredinova 1995, 189–93 – recently excavated eagle-headed buckles from Luchyste (Luchistoye).
15   Ambroz 1968, 10–17
16   Pudovin 1961, 184; ill. 1; 1962, 146
17   Matsulevich 1926, 41–53
18   Rusu 1959, 485–523 (with illustrations of buckles from Koreiz, Nikopol, Suuk-Su, Artek, Chufut-Kale).
19   Repnikov 1906, pl. VIII:1; 3; 4; 5; pl. IX:2; 5; 7; 8; 9; 50 ill. 34; 70 ill. 48; Repnikov 1907, pl.II:1; 2; 3; 5

81   Buckle (Pl. 42)

Originally in three pieces, two of which are composite.
The silver buckle has a rectangular plate with a bird's-head terminal in profile, scrollwork decoration and garnet inlays. The loop is oval, the tongue is hollow and has an animal-head terminal.
End of the 6th–beginning of the 7th century.   Ostrogothic.
Silver, copper, copper alloy, garnet
Inv. no. 1923,7-16,113   Old cat. no. 315
Percentage of silver: tongue: 74   main part: 82
Size: originally possibly 127 x 60mm   Weight: 37.35g
Unpublished

The rectangular, silver attachment-plate is cast and then cleaned up. It may originally have been gilded and some additional tooling of the cast relief design may have been done at this stage. It is decorated with concentric zones forming a frame around the centre. There are four cast, cylindrical collets, each containing a circular cabochon garnet inlay, one in each corner. There are traces of a copper-alloy base or foil beneath two of the garnets. The plate has small perforations beneath the other two inlays. The collets are connected by a double-grooved line along the edge of the rectangle, which borders a frame of cast scrollwork containing conjoined, confronted spirals. It has a double, incised line border on the inside edge framing the central panel, which is now missing. There are silver attachment-rivets at each corner of the scrollwork frame, three of which are missing. The plate has a terminal in the form of a bird's head in profile with an incised, 'herring-bone' pattern on the neck and a cabochon garnet in a cast, cylindrical collet forming the eye. The garnet has no base or foil. There is a perforation in the plate next to the eye, perhaps for a rivet attachment. (Size of the plate originally possibly: 42 x 49mm; D of garnets: 5mm; H: 1-2mm; collet H: 2mm; D of perforation: 2.5mm).

Two silver rivets fix a separate, copper, folded flap attachment to the plate, which consists of a rectangular sheet with a slot cut in the centre to accommodate the buckle-tongue. (W of folded flap attachment under the plate: 26mm; W of its loop: 10mm).

The back of the attachment-plate is plain with a flanged edge all round, except for a 25mm section where the loop-attachment was connected to it. (Size of flange: W: 1.5mm, H: 3.3mm).

The oval buckle-loop is cast in one piece and is of broad, rectangular section, stepped at each end to form an integral, thin, circular-section rod for attachment to the plate. The decoration of the loop starts at a rectangular-section shoulder on either side of the tongue-rest and consists of a cast border of longitudinal ribbing with a cast, foliate, tendril ornament beneath it and an animal-head terminal at each end. The eye of each head is formed by a cabochon garnet in a cast, cylindrical collet (sizes are the same as above), and the nose (or beak?) is suggested by V-shaped engravings. The tongue-rest is plain. (Size of loop: 58 x 39mm; W: 10mm; H: 2mm; D of rod: 2.5mm; tongue-rest: 9.5 x 11mm; H: 1.5mm).

The cast buckle-tongue is of hollow V-section. It is decorated with a line of seven interlocking, chip-carved triangles at the base and has an animal-head terminal with moulded features including very prominent domed eyes (L: 47mm; W: 15mm). The 1.6% of gold detected on the end of the tongue suggests that the buckle was originally gilded but has been heavily cleaned.

Damaged, very fragmentary.

cat. no. 80 is a broadly similar eagle-headed buckle, but differs slightly (e.g. it has glass inlays).

This buckle also belongs to the Bosporan type of eagle-headed buckle. See further the description of **cat. no. 80** above.

82   Buckle (Pl. 43)

In three pieces, each of which is composite.
Silver-copper-alloy buckle has a pentagonal plate decorated with clear glass cabochons, scrollwork and animal-head decoration. The loop is oval, the tongue is hollow.
Second half of the 6th/first half of the 7th century.   Ostrogothic.
Silver-copper alloy, copper alloy (brass), copper, glass,
Prov.: Suuk-Su, Krym (Crimea), Ukraine – 1899
Inv. no. 1923,7-16,71   Old cat. no. 286
Percentage of silver: 46
Size: 182 x 68mm   H: 24mm   Weight: 164.8g
Published: Repnikov 1907, 141, pl. XIV:4; Ambroz 1968, 17–18, pl. 3:1

The three main components were cast. The attachment-plate is of a silver-copper alloy, pentagonal and has a rounded end. Six high cylindrical collets have been cast on as part of the plate, their bases partly projecting from each angle as a lobe. They project from round the edge, three on each side, and each contains a clear glass cabochon. Calcite was identified in the backing paste. The decoration of the plate consists of chip-carved scrollwork on the terminal, multiple incised ribbing in the centre and incised animal heads in profile at the sides. The scrollwork consists of four pairs of spirals, each forming a figure-of-three shape of two opposed scrolls. Two of the pairs are right at the rounded end of the terminal with an incised line between them. The other two are above them between two of the cylindrical collets and are framed by double grooves above and below, triple grooves on the left and four on the right. Between the upper and middle collets the buckle is decorated with transverse, multiple grooves and a stylised animal (bird?) head on each side, their eyes indicated by drop shapes and the jaws (beaks?) by curved multiple grooves side by side. Between the last two grooves is a wide rib which forms the neck of the animal (or bird). This continues as a frame for the zone of incised ribs between the lower and middle collets and the top of the scrollwork. There is another rib alongside the wider one which connects the two upper collets and separates the undecorated folded flap attachment from the plate. These two ribs (a wide and a thin one) form the sides of a sub-rectangle in the centre of the plate which has all-over, transversely incised ribs. There is an applied quatrefoil of four conjoined tear-shaped collets on a separate base-plate at the centre. It is attached by two copper-alloy rivets and may be secondary since it covers the decoration underneath it. It probably contained four glass inlays. (Size of the plate: 134 x 65mm; thickness: 1.8mm; collet of inlays: H: 15mm; D: 11mm; cabochon H: 1.3mm).

The buckle-plate has a flanged edge creating a raised border around the back.

The folded flap attachment is formed of the same piece as the plate. It is extremely long and rectangular in shape with a rectangular slot in the middle. (Folded flap attachment: 28 x 33mm; W of slot: 4mm).

There are base silver and copper strip attachment-fittings on the back and four strips forming the sides of a square behind the upper half of the plate. The ends of the strips overlap behind the upper and middle cylindrical collets. A shorter (fragmentary ?) copper strip is attached from behind to the strip on the left. There is a base silver strip attached to one of the upper corners behind the copper-alloy strip by using the same rivet as for the attachment to the plate. There is a base silver strip behind the terminal of the plate attached to three layers of strips: fragments of a copper-alloy strip; another copper-alloy strip of the same size as the silver strip, and a shorter base silver strip (broken-off end of the other base silver strip?) attached to its top. There are two circular perforations (rivet-holes?) at one end of the copper-alloy strip. Two types of attachment-rivet were used in the whole construction. One is for holding the copper-alloy and silver strips together behind the terminal of the plate. The rivet-ends are turned in on the back and two of them survive inserted from the upper surface of the silver strip at its ends. The other type is used for fixing the strips to the plate. They are inserted from the upper surface of the plate, and the rivet-ends are bent round to form loops on the back. Four of them are attached to the upper half of the plate in a rectangular arrangement, one at each overlapping end of the strips. Another (fifth) rivet of this type fixes the complex of strips to the terminal of the plate. (Size of the strips: W: 14–16mm; L: 49–57mm; D of rivet-heads: 5mm; thickness: 1.5mm).

The loop is oval with a tongue-rest in the middle. It is decorated with multiple, transverse grooves between two incised, longitudinal lines. There are four cylindrical collets (possibly for glass inlays), one on either side of the tongue-rest and one at each end. Here each collet forms the eye of a schematic animal head in profile, recognisable only from its earlier Late-Antique and Ostrogothic prototypes. One of the collets has been applied by an attachment-rivet, the others were cast in one with the loop. The two squared-off ends of the loop are connected by a copper-alloy (brass) bar which passes through the folded flap attachment. It has circular ends by means of which it is fastened to the loop by a copper rivet at each end. The rivet-ends are burred over. (Size of loop: 68 x 52.5mm; W: 8–14mm; H of collets: 6mm; D: 7mm; thickness of the bar for folded flap attachment: 3mm).

The hollow, profiled tongue is decorated with zones of all-over, transverse grooving separated by longitudinal ribs, and there are three incised, transverse lines on the point and 22mm away from it. There is a large, moulded projection on the base cast together with the tongue. The attachment-loop of the tongue consists of a separate, rectangular-section strip. One end of it passes through a perforation at the base of the tongue, and is filed across and hammered flat to burr it over for attachment. (Tongue L: 67mm; W: 7–13mm; thickness of the attachment-loop: 1.5mm; D of the rivet: 3.5mm).

The composition, decoration and technique of the buckle are very crude as may be seen from the fact that the rivet-holes were drilled through the incised decoration, while the quatrefoil collet covers the carving in the centre.

It is in poor condition and only two of the inlays survive.

Similar buckles have been found in the Crimea: at Chufut-Kale (graves 7[1] and 98[2]), at Skalistoe (grave 288),[3] Aromat (grave 1),[4] and at Artek (two buckles).[5] Their construction and the decoration of the loops and tongues are very similar to some of the south Crimean type of eagle-headed buckles, which Aibabin dates to the second half of the 7th century.[6] He supports this idea by the fact that in Skalistoe one was found together with two bronze buckles of this period, and in Chufut-Kale grave 98, with a late 7th-century radiate-headed brooch. Kropotkin dates this grave to the 7th century.[7] The buckle from Aromat is dated to the second half of the 6th/first half of the 7th century by Loboda.[8] According to Ambroz they were made in the second half of the 7th century, after 6th-century Danubian Gepid prototypes, and decorated in a Crimean variant of animal Style I as one of the main ornaments of these buckles.[9]

There are many buckles from the Carpathian Basin, Bulgaria and Italy, which, on the basis of Ambroz's theory, could have served as models for the Crimean ones.[10] They are all slightly different from the south Crimean ones in construction and composition of decoration and are considered to be examples of the late 5th-century, Germanic fashion, combining both Late-Roman and Germanic influences.

Comparative bibliography

1   Kropotkin 1958, ill. 3, 1
2   Kropotkin 1965, ill. 45:5
3   Veimarn and Ambroz 1980, ill. 3; Veimarn and Aibabin 1993, 57–8, ill. 37:1
4   Loboda 1976, ill. 4:1
5   Repnikov 1906, 63; pl. VIII:2; 64; pl. VIII:6
6   Aibabin 1990, 35
7   Kropotkin 1965, 112
8   Loboda 1976, 142
9   Veimarn and Ambroz 1980, 247–62
10   Annibaldi and Werner 1963, 356–73;   Bóna 1974, ill. 18, pls 39–40;   Kiss 1984, 57–76; Dombay 1956, 104–30, pls XVII-XXV

83   Sword-bead fitting (?) (Pl. 44)

Single piece of composite construction.
A globular chalcedony ball within a sling of silver strip.
End of 4th/first half of 5th century   Hunnic era.
Silver, chalcedony
Inv. no. 1923,7-16,149   Old cat. no. ?
Percentage of silver: 93
Size: 31 x 22mm   Weight: 14.93g
Unpublished

The chalcedony ball is drilled through the centre and secured by a long, dome-headed silver rivet which passes through it and is attached to the middle of the rectangular-sectioned silver strip. This is bent to form a sling around the upper part of the ball. At the ends it is bent to form a rectangle, probably for an attachment-slot. The ends overlap by 5mm and are secured by a single rivet flattened at each end. (Size of ball: H: 16mm; W: 20mm; D of perforation: 5–8mm; D of rivet-head: 4mm; D of rivet :2mm; W of strip: 6.5mm; thickness: 1.3mm).

The corroded, central, transverse rivet is of heavily-worked silver wire. The end of the rivet is missing.

The original photograph of the collection does not show this object.

There is a chalcedony sword-bead fitting from Kerch, grave 145, excavated in 1904, which is considered by Zasetskaya to be from the Hunnic era, i.e. the end of the 4th/first half of the 5th century.[1]

According to Aibabin[2] there are similar bead fittings from Skalistoe, graves 422,[2] 434,[3] and 495,[4] which were introduced in the Hunnic period and were still in use in the first half of the 7th century. He dates the chalcedony bead fitting from grave 434 to the first half of the 5th century, the amber bead from grave 495 to the first half of the 6th and the chalcedony bead from grave 422 to the first half of the 7th century.[5]

Comparative bibliography
1 Zasetskaya 1979, 15, pls 4:4; 5
2 Veimarn and Aibabin 1993, 102, ill. 75:17–18
3 *op. cit.*, 107, ill. 77:10
4 *op. cit.*, 126, ill. 92:15
5 Aibabin 1990, 59, pl. 2:33; Veimarn and Aibabin 1993, 181

Provincial Byzantine and related material

84 Earring (Pl. 45, Colour Pl. 1)
Single piece.
Lunate gold earring with punched, engraved and openwork decoration representing a peacock.
6th–7th century.   Provincial Byzantine.
Gold
Prov.: Kerch, Krym (Crimea), Ukraine – 1904
Inv. no. 1923,7-16,67   Old cat. no. 252
Percentage of gold: 95
Size: 32 x 28mm   Weight: 4.77g
Published: Entwistle 1994, 96, no. 101

It was manufactured in the same technique as the earring (**cat. no. 85**) below. The hoop consists of a circular-section wire, bent to form a hook at one end and a loop at the other. The two ends together form a hook-and-eye fastening and it is attached around the inner edge of the half-moon shape with gold solder and is flattened all along the soldering. (D of loop: 16mm; thickness: 1.5mm).

The half-moon shape is formed from a thin, flat sheet of gold which contains the openwork figure of a peacock with outstreched wings and punched and engraved features. The openwork was achieved by crudely cutting holes in the metal. There are punched dots all along the edges. The outer curved edge of the half moon is flattened and has a beaded-wire border soldered on. This was formed one bead at a time by rolling the wire under a single-edged tool. (Size of sheet: W: 12.5mm; L: 25mm; thickness: 0.5mm; thickness of beaded-wire border: 1mm).

The original photograph of the collection does not show this object.

Cat no. 85 is a lunate gold earring of the same type, but with slight differences: **cat no. 84** is bigger and has a more easily distinguishable bird motif. The outer edge of the half moon is flattened for better attachment of the beaded wire. The loop is also flattened for a similar reason, where it is soldered to the inner edge.

85 Earring (Pl. 45, Colour Pl. 1)
Single piece.
Lunate gold earring with punched, engraved and openwork decoration representing two birds.
6th-7th century. Provincial Byzantine.
Gold.
Prov.: Kerch, Krym (Crimea), Ukraine – 1904
Inv. no. 1923,7-16,68   Old cat. no. 253
Percentage of gold: 90
Size: 20 x 26mm   Weight: 2.8g
Published: Entwistle 1994, 97, no. 102

The hoop consists of a circular-section wire attached with gold solder around the inner edge of the half moon. It is bent to form a hook at one end and possibly had a corresponding loop at the other. (D of hoop: 12mm; thickness: 1.5mm).

The half-moon shape is formed from a thin, flat sheet of gold. It has openwork decoration representing two confronted birds, which was achieved by crudely cutting holes in the metal. There are punched and engraved dots and crescents in the middle. The outer curved edge of the half moon has a beaded-wire border soldered on. This was formed one bead at a time by rolling the wire under a single-edged tool. (Size of sheet: W: 9mm; L: 18mm; thickness: 0.5mm; thickness of beaded wire: 1mm).

The loop of the hoop has broken off. The gold solder of the beaded wire was overheated during manufacture and has damaged the lower edge of the earring.

The original photograph of the collection does not show this object.

cat. no. 84 is a lunate gold earring of the same type (for the differences see the description of **cat. no. 84**).

This is a very common type of earring, produced in the early Byzantine period and based on similar shape and motifs, appearing as far apart as southern Germany and the Crimea. The relatively poor technical quality and execution of this earring and of **cat. no. 84** above, however, suggest that they were either made by provincial Byzantine craftsmen, or copies of pieces produced by central workshops.

86 Pendant cross (Pl. 45, Colour Pl. 1)
Single piece of composite construction.
Cruciform gold pendant decorated with garnets and repoussé ornaments. There is an incised cruciform monogram on the back.
6th–7th century.   Byzantine.
Gold, garnet.
Prov.: Kerch, Krym (Crimea), Ukraine – 1900
Inv. no. 1923,7-16,66   Old cat. no. 235
Percentage of gold: 89
Size: 67 x 46mm   Weight: 25.46g
Published: Dalton 1924c, 386–389, pl. 17; Oddy and La Niece 1986, 24 no. , 26. ill. 10; Entwistle 1994, 96, no. 100

The cross consists of three main parts: the front, back and loop, all joined together with gold solder. The suspension-loop of the pendant is made of circular-section wire with the ends bent round and soldered together. The join is the point at which it is soldered to the pendant. It is slightly narrower where it is soldered. (D of loop: 13mm; thickness of wire: 3.2mm; 2.7mm).

The pendant is hollow and the cavity now appears to be empty, except for some sandy soil in the largest break. The front of the cross is decorated in the centre with four rectangular garnet plates in a cruciform pattern. They are set in wax and have no collets around them. The garnets are thick (approximately 2mm) with both well-cut and badly broken edges, suggesting that they are reused fragments. There are no foils beneath them and the back of the inside of the cross can be seen underneath. There is a repoussé palmette on the front, with dots and leaves. In Dalton's words:

> The palmettes upon the arms are not modelled in relief, but rise from the sunk ground in such a way that their flat surfaces are in the same plane as that of the whole object. The details of the leaves are summarily rendered by deeply-incised dots associated with small comma-like or wedge-shaped cavities.

The back has similar almond-shaped panels, but with repoussé scale or feather-like ornament. The meaning of the Greek letters (φωC/ZωH) of the incised central monogram is to be interpreted as: Light, Life. (Thickness of cross: 4.5mm; size of central cross: 11 x 10mm).

The lower arm of the cross is damaged.

Dalton (1924c, 389): 'this object may have been a bishop's pectoral cross'.

A very similar 6th–7th-century cross with an associated breast-chain and openwork pendants was found at Mersin (Turkey) and is now in the Hermitage Museum, St Petersburg.[1] Inlaid gold crosses of this type have also been found in Constantinople.[2]

Comparative Bibliography
1 Kondakov 1896, pl. XVIII:12, same in: Brown 1984, 3, pl. 5
2 Ross 1965, 7-8; 10; pls X:B; XII:B; XIII

87 Temporal-ring (*kolt*) (Pl. 46, Colour Pl. 2)
Single piece of composite construction.
Bifacial crescent-shaped, almost circular, gold sheet decorated with

cloisonné garnets and granulation.

6th–7th century.   Byzantine form. Nomadic??

Gold, garnet

Prov.: Kerch, Krym (Crimea), Ukraine – 1893 (register) – But in Kondakov 1896, 199–200, Kuban is given as the provenance

Inv. no. 1923,7-16,7   Old cat. no. 142

Percentage of gold: 97

Size: 42 x 35mm   H: 14.5mm   Weight: 33.46g

Published: Kondakov 1896, 199–200, ill. 113; Dalton 1924a, 262, pl. XXXVII:20 reproduced from Dalton 1924b; Bálint 1978, 203–4, fig. 15:4

The two faces of the piece were made separately and then soldered together. Each face is made of a lunate, almost circular sheet with a strip soldered around its outer edge. The sheets are convex in the middle. A lunate frame of garnet cloisons is soldered to the top of each face and each of these is made from a strip of gold soldered on edge. The inner cell walls are made of separate gold strips (see further below). The garnets are of irregular shape and have no foils beneath them. Some of the garnets have one well cut edge, but the shapes do not follow any consistent pattern and the majority of the edges are badly cut, all suggesting that the garnets were reused. They are fixed with wax which does not appear to be original. The ends of the strips (i.e. the ones around the sheet) are folded over each other on both faces. Both faces are heavily enriched with zones of granulation in a three-dimensional pattern almost covering the whole surface. The granules appear to have been soldered on in one heating. (H of inner sheet: 4.5mm; H of garnet setting: 2mm, thickness of garnets: c. 1mm, W of outer strip: 4mm; D of granules: 1–2mm).

Around the outer edge between the two faces are the remains of a strip of cloisonné garnet inlays, now damaged and largely missing. The outer walls are soldered to the frame.

There are two suspension loops attached at each end of the top. Each consists of a curved strip of almost semicircular-section wire with both ends within. (W: 2mm).

The surviving garnets are possibly replacements. The cell walls are squashed and seem to be forced around the present inlays. To judge from the parallels, it is possible that originally the cells created a pattern of S-shapes.

The cells around the outer edge are damaged.

A number of temporal-rings of this type have been found, mainly in the Ukraine and Russia. They are all similar in shape, made of gold, and have inlaid glass and granulated decoration.

Similar temporal-rings are published by Kondakov as earrings.[1] They come from the Kuban region (Anapa), from the south Urals area (Simbir province) and Kaibal (Samara province, Russia). There is a pair in Kiev in the collection of M. Botkine.[2] Two were found at Ufa (south Urals region, Russia) and are dated to the 6th–8th century by Akhmerov.[3] A very similar temporal-ring was auctioned in the summer of 1992 by Messrs Sothebys and is now in a private collection.[4] There is a piece with a ring attached to its loops and without inlays from the Don region,[5] while a pair of gold temporal-rings – also without inlaid decoration – was found at Mezőszilas (Hungary), and is considered by Bóna to be evidence for the Central Asiatic links of the Avars.[6] He also refers to close parallels from the Altai region (Kudürge, grave no.) and simpler bronze variants from Odintsovka in the Upper Ob area. Bálint dates them to the 6th–7th century,[7] Aibabin to the 7th century.[8]

Comparative bibliography

1   Kondakov 1896, 199–203; ills 115–19; the piece from Simbir also in: OIAK 1893b, 103; ill. 84
2   Coll. of Botkine 1911, pl. 92
3   Akhmerov 1951, 126–8; ill. 36:1-3
4   Phillips Family Collection
5   OIAK 1908, 101; ill. 134
6   Bóna 1971, 240; ill. 18
7   Bálint 1978, 203
8   Aibabin below

88   Buckle (Pl. 46)

In two pieces.

'Syracuse' type copper-alloy buckle decorated with a palmette on the plate. Oval loop and rectangular-section tongue.

2nd half of the 7th century.   Provincial Byzantine.

Copper alloy (brass), leaded gunmetal

Inv. no. 1923,7-16,82   Old cat. no. 320

Size: 51 x 32mm   Weight: 15.52g

Prov.: Olbia (Mikolayiv, Ukraine)

The plate is of leaded gunmetal and cast in one piece together with the loop. It is shield-shaped with a rounded projection at the base and is decorated in flat relief with two panels of foliate motifs. The back is flat with the remains of two perforated attachment lugs cast on

The loop is oval with a rectangular opening with rounded corners. On either side of the tongue at the centre of the loop are two punched dots.

The tongue is brass and has a rectangular section. It has two cast lugs above the base and is hooked through a perforation in the plate. The hook of the tongue is cast in one piece with it.

(Size of the loop: 32 x 18mm; tongue L: 25mm; thickness of tongue: 4mm; D of perforation on plate: 5mm).

There are two further buckles of this type in the British Museum[1] and there is one in the Ashmolean Museum,[2] all from Kerch.

They belong to the Syracuse type – one of the most typical of Byzantine forms of buckle – and have been found over a large area extending from the Black Sea coast through North Africa, Sicily, and Greece as far as Belgium and England.

Some scholars (Yakobson,[3] Werner,[4] Csallány,[5] Pudovin,[6] and Vinski[7]) date it to the end of the 6th/first half of the 7th century. According to Aibabin there is evidence in Cherson for manufacturing this type of buckle locally using Byzantine models.[8] He dates them to the 7th century,[9] while Ambroz[10] and Kovalevskaya[11] propose the second half of the 7th/first half of the 8th century. According to Kovalevskaya in the North Caucasus area they only appear in the 8th century.

Comparative bibliography

1   Inv. nos: 56,10-4,29; 1910,4-16,70
2   Inv. no. 1909.805. Acquired by Sir John Evans in 1886, and presented to the Ashmolean by Sir Arthur Evans
3   Yakobson 1959, 272–4
4   Werner 1955, 37
5   Csallány 1954a, 113-17, pls II:7–9; III:1-7; Csallány 1954b, 320–32, pls II:7–9; III:1–7
6   Pudovin 1961, 182, ill. 1
7   Vinski 1967, 24–5, pl. XVI
8   Aibabin 1993, 167–8; 1994, 141
9   Aibabin 1990, 43, pls 2:122, 42:6;7; 1993, 172
10   Ambroz 1971, 114;116;118, ill. 7:2, pl. II:29
11   Kovalevskaya 1979, 24, pl. VIII:11; Kovalevskaya 1993, 112; pl. I:32

89   Buckle (Pl. 46)

Consists of two pieces.

Copper-alloy buckle with an openwork palmette on the plate. Oval loop and rectangular-section tongue.

7th–8th century.   Provincial Byzantine.

Copper alloy.

Inv. no. 1923,7-16,81   Old cat. no. 320

Size: 49 x 35mm   Weight: 20.31g

Prov.: Olbia (Mikolayiv), Ukraine – 1909

The copper-alloy plate is cast in one piece together with the loop. It consists of a semicircular frame of flat, rectangular section, with a small rectangular projection at the end. The frame contains an openwork, three-leaved palmette projecting from behind the tongue into the centre. There is an incised line all along the outer edge of the frame which interlocks with another such line below the tongue running round the edge of the palmette. The back is flat with three perforated, cast attachment lugs. (Size of plate: 26 x 27mm, size of lugs: 7 x 7mm; D of holes: 3mm).

The oval loop is rectangular in section, narrowing along both sides and expanding towards the tongue-rest. There is a triangular panel on each side of the tongue-rest, decorated with an incised triangle containing transverse, incised lines. The loop is only slightly flattened for the tongue-rest. (Size of loop: 18 x 35mm; W: 3mm at the sides; 6mm at the top).

The tongue is rectangular in section with a cast lug above the base and a similar, but smaller, lug towards the end of the tongue. The tongue is hooked through a perforation in the top of the plate. The hook of the tongue is cast in one piece with it. (Size of tongue: L: 26mm; W: 3mm; H: 4mm; D of circular cut on plate: 5.5mm).

The hook of the tongue is imperfect.

This buckle has been heavily cleaned, so nothing can be concluded about the decoration.

There is a buckle of the same type said to be from Herpes (Charente, France) in the British Museum.[1]

Byzantine, or so-called Provincial Byzantine, buckles of this type have been found at several places, such as Italy, Spain, Egypt, Hungary, Crimea and the North Caucasus. Yakobson dated them from the second half of the 6th to the first half of the 7th century,[2] Csallány from 620-660,[3] and Vinski to the mid-7th century.[4] In Deopik's opinion they can be dated from the 7th to the 9th century.[5] According to Aibabin's typology, they belong to the first half of the 8th century[6] and by Kovalevskaya's classification to the 8th to 9th centuries.[7] Aibabin and Chajredinova give a reconstruction of a similar buckle and its associated belt-mounts found in Eski-Kermen, vault 181 (Crimea).[8]

Comparative bibliography
1   Inv. no. 1905,5-20,317
2   Jakobson 1959, 273 ill. 139: 17; 18
3   Csallány 1954a, 125–6
4   Vinski 1967, 28, pl. XX:4
5   Deopik 1963, 125–7; ill. 3
6   Aibabin 1990, 43; pls 2:187, 42:22; 1993, 172
7   Kovalevskaya 1979, 23, pl. VII:12;13
8   Aibabin and Chajredinova 1995, 199

90   Strap-end (Pls 47–48)
Single piece of composite construction.
Tongue-shaped silver plate decorated with gold strip collets containing brown and green glass cloisons within a granulated border.
6th–7th century.   Provincial Byzantine
Silver, gold, brown glass, red glass, green glass.
Prov.: Kerch, Krym (Crimea), Ukraine – 1893
Inv. no. 1923,7-16,33   Old cat. no. 159
Percentage of silver: 76
Size: 50 x 29mm   H: 4mm   Weight: 7.04g
Published: Aibabin 1985, 199, fig. 8:40; Aibabin 1990, 57; pl. 52:11; Bálint 1992, 350, pl. 36:6; Bálint 1995, 83, pl. 36:6

Reconstruction of original design, see **Pls 47, 48.**

The silver base-plate is a flat, tongue-shaped frame with a large slot running down the centre, forming an elongated, U-shaped opening that contains a panel of gold and glass inlays. (W: 7–9mm).

The gold, tongue-shaped frame is fastened to the plate, though it is not possible to ascertain if it was soldered in place. It contains three gold strips, each of which is curved to form an 'S' within a ring. They contain brown and red glass cloisons. The strips do not reach to the full depth of the cell: they are about half the height of the tongue-shaped frame. Each ring is soldered to the gold frame which has a border of individual granules. Most of the inlays are of brownish glass with a layer of red ochre beneath them to imitate the colour of garnet (as on no. 91 below). The white paste behind the setting, underneath the ochre, is of crushed chalk (calcite) full of microfossils. One inlay is of red glass, probably coloured by manganese, and has a foil beneath made of metallic tin. No ochre was used beneath this glass, probably because it was once a good colour. The corners of the gold frame are decorated with green glass inlays. (Size of tongue-shaped gold frame: 36 x 11mm; thickness: 0.5mm; D of rings: 9.5mm; 10mm; 12mm; D of granules: 1mm).

There is a tongue-shaped, grey-brown area beneath the decorative panel. The XRF analysis of this revealed silver with some copper, gold, chlorine and bromine. This analysis, and the appearance of the material, suggests that the area is probably a substantially corroded silver-copper alloy, perhaps originally a separate sheet acting as a backing to the inlaid gold panel. The material has probably been corroded to silver chloride and some silver bromide; the latter is occasionally found associated with corroded silver. It is not clear, however, why this area should be so preferentially corroded.

See **Pl. 48** for construction, and **Pl. 47** section showing the several layers of its composition.

Damaged, very fragmentary.

The original photograph of the collection does not show this object.

There are similar belt-fittings from Kerch,[1] Portovoe (Razhdol'noe, Crimea),[2] and Kabardino-Balkaria (Caucasus).[3] They have a similar construction consisting of a silver base-plate and gold decorative panel with curved strips as collets. They are products of the Hunnic period according to Fettich.[4] Bálint considers the inlaid belt-fittings from the Crimea as the products either of Byzantine workshops, or of local craftsmen adopting Byzantine style.[5] He dates the grave from Portovoe

to the period between the mid-6th and the end of the 7th century. Ambroz[6] and Aibabin[7] date it to the second half of the 7th century. According to them they represent the nomadic fashion for the polychrome style, and this technique was adopted and spread by the nomads after Byzantine prototypes.

There are belt-ends with glass-plate inlays and granulated borders from the rich, early-Avar graves of Bócsa[8] and Kunbábony,[9] and also from the grave of Mala Pereshchepina[10] (dated c. 640 according to Werner[11]).

Comparative bibliography
1   Fettich 1951, pl. XLVI:1–7
2   Aibabin 1985, ill. 8:23; Seipel (ed.) 1993, 244, 245 (good quality photograph)
3   Fettich 1951, pl. XLVI:11–22
4   Fettich op. cit.
5   Bálint 1992, 348–50; Bálint 1995, 82–3, pl. 34:1–11
6   Ambroz 1971, 106; ill. 6:30;31;33–6
7   Aibabin 1985, 199–200; Aibabin 1990, 57
8   László 1955, pls XXXV:18; XXXVI:18
9   Tóth and Horváth 1992, 108–10; pl. IV:1
10   Bobrinsky 1914, pl. XIV:46
11   Werner 1984

91   Belt suspension mounts (Pl. 49)
Two, each of composite construction.
Silver shield-shaped mounts with a T-shaped projection beneath, each decorated with a gold strip collet containing a brown glass inlay bordered by granulation.
6th–7th century.   Provincial Byzantine
Silver, brown glass, gold
Prov.: Kerch, Krym (Crimea), Ukraine – 1893
Inv. no. 1923,7-16,36 and 37   Old cat. no. 159
Percentage of silver: no. 36: 92   no. 37: 93
Size: no. 923,7-16,36: 28 x 20mm   Weight: 4.94g
        no. 923,7-16,37: 28 x 20mm   Weight: 5.09g
Published: Roes 1953a, 31, fig. 9 left; Aibabin 1985, 199, fig. 8:27; Aibabin 1990, pl. 52:2; Bálint 1992, 350, pl. 36:16;17; Bálint 1995, pl. 36:16,17

Each is cast in one piece. The shield-shaped frame has a pointed end and pointed corners. A horizontal groove is cast across its base. It has a bevelled, flanged edge projecting around the back. There is a semicircular opening in the centre containing a semicircular, brown glass plate in a gold setting. It has a silver base-plate. There is a layer of red ochre behind the setting, to imitate the colour of garnet (as on no. 90 above). The collet of no. 1923,7–16,36 is made of one gold strip, and that of no. 1923,7–16,37 of two. The edge of the strip is folded around the glass inlay and the collets are bordered by gold granulation. The granules and collet are applied to the base-plate with a silver solder which secures the inset as well. This appears to be an original feature. (Size of shield shape: 15.5 x 15.5mm; size of glass inlay; 6 x 4.5mm; D of granules: 1mm; H of edge: 2mm).

Beneath the shield shape there is a T-shaped projection with solid, hemispherical ends and two cast, longitudinal lines on top in the centre. The 'neck' of the T has a bevelled, flanged edge. (Size of T shape: W: 20mm; L: 12mm; D of hemispheres: 6mm; W of 'neck': 4.5mm; H of edge: 2mm).

There are two circular-section attachment-shanks on the back. It is hard to tell whether they are cast or soldered, but casting seems more likely. The end of each is burred over. (D: 2mm; L: 3.5mm).

The two mounts were probably cast using the same mould.

The glass inlay of no. 6 is missing. The gold setting is fragmentary. The glass inlay of no. 7 is fragmentary.

The original photograph of the collection does not show these mounts.

According to Bálint neither the origin of the shape, nor the function of these objects is clear.[1] It is unlikely that they served as suspension mounts. It is also possible, however, that they had no special function on the belt, and were only copying a particular shape. T-shaped mounts also appear among the Italian, Langobardic belt-sets, but usually with a single mount in each set.

The gold examples from Nocera Umbra (Italy)[2] and the cemetery of Cebelda 1a (Georgia)[3] were constructed in a special way: the horizontal part is a separate bar going through a hook below the shield-shaped part of each mount. Whether this feature on its own was of any significance in terms of the function of this type of mount, we do not know. If there was, the later, cast-in-one variants like those in the Berthier-Delagarde Collection are presumably simply copying that type, and play a part only as a decorative element on each belt. That would also explain why these belts have more than one T-shaped mount.

This type of mount has been found at several places in the south Russian and Danubian regions. They vary in the size, shape and decoration of the shield-shaped part. Bálint surveyed a number of different kinds of T-shaped mount and considers the inlaid ones to be 6th–7th-century products manufactured under Byzantine influence.[4] Belt-mounts from the Crimea, inlaid with enamel or glass, were made by Pontic Byzantine workshops, or by local workshops adopting Byzantine style.[5] Aibabin established eight different variants of the same type, and dated them from the end of the 6th to the 7th century.[6] According to him, both the Berthier-Delagarde pieces and the very similar ones from Portovoe (Crimea) are of the second half of the 7th century.[7] Bálint dated the Portovoe grave to the period between the mid-6th century and the end of the 7th century, or rather to the first half/second third of the 7th century.[8] Ambroz dated this type of belt-mount to the second half of the 6th–7th century.[9]

There are similar, inlaid, T-shaped mounts from the rich, early-Avar graves of Bócsa[10] and Kunbábony[11] (Hungary) and also in the Fleissig Collection[12] and from Mala Pereshchepina (Ukraine).[13] They are made of gold and are related to the so-called pseudo-buckles which show the high rank of their owner. These probably represent a richer variant of the same type of belt-mount.

A belt-set from Vasilevka (Ukraine) has similar T-shaped mounts, but without inlays, and also belt-ends resembling **cat. no. 90** in the collection, and appliqués similar to the inlays of the shield-shaped mounts (**cat. no. 92**) below.[14]

Different variants of this type of mount (from the Kama region; from Ufa, Turbasli, Bakhmutino and Urya) are dated to the first half of the 7th century by Gening.[15]

Silver mounts with semicircular openings have been found in the Caucasus[16] and in Chufut-Kale, grave no. 1 (Crimea).[17] There are further T-shaped mounts with semicircular or lunate openings from Kerch in the British Museum[18] and a pair with rectangular openings is in the Ashmolean Museum.[19]

The relative chronology of this type of mount is discussed by Ambroz.[20]

Comparative bibliography
1   Bálint 1995, 142–3
2   Werner 1974b, pl. V:9
3   Bálint 1995, 143, pl. 38:14
4   Bálint 1992, 348–50, 381–4, pls 47–50; Bálint 1995, 138–43, pls 47, 48 – T-shape as a type has a European (Byzantine) origin
5   Bálint 1995, 83
6   Aibabin 1990, 53; Aibabin 1985, 199; ill. 8:9
7   Seipel (ed.) 1993, 242–3 (good quality photographs)
8   Bálint 1995, 82–3, pl. 34:1–11
9   Ambroz 1971, 118
10   László 1955, pls XXXV:12; 14; XXXVI:12;14
11   Tóth and Horváth: 1992, 110-111; pl. IV:4;5
12   Kalmár 1943, pls XXII-XXIV
13   Bobrinsky 1914; Werner 1984
14   Bálint 1992, pl. 49
15   Gening 1979, 96–106
16   Sakhanev 1914, 131 ill. 22:6
17   Kropotkin 1965, 112, pl. 44:13
18   Inv. no. P&E 56,10-4,40-52 – given by Dr D. McPherson, 1856
19   Inv. no. 1910.69c
20   Ambroz 1973, 294

92   Belt-mounts (Pl. 49, Colour Pl. 2)

Two, each of composite construction.
Silver shield-shaped mounts, each with a gold strip collet containing a cabochon garnet, bordered by granulation.
6th–7th century.   Provincial Byzantine

Silver, copper, gold, garnet
Prov.: Kerch, Krym (Crimea), Ukraine – 1893 according to the register, but possibly from the Dnieper region according to Fettich, 1953 (see below).

Inv. no. 1923,7-16,34 and 35   Old cat. no. 159
Percentage of silver: no. 34: 92   no. 35: 89
Size: 1923,7-16,34: 25 x 24mm   Weight: 3g
    1923,7-16,35: 29 x 25mm   Weight: 4.4g
Published: Aibabin 1985, 199, fig. 8:32; Bálint 1992, 350, pl. 36:14;15; Bálint 1995, pl. 36:14,15

Each flat, shield-shaped plate is pointed at the end and at the two top corners. There is a circular opening in the centre of the top which contains a cabochon garnet in a cylindrical collet bordered by gold granulation. There is no access by means of which to identify whether there is a foil present beneath the garnet. The collet of the cabochon consists of a curved gold strip, which is soldered to a silver disc together with the granulated border. (D of opening: 10mm; D of garnet: 5mm; H of garnet: 2mm; collet H: 2mm; D of granules: 1.5mm).

The mounts have bevelled, flanged edges projecting around the back. (H: 3mm).

There are three silver attachment-shanks cast on the back in a triangular arrangement. One copper attachment-shank is situated in the centre of the silver disc base-plate of the central inlay. The end of each is burred over. (D of disc shank: 2mm; L: 3mm; D of the other three shanks: 2mm; L: 4mm).

No. 1923,7-16,34 is fragmentary. One attachment-shank is missing.

The original photograph of the collection does not show these mounts. One photograph of the museum shows no. 1923,7-16,34 complete (the left corner has been broken since).

This type of shield-shaped belt-mount very often occurs together with T-shaped mounts like **cat. no. 91** in the collection. They also vary in size and decoration. Bálint dates them to the 6th–7th century,[1] Aibabin to the second half of the 7th century.[2] According to Bálint the enamel- or glass-inlaid belt-fittings from the Crimea are products either of Pontic Byzantine workshops, or of local workshops adopting Byzantine fashion (see also **cat. nos 90 and 91** above).[3]

An identical mount, published by Fettich, is said to be from the Dnieper region and is now in the Museum of Warsaw.[4] It could possibly be a piece from the same set and its provenance therefore indicate the provenance of the Berthier-Delagarde pieces, too.

Shield-shaped gold mounts decorated with inlays and granulation have been found in the rich, early-Avar graves at Kunbábony[5] and Bócsa[6] (Hungary) and also appear in the grave of Mala Pereshchepina (Ukraine).[7] They were found together with T-shaped mounts and an inlaid belt-end similar to **cat. no. 90** in the collection. These graves can be dated to the first half of the 7th century and the mounts could be considered to be richer variants of the same type.

There are appliqués very similar to the inlay of our mounts from a belt-set found in Vasilevka (Ukraine), which also contains a T-shaped suspension mount and belt-ends decorated with gold foil and granulation.[8]

There are further silver mounts with circular openings in the British Museum from Kerch,[9] and a similar one from Chufut-Kale (Crimea), dated to the 6th century by Kropotkin.[10] Similar mounts, made of bronze, have also been found at Kerch.[11]

Comparative bibliography
1   Bálint 1992, 348–50
2   Aibabin 1985, 199; ill. 8:32; Aibabin 1990, 54; pl. 50:26–31
3   Bálint 1995, 85
4   Fettich 1953, pl. XXXI:9
5   Tóth and Horváth 1992, 29–30; pl. III:4
6   László 1955, pls XXXV:10; XXXVI:10
7   Bobrinsky 1914, pl. XVI:59, Werner 1984
8   Bálint 1992, pl. 49
9   Inv. no. P&E 56,10-4,40-52 – given by Dr D. McPherson, 1856
10   Kropotkin 1965, 112, ill. 44:11
11   Artamonov 1962, 60 ill.

Plate 1

Jewellery

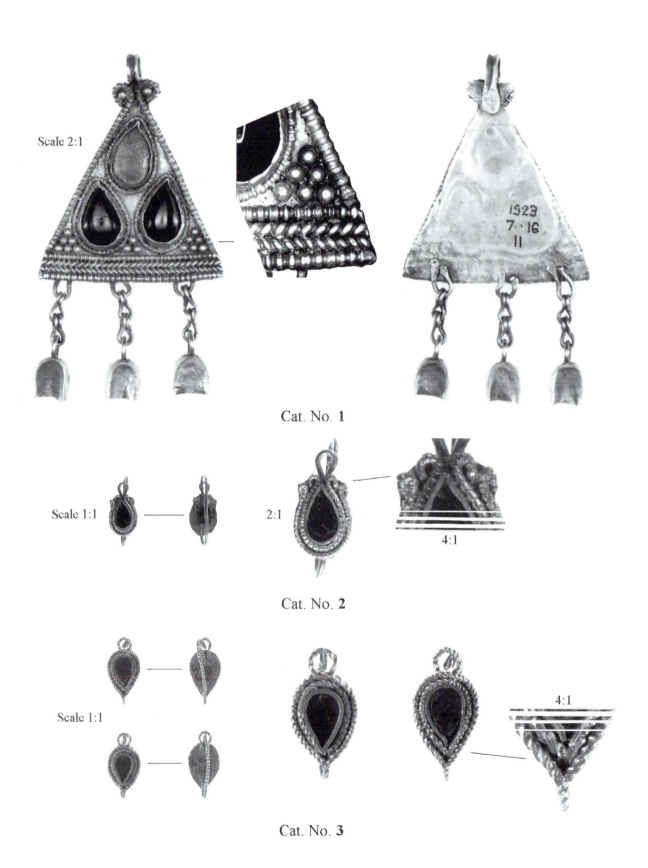

Scale 2:1

1923
7 · 16
11

Cat. No. **1**

Scale 1:1

2:1

4:1

Cat. No. **2**

Scale 1:1

4:1

Cat. No. **3**

Plate 2

Jewellery

Cat. No. 4

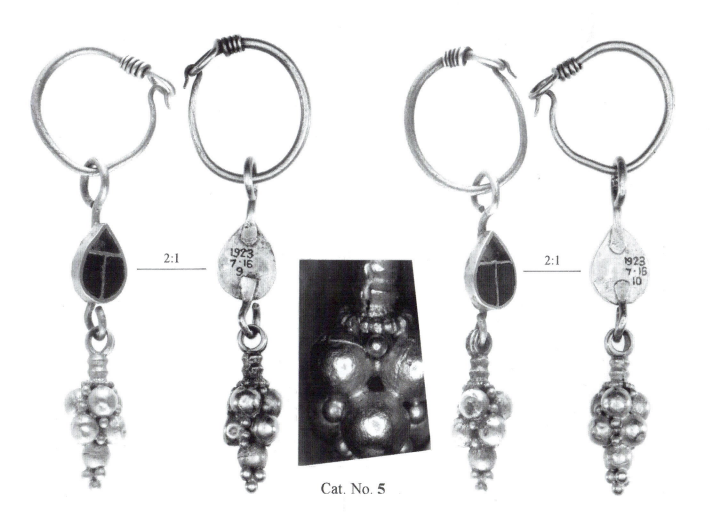

Cat. No. 5

Plate 3

Jewellery

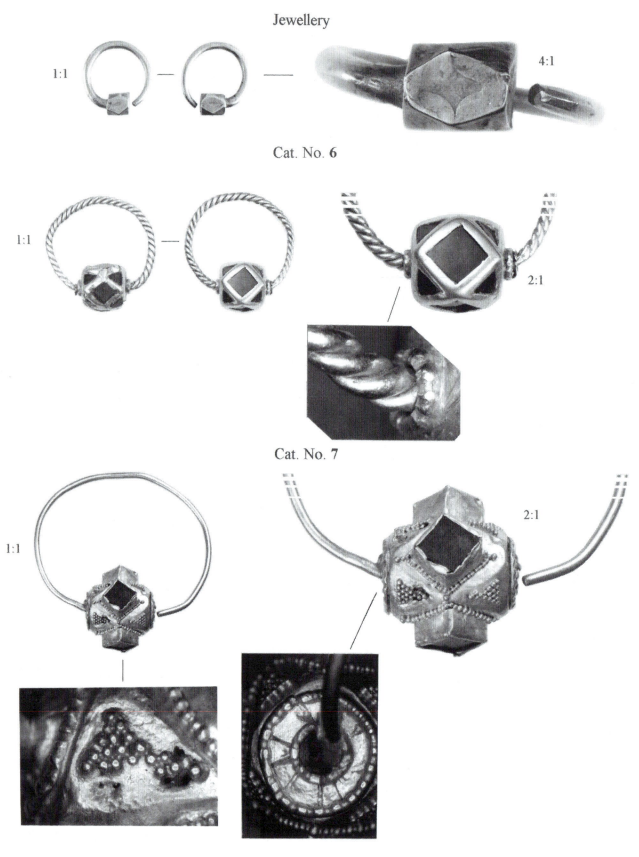

1:1   4:1

Cat. No. **6**

1:1   2:1

Cat. No. **7**

1:1   2:1

Cat. No. **8**

Plate 4

Jewellery

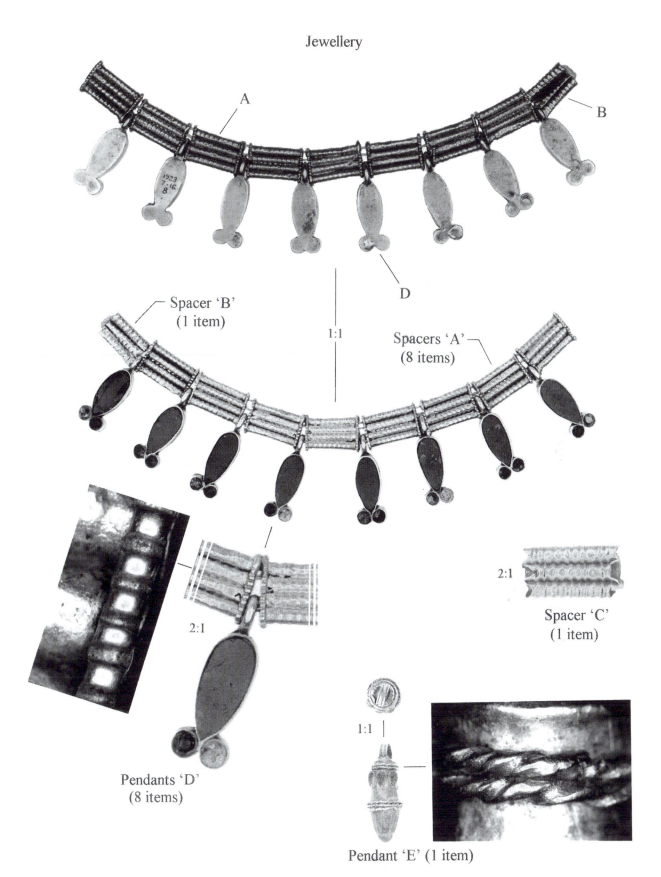

Spacer 'B'
(1 item)

1:1

Spacers 'A'
(8 items)

2:1

Spacer 'C'
(1 item)

2:1

Pendants 'D'
(8 items)

1:1

Pendant 'E' (1 item)

Cat. No. 9

Plate 5

Jewellery - Addendum

Spacer 'B'   Spacers 'A'

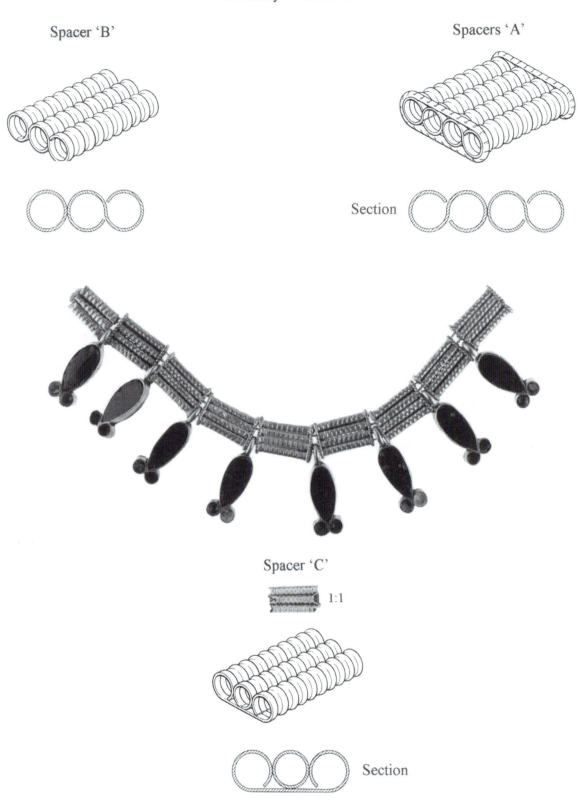

Section

Spacer 'C'

1:1

Section

Spacers of Necklace Cat. No.**9**

Plate 6

Jewellery

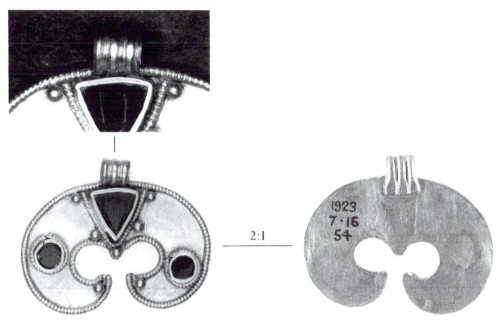

Cat. No. **10**

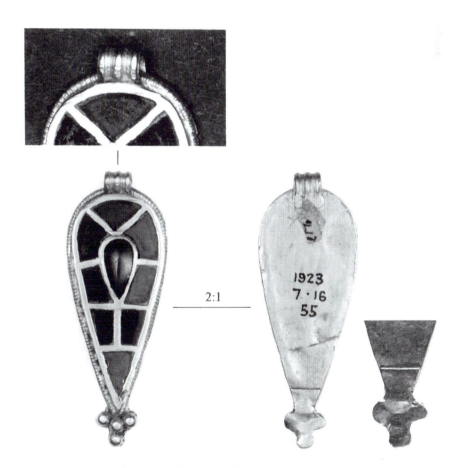

Cat. No. **11**

Plate 7

Jewellery

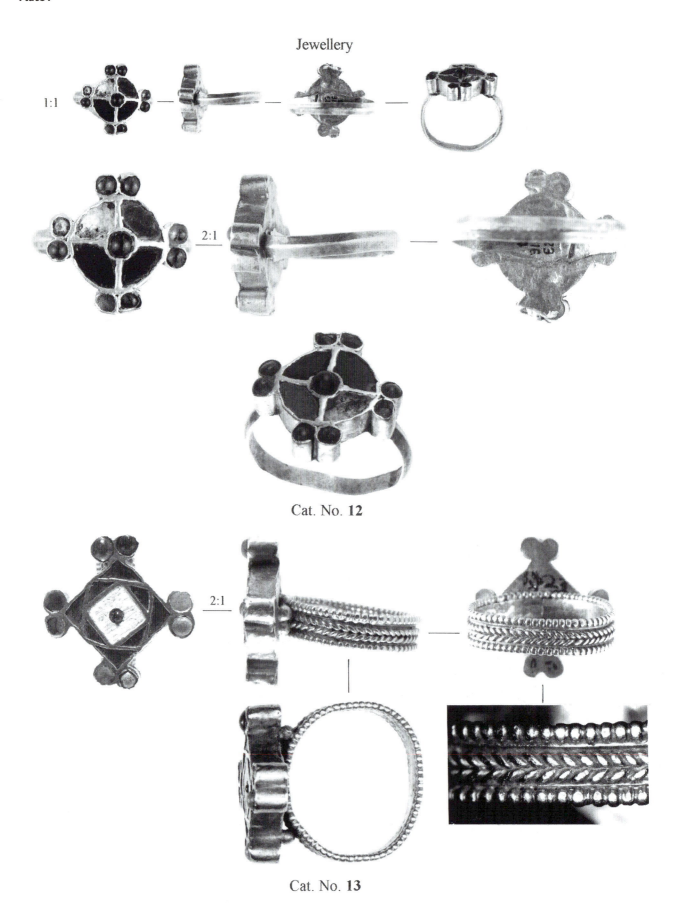

1:1

2:1

Cat. No. **12**

2:1

Cat. No. **13**

Plate 8

Jewellery

2:1

3:1

Cat. No. **14**

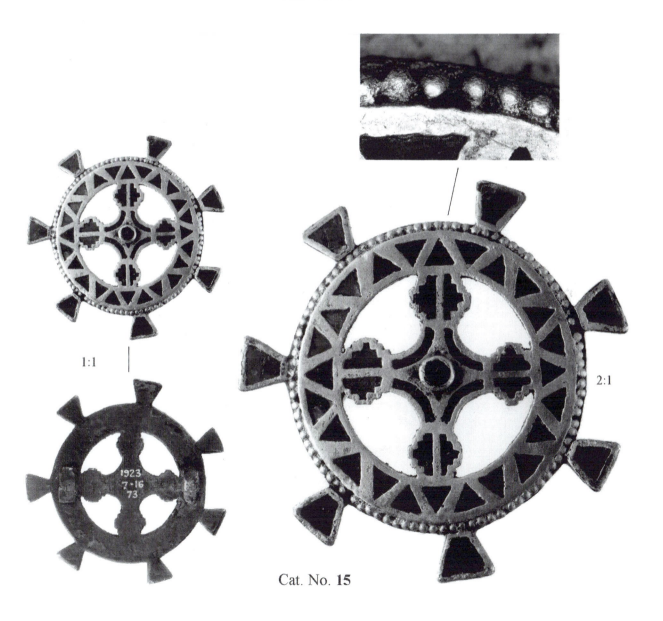

1:1

2:1

Cat. No. **15**

Plate 9

Jewellery

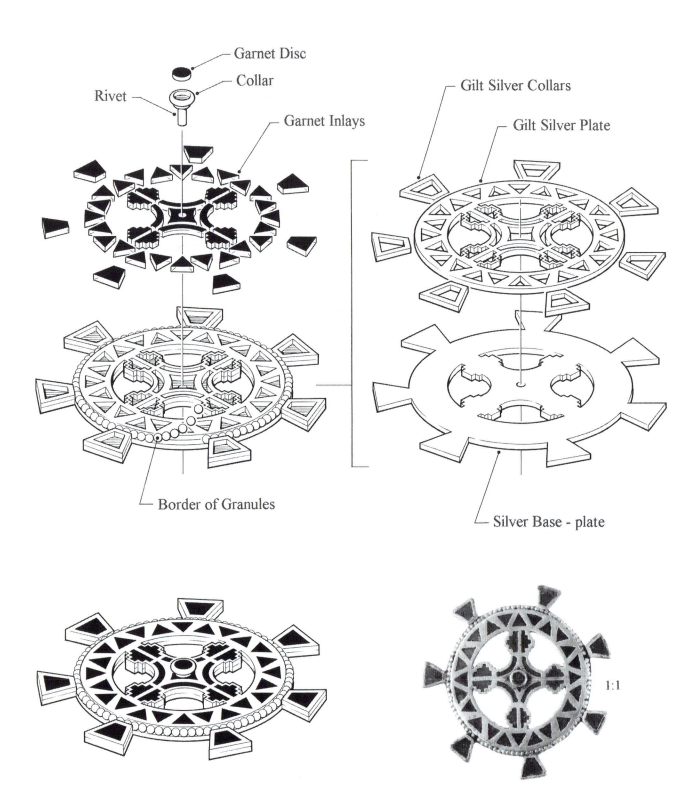

Construction of Brooch Cat. No. **15**

Plate 10

Jewellery

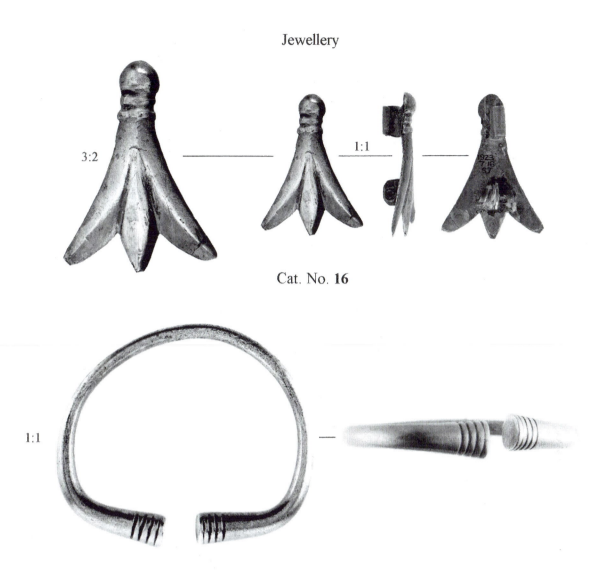

3:2   1:1

Cat. No. **16**

1:1

Cat. No. **17**

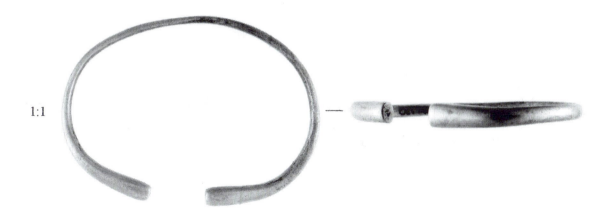

1:1

Cat. No. **18**

Plate 11

Jewellery

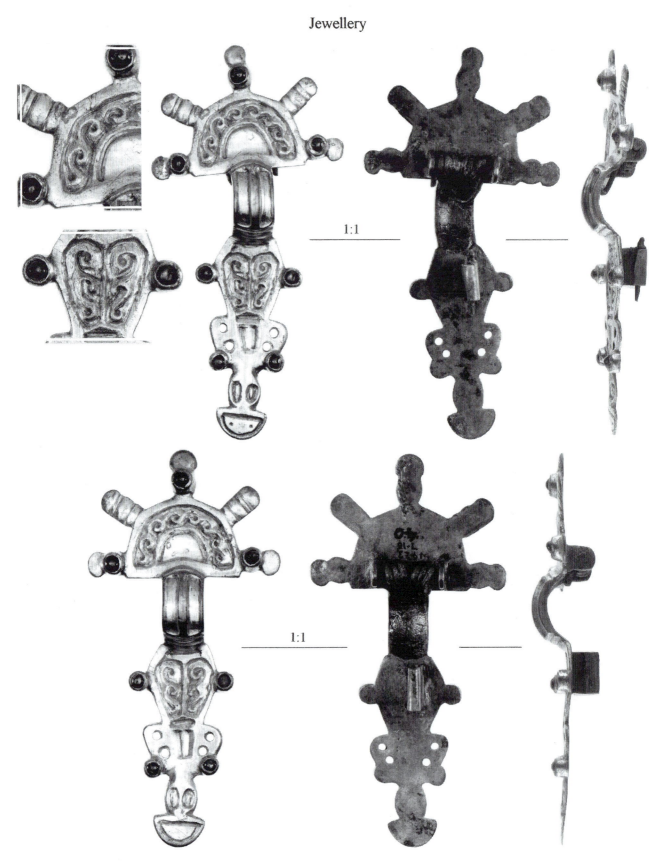

1:1

1:1

Cat. No. **19**

Plate 12

Jewellery

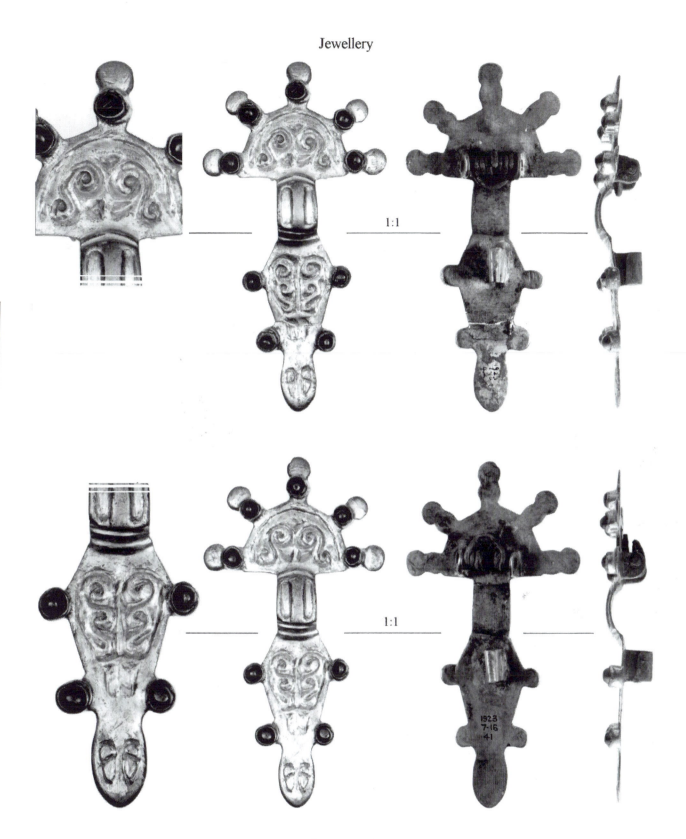

1:1

1:1

Cat. No. 20

Plate 13

Jewellery

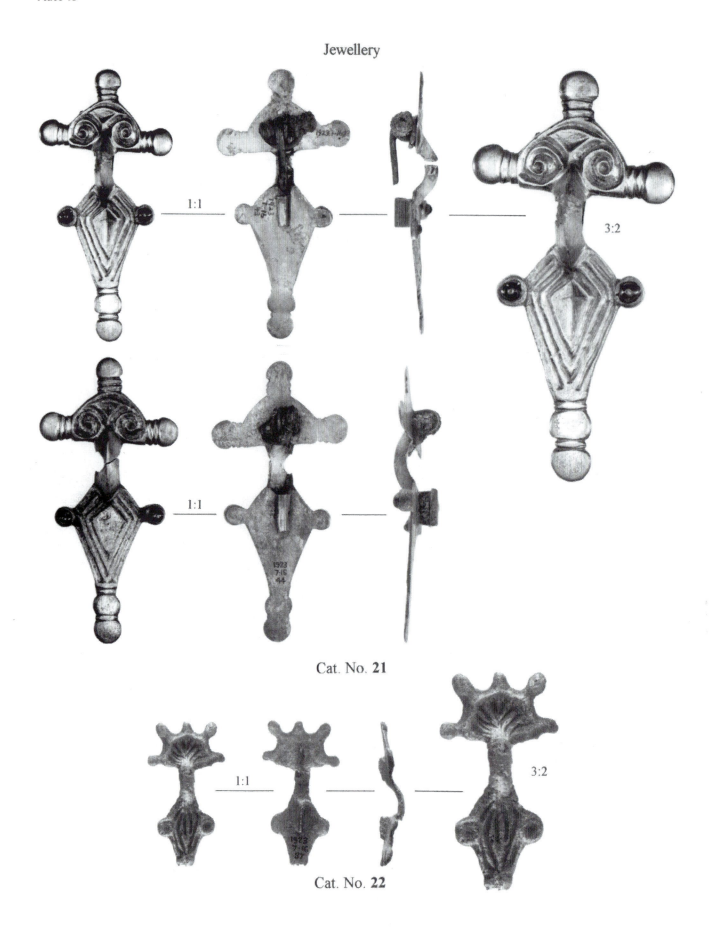

Cat. No. **21**

Cat. No. **22**

Plate 14

Mounts

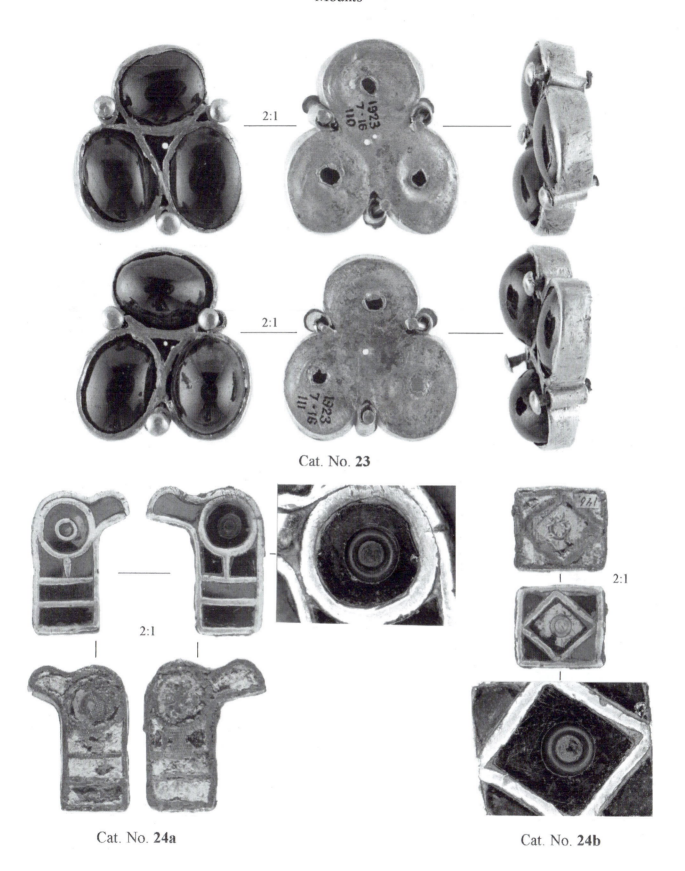

2:1

2:1

Cat. No. **23**

2:1

2:1

Cat. No. **24a**

Cat. No. **24b**

Plate 15

Mounts

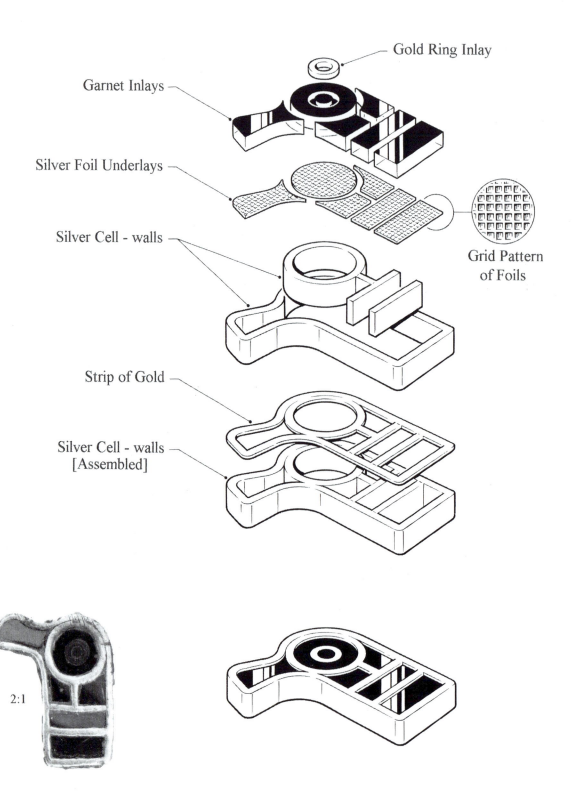

Gold Ring Inlay

Garnet Inlays

Silver Foil Underlays

Grid Pattern
of Foils

Silver Cell - walls

Strip of Gold

Silver Cell - walls
[Assembled]

2:1

Construction of Mount Cat. No. **24a**

Plate 16

Mounts

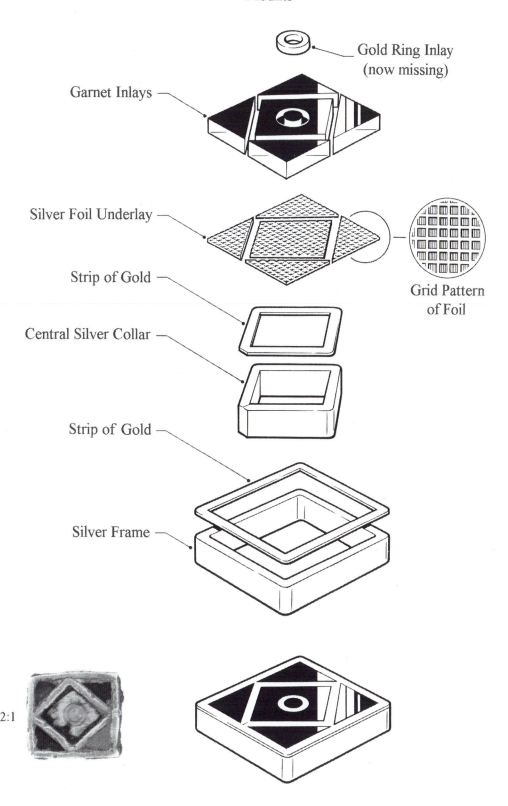

Gold Ring Inlay
(now missing)

Garnet Inlays

Silver Foil Underlay

Grid Pattern
of Foil

Strip of Gold

Central Silver Collar

Strip of Gold

Silver Frame

2:1

Construction of Mount Cat. No. **24c**

Plate 17

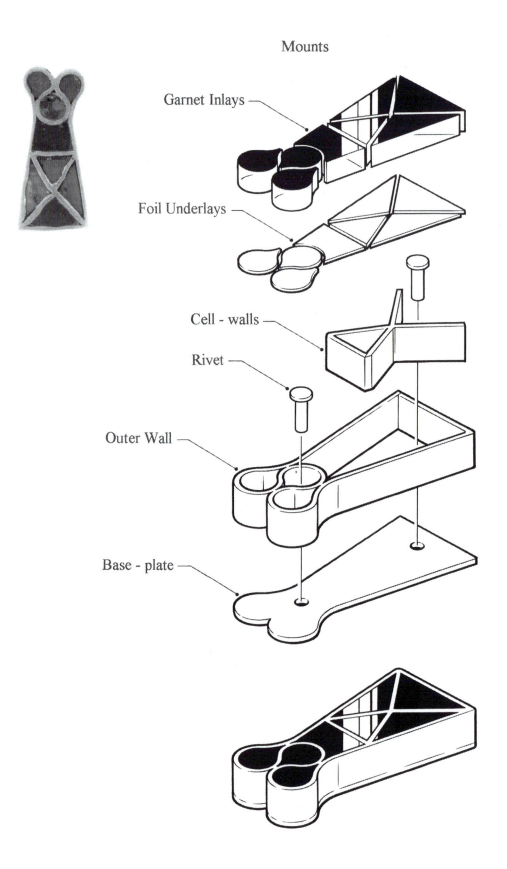

Mounts

Garnet Inlays

Foil Underlays

Cell - walls

Rivet

Outer Wall

Base - plate

Construction of Mount Cat. No. **25**

Plate 18

Mounts

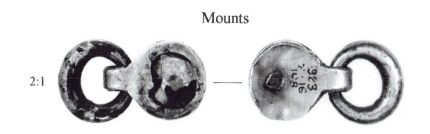

2:1

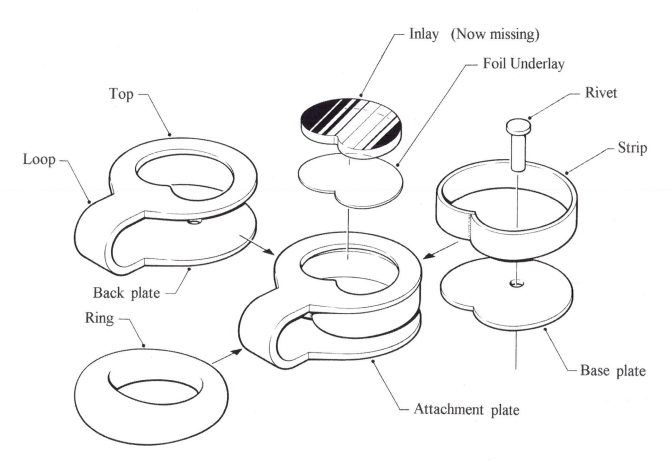

Inlay (Now missing)

Foil Underlay

Rivet

Top

Strip

Loop

Back plate

Ring

Base plate

Attachment plate

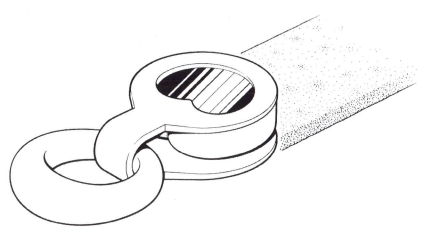

Construction of Mount Cat. No. **26**

Plate 19

Mounts

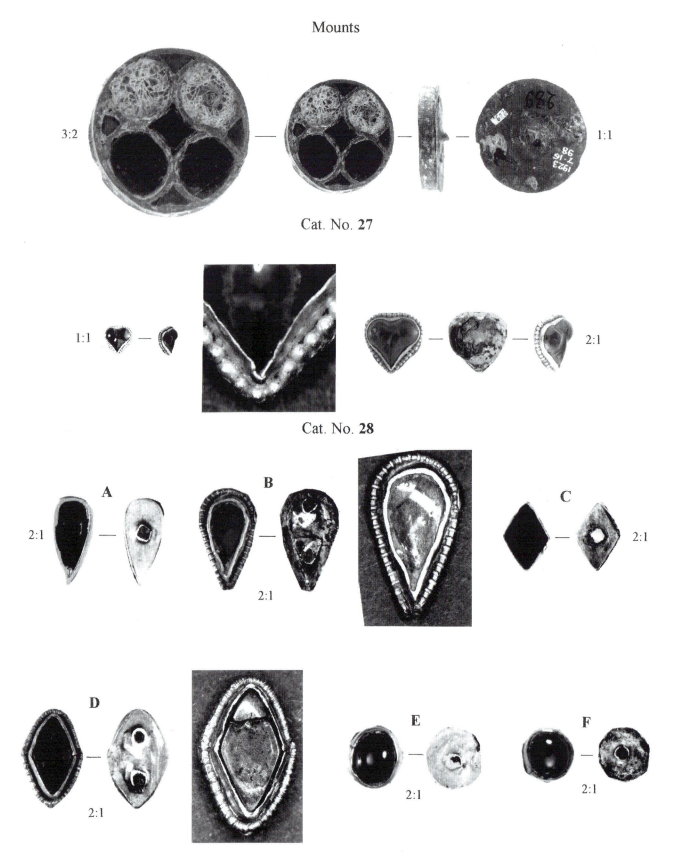

Cat. No. **27**

Cat. No. **28**

Cat. No. **29**

Plate 20

Mounts

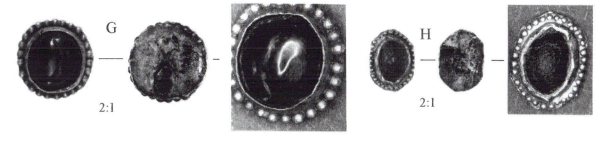

G   2:1   H   2:1

I   2:1   J   2:1

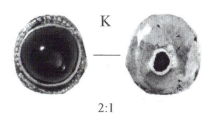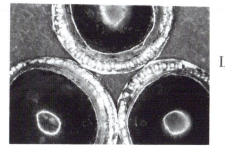

K   2:1   I, J and K

Cat. No. **29** continued

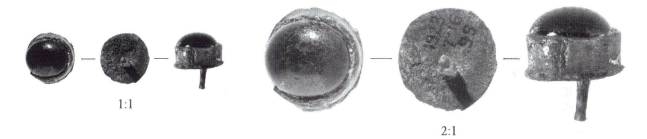

1:1   2:1

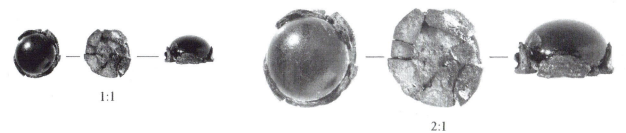

1:1   2:1

Cat. No. **30**

Plate 21

Horse Harness

All 1:2

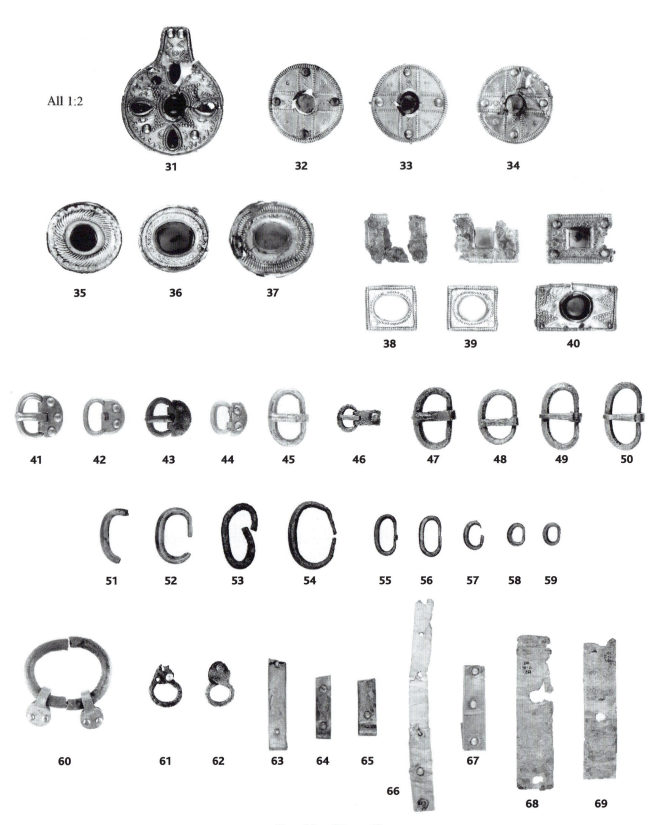

Cat. No. **31** to **69**

Plate 22

Horse Harness

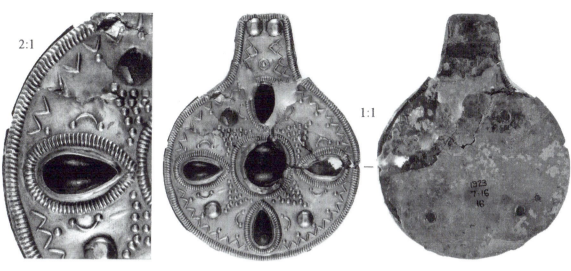

2:1

1:1

Cat. No. **31**

Section

LEGEND - this also applies to Cat. Nos **31** to **43**

——— Overlay - Silver Gilt   ⧹⧹⧹⧹ Back Plate - Silver

≡≡≡ Patterned Base - Copper Alloy   Possible Position of Leather Strapping

⧹⧹⧹⧹ Plain Sheet - Copper Alloy   * *Chabochons not shaded for clarity*

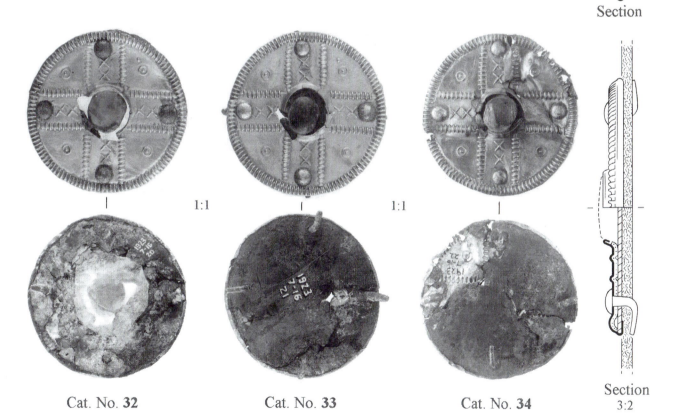

1:1   1:1

Cat. No. **32**   Cat. No. **33**   Cat. No. **34**

Section
3:2

Plate 23

Horse Harness

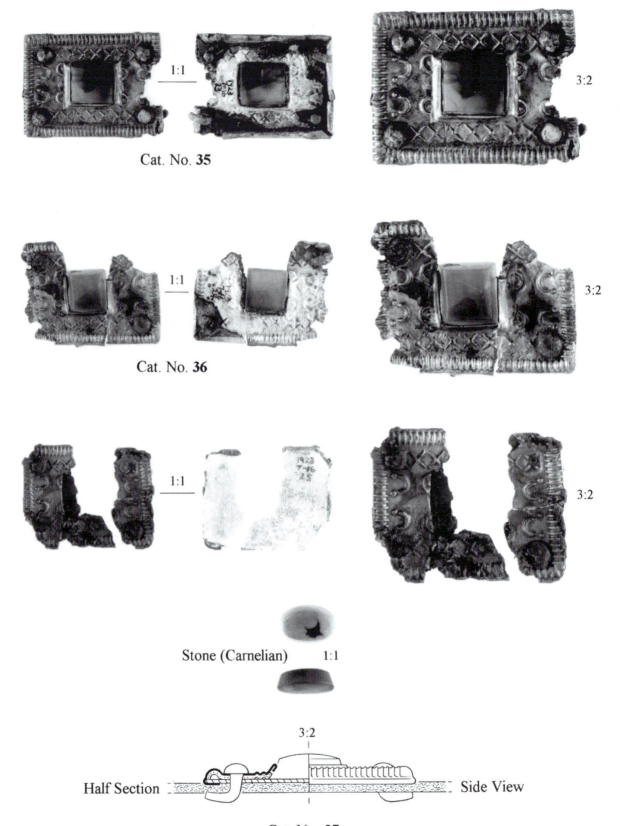

Cat. No. **35**

Cat. No. **36**

Stone (Carnelian)   1:1

Half Section   Side View

Cat. No. **37**

Plate 24

Horse Harness

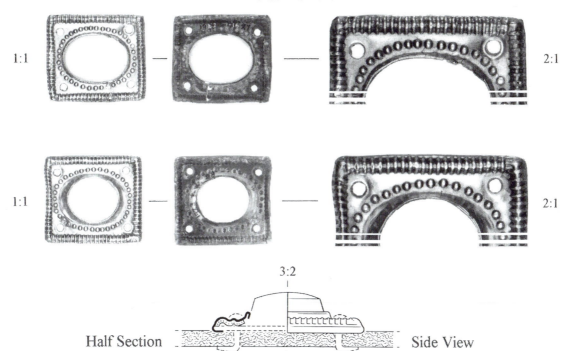

1:1 — 2:1

1:1 — 2:1

3:2

Half Section — Side View

Cat. No. **39**

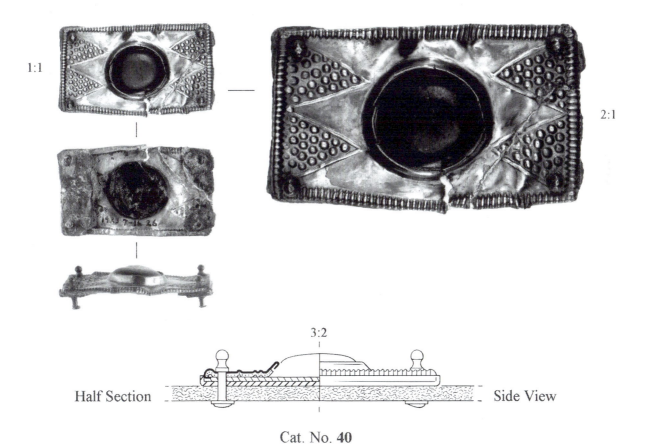

1:1 — 2:1

3:2

Half Section — Side View

Cat. No. **40**

Plate 25

Horse Harness

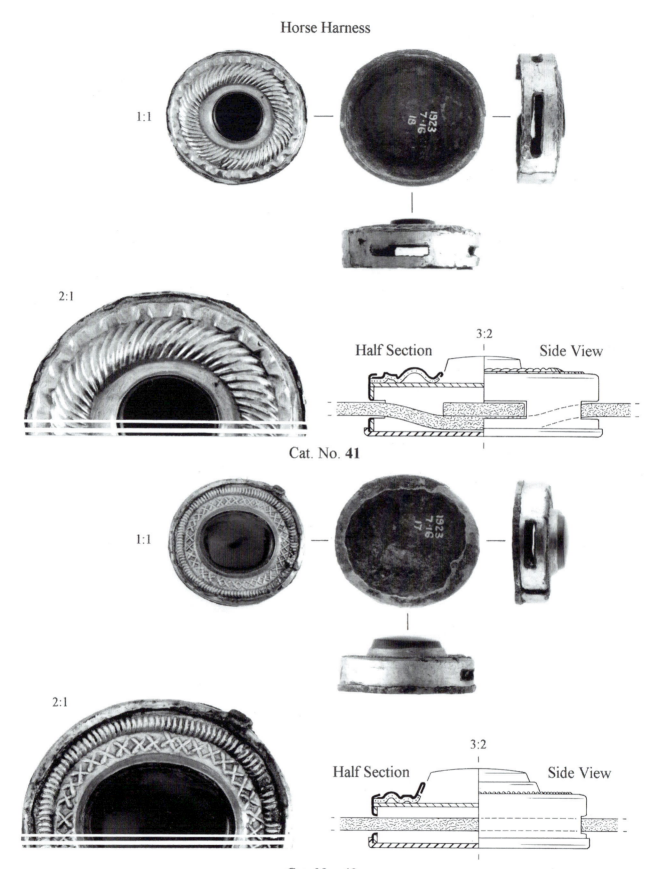

Cat. No. **41**

Cat. No. **42**

Plate 26

Horse Harness

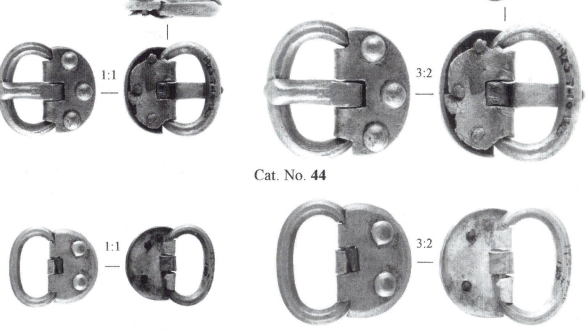

1:1

3:2

Half Section   Side View

Cat. No. **43**

1:1   3:2

Cat. No. **44**

1:1   3:2

Cat. No. **45**

Plate 27

Horse Harness

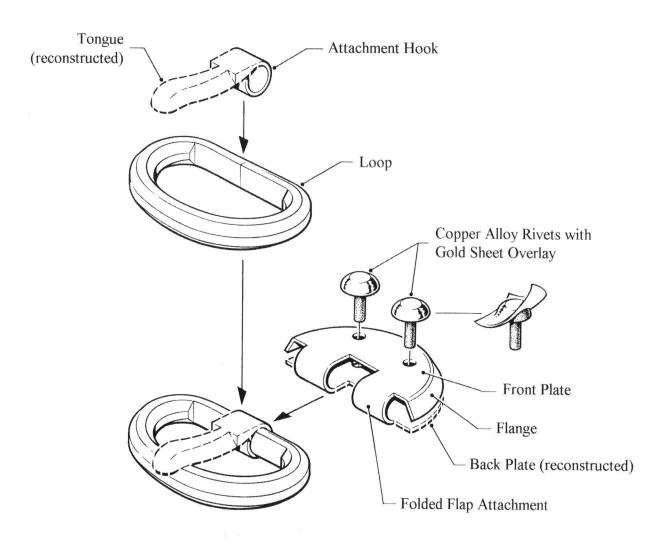

Tongue
(reconstructed)

Attachment Hook

Loop

Copper Alloy Rivets with
Gold Sheet Overlay

Front Plate

Flange

Back Plate (reconstructed)

Folded Flap Attachment

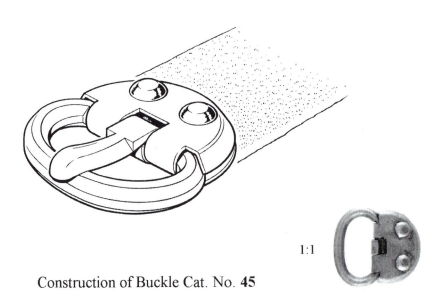

Construction of Buckle Cat. No. **45**

1:1

Plate 28

Horse Harness

1:1  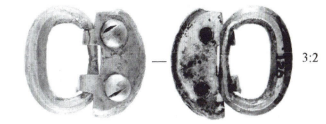 3:2

Cat. No. **46**

1:1   3:2

Cat. No. **47**

1:1   2:1

Cat. No. **48**

1:1   3:2

Cat. No. **49**

Plate 29

Horse Harness

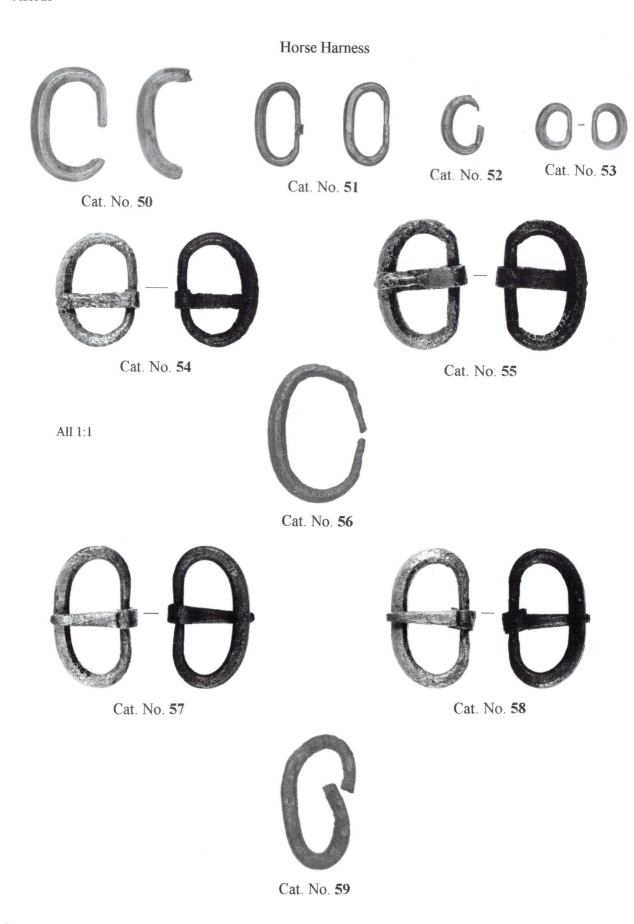

Cat. No. **50**

Cat. No. **51**

Cat. No. **52**

Cat. No. **53**

Cat. No. **54**

Cat. No. **55**

All 1:1

Cat. No. **56**

Cat. No. **57**

Cat. No. **58**

Cat. No. **59**

Plate 30

Horse Harness

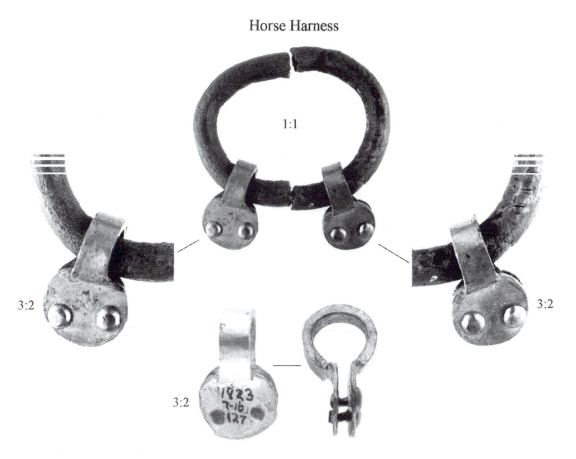

1:1

3:2

3:2

3:2

Cat. No. **60**

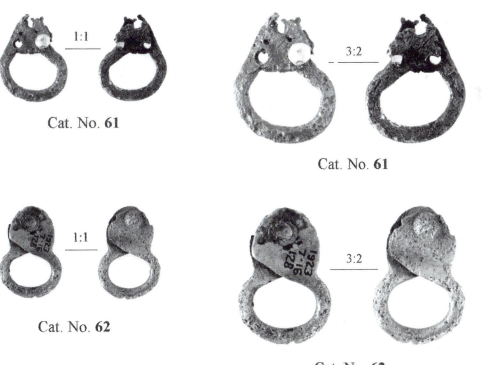

1:1

Cat. No. **61**

3:2

Cat. No. **61**

1:1

Cat. No. **62**

3:2

Cat. No. **62**

Plate 31

Horse Harness

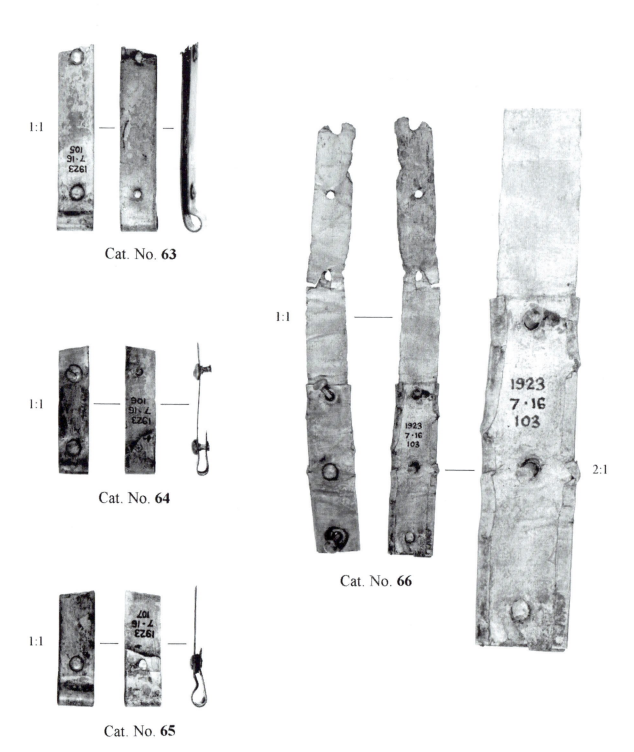

Cat. No. **63**

Cat. No. **64**

Cat. No. **65**

Cat. No. **66**

Plate 32

Horse Harness

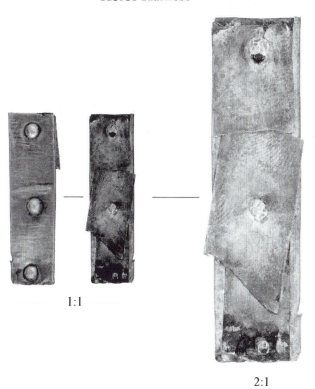

1:1

2:1

Cat. No. **67**

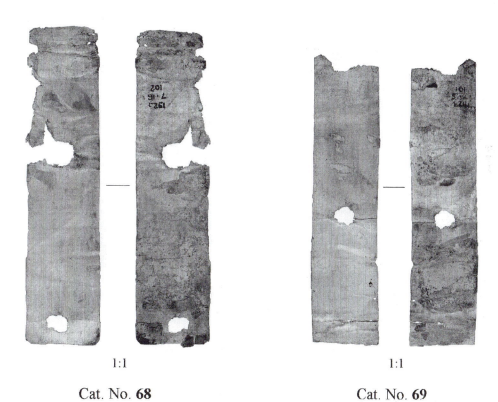

1:1

1:1

Cat. No. **68**

Cat. No. **69**

Plate 33

Buckles

1:1

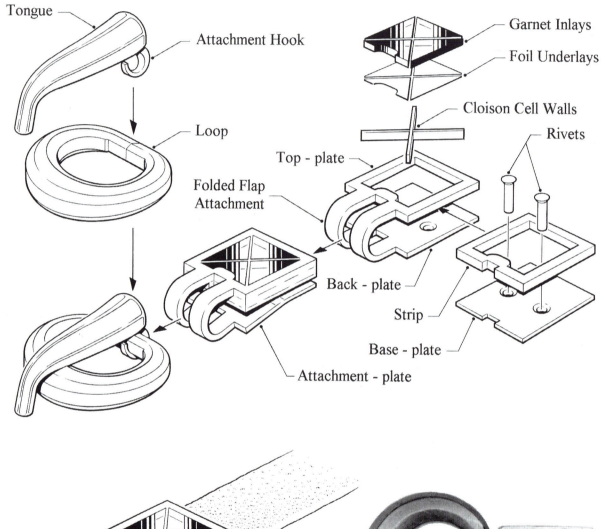

Tongue

Attachment Hook

Loop

Folded Flap
Attachment

Top - plate

Back - plate

Strip

Base - plate

Attachment - plate

Garnet Inlays

Foil Underlays

Cloison Cell Walls

Rivets

2:1

Construction of Buckle Cat. No. **70**

Plate 34

Buckles

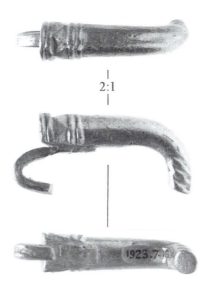

2:1

Cat. No. **71**

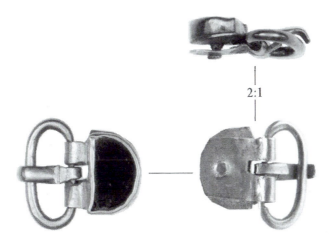

2:1

Cat. No. **72**

Plate 35

Buckles

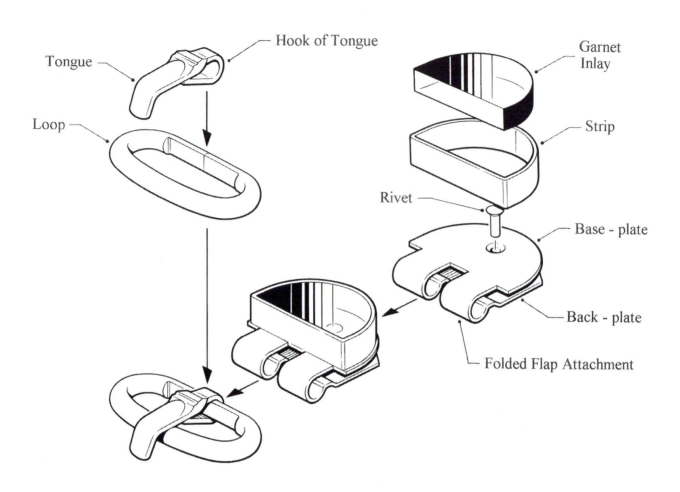

Tongue

Hook of Tongue

Garnet Inlay

Loop

Strip

Rivet

Base - plate

Back - plate

Folded Flap Attachment

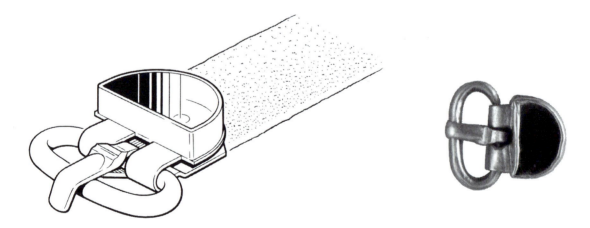

Construction of Buckle Cat. No. **72**

Plate 36

Buckles

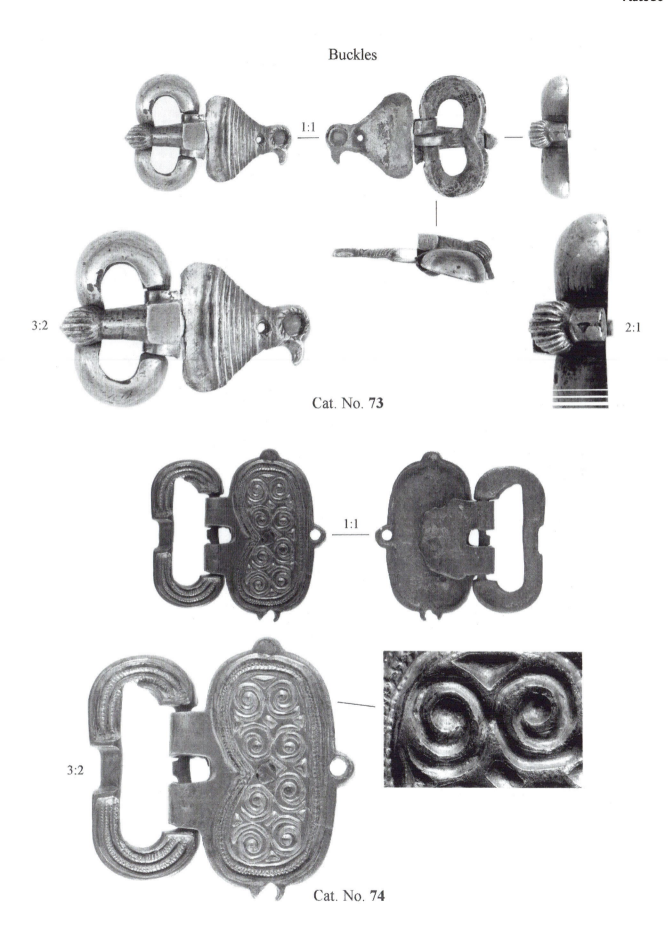

Cat. No. **73**

Cat. No. **74**

Plate 37

Buckles

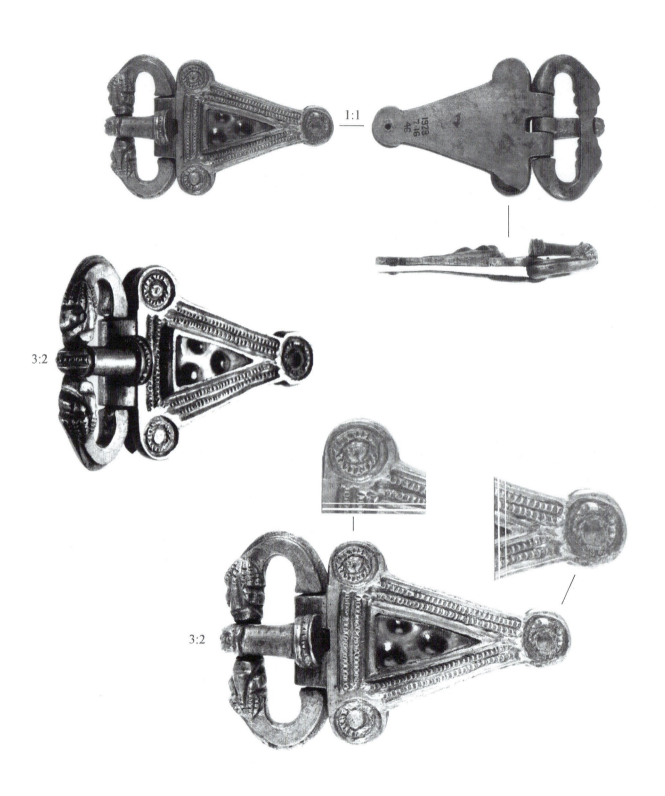

1:1

3:2

3:2

Cat. No. 75

Plate 38

Buckles

1:1

2:1

Cat. No. **76**

Plate 39

Buckles

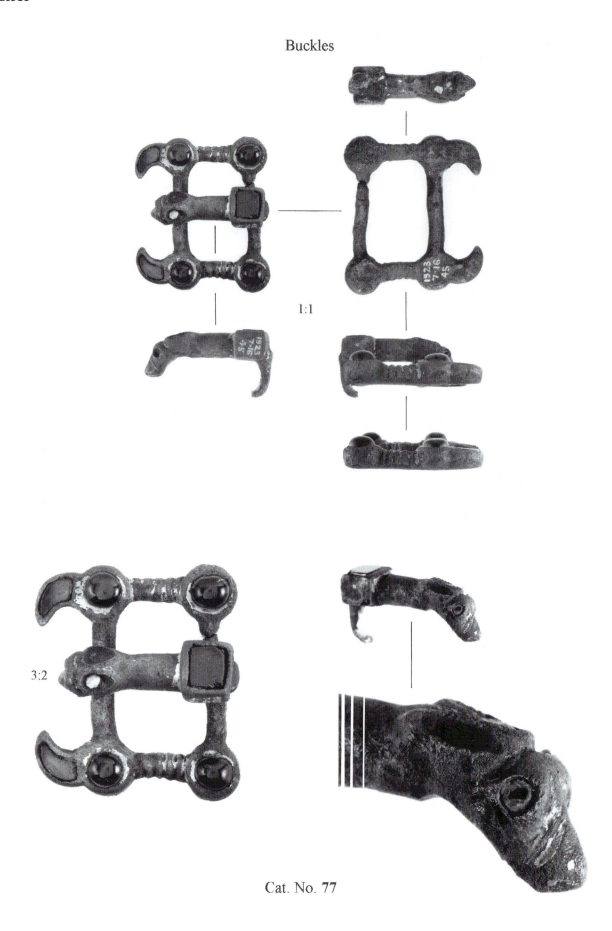

1:1

3:2

Cat. No. 77

Plate 40

Buckles

1:1

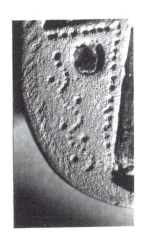

Cat. No. 78

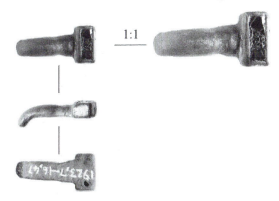

1:1

Cat. No. 79

Plate 41

Buckles

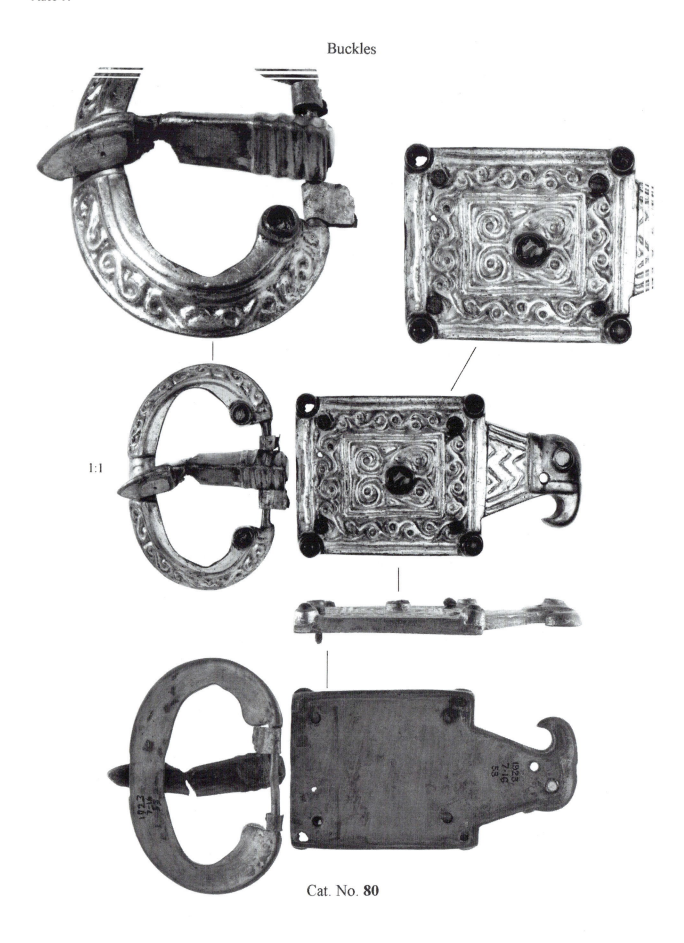

1:1

Cat. No. **80**

Plate 42

Buckles

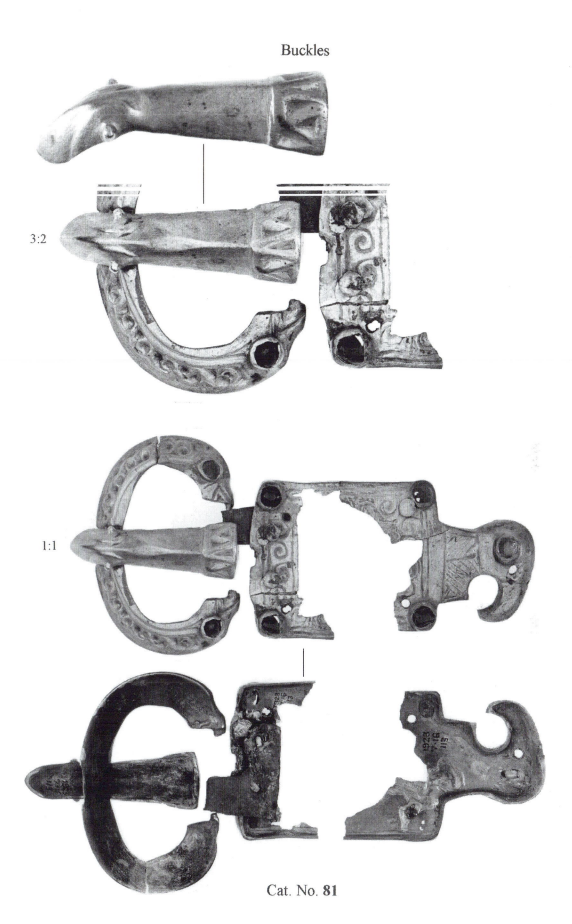

3:2

1:1

Cat. No. **81**

Plate 43

Buckles

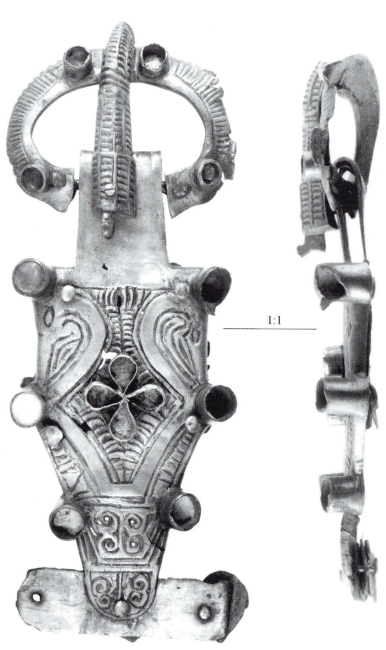

1:1

Cat. No. **82**

Plate 44

Buckles

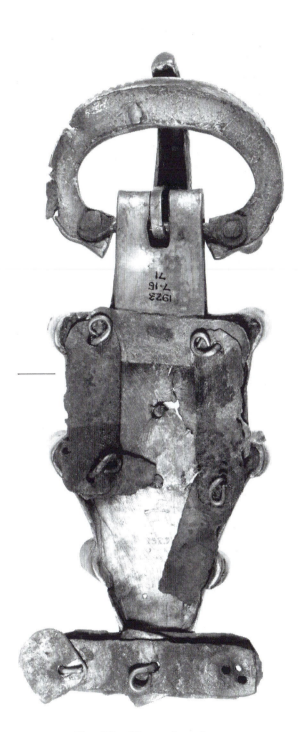

Cat. No. **82** continued

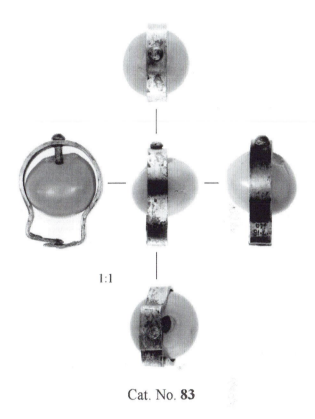

1:1

Cat. No. **83**

Plate 45

Provincial Byzantine

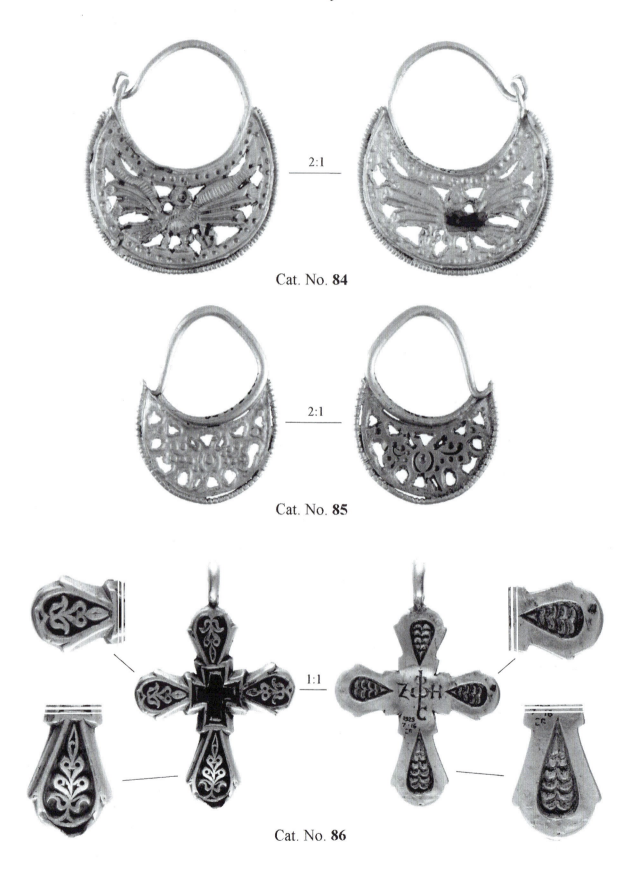

Cat. No. **84**

2:1

Cat. No. **85**

2:1

Cat. No. **86**

1:1

Plate 46

Provincial Byzantine

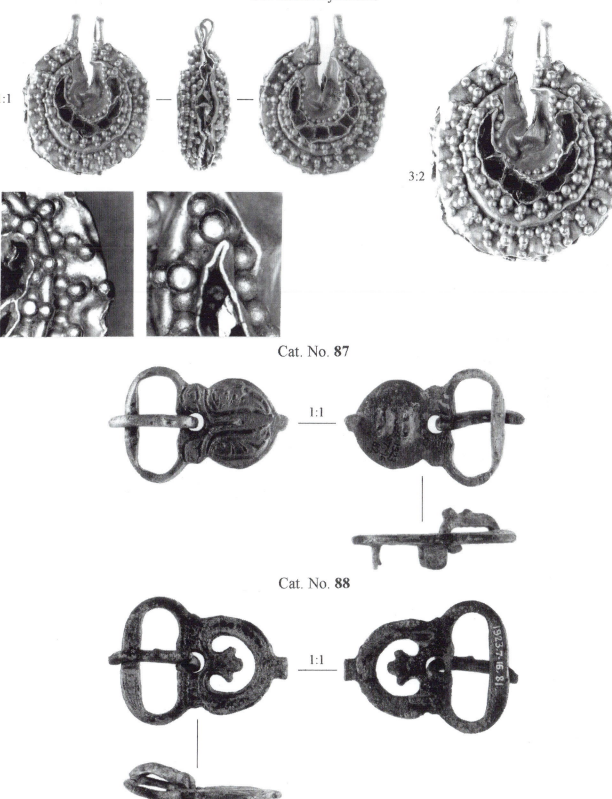

1:1

3:2

Cat. No. **87**

1:1

Cat. No. **88**

1:1

Cat. No. **89**

Plate 47

Provincial Byzantine

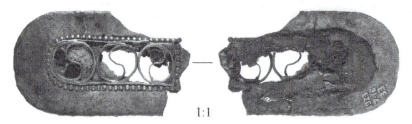

1:1

Reconstruction of Original Design

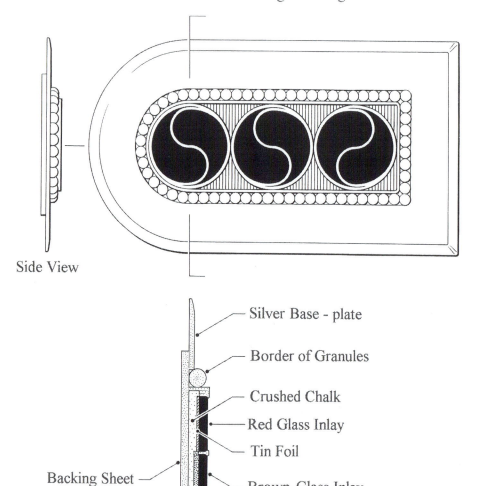

Side View

Silver Base - plate

Border of Granules

Crushed Chalk

Red Glass Inlay

Tin Foil

Backing Sheet

Brown Glass Inlay

Red Ochre

Gold Strips

Gold Frame

Section to Illustrate Construction Layers

Cat. No. **90**

Plate 48

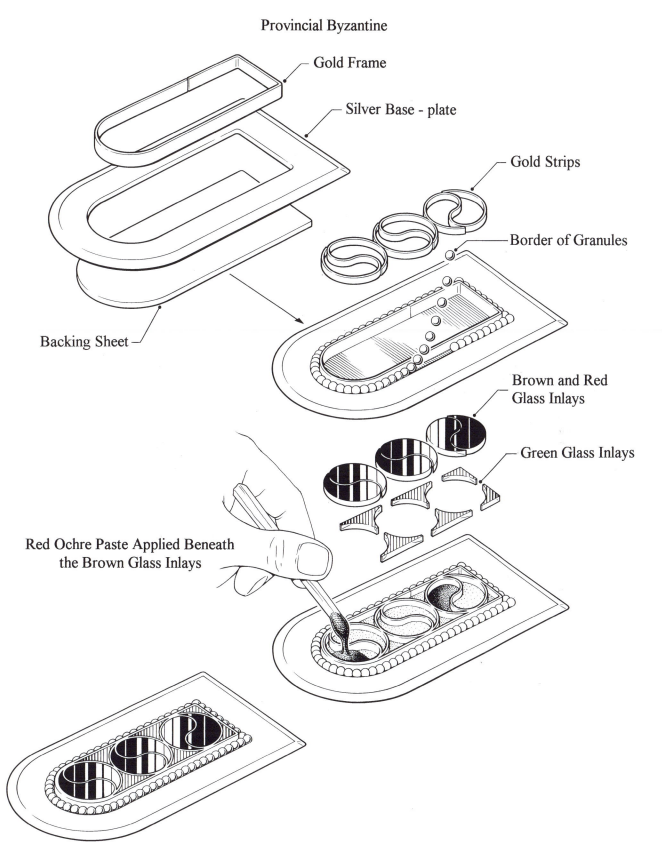

Provincial Byzantine

Gold Frame

Silver Base - plate

Gold Strips

Border of Granules

Brown and Red Glass Inlays

Green Glass Inlays

Backing Sheet

Red Ochre Paste Applied Beneath the Brown Glass Inlays

Construction of Strap-end Cat. No. **90**

Plate 49

Provincial Byzantine

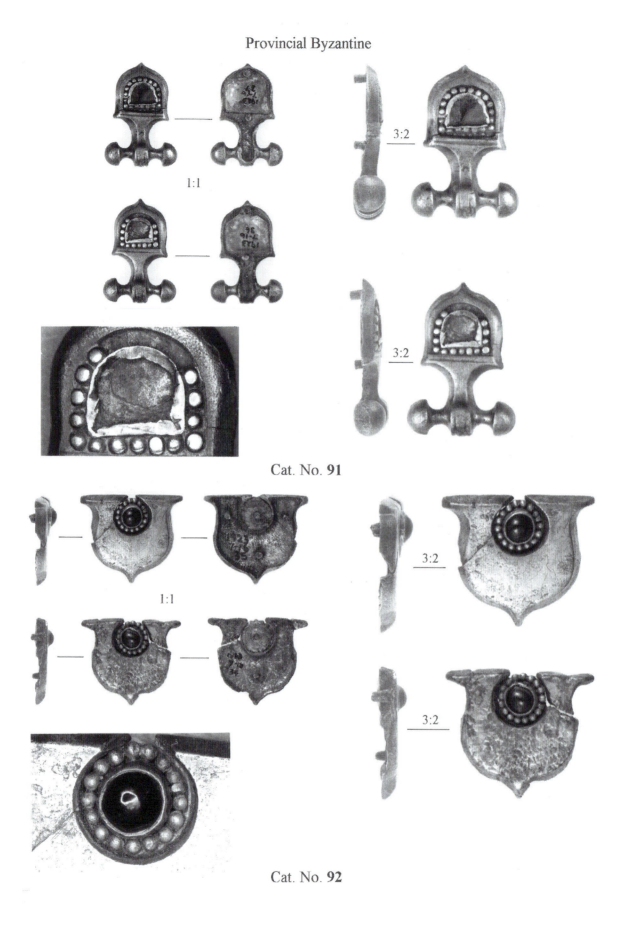

1:1

3:2

3:2

Cat. No. **91**

1:1

3:2

3:2

Cat. No. **92**

Appendix 1

Provincial Roman jewellery of the 2nd–3rd centuries AD

Six brooches (**cat. nos 93–98**) are all of familiar types. Six are enamelled bronze brooches typical of the Middle Empire period (2nd–3rd century AD), and particularly common in the north-western provinces of the Empire, while the seventh (**cat. no. 99**) is a silver fibula of cross-bow type, a Late-Roman form.

Though enamelling on gold was an ancient tradition in the Classical world, the use of enamel on base metal ornaments was established before the Roman conquest in many of the Celtic areas of Europe and continued to be popular in those regions when they became provinces of the Empire. Enamelled brooches and studs, as well as small bronze vessels with enamel decoration, were probably made at numerous centres in provinces from Britannia to Pannonia (Hungary), and certainly including many areas of Gaul.[1]

Note

1 Catherine Johns, former curator in the Department of Prehistoric and Romano-British Antiquities, British Museum. The notes and descriptions of cat. nos 93–99 below are also written with the benefit of her expertise and advice.

93 Brooch (Pl. 50)

Single piece of composite construction.
Copper-alloy brooch in the shape of a leopardess, enriched with enamel and glass inlays.
2nd–3rd century
Copper alloy, enamel, glass, iron
Prov.: unknown
Inv. no. GR 1924,5-2.1 – transferred to Greek and Roman Department in 1923   Old cat. no. 167
Size: L: 45mm   W: 20mm   Weight: 13.29g

The copper-alloy brooch is three dimensional, cast. It represents a reclining pantheress or leopardess, its head raised and thus cast fully in the round. The three projections along the animal's belly indicate teats, identifying it as a female. The eyes are inlaid with small beads of yellow glass, while the body is ornamented with 14 circular spots of enamel, all apparently red. The figure is carefully executed with cast features, such as the ears, the forehead, the mouth, the paws and the incised twisting on the tail.

The back is flat.

The catchplate and the spring-holder are cast. The spring-holder is a pair of semicircular lugs, centrally perforated for an iron (?) pin-spring axis.

(H at body: 4–5mm, H at head: 15mm).

The catchplate and the pin-spring axis are fragmentary. The pin is missing.

Plate-brooches in a variety of shapes, including zoomorphic forms, were probably intended as much for pure decoration as for use in securing garments. Of the examples present in this collection, the spotted panther or leopard is a well-known form, and is one of comparatively few zoomorphic designs which have an obvious symbolic meaning in the context of Roman religion: leopards, panthers and tigers were all animals associated with the god Bacchus. Many zoomorphic plate-brooches are completely flat, with large areas of solid enamel colour, but the leopards belong to a distinctive group which are more three-dimensional, the heads in particular being rendered completely in the round and the enamel taking the form of small spots in the metal background. The body spots are generally in two colours, e.g. black and red, but appear here to be in red alone.

94 Brooch (Pl. 50)

Single piece of composite construction.
Copper-alloy rectangular plate-brooch with enamel inlays.
2nd–3rd century
Copper alloy, enamel
Prov.: Olbia (Mikolayiv), Ukraine – 1897
Inv. no. GR 1924,5-2.2 – transferred to Greek and Roman Department in

1923   Old cat. no. 196
Size: L: 49mm   W: 26mm   Weight: 7.74g

Convex, rectangular, cast plate-brooch of copper alloy with a projecting, discoid lobe below each corner. There is a triangular plate projection at each of the two shorter sides with a similar discoid lobe at their top. There is a rectangular, raised panel in the centre of the front, inlaid with three different-coloured strips of enamel (red, blue and amber yellow). There is a notched, rectangular framing rib around the raised area. Each peripheral lobe is decorated with concentric, engraved circles.

The back is plain.

The catchplate and spring-holder are cast, the latter consisting of a pair of semicircular lugs centrally perforated for the pin-spring axis.

(H: 6mm, size of enamelled zone: 8 x 20mm, D of lobes: 5mm).

The pin-spring axis and catchplate are fragmentary.

95 Brooch (Pl. 50)

Single piece of composite construction.
Copper-alloy lozenge-shaped plate-brooch with enamel inlays.
2nd century
Copper alloy, enamel, iron
Prov.: Olbia (Mikolayiv), Ukraine, 1897
Inv. no. GR 1924,5-2.3 – transferred to Greek and Roman Department in 1923   Old cat. no. 261
Size: L: 42mm   W: 32mm   Weight: 5.87g

Lozenge-shaped, cast plate-brooch with a discoid lobe at each corner. There is a lozenge-shaped, central, raised panel divided into four lozenge-shaped zones of equal size. Each zone is inlaid with enamel, two opposed red and two opposed, vivid, hyacinth-blue enamels. There is a notched rib running between the enamelled zones, and a similar rib all around them. Each peripheral lobe is decorated with concentric, engraved circles.

The back is plain with a circular, central depression.

The pin-catch and spring-holder are cast, the latter consisting of a pair of semicircular lugs centrally perforated to secure an iron spring axis.

(H: 3mm, size of enamelled zone: 15 x 15mm, D of lobes: 6mm).

The surface of one of the red enamels has deteriorated to green. The catchplate and pin-spring axis are fragmentary. The pin is missing.

96 Brooch (Pl. 50)

Single piece of composite construction.
Copper-alloy hexagonal plate-brooch with enamel inlays.
2nd–3rd century
Copper alloy, enamel, iron
Prov.: Kerch, Krym (Crimea), Ukraine – 1900
Inv. no. GR 1924,5-2.4 – transferred to Greek and Roman Department in 1923   Old cat. no. 233
Size: L: 35mm   W: 23mm   Weight: 7.88g

Hexagonal, cast plate-brooch with a discoid lobe at each corner. There is a central, hexagonal zone decorated with enamel inlays of various colours and shapes: a central, orange disc surrounded by black and red dots on a turquoise background. One of these is damaged and it is neither red nor black. The fact of its complete decay suggests a different composition. The centre of each peripheral lobe is inlaid with a red enamel disc.

The back is plain and flat. The pin-catch and spring-holder are cast on the back, each being behind the lobe at either end. Fragments of the iron pin-spring axis are preserved. (H: 2.5mm, D of lobes: 5.5mm).

The pin-catch is fragmentary. The pin is missing.

97 Brooch (Pl. 50)

Single piece of composite construction.
Copper-alloy disc-brooch with a central, riveted boss and millefiori enamel inlays.
2nd century
Copper alloy, millefiori enamel
Prov.: Olbia (Mikolayiv), Ukraine – 1897
Inv. no. GR 1924,5-2.5 – transferred to Greek and Roman Department in 1923   Old cat. no. 197
Size: D: 37mm   Weight: 10.44g

Copper-alloy, cast disc-brooch with eight peripheral, discoid lobes. There is a raised, disc-shaped panel at the centre with a central, projecting, riveted boss decorated with red enamel inlay on the top. The central, raised panel is decorated with two concentric, enamelled rings with copper-alloy borders. The inner ring is inlaid with red enamel, the outer one with millefiori enamel. There are three patterns of millefiori enamel as follows: (a) eight squares of turquoise with a ?red and black 5 x 5 chequerboard centre; (b) four squares of red with black and ?white 5 x 5 chequerboard; (c) four squares of white with a central, floral element consisting of a red dot and circle surrounded by eight black petals. Each peripheral lobe is decorated with concentric, engraved circles.

The back is plain and concave. The pin-catch and spring-holder are cast on the back, each behind a lobe at either end. The spring-holder consists of a pair of semicircular lugs centrally perforated to secure the pin-spring axis.

The pin-catch is fragmentary. The pin is missing.

(D of raised panel: 21.5mm, D of boss: 6mm, H with boss: 10mm, H without boss: 5mm).

Millefiori enamelling is represented on this wheel-brooch. This intricate technique required specialised glassmaking and gem-cutting skills, as well as those of the bronzesmith and enameller, and was used on some highly specialised, small bronze vessels, as well as on personal ornaments. The very wide distribution of the rare, hexagonal ink-pots (pyxides) with millefiori enamelling extends as far as Palmyra and Kerch (the latter apparently from a Sarmatian grave), suggesting that they were seen as exotic curios.

98   Fibula (Pl. 51)

Single piece of composite construction.
Copper-alloy composite plate-brooch, inlaid with enamel.
2nd century
Copper alloy, enamel
Prov.: Kerch, Crimea (Krym), Ukraine – 1900
Inv. no. GR 1924,5-2.6 – transferred to Greek and Roman Department in 1923   Old cat. no. 232
Size: L: 50mm   Weight: 21.76g

Cast, copper-alloy brooch with a lozenge-shaped upper section and lobed lower section, both inlaid with enamel. There is a projecting, cast, discoid boss in the centre of the upper section, with red and blue enamel inlays.

It is enclosed by two lozenge-shaped strips with gilt-copper-alloy dividers. The pattern of the enamel is of alternating red and turquoise squares. The turquoise areas in the corners of both the inner and outer lozenges have had directly inset enamel spots of contrasting colour – all lost, but their positions can clearly be seen. The border rib is notched transversely. The bottom part of the brooch consists of four zones of red enamel inlays: a central triangle with a tear-shaped zone below, flanked by a semicircular zone at each side. Each zone of enamel has a gilt-copper-alloy frame.

The back is plain. The pin-catch and spring-holder are cast, the latter consisting of a tube divided in two by a slot which accommodates the base of the pin. The pin-catch is cast on the back of the lower part of the brooch and is perforated to accommodate a chain, or string of beads, when worn as one of a matching pair. (L of top part: 28 x 31mm, L of bottom part: 22mm, D of boss: 8mm, H with boss: 8mm, H without boss: 3mm).

Unlike the other enamelled brooches above, this is effectively a fibula rather than a plate-brooch, but its decoration is much influenced by the many geometric forms of plate-brooches. The closest parallels to this example would seem to be from Pannonia rather than Gaul.

99   Brooch (Pl. 51)

Single piece of composite construction.
Silver crossbow-brooch with three knobs at the head-end and niello decoration on the bow.
late 3rd/early 4th century
Silver, niello
Prov.: Olbia (Mikolayiv), Ukraine – 1896
Inv. no. GR 1924,5-2.7 – transferred to Greek and Roman Department in 1923   Old cat. no. 193
Size: L: 58mm   W (of head): 31mm   Weight: 7.82 g

Small silver brooch of crossbow type. The bow is decorated with a running chevron pattern inlaid with niello, and the relatively short, narrow foot has two pairs of cross mouldings and lightly chamfered

sides at the tip. The catchplate is a simple, open one. The simple tubular cross-bar terminates in very small rounded knobs, and the central knob terminal is also small, though slightly pointed.

(Thickness of the bow: 4mm).

It is a type which was found throughout the Empire in the 4th century AD, and, unlike most earlier fibula types, was quite often made in gold, silver or gilded bronze, as well as plain bronze. It was, indeed, the only fibula type which was commonly used in the Late-Roman period. The silver specimen in this collection has all the typical features of an early example in the type-series: it is small and slender, has a short, narrow foot, small knob terminals and a simple, open catchplate. Later crossbow-brooches are larger, often excessively so, with proportionally longer and wider feet, very large knob terminals, and often have elaborate decoration and an ingenious fastening mechanism.

Late-Antique and Sarmatian material

100   Fibula (Pl. 52)

Single piece.
Gold fibula.
2nd–3rd century
Gold
Prov.: Kerch, Krym (Crimea), Ukraine – 1893
Inv. no. GR 1981,9-5.1 – transferred to Greek and Roman Department in 1981   Original Inv. no. 1923,7-16,2   Old cat. no. 65
Percentage of gold: 82
Size: W: 16mm   L: 41mm   Weight: 2.9g

The fibula is made from a single wire of gold, shaped by hammering. The pin is of circular section with a pointed end, the other end coiled to form the spring. The spring itself is also of circular section and consists of two spirals outwards, a loop around the front, and forms three spirals inwards to the bow. The bow is a rectangular-section strip, bent to shape. It is hammered flat at the end to form a triangular foot-plate. At the back this is folded back and its edges are turned in to form the pin-catch. The end of the pin-catch is hammered to form a plano-convex-section wire, which is returned and wrapped seven times round the base of the bow.

There are three other similar fibulas in the collection (**cat. nos 101, 102 and 103** below). The technique of making these fibulas from a single strip of gold is skilfully executed. There is no similarity between the four fibulas in their alloy composition. The circular-section wire of cat. no. 100 is formed by hammering, but that of **cat. nos 101 and 102** was made by twisting the strip tightly and rolling it between two hard, flat surfaces to smooth it. However, both of the above-mentioned methods were used for the construction of the fibula, **cat. no. 103**.

A similar gold fibula from Kerch is published by Rostovtsev[1] and a pair also from Kerch is in the Louvre.[2] There is one from south Russia, but with no exact provenance, published by Greifenhagen[3] and one in the museum of Hamburg with no known provenance.[4]

Comparative bibliography
1   Rostovtsev 1923b, 107 no. 10, pl. 4
2   De Ridder 1924, 82 nos 945, 946, pl. XV
3   Greifenhagen 1975, I, 47, pl. 24:10–12
4   Hoffmann and von Claer 1968, 155 no. 97

101   Fibula (Pl. 52)

Single piece.
Gold fibula.
2nd–3rd century
Gold
Prov.: Kerch, Krym (Crimea), Ukraine – 1893
Inv. no. GR 1981,9-5.2 – transferred to Greek and Roman Department in 1981   Old Inv. no. 1923,7-16,3   Old cat. no. 66
Percentage of gold: 91
Size: W: 16mm   L: 36.5mm   Weight: 2.65g

Very similar to **cat. no. 100** above, and made in the same way, though smaller. It is hammered from a single piece of block-twisted wire. The pin-spring consists of a single spiral outwards, a loop around the front, and forms two spirals inwards to the bow. This is of circular-section wire only lightly flattened along two sides. The end of the pin-catch is a circular-section wire which is wrapped five times around the base of the bow.

102   Fibula (Pl. 52)

Single piece.
Gold fibula.
End of the 1st/beginning of the 2nd century
Gold
Prov.: Kerch, Krym (Crimea), Ukraine – 1897
Inv. no. GR 1981,9-5.6 – transferred to Greek and Roman Department in 1981   Old Inv. no. 1923,7-16,50   Old cat. no. 200
Percentage of gold: 88
Size: W: 9mm   L: 23mm   Weight: 1.28g

Very similar to **cat. no. 100** above, and made in the same way, though smaller. It is also hammered to shape, but the wire itself was formed by twisting. The pin-spring consists of a single spiral outwards, a loop beneath the bow, and forms two spirals inwards to the bow. The end of the pin-catch is a circular-section wire which is wrapped only three times around the base of the bow.

103   Fibula (Pl. 52)

Single piece.
Gold fibula with decoration on the bow.
Second half of the 2nd century
Gold
Prov.: Kerch, Krym (Crimea), Ukraine – 1900
Inv. no. GR 1981,9-5.9 – transferred to Greek and Roman Department in 1981   Old Inv. no. 1923,7-16,61   Old cat. no. 226
Percentage of gold: 66
Size: W: 15.5mm   L: 42mm   Weight: 3.71g

The pin-spring consists of a single spiral outwards, a loop around the front, and forms two spirals inwards to the bow. The wire forming the spring is hammered to shape. The loop connecting the two outermost spirals of the spring is soldered to the bow. The foot-plate is narrow and almost rectangular. The end of the pin-catch is a hammered circular-section wire which is wrapped four times around the base of the bow.

The decoration consists of a single, circular-section gold wire, made by twisting. It is wound around the bow, forming a pattern of alternate transverse zones and wavy vertical lines along its whole length. There is no trace of solder which would support this decorative wire.

Both methods of shaping a wire by hammering and twisting are present, which suggests that they were in use at the same time and, presumably, in the same workshop.

  cat. no. 102 is similar and made in the same way, but with no decoration on its circular-section bow.

104   Pendant (Pl. 53)

Single piece of composite construction.
Gold, three-dimensional pendant in the form of a clenched fist.
Gold, enamel
Prov.: Kerch, Krym (Crimea), Ukraine – 1899
Inv. no. GR 1981,9-5.7 – transferred to Greek and Roman Department in 1981   Old Inv. no. 1923,7-16,51   Old cat. no. 206
Percentage of gold: body: 83   loop: 81
Size: L: 40mm overall   Weight: 2.57g

The main suspension attachment is of circular-section wire, irregularly grooved and bent to form an oval loop at the top. The other end is bent to form a smaller loop with its end wrapped around the base of the wire. To it is attached a single loop of circular-section wire. This is fastened to a loop at the base of the pendant, a circular-section wire with both of its ends soldered to a disc which is attached to the base of the pendant by means of folding the edges of the pendant all around it. There is a beaded-wire border soldered around the edge. The wire is probably shaped by a two-edged tool.

The pendant itself is in the form of a closed hand and is hollow inside. It is constructed of two longitudinal halves of repoussé work, hammered into a former and joined together. The finger-nails and joints are indicated by incised lines. The thumb projects between the first and second fingers in a gesture of 'ficus'. Soldered onto the front of the wrist is a single wire bent into a leaf shape. It contains traces of enamel, which is now opaque and white (originally it may not have been white).

The suspension attachment and the beaded wire are both heavily worn.

There is a similar pendant in the British Museum from Olbia (Ukraine)[1] and another in the Hermitage.[2]
Comparative bibliography
1   Marshall 1911, 353 no. 2964, pl. LXVIII
2   Comptes Rendus 1872, pl. 3:11

105   Pendant (Pl. 53)

Single piece of composite construction.
Miniature gold pendant of pyramidal shape with suspension loops.
Gold
Prov.: Kerch, Krym (Crimea), Ukraine – 1900
Inv. no. GR 1981,9-5.8 – transferred to Greek and Roman Department in 1981   Old Inv. no. 1923,7-16,56   Old cat. no. 218
Percentage of gold: pyramid: 97   suspension loop: 73   loop: 69
Size: L: 29mm overall   Weight: 1.28g

There is a suspension loop of circular-section, beaded wire at the top. To its base is soldered a hinge, which consists of two loops with a rod passing through it securing a ribbed strip with a median groove. Both ends are bent round to form a loop and between the two ends is soldered a large granule. To the lower loop is hooked a loop of plain, circular-section wire which has another similar strip attached. A small loop of beaded wire is hooked through the lower section and from it a miniature pendant of pyramidal shape is suspended by a soldered-on loop of beaded wire.

The suspension loop is heavily worn on the top inside edge. The pyramid is covered with platinum group metallic inclusions, which suggest an alluvial source for the gold.

The XRF analyses of the pendant show that the metal-composition of the pyramid is quite different from that of the rest of the component parts. It is therefore possible that the pyramid has been re-used from another item of jewellery.

106   Earring (Pl. 53)

Single piece of composite construction.
Gold hoop with a pyramidal pendant of gold spheres enriched with granules.
2nd–3rd century
Gold
Prov.: ?1894
Inv. no. : GR 1981,9-5.16 – transferred to Greek and Roman Department in 1981   Old Inv. no. 1923,7-16,109   Old cat. no. 155
Percentage of gold: body: 72   cylinder attachment: 74   hoop: 76
Size: W: 14mm   L overall: 35mm   Weight: 1.9 g

The hoop consists of a ring of circular-section wire, made by twisting and rolling. It narrows towards the ends. One end is bent to form a hook, the other is bent to form a loop then twisted cylindrically around itself in a return. The two ends together form a hook-and-eye fastening.

The pendant is a pyramid of spheres and granules. Each of the five spheres is hollow and constructed of two hemispheres soldered together. The three at the top and the one at the bottom each have a pyramid of four granules soldered to their base and there are two granules soldered between each of the spheres at the top. There is a twisted wire soldered around the top of the lowermost sphere, and a beaded wire to its base directly above the pyramid of granules. To its top is soldered a cylindrical, ribbed strip which is in turn soldered to a loop of ribbed strip with a groove along the middle by means of which the pendant is attached to the earring hoop.

There is an earring with a similar pendant from Dura Europus (Syria) now in Yale University Art Gallery, New Haven,[1] and a pair of earrings of the same type in the Brooklyn Museum.[2] A pair from south Russia is published by Greifenhagen.[3]
Comparative bibliography
1   Baur *et al.* 1933, 246, pl. IX:2
2   Davidson and Oliver, JR 1984, 117 no. 126 A–B
3   Greifenhagen 1975, I, 46, pl. 23:14, 15

107   Earring (Pl. 53)

A pair, each of composite construction.
Cabochon garnet inlay on the hoop and pyramidal pendant of granules.
3rd century

Gold, garnet
Prov.: 'Eltine' according to register (probably to be identified with Eltigen, Heroyivske (Geroyevskoye), the antique Nymphaion, a Greek town in the Krym near Kerch) – 1899
Inv. no. GR 1981,9-5.14 and 15 – transferred to Greek and Roman Department in 1981   Old Inv. no. 1923,7-16,90 and 91   Old cat. no. 204
Percentage of gold: base-plate: 83   body: 84
Size: W: 19mm   L overall: 34mm   Weight: no. 14: 4.78g   no. 15: 4.74g

The hoop consists of a ring of circular-section wire, narrowing towards both ends. One end is bent to form a hook. The other end is soldered to the base-plate of the setting, flattened and folded double to create a projecting loop. The two ends together form a hook-and-eye fastening. The base-plate is circular with a circular cabochon garnet at its centre. The collet is a gold strip soldered onto the base-plate, bent around the garnet. There is no solder-joint visible on the collet. It is bordered by beaded wire soldered onto the base all around its edge. It is uneven, so possibly formed with a single-bladed tool.

The pendant is a bunch of granules eight deep which are soldered to each other forming a hollow, inverted pyramid with a circular base. To its base is soldered a cylindrical strip decorated with a double grooved line all around. It is soldered to a loop of ribbed strip with a median groove by means of which the pendant is attached to the earring hoop.

The beaded wire is very worn. There is considerable evidence of wear on these earrings.

There are earrings with a similar type of pendant (so-called Bulgarian type) from Bulgaria and south Russia, published by Ruseva and Slokoska.[1]

Comparative bibliography
1   Ruseva and Slokoska 1991, nos 32–5, 40

108   Earring (Pl. 54)
Single piece of composite construction.
Gold hoop with a carnelian inlay and pyramidal pendant of granules.
2nd–4th century
Gold, carnelian
Prov.: Kerch, Krym (Crimea), Ukraine – 1895
Inv. no. GR 1981,9-5.3 – transferred to Greek and Roman Department in 1981
Old Inv. no. 1923,7-16,5   Old cat. no. 140
Percentage of gold: body: 76   loop: 76
Size: L: 50mm overall   34mm upper part, 16mm pendant-part
Weight: 2.7g

The hoop is of circular-section wire, which forms an elongated hook at the upper end for suspension from the ear. It passes behind the setting and its other end is a round loop which secures the pendant. Is is flattened where a thin, gold, oval sheet is soldered above the lower loop. This serves as a base-plate for a setting with its collet formed of a single strip soldered on and curved around the inlay with overlapping ends. It contains an oval, faceted inlay of carnelian with a flat top and a central, wheel-cut intaglio. The intaglio depicts a pedestal-vase with corn, or leaves, projecting from either side of its top as possibly a symbol of vegetation. At least two different sizes of wheel were used for cutting it. The depth of the stone extends to the bottom of the setting. There is a double-twisted wire – in a herring-bone pattern – forming a broad border around the collet, soldered onto the base-she*et all* around its edge.

The pendant is a bunch of granules seven deep forming an inverted pyramid. The granules were made individually and soldered together. To its base is soldered a cylindrical, ribbed sheet which is soldered to a circular loop of circular-section wire, by means of which the pendant is attached to the earring hoop.

The inverted pyramidal pendant is a long-lived feature, which was popular all over the classical world.

The engraved gem decoration on such an earring is an unusual combination. The gemstone itself is of the middle Roman period, but it was associated with the earring possibly at a later time, around the 2nd to 4th centuries.[1]

Comparative bibliography
1   C. Jones, pers. comm.

109   Earring (Pl. 54)
A pair, each of composite construction.
Gold hoop and a pendant decorated with a garnet inlay and enriched with wires, rosettes and three pendants.

1st century BC
Gold, garnet
Prov.: Kerch, Krym (Crimea), Ukraine – 1900
Inv. no. GR 1981,9-5.10 and 11 – transferred to Greek and Roman Department in 1981
Old Inv. no. 1923,7-16,62 and 63   Old cat. no. 230
Percentage of gold: back sheet: 92   twisted wire: 95   hoop: 93
Size: no. 10: W: 19mm   Weight: 3.38g
          no. 11: L overall: 48mm   Weight: 3.44g

The hoop is an elongated hook of circular-section wire with a small, dome-headed knob at its end. The other end is flattened where it is soldered to the hexagonal base-plate of the pendant, onto which is soldered a central, box-shaped setting. The four sides of it are constructed from a single strip with a soldered join adjacent to the suspension hoop. Around its top edge a rectangular sheet is fixed by wax with a rectangular opening cut into the centre and its edges turned in to hold the inlay. The setting contains a rectangular garnet plate. There is no foil visible behind the garnet, although it is difficult to see through. The garnet and its surround are now held in place by a white, waxy paste, which is unlikely to be part of the original construction (it blocks and has squeezed out of the small holes in the sides of the box, which must once have anchored some missing attachment). The garnets are too small for their settings and would fall out without the adhesion of the white paste. To the top of no. 1981,9-5,10 is soldered vertically a thin sheet bent to form a cylinder containing a small, circular-section wire with a rosette of granules soldered onto the end. No. 1981,9-5,11 has remains of a similar construction, but its cylindrical sheet is held in place by the wax. There are three similar wires (but with no sheet around them) soldered onto the base-plate, each of them enriched with similar rosettes. The lower edge of the base-plate is bent in to secure a beaded wire formed by a multiple-bladed tool. It serves to support three pendants. Each of these is suspended by a loop, one end of which is flattened where it is soldered on, while the other is free. On no. 1981,9-5,10 the central pendant has a replacement suspension loop. Each pendant consists of a single wire bent round at the top to form a suspension loop, with the return wrapped cylindrically around the body for three-quarters of its length. The wires were all made by twisting strips or rods of gold and rolling them to form a round section. Each pendant terminates in a circular sheet with granules soldered onto it in the form of a rosette.

The garnets are probably replacements; the white paste is not original.

The heavy wire scrollwork of this earring is similar to the decoration of several pieces of late Hellenistic (1st century BC) jewellery such as an earring in the Jewellery Museum, Pforzheim (Germany),[1] an armband from Palaiokastro (Greece),[2] and the armbands in the Museum of Fine Arts, Boston.[3]

Comparative bibliography
1   Deppert-Lippitz 1985, ill. 225
2   *Op. cit.* ill. 217
3   *Op. cit.* pl. XXXII

110   Earring (Pl. 54)
Single piece of composite construction.
Gold hoop and a pendant of a lunate gold sheet decorated with three cabochon garnets, and enriched with bordering wires and granules.
2nd century?
Gold, garnet
Prov.: Olbia (Mikolayiv), Ukraine
Inv. no. GR 1981,9-5.13 – transferred to Greek and Roman Department in 1981   Old Inv. no. 1923,7-16,74   Old cat. no. 310
Percentage of gold: base-plate: 95   body: 93
Size: W: 22m   L: 26mm   Weight: 2.89g

The hoop consists of a circular-section wire formed by twisting. It is bent to form a hook at one end. The other end is bent to form a loop then twisted cylindrically around itself in a return. The two ends together form a hook-and-eye fastening.

The lunate pendant is soldered to the hoop and also secured by a triangular projection from the base-plate, which is folded over it. The base-plate is a single sheet of lunate form with seven triangular projections around its outer edge. Each projection contains three soldered-on granules in a triangular arrangement. The edge of the base-plate is folded up, except where the groups of granules are. Within the edge of the base-plate is soldered a strip forming a vertical collar. It has two twisted wires in a herring-bone pattern all along the inside edge. A thin, plain, circular-section wire is soldered onto the plate within the twisted wires. All the wires are made by twisting. There is a hemispherical sheet at each point of the base-plate covering the wires with a granule soldered onto the centre of each. The main field is decorated with three cabochon garnets in a triangular arrangement, each in an individual collet. The two smaller ones have their collets squashed to size, since the latter were originally tear-shaped, but the present stones are circular and may be replacements. The collet of the bigger cabochon is notched around the edge and folded around it. This has a twisted-wire border with a granule soldered onto the base-plate above the centre of it.

There is a very similar pair of crescent-shaped gold earrings decorated with garnet inlays in the Collection of Burton Y. Berry.[1]

Comparative bibliography

1   Rudolph and Rudolph 1973, 92 no. 71b, pl. 71

111   Earring (Pl. 55)

Single piece of composite construction.
Gold hoop and a pendant of triangular gold sheet containing a tear-shaped garnet enriched with granules and beaded wire, and three garnet bead pendants.
2nd–1st century BC
Gold, garnet
Prov.: Kerch, Krym (Crimea), Ukraine – 1893
Inv. no. 1923,7-16,13   Old cat. no. 147
Percentage of gold: body, side: 95   base-plate: 93   base-plate abraded: 94
Size: W: 20mm   L: 38mm   Weight: 5.65g

The hoop consists of a circular-section wire with one end bent to form a hook. The other end is flattened and soldered to the base-plate of the pendant. This consists of a triangular sheet with a box-shaped setting soldered on. The sides of the setting are formed by a broad strip bent to a tear shape. From the limited access available, there is no evidence of any material inside the box-shaped setting. To the top of the box is soldered a ribbed strip bent to form a cylinder, soldered to the top surrounding a small perforation where the two ends of the strip meet. The broken ends of at least three gold wires can be seen through the perforation. They appear to be twisted together in a rope-like fashion and presumably formed another decorative feature, similar to the protruding wire decoration of **cat. no. 109** above. The tear-shaped strip has a thin strip soldered around its top edge supporting a line of granules soldered on. There is a further strip soldered at right angles to the top inside edge of the side-strip, which is bent along its central line around the garnet to secure it. The garnet is of a three-dimensional tear shape (?face-like or representing an ivy leaf, very similar to that of **cat. no. 28** above). There is a small loop of beaded wire soldered to each lower corner of the base-plate, directly next to the setting. The beading is uneven and poorly executed. It was probably made with a single-bladed tool. The lower edge of the base-plate has a strip soldered on, which is bent to a semicircular section in order to secure a line of granules soldered on top.

There are three loops of ribbed strip soldered to the base-plate, each with a median groove. One end of each is flattened where it is fastened to the base-plate. The other end is free. From each of these is suspended a pendant by a circular-section wire, the top end of which is bent to form a loop. The wire passes through the centre of an ovoid garnet bead, which has a flower-shaped sheet washer at the top and bottom. The washers are held in place by pressure from the burred end of the suspension wire.

The lower edge of the base-plate has been overheated during the solder work and has melted in several places.

Earrings of this type are published by Ondřejová and dated to the 2nd–3rd century.[1] There is an earring with similar ovoid garnet pendants from Palaiokastro (Greece) in the Museum of Hamburg.
See **cat. no. 28** above for similar three-dimensional garnet inlays.

Comparative bibliography

1   Ondřejová 1975

112   Buckle-loop (Pl. 55)

In two pieces.
Copper-alloy, elongated buckle-loop with animal-head decoration on the tongue.
1st–3rd century. Sarmatian

Copper alloy
Prov.: Olbia (Mikolayiv), Ukraine
Inv. no. 1923,7-16,84   Old cat. no. 320
Size: loop: 55 x 27mm   tongue L: 40mm   Weight: 13.77g

The loop is cast, oval. It has an oval-section head, which is opened at the base, each end of which is decorated with an openwork spiral inwards and elongated into a rectangular-section rod for accommodating the tongue. The elongated part has a pattern of three circles on the top of each arm followed by a rectangular projection with a central circular perforation for attachment of the tongue. There is a circular projection at both ends of the loop with a circular perforation for attachment to the plate.

The tongue is of semicircular section with a T-shaped base by means of which it is hinged into the perforations on the arms of the loop. The base of the tongue is decorated with an elaborate, cast, projecting animal-head (dog, or wolf?). The tongue is further decorated with four deep lines crosswise and an animal-head (bird ?) terminal in profile.

The tongue is loose. One of the perforations preserves fragments of the plate-attachment and another one of the tongue. The plate is missing.

113   Buckle-loop (Pl. 56)

In two pieces.
Copper-alloy loop with openwork decoration, and tongue.
1st–3rd century.   Sarmatian.
Copper, copper alloy
Prov.: Olbia (Mikolayiv), Ukraine
Inv. no. 1923,7-16,83   Old cat. no. 320
Size: 29.5 x 34mm   Weight: 13.94g

The cast, copper-alloy loop is oval with an openwork, rectangular projection at its base for attachment to the plate. The oval part is decorated with two openwork scrolls at the base, below which is a small, cast bar for the attachment of the tongue.

The narrow tongue is of copper with an elongated, rectangular base decorated with a carved, zig-zag pattern on the top. It has a circular opening at the back of the base with both of its ends flattened to form a closed, circular fitting around the bar of the loop.

The tongue is probably a replacement. The plate is missing, or the loop may belong to the attachment-plate (**cat. no. 114**) below.

Similar buckle-loops were found in Kerch[1] and Cherson.[2] They are attached to buckle-plates of the type **cat. no. 114**. They are considered to be Sarmatian and dated to the 1st–3rd centuries by Shkorpil[3] and also by Solomonik.[4] There are two buckle-loops of this type from Kerch in the Ashmolean Museum,[5] and one of unknown provenance in the Odessa Museum.[6]

Comparative bibliography

1   Shkorpil 1910b, 32 ill. 8; Solomonik 1959, 132, 133, nos 71, 76, 78 – no. 71 is of gold
2   OIAK 1893a, 34 no. 18
3   Shkorpil 1910b, 32
4   Solomonik 1959, 132
5   Inv. nos 1909.805 (with a plate attached) and 1909.809. Both acquired by Sir John Evans in 1886 and presented to the Ashmolean by Sir Arthur Evans in 1909.
6   Pósta 1905, 433 ill. 244: 4

114   Buckle-plate (Pl. 56)

Single piece.
The copper-alloy buckle-plate is a rectangular frame containing an openwork tamga.
1st–3rd century. Sarmatian.
Copper, copper alloy.
Prov.: Olbia (Mikolayiv), Ukraine – 1909
Inv. no. 1923,7-16,85   Old cat. no. 320
Size: 43 x 22mm   Weight: 7.58g
Published: Sulimirski 1970, 152, pl. 37 left

The copper-alloy (brass) plate is cast in one and has a folded flap attachment at one end to secure it to the loop or to a plate, like **cat. no. 115** below. Two copper attachment-rivets survive in two perforations drilled through the end of the plate.

Thickness of plate: 2mm; W of folded flap attachment: 11.5mm; D of rivet-heads: 3mm.

The folded flap attachment is imperfect. There are traces of corrosion on the plate and the loop is missing.

There are many similar Sarmatian buckle-plates from the Black Sea region.[1] In some cases they bear different tamga-motifs,[2] or they may be attached to various kinds of loop, including loops like that of **cat. no. 113** above.[3] One such plate was attached to a belt-mount identical to **cat. no. 115** below.[4] In some cases they are made of gold.[5]

At Chorna/Chernaya Rechka (Crimea, Ukraine) a similar buckle was found with objects considered to be of the second half of the 3rd century by Aibabin.[6] Solomonik[7] and Shkorpil[8] dated them to the 1st–3rd centuries, while according to Aibabin they should be dated to the 2nd and 3rd centuries.[9]

In view of the joint appearance of this type of object with **cat. nos 113** and **115** in the collection, the information above should apply to them too.

Comparative bibliography
1 OIAK 1893a, 34, ill. 18; OIAK 1893b, 53, ill. 29; Shkorpil 1907, 14, ill. 5; Shkorpil 1910b, 23–35, ills 8–12; Pósta 1905, 55 ill. 244; also in: Solomonik 1959, 133 no. 5; Solomonik 1959, 132–7 also list of similar buckles with literature, ills 71; 72; 76;78–80; 84–6; Babenchikov 1963, 108–9, pls VII:11 and XV:3
2 OIAK 1893a, 34, ill. 18 – Cherson; Shkorpil 1910b, 32, ill. 8 – Gulf of Kerch together with coins of Choti I (1st century); Solomonik 1959, 78 – Kerch
3 Shkorpil 1910b, 32, ill. 9 – in Gulf of Kerch gulf together with buckle under footnote 2
4 Solomonik 1959, 132, nos 71–2; Römisch-Germanisches Museum, Cologne – Inv. nos: D 100 and D 99
5 Babenchikov 1963, 108-109, pls VII:11 and XV:3
6 Aibabin 1990, pl. 2:1–2
7 Solomonik 1959, 132–7
8 Shkorpil 1910b, 31–4
9 Aibabin below

115   Belt-mount (Pl. 56)
Single piece.
Copper-alloy, tongue-shaped frame with openwork decoration based on the pelta and volutes.
1st–3rd century.   Sarmatian.
Copper alloy.
Prov.: Olbia (Mikolayiv), Ukraine – 1909
Inv. no. 1923,7-16,86   Old cat. no. 320
Size: 52 x 15mm   Weight: 6.11g
Unpublished

The mount is a single casting in the form of an elongated, tongue-shaped frame containing openwork decoration. There is a rectangular attachment slot at the base. The openwork comprises a lunate cut-out below the base, followed by a rectangle with an opened circle on either side. Below is a circular section containing an openwork rectangle in the centre surrounded by four segments. There is a tear-shaped section below, containing an openwork, lunate shape, two circles next to each other below that, and a triangle at the end above a small disc terminal. The front and back are both flat. (Thickness of plate: 2.5mm).

The rectangular attachment slot is broken.

An almost identical mount was found near Kerch in 1909 and is dated to the 1st–3rd century by Shkorpil[1] and Solomonik.[2] There is a similar mount in the British Museum[3] and a further two mounts of the type in the Römisch-Germanisches Museum, Cologne[4], all from Kerch and attached to openwork plates similar to **cat. no. 114** above by means of rectangular attachment slots at the base.

Aibabin dates this group of Sarmatian belt-mounts to the 2nd–3rd century.[5]

Comparative bibliography
1 Shkorpil 1910, 31; ill. 9
2 Solomonik 1959, 133; ill. 76
3 Inv. no. 56,10-4,56
4 Inv. nos: D 99 and D 100
5 Aibabin below

116   Sword-sheath slide (Pls 57–58)
Single piece.
Rectangular jade bar with attachment slot at the back, decorated with scrollwork carved in low relief.
Late 2nd–end of 1st century BC   Chinese. Late Han Dynasty (?) – date of manufacture
3rd century.   Sarmatian – later use

Jade.
Prov.: Kuban area – 1894
Inv. no. 1923,7-16,88   Old cat. no. 29
Size: 94.5 x 26.5mm   Weight: 59.79g
Published: Rostovtsev 1923a, 38 note 2; Rostovtsev 1930, 339–40 no. 2, figs 256–7; Werner 1956, 27 note; Trousdale 1969, 61, fig. 8; Trousdale 1975, 25, 102–3, 237–8, 264 table 2, pl. 19c; Khazanov 1971, 25, 149, pl. XV:7

One end of the bar is flat and expanded, the other narrows to a rounded terminal. (Thickness of one end: 11mm; other end: 2mm).

The front surface is decorated with incised, low-relief scrollwork. See **Pl. 58** for details of the design.

From the back projects a large, cuboid block. It is perforated by a transverse, rectangular slot for attachment, 17mm from one end and 41mm from the other end of the bar. (Size of the slot: 8 x 35mm; the bar is 3.5mm thick under the slot.)

There are traces of metal on the back (iron corrosion).

A very similar Chinese jade slide was found in Kerch in the Messaksoudi find, which is dated to the second half of the 3rd century.[1] Beck, Kazanski and Vallet date it to the first half of the 4th century.[2] A sword found in Pokrovsk (Voshkhod, Russia) dating to the Hunnic era has a similar slide made of nephrite, and a hilt decorated with garnet inlays.[3] Another slide of the same type from Alt-Weimar (lower Volga region, Russia) is said to be late Sarmatian.[4] According to Werner this fashion was spread from the East by the Alans coming from the Volga region in the period of the late Roman Empire.[5] Maksimenko and Bezuglov date the nephrite sword slide from the Sarmatian kurgan of Sladovsky (Rostov district, Russia) to the end of the 2nd–first half of the 3rd century.[6] Ginters associates the origin of this type of object with the Iranian people, while the ornaments and the use of jade are Chinese characteristics.[7] A similar nephrite slide from the Perm area (Russia) is published by Spitsin.[8]

Trousdale's monograph on sword and scabbard slides surveys a large number of this type of object discussing their history, origin, development and bibliography.[9] According to his idea the long sword and scabbard slide were first used by the equestrian people of the southern Ural steppe during the 7th–6th centuries BC, antedating the earliest appearance of the Chinese jade slides in the 5th century BC. The scabbard slide was brought westwards from China by the Yüeh-chih, a nomadic people living on the north-northwest frontier of China until the third decade of the 2nd century BC, who occupied Russian Central Asia in the third quarter of the same century. The Berthier-Delagarde piece was carved in China in the late 2nd/end of the 1st century BC and was found in a Sarmatian grave of the 3rd–4th century AD. In the 3rd and 4th centuries AD the scabbard slides manufactured in south Russia imitate the Chinese ones.

The scabbard slides were then imported to the Ural steppe from south Russia. The history of this type of object therefore began in the southern Ural steppe and ended some thousand years later in the same region. Trousdale rules out the possibility that the scabbard slides could be associated with the Huns.[10] But Zasetskaya, as a proponent of this theory, dates the slide from Pokrovsk to the 2nd half of the 5th century.[11]

The 'in situ' finds of two sword slides of this type, one from the Han period from Korea,[12] the other from the above-mentioned kurgan in Alt-Weimar, solved the problem of how these objects were used (see **Pl. 58 right side**).

Comparative ibliography
1 Rostovtsev 1923a, 10–11, ills 3–5
2 Beck, Kazanski and Vallet 1988, 63 et seqq. – with further literature and references.
3 Werner 1956, 26–7, pl. 40:3; Bóna 1991, 1993, ill. 22/1; Menghin 1994/95, 178, 185, ill. 35 – with further literature and references.
4 Rau 1927, 39
5 Werner 1956, 26–7, 42, pl. 38:4
6 Maksimenko and Bezuglov 1987, 183–92, 187–8, ill. 2:7
7 Ginters 1928, 173 – pl. 29a is wrongly attributed to the Berthier-Delagarde Collection
8 Spitsin 1902, 28, pl. II:1
9 Trousdale 1975, 1–332
10 Trousdale 1975, 112
11 Zasetskaya 1986, 79–91, 85–6, ill. 1:55
12 Yetts 1926, 197–201

117   Earring (Pl. 59)

Single piece.
Ribbed wire hoop with a flat, tear-shaped terminal.
3th-4th century?   Sarmatian.
Silver.
Prov.: 'Ecaterinos tertre' (in register; 'tertre' is French for 'mound' or 'barrow') – 1893
Inv. no. 1923,7-16,116   Old cat. no. 158
Percentage of silver: 93
Size: 44 x 30mm   Weight: 6.35g
Unpublished

The earring is made from a single piece. The hoop consists of a spirally ribbed wire. It narrows towards a hook at the end which is plain. The terminal is a thin, flat, tear-shaped plate, with a perforation at the tip. There are traces of a tear-shaped setting having been soldered in the centre of it.

Size of sheet: L: 34mm; W: 18mm; thickness: 0.2mm; size of central tear shape: 12 x 7mm; D of hole at the tip: 2mm; thickness of hoop: 3.5–1.3mm.

The terminal is damaged.

The original photograph of the collection does not show this object.

According to Aibabin these earrings are typically Sarmatian, of the second half of the 3rd/early 4th century.[1] They are made of gold, silver or bronze, and are often decorated with a central, tear-shaped glass, or semi-precious stone inlay.

Similar earrings of gold with a central sard inlay have been found in Chorna/Chernaya Rechka (Crimea, Ukraine), and are dated to the 3rd century by Babenchikov.[2] A bronze variant of this type from the site Kaborg IV (Ukraine) is dated to the same period by Magomedov[3] and a pair of silver earrings with glass inlay from Balka (Ukraine) is published by Savovs'ky.[4] Bichir dates a similar pair of earrings from Tîrgşor (Romania) to the 2nd–3rd century.[5] They are made of silver and inlaid with a violet-coloured cabochon. A similar earring has been found at Dnipropetrovsk (Ukraine).[6] It is made of bronze, and contains a central glass inlay.

Comparative bibliography
1   Aibabin below
2   Babenchikov 1963, 93, 98; pl. II:13–14
3   Magomedov 1979, 59, 61; pl. X:3
4   Savovs'ky 1977, 65–6; ill. 5:2
5   Bichir 1977, 193; pl. 24:12
6   OIAK 1893b, 87, ill. 68

118   Brooch (Pl. 59)

Single piece of composite construction.
Base silver bow brooch.
3rd-4th century?   Chernyakhovsk culture.
Base silver, iron.
Inv. no. 1923,7-16,121   Old cat. no. unknown
Percentage of silver: pin: 65   body: 69
Size: L: 5.6mm   Weight: 5.68g
Unpublished.

The body of the brooch is made from two pieces. The spring and pin are made of the same piece of circular-section wire with a pointed end. The bow, foot-plate and pin-catch are made from another, separate piece of metal. The bow is a strip of square section. At the head-end it is bent over to form a loop to secure the pin-spring axis, which is of iron. The foot-plate consists of a rectangular sheet, formed by hammering flat the end of the bow. The pin-catch element is missing, but its end is a plano-convex-section wire which is returned and wrapped six times round the base of the bow.

W of bow: 3mm; thickness: 2mm; pin: L: 40mm; D: 2mm; foot-plate: 6 x 20mm.

It is broken in two. The pin-spring is fragmentary and the pin-catch is missing.

The pin-catch has not been restored properly and a fragment of it has been fixed to the foot-plate.

The main feature of this type of brooch is that its spring and pin are made of a separate piece of wire and the pin-spring axis is secured by a loop created by bending the head-end of the bow. They were made either of silver, or copper alloy.

According to Aibabin many brooches of this type were found in 3rd–4th-century cemeteries of the Chernyakhovsk culture and also in late Sarmatian burials of the 3rd–beginning of the 4th century.[1] According to Skripkin they appear in the second half of the 3rd century,[2] but Ambroz dates the pieces from the Caucasus and Volga regions into the 4th century.[3]

Brooches of this type were found e.g. in Budjeşti (Romania),[4] in the Lower Don region,[5] in Kislovodsk (south Russia),[6] in the Lower Volga region,[7] and in Sîntana de Mureş (Marosszentana, Romania).[8]

Comparative Bibliography
1   Aibabin below
2   Skripkin 1977, 102–3
3   Ambroz 1966, 52
4   Rikman 1975, 109, ill. 28:4 (Chernyakhovsk culture)
5   Bezuglov and Kopylov 1989, 176, ill. 2:4–6 (Sarmatian)
6   Kuznetsov 1990, 253, ill. 1:14–16 (Sarmatian)
7   Skripkin 1977, 102–103, ill. 3:10–17 (Sarmatian)
8   Bóna 1986a, 116, ill. 6:1–3 (Chernyakhovsk culture)

Plate 50

Appendix 1 - Provincial Roman

1:1

Cat. No. **93**

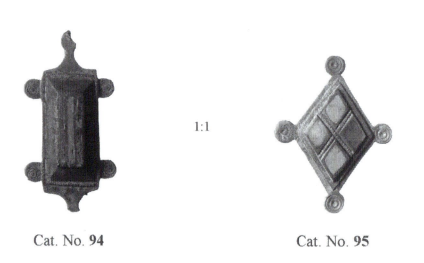

1:1

Cat. No. **94**   Cat. No. **95**

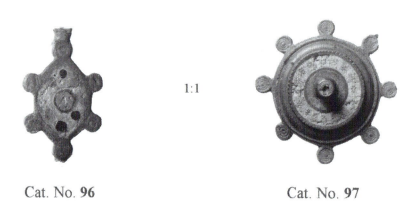

1:1

Cat. No. **96**   Cat. No. **97**

Plate 51

Appendix 1 - Provincial Roman

1:1

Cat. No. **98**

1:1

Cat. No. **99**

Plate 52

Appendix 1 - Late Antique and Sarmatian

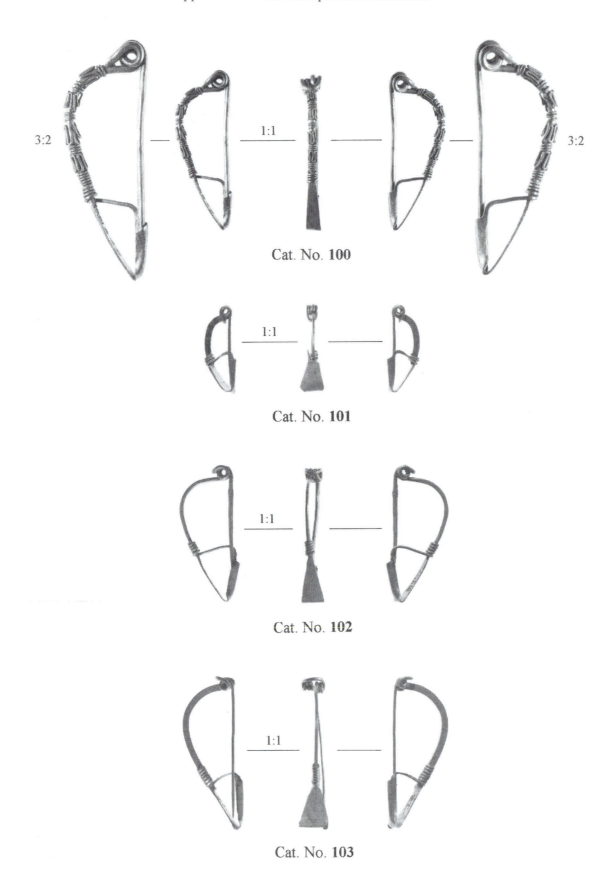

Cat. No. **100**

Cat. No. **101**

Cat. No. **102**

Cat. No. **103**

Plate 53

Appendix 1 - Late Antique and Sarmatian

1:1

Cat. No. **104**

Cat. No. **105**

1:1

Cat. No. **106**

1:1

1:1

Cat. No. **107**

Cat. No. **107**

Plate 54

Appendix 1 - Late Antique and Sarmatian

1:1

Cat. No. **108**

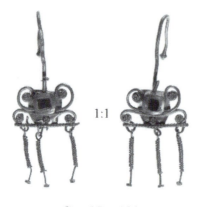

1:1

Cat. No. **109**

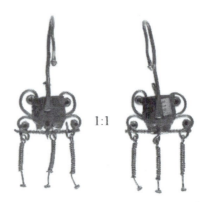

1:1

Cat. No. **109**

1:1

Cat. No. **110**

Plate 55

Appendix 1 - Late Antique and Sarmatian

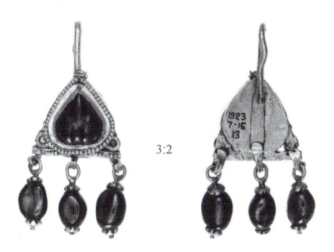

3:2

Cat. No.111

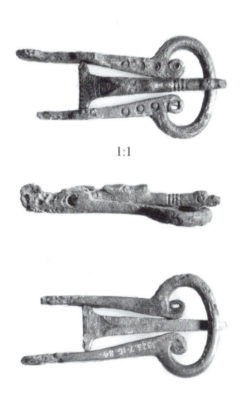

1:1

Cat. No. 112

Plate 56

Appendix 1 - Late Antique and Sarmatian

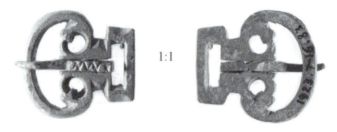

1:1

Cat. No. **113**

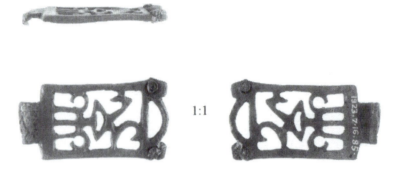

1:1

Cat. No. **114**

1:1

Cat. No. **115**

Plate 57

Appendix 1 - Late Antique and Sarmatian

1:1

Cat. No. 116

Plate 58

Appendix 1 - Late Antique and Sarmatian

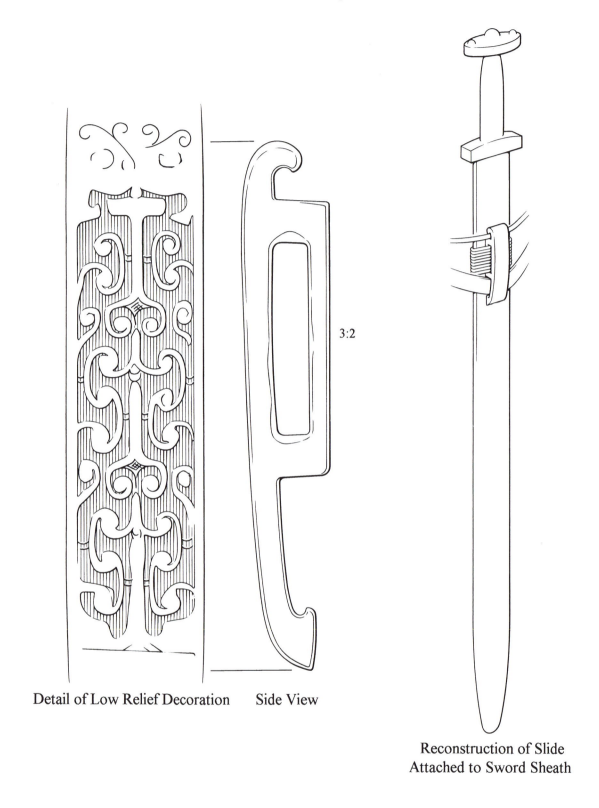

3:2

Detail of Low Relief Decoration   Side View

Reconstruction of Slide
Attached to Sword Sheath

Cat. No. **116** - continued

Plate 59

Appendix 1 - Late Antique and Sarmatian

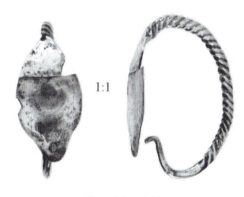

Cat. No. **117**

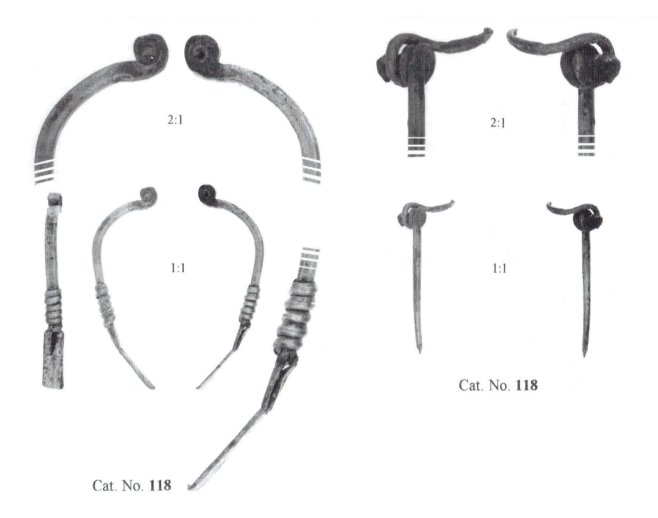

Cat. No. **118**

Cat. No. **118**

Appendix 2

Other early material

119   Pendant (Pl. 60)
Single piece of composite construction.
Silver lunate pendant decorated with three gold studs.
1st century?
Silver, gold
Prov.: Kerch, Krym (Crimea), Ukraine – 1893
Inv. no. GR 1969,11-1.1 – transferred to Greek and Roman Department in 1969
Old Inv. no. 1923,7-16,38   Old cat. no. 160
Size: 31 x 27mm   Weight: 5g

The pendant is cast and of flattened rectangular section, narrowing towards the terminals. There is a gold (or gilt-silver?) stud soldered to each terminal and to the centre, where the suspension loop is attached.
The suspension loop is oval and of flat, rectangular section.
The surface of the pendant is very corroded.

120   Coil (Pl. 60)
Single piece.
Silver coil decorated with granules and S-scrolls.
c. 400 BC?
Silver
Prov.: Olbia (Mikolayiv), Ukraine
Inv. no. GR 1969,11-1.2 – transferred to Greek and Roman Department in 1969
Old Inv. no. 1923,7-16,75   Old cat. no. 317
Size: 30 x 22mm   Weight: 14.64g

The coil is a double spiral of oval shape, made of a silver wire of circular section. Both ends have a cylindrical silver strip soldered on to support the decoration. Each is decorated with a soldered-on rim of beaded wire followed by opposed pairs of S-scrolls and a similar beaded wire below. Each terminal consists of a pyramid of granules, soldered on. (D of wire: 4mm).

There are two pairs of gold earrings of this type in the Hermitage, one found in Kerch (Crimea),[1] and the other pair said to be from Kyme.[2] The earrings from Nymphaion (Crimea, Ukraine) are also similar.[3] According to Silantyeva 'there were probably several centres of production of this type, including one in the North Pontic region'.[4]

Comparative bibliography
1   Williams and Ogden 1994, 152, ill. 93
2   Silantyeva 1976, 126, ill. 3b, 95, ill. 47
3   Vickers 1979, pl. 11c
4   Silantyeva op. cit. , 123–127

121   Coil (Pl. 60)
Single piece.
Silver coil, similar to cat. no. 120 above.
c. 400 BC?
Silver
Prov.: Olbia (Mikolayiv), Ukraine
Inv. no. GR 1969,11-1.3 – transferred to Greek and Roman Department in 1969
Old Inv. no. 1923,7-16,76   Old cat. no. 317
Size: 30 x 20mm   Weight: 12.79g

Similar construction, shape and decoration to cat. no. 120 above, except it is slightly more open. It is possibly its pair. (D of wire: 4mm).
One of the two terminals is missing. The object has been damaged by a cleaning agent.

122   Coil
Single piece.
Siver coil decorated with patterned strip of silver and pyramid of granules.
c. 400 BC?
Silver
Prov.: Olbia (Mikolayiv), Ukraine
Inv. no. GR 1969,11-1.4 – transferred to Greek and Roman Department in 1969   Old Inv. no. 1923,7-16,77   Old cat. no. 318

Size: 23 x 18mm   Weight: 8.65g

Similar to the coils above, but slightly smaller and with different decoration. Both ends have a soldered-on, cylindrical silver strip decorated with two lines of transverse grooves all round and a median rib between them. To each end is soldered a pyramidal terminal of granules. (D of wire: 4mm).
One of the two terminals is missing.

123   Coil (Pl. 60)
Single piece.
Silver coil, similar to cat. nos 120 and 121 above.
c. 400 BC?
Silver
Prov.: Olbia (Mikolayiv), Ukraine
Inv. no. GR 1969,11-1.5 – transferred to Greek and Roman Department in 1969   Old Inv. no. 1923,7-16,78   Old cat. no. unknown
Size: L: 27mm   Weight: 3.39g

Construction, shape and decoration are very similar to cat. nos 120 and 121 above, except it is made of a thinner wire. The pattern of decoration is slightly different: it consists of a plain wire rim with single S-scrolls below, and a pyramid of granules. (D of wire: 3mm).
Approximately half of the coil is missing.

124   Coil (Pl. 60)
Single piece.
Silver coil decorated with granules and beaded wire.
c. 400 BC?
Silver
Prov.: Olbia (Mikolayiv), Ukraine
Inv. no. GR 1969,11-1.6 – transferred to Greek and Roman Department in 1969   Old Inv. no. 1923,7-16,79   Old cat. no. unknown
Size: 26.5 x 18mm   Weight: 3.9g

Silver coil with the ends decorated differently from **cat. nos 120–123** above. All that remains of the pattern of beaded wires and granules is soldered directly onto the wire. To it is soldered a pyramidal terminal of granules. (D of wire: 2.5mm).
One end of the coil is missing, the wire is damaged, and the decoration is fragmentary.

125   Armlet (Pl. 61)
Single piece.
Silver armlet of circular section.
4th century BC?
Silver
Prov.: Olbia (Mikolayiv), Ukraine
Inv. no. GR 1969,11-1.7 – transferred to Greek and Roman Department in 1969   Old Inv. no. 1923,7-16,80   Old cat. no. 319
Size: D: 51mm   Weight: 13.75g

The armlet has a circular section tapering towards the ends. It is constructed of two parts: a solid silver core of wire and a strip wound round it. The strip is constructed of four wires soldered alongside each other. (D at the centre: 7mm, at the ends: 3mm).
The armlet is fragmentary.

126   Amulet (Pl. 61)
Single piece.
c.1350–1250 BC   Egyptian – 18th to 19th Dynasties
Quartzite
Prov.: Chersonesus (Hersonès), Krym (Crimea), Ukraine – 1908?
Inv. no. 1923,7-16,93   Old cat. no. 275
Size: 40 x 18mm   Weight: 5.1g
Unpublished

Amulet called a *tit* or Girdle of Isis. It is in the form of a standing human figure with carved features. The back is flat. There is a suspension loop at the top.
The suspension loop is broken.
According to a later note in the register: 'Examined by Dr. F.A. Bannister, Dept of Mineralogy, Brit. Mus. Nat. Hist., Nov. 1946, and substance identified as quartzite.

According to Carol Andrews, Department of Egyptian Antiquities in the British Museum: 'An Egyptian funerary amulet called the *tit* or Girdle of Isis. It takes the form of a loop of material from whose bound lower end hangs a long divided sash flanked by two folded loops, perhaps representing a cloth worn during menstruation. Chapter 156 of the Egyptian *Book of the Dead* prescribed that this amulet be made from red jasper, the colour of the blood of the goddess Isis, but any similarly coloured material, such as red quartzite, was an acceptable substitute. According to Chapter 156 if a *tit* was placed on the neck of the mummy 'the power of Isis will be the protection of his body'.[1]

Comparative bibliography

1 Andrews 1994, 44–45

127 Figure of a hare (Pl. 61)

'Gold embossed figure of a hare, oval outline' according to the register. Present location of the object within the British Museum is untraced.
Prov.: 'Tertre Coul Obas, Kerch' according to register, i.e. Kuloba ('tertre' is French for 'mound' or 'barrow')
'1st century B.C.' (register)
Inv. no. 1923,7-16,1
Size: L: 12.5mm

128 Figure of an animal (Pl. 61)

Single piece
Gold figure of an animal (horse ?)
3rd century BC   Scythian
Gold
Prov.: Maikop (south Russia) – 1909
Inv. no. 1923,7-16,95   Old cat. no. 95
Size: 17 x 19mm   H: 3mm   Weight: 6.7g

Gold figure of an animal cast in low relief. The back is plain and slightly concave. There is a cast attachment loop on the back. (Thickness of loop: 3mm).

Late material, 9th–13 centuries AD

129 Cross (Pl. 62)

Single piece of composite construction.
Gold pendant cross decorated with filigree wires and a central, circular, amethyst cabochon inlay.
12th century?   Byzantine
Gold, amethyst
Prov.: Cherson (Hersonès), Krym (Crimea), Ukraine – 1895
Inv. no. 1923,7-16,89   Old cat. no. 33
Size: L: 46mm   W: 37.5mm   Weight: 5.4g

The cross is constructed of three gold sheets, each bent to form a cylinder. A central, vertical cylinder supports the soldered-on arms at either side. Each arm of the cross is decorated on the whole of its surface with four longitudinal zones decorated with two concentric, filigree wire rings that are soldered on separately. Between each zone is a filigree wire soldered on. There are two further filigree wires soldered around the end of each arm of the cross: one running across the last row of rings, the second one along the end of each cylinder. Five plain wires are attached equidistant from each other to the end of each arm of the cross. Both ends of each of these wires are bent to form a loop, and are hooked into either filigree wire mentioned above. They are also soldered to the surface of the cross. Each arm of the cross terminates in an openwork basket of bent, plain wires in the form of a hemisphere. Around the top of each hemisphere is soldered a ring of filigree wire. The cross is further decorated with a central, circular amethyst cabochon within a cylindrical collet. The collet is a single strip of gold notched around its upper edge, soldered on where the arms of the cross meet. (D of each arm: 5.5mm, H of collet: 2.5mm, D of cabochon: 4.5mm, thickness of filigree wires: 2mm, thickness of plain wires: 8mm).

The suspension loop of the pendant is soldered onto the terminal of the top arm of the cross. It is a strip of gold bent circular with the ends overlapping. (D of loop: 2.5mm).

Some wires, especially around the ends, are missing. Otherwise it is in good condition.

130 Cross (Pl. 62)

Single piece of composite construction.
The obverse of a cast, silver reliquary pectoral cross, decorated with niello and five busts in relief.
12th century?   Byzantine

Silver
Prov.: Cherson (Hersonès), Krym (Crimea), Ukraine – 1908
Inv. no. 1923,7-16,94   Old cat. no. 276
Size: L: 58mm   W: 39mm   thickness: 2.5mm   Weight: 11.77g

This half of the cross is cast in one piece. It is flat and rectangular in section, and has rectangular arms, each with a circular end. The end of each arm and the centre of the cross are decorated with a circular, cast bust in relief, each within a narrow, circular rib border. There is a small lobe projecting from either side of this circular border, at the end of each arm. Between the busts the cross is decorated with geometrical niello ornament. (D of circular fields of bust reliefs: 11mm).

The back is plain with a narrow, raised edge all around.

Traces of the cast loop attachment are on the top, projecting from the rib border of the uppermost bust.

There is also a cast hinge attachment at the bottom of the pendant. It consists of a pair of lugs, each perforated through its centre to secure a rod, which holds the remains of the reverse side of the cross.

Damaged at the top. The niello is hardly visible. The reverse side is missing.

131 Earrings (Pl. 63)

A pair, each of composite construction.
Silver earrings with bead pendants decorated with twisted wires and granulation. The hoop is enriched with spherical beads.
9th–11th century.
Silver
Prov.: unknown, but found in 1893 according to register.
Inv. no. 1923,7-16,114 and 115   Old cat. no. 157
Percentage of silver: large sphere of no. 114: 95   hoop: 96
      no. 115: 95
Size: no. 923,7-16,114   L: 60mm overall   Weight: 4.75g
      no. 1923,7-16,115   L: 56mm   Weight: 4.48g
Unpublished

The earring hoop is made of a circular-section wire with pointed end. It is decorated at the top with a small, hollow bead capped by a granule. The hoop is further decorated with a similar bead pierced by a D-sectioned wire, which also encircles another small bead pierced by the earring hoop. All these small beads are constructed of two hollow hemispheres. (D of hoop: 21mm, thickness: 1.5mm, D of beads: 6mm).

The pendant is a large bead made of two hollow hemispheres. The join of the two halves is covered by three horizontal strips of twisted wire. A circlet of similar twisted wire is soldered at the top and bottom of the bead. There are granules soldered to this wire forming a terminal at the bottom, and in a circular arrangement at the top. The pendant is attached to the hoop by four columns each consisting of two granules, the tops of which are soldered to the bead of the hoop. Each column is enriched with a ring of circular-section wire soldered to the middle, between the granules. (D of bead: 13mm, thickness of twisted wires: 0.5mm, D of granules: 2mm).

There is a blob of solder stuck on the hoop of no. 1923,7-16,115 and two small beads are missing from the same earring. The bead at the top of no. 1923,7-16,114 is repaired with soft solder.

The original photograph of the collection does not show these earrings.

Similar earrings of gold and silver were found in the North Caucasus area (in Kuban, Lizgor, Kumbulta, and Makhchesk).[1]

Comparative Bibliography

1 Uvarova 1900, 222–3, 260; pls XLVIII:5, LXXXII:5; 6, LXXXIX:22, CVII:5; 6, CIX:3 – all said to be in the collection of Uvarova

132 Earrings (Pl. 63)

A pair, each of composite construction.
Copper hoop with shell-shaped bead enriched with a gilt-silver overlay and repoussé decoration.
11th–13th century
Gilt-silver, impure copper
Prov.: Caucasus area – 1909
Inv. no. 1923,7-16,96 and 97   Old cat. no. 283
Percentage of silver: no. 6 gilding: 22 no. 7 inside: 67
Size: no. 96: 38 x 24mm   Weight: 4.52g;
      no. 97: 23 x 20mm   Weight: 3.16g
Unpublished

The hoop consists of a circular copper wire of circular section. One of its ends is bent to form a hook; the other is slightly pointed and is either corroded, or broken off (remains of a hook-and-eye fastening?).

Each bead is made of two hollow shells of impure copper onto which is pressed a gilt-silver overlay. It is decorated with triangular groups of repoussé circles on the surface, and a pseudo-filigree wire border. There is a threefold pseudo-filigree wire around each perforation where the hoop passes through the pendant, and a double wire of the same type masks the join around the centre of the shell, one around the edge of each half.

(Size of bead: D: 21mm; W: 20mm; D of circle motifs: 2.5mm; W of filigree: 0.7mm; D of hoop: 20mm).

No. 1923,7-16,97 is fragmentary and its hoop is missing.

The original photograph of the collection shows no. 923,7-16,97 with a hoop.

A very similar pair of earrings has been found at Kerch.[1]

Comparative bibliography

1   OIAK 1906, 155-156, ill. 311a-b

133   Armlets (Pl. 64)
Two Penannular silver armlets made of twisted wires.
12th–13th century?
Silver.
Prov.: unknown; according to register found in 1894.
Inv. no. 1923,7-16,117 and 118   Old cat. no. 156
Percentage of silver: no. 117: 89   no. 118: 96
Size: no. 923,7-16,117: 58 x 49mm   Weight: 22.58g
        no. 923,7-16,118: 54 x 51mm   Weight: 21.03g
Unpublished

Each piece is made from a single wire bent double, and twisted together with another wire to form a triple-twisted wire. Both ends are bent and flattened into circular terminals, which are decorated with a line of punched dots along the central line of each wire. Each end of the third wire is clearly visible within the loop.

Thickness of the wires: three together: 5.5mm; each: 2.5mm; D of terminals: 16mm.

Both are damaged.

The original photograph does not show these armlets.

Similar bracelets were found in the towns of Kievan Rus. Sedova dated them to the 12–13th century.[1]
Makarova gives a typology of this kind of bracelet.[2]
Kepeska gives a bibliography for pieces listed from Macedonia, Serbia and Bulgaria.[3]
For armlets of this type, see also articles by Korzukhina,[4] Levashova[5] and Ryndina.[6]

Comparative bibliography

1   Sedova 1981, 97, pl. 34:4, 8
2   Makarova 1986, 33–8, ills 13–14
3   Kepeska 1995, 35, 62–62, ill. 16b:8–12, pl. VI:38/8–12
4   Korzukhina 1954, 62–71
5   Levashova 1967, 207–52
6   Ryndina 1963

134   Finger-ring (Pl. 64)
Single piece.
Copper-alloy finger-ring with an oval bezel engraved with a pentagram.
10th century.
Copper alloy
Prov.: Kerch, Krym (Crimea), Ukraine – 1909
Inv. no. 1923,7-16,70   Old cat. no. 284
Size: 20 x 21.5mm   Weight: 2.81g

The bezel and hoop are made of a single piece cast and hammered to shape. The bezel is oval. It is decorated in the centre with an engraved pentagram with a carved dot at each tip. There are smaller carved dots all around the edge of the bezel.

The hoop is a flat strip decorated with engraved, transverse lines.
(Size of bezel: L: 13.5mm; W: 10mm; H: 2mm; hoop: W: 3mm; thickness: 1-2mm).

135   Finger-ring fragment (Pl. 64)
Single piece
Silver hoop of a finger-ring with one expanding shoulder remaining.
Silver
Prov.: Kerch, Krym (Crimea), Ukraine – 1900

Inv. no. 1923,7-16,72   Old cat.no. 287
Percentage of silver: 91
Size: 20 x 10mm   Weight: 1.37g
Unpublished

The fragmentary hoop consists of a band of rectangular section expanding at the shoulder, which has two engraved V-shapes, one inside the other. All that remains of the bezel is part of a plain, thin plate, integral with the hoop. (Thickness of hoop: 2mm; thickness of shoulder: 1mm).

The original photograph of the collection does not show this object.

Objects of unknown date

136   Mount or buckle-plate? (Pl. 65)
Single piece of composite construction.
Trapezoidal plate.
Silver, copper alloy.
Prov.: unknown
Inv. no. 1923,7-16,145   Old cat. no. unknown
Percentage of silver: 96
Size: 32 x 41mm   Weight: 11.6g
Unpublished

Trapezoidal copper-alloy plate with an applied silver sheet on the front. The edge of the latter is wrapped around the edges of the plate. There are three attachment shanks in a triangular arrangement soldered onto the back. (Sides: 32mm, 9.5mm, 2 x 41mm).

The silver sheet is imperfect.

137   Bindings or mounts? (Pl. 65)
Three.
4th–6th century.
Silver.
Prov.: unknown
Inv. no. 1923,7-16,146 to 148   Old cat. no. unknown
Percentage of silver: no. 46: 90   no. 47: 94   no. 48: 90
Size: no. 146: 31 x 25.5mm   Weight: 1.73g
        no. 147: 29 x 26mm   Weight: 1.53g
        no. 148: L: 23mm; 18mm surviving   Weight: 0.9g
Unpublished

Each is a narrow silver strip bent to form a square frame with overlapping ends. (W of strip: 2mm; thickness: 1mm).
No. 1923,7-16,148 is broken in two.

138   Bead (Pl. 65)
Single piece.
Oval, perforated.
Agate.
Prov.: Unknown
Inv. no. 1923,7-16,150   Old cat. no. unknown
Size: 12 x 25mm   Weight: 4.5mm
Unpublished

Elongated oval with polished surface. It has been perforated longitudinally, drilled from both ends, and the two holes are slightly misaligned where they meet. (D of perforation: 2.5mm).

Objects without numbers, apparently Berthier-Delagarde Collection

a. Base silver penannular loop. (23mm).
b. Bronze fragment of wire, bent one end. (15mm).
c. Bronze overlaid with silver. Silver rivet. (L: 17mm); from 1923,7-16,71?
d. Two silver fragments with filigree.

Plate 60

Appendix 2 - Early Material

1:1

Cat. No. **119**

1:1

Cat. No. **120**

1:1

Cat. No. **121**

1:1

Cat. No. **122**

1:1

Cat. No. **123**

1:1

Cat. No. **124**

Plate 61

Appendix 2 - Early Material

Cat. No. **125**

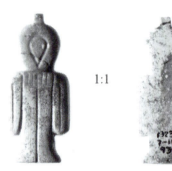

Cat. No. **126**

Cat. No. **127**

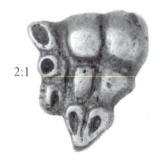   

Cat. No. **128**

Plate 62

Appendix 2 - Late Material

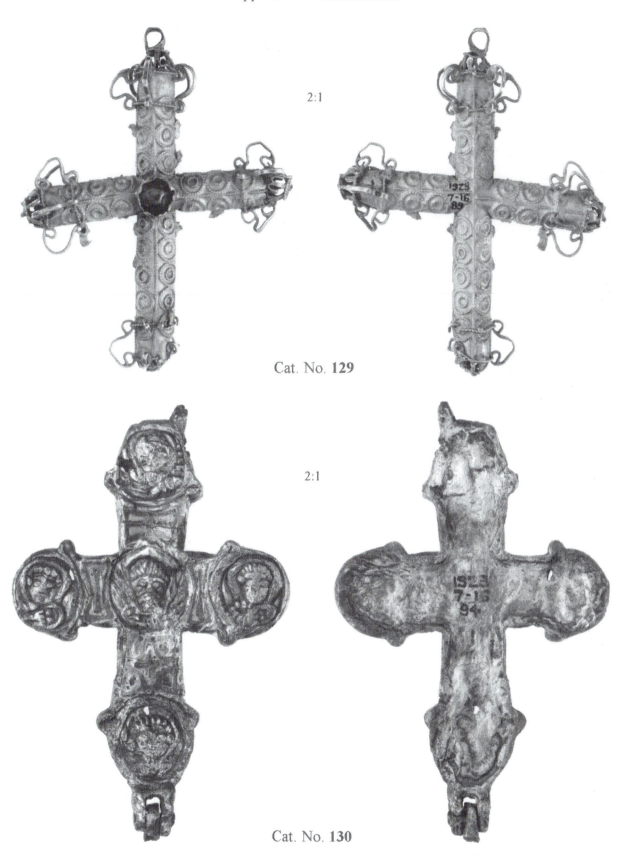

2:1

Cat. No. **129**

2:1

Cat. No. **130**

Plate 63

Appendix 2 - Late Material

2:1

1:1

1:1

2:1

1:1

Cat. No. **131**

1:1

Cat. No. **132**

Plate 64

Appendix 2 - Late Material

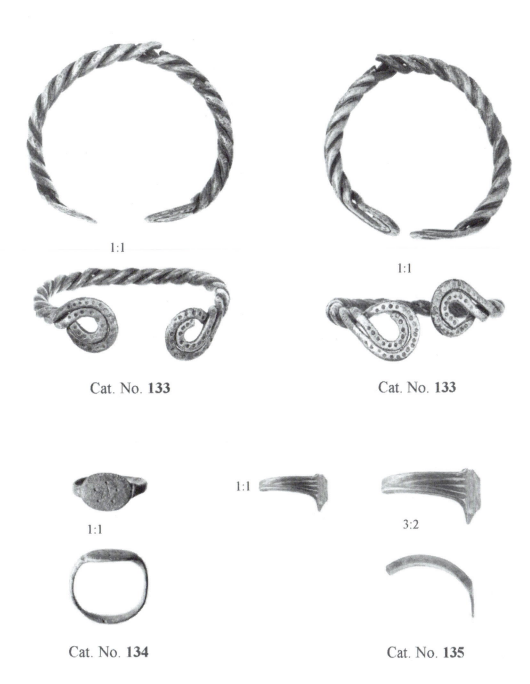

1:1

1:1

Cat. No. **133**

Cat. No. **133**

1:1

1:1

3:2

Cat. No. **134**

Cat. No. **135**

Plate 65

Objects of Unknown Date

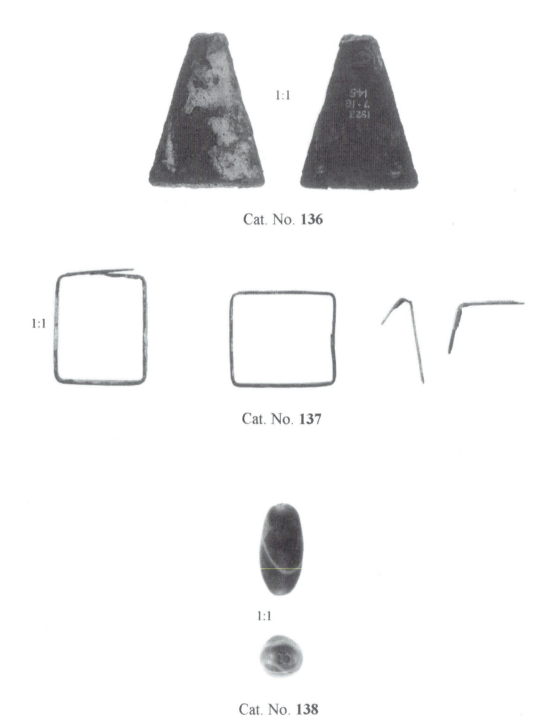

Cat. No. **136**

Cat. No. **137**

Cat. No. **138**

Commentary on Select Items and Groups in the Collection

Aleksander Aibabin

The Sarmatian and Alan objects

The Berthier-Delagarde Collection contains an interesting group of artefacts dating between the 1st and 4th centuries AD that are typical of the Sarmatians and Alans of the northern Black Sea coast. These tribes were neighbours who lived together in Bosporus and shared an identical polychrome style of jewellery.

One of the most important pieces in this group, and indeed of the whole collection, is of star quality: a jade scabbard-slide ornamented with scroll-work (**cat. no. 116, Pls 57–58**). It is said to be from the Kuban area, presumably from a Sarmatian burial, and was shown to be of Chinese manufacture by Rostovtsev, demonstrating the immense distances that prestige objects travelled across the steppe.[1] These slides are of a long-lived type and found on swords from Sarmatian cemeteries of the 2nd to 3rd centuries,[2] occurring also in a grave of the second half of the 5th at Voskhod kolkhoz.[3] A similar slide was found together with other objects on the Messaksudi estate, Kerch, in 1918, and is now exhibited in the Musée des Antiquités Nationales, St.-Germain-en-Laye. The finds were identified as a grave assemblage of the second half of the 3rd century by Rostovtzeff.[4] In addition it has been shown recently that Messaksudi also sold an oval buckle with a long tongue of Variant 3.[5] These buckles occurred in the Crimea from the last quarter of the 4th century[6] and other buckles from the grave complex (with an attachment-plate hinged by means of a folded flap) were made in the earlier half of the century,[7] suggesting that Kazanski's dating of the assemblage to the last 3rd of the 4th century is most likely correct.[8]

A pair of garnet-inlaid gold earrings (**cat. no. 109, Pl. 54**) is similar in construction, decoration and technique to those found in Sarmatian graves of the second half of the 1st century, in the northern Black Sea coastal steppe.[9] A much later piece, a temporal-pendant from Kerch (**cat. no. 1, Pl.1**), has a triangular, gold sheet base, decorated with garnet and green glass cabochons, twisted and beaded wire, granulation, and three pendants on chains. A similarly-decorated piece in the Diergardt Collection has been ascribed to the 4th century.[10] The period of manufacture of these pendants may be established from the burial found at the village of Novaya Norka, in 1887, which contained an example with conical pendants that is close to the published pieces in technique and style of ornament.[11] The burial is dated by a Type II profiled brooch to the second half of the 3rd century.[12] A silver earring with a hoop of twisted wire and a hammered, decorative oval plate (**cat. no. 117, Pl.59**) is similar to those from Sarmatian burials of the second half of the 3rd/beginning of the 4th century from the Danube and Dnieper steppes.[13]There is a further example from a contemporary grave in the Chernyakhovo-culture cemetery at Kaborga IV.[14] These earrings are a simpler variant of gold and silver types with cornelian and coloured glass inlays on the

plates from female Sarmatian graves of the same period in the Don,[15] Crimean[16] and Danube regions.[17]

Another remarkable aspect of the collection is the large number of gold bow brooches. While copper-alloy types are common, gold examples are rare. The gold brooch with a wire-enriched bow (**cat. no. 100, Pl. 52**) belongs to Ambroz's variant 15/I–5,[18] which is typical of late 2nd/early 3rd-century Sarmatian burials.[19] The three gold bow brooches with rectangular-section bows, short spring spirals, and triangular feet (**cat. nos 101–103, Pl. 52**), are similar to examples of Ambroz's Variant 15/II-1, dating to the latter half of the 2nd and the 3rd centuries.[20]

The silver bow brooch (**cat. no. 118, Pl. 59**) belongs to a separate, Dacian group of Variant I, on the basis of the attachment of the pin-spring axis to the bow.[21] Brooches of the same type with various forms of foot-plate existed from the beginning of the 4th century, occurring in both Chernyakhovo-culture cemeteries[22] and Sarmatian burials,[23] and one was found at Sovkhozne (Sovkhoz no. 10), grave 55 (**Map B: 4**), associated with a coin of 305–311.[24]

Two openwork, cast copper-alloy attachment-plates from belt buckles are decorated with Sarmatian emblems (**cat. nos. 114–115, Pl. 56**). Almost all the analogous pieces have been found in Kerch, leading Shkorpil and Solomonik to assume that mounts of this type were made in Bosporus in the 1st to 3rd centuries.[25] In a grave at Chersonesus a buckle with a similarly-decorated attachment-plate was found with a coin struck between 180–192[26] and at Chernaya Rechka, vault 35,[27] one was associated with brooches of the second half of the 3rd century.[28] Belt-ends and buckles with Sarmatian emblems can probably be dated to the latter half of the 2nd and the 3rd centuries and appear all over the area of Sarmatian settlement, particularly in the Bosporan Kingdom.The emblems on serially-produced buckles are probably a general feature, while those on gold objects and harness mounts may have a more personalised significance. Copper alloy buckles (**cat. nos. 48–49, 54–55, 57–58, Pls 28–29**) (**nos. 130–135**), and silver examples (**cat. no. 44, Pl. 26**) (**no. 123**), with cast, oval loops expanding to the centre and flat tongues with rectangular, or oval, attachment-plates are similar to those from Sarmatian burials of the 3rd century in the Crimea, and the Don and Kuban regions.[29] The copper-alloy buckle (**cat. no. 47, Pl. 28**) is of a somewhat different form typical of the first half of the 4th century, although also found in graves of the second half.[30]

Another significant group in the collection is an assemblage of horse harness-mounts with repoussé decoration and collared glass or stone settings (**cat. nos. 31–43, Pls 21–6**). Mounts of similar type were found at Kerch in the graves of 1837 and 1841,[31] in a burial mound of the second half of the 3rd/first half of the 4th centuries in the town of Azov[32] and at Kishpek.[33] Similar mounts also appear on buckles from Chersonesus[34] from graves on the Messaksudi estate at Kerch,[35] from burials at Timashevskaya, of the second half of the 3rd century,[36] and from the Stavropol region.[37] There are also temporal-pendants, bracelets and a buckle from contemporary graves in the Dnieper, Don, and Kuban regions.[38] Comparable material comes from Crimean graves of the first group such as Chernaya Rechka 2, 3, 35 and 45; from Druzhne (Druzhnoye), vault 1 and grave 24 (with a coin of 251)[39] and Belbek III, grave 2.[40] The grave at Kishpek was dated by the author to the Hunnic period, that is to the end of the 4th to 5th centuries, and is an assemblage of major importance which was well excavated, but poorly published. Ambroz and Kuznetzov dated it to the second half of the 3rd/beginning of the 4th century,[41] but on the basis of its buckles of Keller type A it belongs rather to the first half of the 4th century.[42] Ambroz ascribed its decorative details to the early polychrome style, which appeared in the Roman provinces in the second half of the 3rd century.[43] It should be noted that prototypes of the Kishpek-type mounts were found in 1986 in a Sarmatian grave dated to the end of the first/ beginning of the 2nd centuries, in a burial mound on the outskirts of the town of Azov. The oval gold mounts from Azov, like mounts nos. 17 and 19, are each decorated with a large, red, oval chalcedony (cornelian) with bevelled edges and such objects probably combined elements from both Late-Roman and early-Alanic jewellery traditions.[44] In conclusion it should be noted that such ornaments and horse harness-mounts of the second half of the 3rd–4th centuries enable us to advance stronger arguments for the existence of an early-Alanic polychrome style in Bosporus and the North Caucasus. The appearance of such objects, and the fashion for them, may be connected with the alliance between the Roman Empire and the Bosporan Kingdom.

The copper-alloy horse bridle-ring (**cat. no. 60, Pl. 30**) appears on an archival photograph of the collection in the Crimea, supporting three small silver attachment mounts. Rings with such small mounts were found in burials of the second half of the 3rd century at Kerch,[45] and in a contemporary catacomb at Budyonovskaya Sloboda.[46] In the North Caucasus iron rings with small attachment mounts continued in use later.[47] Elongated mounts cut from thin silver sheet for use on horse-harness are similar to those from Sarmatian burials of the second to third centuries (**cat. nos. 63–69, Pls 31–32**) and are considered by some to be for funerary use.[48]

The Hunnic polychrome style and the Kerch vaults
Mounts and jewellery of gold and gilt silver abundantly decorated with garnet in the Berthier-Delagarde Collection are typical of the polychrome style which arose among the tribes of the Hunnic alliance, according to Werner and Ambroz. The old idea that the Huns caused great destruction in the Crimea is incorrect, and Bosporus, for instance, was occupied by them. The Kerch tombs contained the bodies of the Bosporan royalty or elite, who had adopted elements of Hunnic fashion and also had access to Late-Roman imports, such as glass vessels, silver plates and costume accessories. Items like shoe-buckles do not, therefore, serve as ethnic identifiers. The main distinction between the older Bosporan style of jewellery, with individual inlays (often cabochon garnets, or glass paste in single collets), and the new style is the innovation of multiple flat inlays

mounted in cloisonné cell-work. It is therefore significant that the Hunnic occupation of the Crimea occurred after they had reached the middle Danube (see below).

A gold buckle with an attachment-plate inlaid with a garnet (**cat. no. 72, Pl. 34**) is similar to the buckle (**cat. no. 47, Pl. 28**) in the form of its loop and tongue. Buckles with inlaid plates of similar type have been found in Hunnic-period graves in the north-western Black Sea coast, the North Caucasus and the Urals.[49] A gold buckle with a faceted circular loop, tongue, and plate inlaid with garnets (**cat. no. 70, Pl. 33**), and a buckle-tongue grooved at each end (**cat. no. 71, Pl. 34**), are typologically close to objects of 5th-century date.[50] These and the other Hunnic-period pieces in the collection lack context and associations. However, previous scientific excavations provide rich data that help establish the cultural milieu of closely related pieces. Zasetskaya attributes the Kerch vaults 154/1904 and 165/1904, in which buckles of the same type as those of the Berthier-Delagarde Collection were found, to the end of the 4th and first half of the 5th century.[51] These two family burial-places contained, respectively, 11 and 10 skeletons.[52] At first the dead were interred on ledges, and later on the floor.

On the central ledge of vault 154/1904, with skeletons 5 and 6, were found circular buckles of Variant 3 of the last quarter of the 4th to first half of the 5th century.[53] On a ledge to the left in burials 7 and 8 were glasses with blue spots of types I-B and I-E,[54] which can be assigned to much the same period,[55] contemporary circular buckles of Variant 3,[56] a fragment of a sheet brooch with settings for inlays,[57] and gold spacer-tubes.[58] On the right-hand ledge in burials 9, 10 and 11 were found a glass with blue spots of I-B Type[59] from the first half of the 5th century,[60] gold spacer-tubes, and earrings with amber and cornelian inlays.[61] On the floor in burial 1 were found circular buckles of Variant 3,[62] while in burial 2, which overlay the first one, were two sheet brooches with feet of Variant 21/IIAA,[63] a gold wreath with an impression of a coin of Valentinian I (**364–375**), spacer-tubes and mounts,[64] and a large buckle with an attachment-plate decorated with a rosette.[65] In burial 3 were circular buckles of Variants 3[66] and 5, made in the first half of the 5th century.[67] In burial 4 were a large buckle with an animal head on the tongue of Variant 1[68] and a circular buckle of Variant 3.[69]

On the central ledge of vault 165/1904 lay burial 4[70] with a sheet brooch of Variant IBB,[71] a brooch similar to Danubian examples from graves of period D2 (**410–440**),[72] and a bone pyx. In burial 5 were a gold wreath decorated with an impression of a coin of Sauromatus II (**173/174–210/211**),[73] circular buckles of Variant 3[74] and 5,[75] buckles with imitations of the animal heads on the tongues of Variant 2,[76] and a saddle with bells.[77] On the right-hand ledge of burial 6 were sheet brooches of Variant 21/IIAA.[78] On the left-hand ledge of burial 9 was a circular buckle[79] of Variant 4 of the first half of the 5th century[80] and in burial 10 there were two sheet brooches of Variant 21/IIAA.[81] On the floor of burial 3 lay circular buckles of Variants 3 and 4,[82] belt-ends with turned-up edges,[83] and fragments of a pair of sheet brooches with appliqués of Smolín type.[84]

It is assumed that buckles with rosettes on the attachment-plates (**cf. cat. no. 76, Pl. 38**) were in use in the Danube region around 420–454,[85] or in period D2 of 410–440,[86] and sheet brooches of Variant 21/IIAA, with feet expanding at the top, in the first third of the 5th century,[87] or in period D2.[88] Two sheet brooches of Smolín type are dated by Werner and Ambroz to the second half of the 5th century,[89] and by Tejral to period D2/D3 of 430–455,[90] while Bierbrauer dates them to the first half of the 5th century.[91] Judging by the location of the burials similarly dated by the buckles, glasses, and brooches of Variants 21/IBB and 21/IIAA, interments began on the central ledges of both vaults. In vault 154 this took place at the end of the 4th or the beginning of the 5th century, and in vault 165 in the first quarter of the 5th century. During the first half of the 5th century burials were interred on side ledges. The latest burials were placed on the floor: in vault 154 at the beginning of the second half of the 5th century; and in vault 165 in the second half of the century. At Kerch a rosette-decorated Danubian buckle and brooches of Variant 21/ILAA were in use at least at the beginning of the second half of that century, and brooches of Smolín type were in use during its second half.

The necklace (**cat. no. 9, Pl. 4**) consists of gold spacers, garnet pendants and a biconical pendant set with a blue stone. Two similar spacers come from Luchyste (Luchistoye), vault 41 (**Map B: 16**), and a necklace of 11 spacers from Chernaya Rechka, vault 11/1980, together with a buckle with an oval loop, attachment-plate and long tongue, and red-slipped pottery of the first half of the 5th century. Others were found in Kerch, vault 154/1904 (burial 2), of the early second half of the century, with two sheet brooches of Variant 21/ILAA (according to Ambroz), and a buckle with a rosette-decorated attachment-plate.[92] Similar garnet pendants were found on a necklace from Maikop[93] with a 5th-century pendant in the form of a cicada.[94] The garnet-inlaid gold earring (no. 6) closely parallels those from Kerch, vault 154/1904, on the right-hand ledge of burial 9 of the first half of the century.[95]

Further exceptional Hunnic-period pieces include a gilt copper-alloy mount with polychrome inlays (**cat. no. 27, Pl. 19**), thought to be a belt-fitting with parallels at Kerch, Muslyumovo, and in the Diergardt Collection.[96] Another type of belt mount, with circular attachment-plate and suspension loop (**cat. no. 26, Pl. 18**), came into fashion at the beginning of the 5th century.[97] Other pieces, such as the garnet or glass-inlaid studs (**cat. nos 28–29, Pls 19–20**), may be of this period, but appear later, too.

The mid-Danubian connections

A small group of gold and garnet pieces in the Berthier-Delagarde Collection are unusual or unparalleled in the Crimea, but find analogies farther west. They include a gold oval brooch inlaid all over with garnets from Kerch (**cat. no. 14, Pl. 8**) which is unique in the Crimea. It may belong to a 5th-century group of south-Russian/Danubian brooches identified by Werner.[98] Gold lunate and tear-shaped pendants with garnet settings (**cat. nos 10–11, Pl. 6**) are dated to the second half of the century by analogy with an Ostrogothic burial at Gáva.[99] Parallels to the gold finger-rings with garnet-inlaid, geometric bezels soldered to sheet bases (**cat. nos 12–13, Pl. 7**) have not been found in the Crimea, but related examples occur in Gepid burials of the second half of the 5th century.[100]

A gilt-silver, garnet-inlaid, wheel-shaped brooch with trapezoid projections (**cat. no. 15, Pls 8–9**) was among the objects sold by A. Volgeninoff in 1923.[101] It is similar to brooches

thought by Werner to be 7th-century Frankish,[102] but, as noted by Andrási (Catalogue above), the best parallel is from the Danube region (unpublished). A pair of gold earrings have hoops of twisted wire and polyhedral beads inlaid with lozenge-shaped and triangular garnets (**cat. no. 7, Pl. 3**). Similar pieces appear in other museums[103] and have been found in Ostrogothic burials of the second half of the 5th/beginning of the 6th centuries.[104] They contrast with the local Crimean products and only one other example has been found in the Crimea, which must be seen as an import, perhaps from the mid-Danube region. Local forms of earring are represented in the collection, such as the garnet-set gold example with a smooth wire hoop most probably from Suuk-Su (**cat. no. 8, Pl. 3; Map B: 14**). In graves here[105] and at Luchyste (Luchistoye)[106] gold earrings with polyhedral beads inlaid with red and blue glass were associated with sheet brooches and eagle-headed buckles of the second half of the 6th and 7th centuries. At Luchyste some 20 gold examples were found and it was noted that, while the 6th-century pieces had garnet inlays, those of the 7th were inlaid with glass. A wider date range is provided by the gold earrings with smooth hoops and solid polyhedral beads in the collection (**cat. no. 6, Pl. 3**). This very simple cast form is a long-lasting type in the Crimea, where it is associated with grave-goods from the 5th to the first half of the 7th centuries.[107]

It is generally accepted that cicada brooches of the same type as that in the collection (**cat. no. 16, Pl. 10**) were worn in western Europe, the Balkans, and the Caucasus during the 5th to 6th centuries.[108] In the Crimea, however, they were in use from the mid-5th century to the beginning of the 7th and their appearance may be associated with the introduction of mid-Danubian elements by the Huns.[109] In addition to this influence on brooch styles, cast radiate-headed brooches of Variant 1 were manufactured in the Crimea using Danubian prototypes in the first half of the 6th century and brooches of Variant 2 in the second half of the 6th to the 7th centuries (see p.145 below).

A large silver buckle from Suuk-Su has a rhomboidal attachment-plate decorated with a four-petalled setting containing light-coloured glass (**cat. no. 82, Pls 43–4**). Its S-shaped scrolls and zoomorphic figures were retouched with a graver after casting. In its construction, method of attachment to the belt, and form and decoration of the loop and tongue it closely resembles eagle-headed buckles of south-Crimean type. Ambroz considered that south-western Crimean buckles of this type from Skalyste (Skalistoye), Suuk-Su, Aromatne (Aromat) (**Fig. 7: 3**), and Chufut-Kale (**Map B: 28, 21, and 24**), were the products of Crimean jewellers descended from Gepid craftsmen who had migrated to the peninsula, and he regarded their decoration as a much devolved variant of the mid-Danubian style.[110] The Crimean craftsmen used not only elements of Gepid style, such as animal heads, coloured inlays, and pecking eagles, but also motifs from Scandinavian animal Style I, including animal heads with gaping mouths at the bases of the attachment-plates and pairs of *couchant* animals at the terminals. Local jewellers used only the general outlines of this borrowed decoration, altering some minor details and greatly distorting others. The buckles have folded plates, not shorter than 30mm, at one end of the attachment-plates to secure the loops; i.e. the same length as on the attachment-plates of the eagle-headed, south-Crimean buckles of Variant V.

Ambroz considered this feature demonstrated the existence of these buckles in the second half of the 7th century.[111] At Chufut-Kale one was found with an eagle-headed buckle of Variant V in vault 7, while another was found at Skalyste associated with a buckle of that date in vault 288 (**Fig. 7: 1, 2, 4**).[112]

The chronology of select brooches and buckles

There is considerable discussion concerning the chronology of some types of Crimean brooches and buckles, which is reflected in the evident discrepancies between the dates ascribed to the same objects by western and eastern-European scholars. The situation is briefly summarised below.

There is a pair of radiate-headed brooches in the Berthier-Delagarde Collection with triple-knobbed, semi-circular head-plates and lozenge-shaped foot-plates (**cat. no. 21, Pl. 13**). They are garnet inlaid and decorated with cast, chip-carved, concentric rhomboidal patterns on the foot-plates, and scroll-work on the heads. Such brooches are divided into two variants according to the decorative techniques used. In the first part of the 6th century brooches of Variant 1 in the Danube region and Italy were chip-carved.[113] At Cherson, vault 14/1914, such brooches were associated with grave-goods of this period and examples from Kerch are to be similarly dated.[114] The decoration of Crimean Variant 2 brooches was retouched with a graver after casting and their later dating has been established by association in closed assemblages from the southern Crimea. At Suuk-Su burial 155 contained grave goods of the first quarter of the seventh century,[115] and at Luchyste (Luchistoye), vault 77 (skeleton 8), there was a buckle with a repoussé cross on its large rectangular attachment-plate (**Fig. 1: 1, 3**), which is characteristic of that century.[116] In the Crimea brooches of Variant 1 were probably made using Danubian prototypes in the first half of the 6th century, and brooches of Variant 2 were produced there in the second half of the 6th to the 7th centuries.

Another pair of silver brooches differ from the above in the scroll decoration of their foot-plates (**cat. no. 20, Pl. 12**). Kühn named them the Kerch-type.[117] Brooches of this type have been found mainly at Kerch, but also at Cherson, Suuk-Su, vault 162, Luchyste, vault 54 in burial 12 (**Fig. 2**), in the Dnieper region,[118] the Danube region, and Germany.[119] The Danubian prototypes of Kerch-type brooches were decorated with deep chip-carving and were made in the second half of the 5th and first half of the 6th centuries.[120] The controversy over the chronology of Kerch-type brooches is reviewed in one of my articles.[121] Ambroz stated that Kerch-type brooches came into fashion not earlier than the first half of the 6th century, remaining in use into the second half of the 7th and somewhat later.[122] Only three closed assemblages with Kerch-type brooches are known. At Kerch, grave 19, they were associated with a red-slipped bowl[123] of Hayes 3-type H (**Fig. 3: 5**)[124] and analogies to Form 3H from Greece are attributed both to the first half of the 6th century,[125] and also to its latter half.[126] At Suuk-Su, vault 162, and Luchyste, vault 54, in burial 12 (**Fig. 2**) these brooches were found with eagle-headed buckles,[127] which have rectangular attachment-plates cast with a bird's head, such as an eagle or falcon, on the terminal. They are divided according to ornament and size into the south-Crimean forms, known only in the south-west, and the Bosporan ones.

Silver buckles from south-western Crimea have massive loops with a row or two of cast, S-shaped scrolls and opposed, stylised animal heads, faceted tongues, and rectangular or trapezoidal attachment-plates with bird-headed terminals. The flap hingeing the loop to the plate is moulded and riveted, and a wide leather belt was inserted, secured by copper-alloy studs. These studs also connected it to copper-alloy strips behind for additional attachment. Onto the loop and tongue, around the edges of the attachment-plate, and on the eagle head, were soldered cylindrical settings inlaid with red and blue glass, garnet or cornelian. Sometimes animal figures were cast at the bases of the tongues. There are eight decorational variants of attachment-plate[128] and the buckles are divided into five variants according to the length of the folded attachment-flap: I - 10–14mm; II - 16–22mm; III - 23–27mm; IV - 28–30mm; V - 31–38mm (**Figs 4 and 5**).[129] Buckles of Variant I are dated by a coin of Justinian I (527–565) and by objects of the second half of the 6th century at Suuk-Su.[130] The period of buckles of Variant II is defined by the grave-groups from Suuk-Su, grave 77, with a coin of 597–602[131] and from grave 124 with large silver sheet brooches of Variant IIB-2, of the first half of the 7th century.[132] Buckles of Variant III from Suuk-Su, graves 61 and 89, were found together with sheet brooches of Variant IIB-1, of the first half of the 7th century, and at Luchyste, vault 10, layer 4, with sheet brooches of Variant IIB-2 (**Figs 3: 2, and 5: 1**).[133] Buckles of Variants IV and V, with long folded hinge-flaps, come from grave-groups with objects of the second half of the 7th century.[134] In vault 257 on the slope of Eski-Kermen (**Map B: 17**) one burial contained an eagle-headed buckle of Variant V with a pendant made from half a Byzantine gold coin of 629–641, and a bronze Byzantine cross of the second half of the century; the other burial contained a silver coin of 668–685.[135] As mentioned above, there were buckles of Variants IV and V in the upper layers of the multi-layer vaults 10 and 38 at Luchyste, and buckles of Variants II and III, with shorter folded flaps, in the lower layers.[136]

The radiate-headed brooches of Kerch type from Suuk-Su, vault 162, and Luchyste, vault 54, burial 12, are of interest since they were associated with eagle-headed buckles of Variant IV.[137] These brooches were probably used in Bosporus in the second half of the 6th and the first half of the 7th centuries, and in the south-western Crimea in the second half of the 7th century.

Gilt-silver brooches of Aquileia type (**cat. no. 19, Pl. 11**) are larger than the previous type. On both the head and foot-plates there are schematic running foliate scrolls, finished with a graver, and settings with red inlays. The foot is pierced by two holes and cast with knobs: an important feature of the Aquileia type, which is divided into three variants according to the decorative technique. Variant 1 includes brooches from the end of the 5th and the first half of the 6th century with deep chip-carved and punched decoration, found in Italy, France and the Danube region. Pecking birds cast on the sides of the foot-plate replace the knobs.[138] Variant 2 includes examples from the Berthier-Delagarde Collection, the Danube region,[139] and Luchyste, vault 77, on which the decoration is finished with a graver; and Variant 3 includes brooches from Kerch and the Kuban region with cast ornament.[140] Kühn dates brooches of Variants 2 and 3 to 450–550,[141] Werner to the first half of the 6th century,[142] and Ambroz to the second half of the 6th to the 7th centuries.[143] The brooches from Luchyste were found with a

7th-century silver buckle with a large rectangular attachment-plate decorated with a repoussé cross.[144] Examples of Variant 3 were found at Kerch with a B-shaped buckle of Variant 1-2, of around 550–650, on a ledge in vault 78/1907; also in vault 152/1904 in the upper layer, above the layer with a burial of the late 6th century; and, in vault 180, with a belt-set of the second half of the 7th century (**Fig. 3: 4**).[145] These data enable us to define the period of Aquileia-type brooches, Variants 2 and 3, as from the end of the 6th and the 7th centuries.

The silver-gilt buckles in the collection inlaid with either red glass (**cat. no. 80, Pl. 41**), or garnet (**cat. no. 81, Pl. 42**), should be included in a typological group of the Bosporan eagle-headed buckles. These are almost all from Kerch (**Fig. 6: 5–6**), with two from the slope of the Eski-Kermen plateau in highland Crimea, and are shorter than the south-Crimean ones, not exceeding 134mm in length. Their loops are decorated with rows of scrolls and the attachment-plates with cylindrical collets inlaid with almandine or red glass, which are imitated on some buckles by solid cylinders with engraved circles representing the inlays. The plate of one of the buckles is cast with a central rectangular opening, which is filled by a support for a cornelian-inlaid setting inserted from beneath. The plates of some buckles are cast with trapezoidal panels and eagle heads, and others with rectangular panels, as on the south-Crimean buckles.[146] In the proportions of their rectangular plates, the S-shaped scrolls, rectangular or trapezoidal panels, and eagle-headed terminals, the Bosporan buckles are close to those from the Danube region, Kovin and northern Serbia,[147] Cipau,[148] and the 6th-century layer at Iatrus.[149] A rectangular opening in the plate of one of the Kerch buckles (**Fig. 6: 5**) is characteristic of Gepid buckles.[150] The Danubian eagle-headed buckles are usually dated to the first half of the 6th century,[151] but some burials containing similar buckles are dated to 567–600.[152] The Bosporan buckles from the slope of Eski-Kermen, grave 315, were found with sheet brooches of Variant 2B-3 of the 7th century (**Fig. 3: 3**); at Kerch, in the vault of 1875, with buckles of Variant III with rectangular attachment-plates of the first half of the century; in vault 152 in a layer covering a burial of the second half of the 6th century; and, in vault 180, with a belt-set of the second half of the 7th century.[153] In the upper layer of Kerch vault 163, two burials were found, with an eagle-headed buckle in the first (**Fig. 6: 1**) and a buckle with two bird heads on the terminal of the plate in the other, just opposite the entrance to the chamber.[154]

Bierbrauer considers that Ostrogothic eagle-headed buckles were in use in Italy until the arrival of the Lombards in 568.[155] A buckle of similar type was found, however, in the cemetery at Kranj, Slovenia, which was in use between 500–600 and where, in the upper layer of vault 163, burials were probably deposited in the second half of the 6th century.[156] As in Bosporus eagle-headed buckles began to be made locally using Danubian prototypes, but later than in the Danube region and not before the second half of the 6th century. At Kerch they were in use until the end of the 7th century.

The Byzantine connection
Some Byzantine objects in the Berthier-Delagarde Collection have provenance of Kerch and are unique in Bosporus (**cat. nos 74–75, 78, 90–92**). They are discussed individually below,

with several of the more outstanding, unprovenanced pieces.

The Byzantine buckles first appear in the first half of the 6th century (**cat. nos 73–74, Pl. 35**), which seems to agree with details in Procopius about the subjection of this region to Byzantium under the Emperors Justin I (518–527) and Justinian I (527–565).[157] The second buckle has an oval loop, the ribbed decoration of which imitates twisted and beaded wire, and an attachment-plate with S-shaped scrolls cast and finished with a graver. It is recorded on a photograph in the Berthier-Delagarde archives, showing a tongue with a rectangular base containing two inlays (**Fig. 6: 4**).[158] Similar buckles were in use in the second half of the 5th and the first half of the 6th centuries in the Danube region, Germany and other areas.[159] A cast, copper-alloy buckle with an oval loop, triangular-section tongue, and an oval attachment-plate with a cross-shaped setting inlaid in red and green glass is typical of the Byzantine periphery (**cat. no. 78, Pl. 40**). In the Crimea such buckles came into fashion from the beginning of the 6th century and, in the Caucasus, in the first half of the 7th.[160] A gilt-silver buckle (**cat. no. 75, Pl. 37**) consists of a broad oval loop, a faceted tongue with a lion's head terminal, and a triangular attachment-plate with round lobes, ribbed decoration and a central triangular panel containing a clear glass inlay with three blue spots. It is similar to Byzantine buckles from Skalyste (Skalistoye) and Cherson, vault 62/1909 (**Fig. 6: 2–3**), in a burial of the first half of the 6th century,[161] and to a buckle with a triangular plate in a contemporary grave from Dyurso.[162] A gilt-silver buckle with a broad, B-shaped loop, a tongue with a dog's head on the front, and a plate with an eagle-headed terminal and garnet inlay (**cat. no. 73, Pl. 36**) is similar to those found in Kerch, vaults 113/1904 and 78/1907.[163] As such buckles were not known beyond the frontiers of Bosporus, we may assume that they were manufactured there. In these pieces local craftsmen combined details from Byzantine types, such as the forms of the loops and tongues, with Germanic styles such as the eagle-headed terminals of the attachment-plates.

One of the two cast, copper-alloy Byzantine buckles in the collection, with acanthus leaves on a pelta-shaped attachment-plate, belongs to the Syracuse type (**cat. no. 88, Pl. 46**), which forms the most numerous group of the 6th to 7th century found on Byzantine territory.[164] In the north-western part of Cherson, in two properties of district III, the remains of bronze-casting workshops were found, and the chemical analyses of the slag, bars and half-finished products from the sites are identical to those of the Syracuse-type buckles kept in reserve collections. In 1996-7 skin-divers found many pieces of slag, defective Syracuse-type buckles, and 'heraldic' mounts from belt-sets, etc., on the sea-bed off the south-eastern coast of Cherson, and there were, no doubt, jewellers' workshops making such pieces in this district of the city.[165]

A Byzantine polychrome belt-set of the second half of the 7th century from Kerch (**cat. nos. 90–92, Pls 47–49**) is identical to those found in the graves of nomad nobles from the neighbouring steppes at Portove (Portovoye) (**Map B: 43**) and Belozerka. These pieces are particularly important and rare, and are characterised by the use of silver for the main parts and the sparing use of gold for granulation or cloison-work. Only one is known from the north-Crimean steppe, at Portove, and such sets probably reached the nomads via Bosporus.

According to Malalas the nomads traded their goods for Byzantine merchandise there.[166] Such mounts for belts and horse-harness came from Kerch[167] and Cherson, from the burials of nomad nobles on the Crimean steppe, as at Portove, and from the northern Black Sea steppe, as at Belozerka, Hladkivka (Kelegei), and Pereshchepino.[168] Their broader distribution extends from Hungary, as at Tépe and Bócsa[169] to Iran,[170] and the Alanic catacombs of the North Caucasus at Upper Rutkha, and Kudentovo.[171] The general fashion for this kind of decoration, combining polychrome glass inlays with granulation, spread from Byzantium to the nomads in the second half of the 7th century[172] and there is a gold temporal-pendant decorated in the same style in the collection (**cat. no. 87, Pl. 46**). Similar pendants have been found in destroyed graves of the 7th century at the village of Michaelsfeld on the Black Sea Coast of the Kuban[173] and at Ufa,[174] and further finds have been made recently in the eastern Crimea, between Kerch and Feodosiya.[175] The gold cross in the Berthier-Delagarde Collection is an outstanding piece of Byzantine jewellery (**cat. no. 86, Pl. 45**) with a parallel from Kerch in the Römisch-Germanisches Museum, Mainz.[176] Similar crosses have been found at Hladkivka and in Byzantium together with coins of 641–668.[177]

Medieval material

The provenances of later objects in the collection, such as a pair of silver earrings of the 10th to 11th centuries (**cat. no. 132, Pl. 63**) and a pair of bracelets of twisted silver wires (**cat. no. 133, pl. 63**), remain unknown. Similar bracelets were made in the towns of Kievan Rus' in the 12th to 13th centuries,[178] while in the south-western Crimea, in Luchyste, vault 6, one was found with a coin of 1143–1180,[179] and at the settlement site of Bakla (**Map B: 27**) in a jug with jewellery of the 12th to 13th centuries.[180] Talis considers that ancient Rus' jewellery was brought to highland Crimea by the Polovtsi, who migrated into the Crimean and northern Black Sea steppe.[181]

Conclusion

It was O.M. Dalton who first reported in the West, in 1924, that the British Museum had purchased the Berthier-Delagarde Collection, which still rightly attracts the attention of specialists today.[182] A large part of the collection, however, has been neither published, nor properly attributed, until the present catalogue. A careful study of the artefacts gives us new information regarding the ethnic history of the Crimea, and the male and female costumes typical of different ethnic groups. The objects in the collection illustrate different stages of the jeweller's craft in both the peninsula and the northern Black Sea coast as a whole, and their analysis helps us trace the influences of the Roman Empire, Byzantium and the Danube region on local centres. As noted above, some pieces appear quite unique for the Crimea. The Kerch provenance of some imported Ostrogothic and Gepid objects illustrates the contacts between Crimean Gothia, the Danube region and Italy during the Migration period. In particular, the large silver buckle with a lozenge-shaped plate broadens our understanding of the work of south-Crimean jewellers, as its decoration bears witness to the later relations between the craftsmen of the Crimea and the middle Danube. The publication of this collection thus extends scientific knowledge both of local jewellery production, and of the character of imports into the Crimea, and is of great importance for the evaluation of Late-Antique and early-medieval culture along the northern Black Sea coast.

Notes

1. Rostovtsev 1930, 339, figs 255–6
2. Khazanov 1971, 12, 14, 25, figs XIV:9; XV:5, 8, 9; Maksimenko and Bezuglov 1987, 186–7, 190, fig. 2:7
3. Zasetskaya 1986, fig. 1:55; Ambroz 1989, 44
4. Rostovtzeff 1923a, 122–37
5. Beck *et al.* 1988, fig. 1:1
6. Aibabin 1990, 28, figs 2:26; 22:8–11
7. Aibabin 1990, 27–8, figs 2:10; 22:3; Kazanski and Legoux 1988, 13–14, fig. 9:44
8. Beck *et al.* 1988, 70
9. Kovpanenko 1980, 183, fig 9:2; Medvedev 1981, 257, 259, 300; Simonenko and Lobai 1991, 56, fig. 24
10. Damm 1988, 126–7, figs 75–6
11. Berkhin (Zasetskaya) 1961, 148, 150, fig. 4:2
12. Skripkin 1977, 113–4, fig.3:42
13. Savovsky 1977, fig. 5:2; Bezuglov and Zakharov 1989, 55
14. Magomedov 1979, 59, 61, fig. X:3
15. Bezuglov and Zakharov 1989, 55, fig. 2:1
16. Gushchina 1974, 41, fig. IV:4
17. Bichir 1977, pl. 24:12
18. Ambroz 1966, 51, pl. 9:12
19. Skripkin 1977, 102, fig. 2:20–2; Bezuglov 1988, fig 2:17
20. Ambroz 1966, 52; Skripkin 1977, 107, fig. 2:9, 12
21. Diaconu 1971, 240, pl. VII:7–8; Aibabin 1990, 18, fig. 8:5
22. Diaconu. 1971, 240, pl. VII:7–8; Ambroz 1966, 69, pl. 12:12; Magomedov 1979, fig. X:2; Rikman 1975, fig. 28:4
23. Vinogradov and Petrenko 1974, fig. 2:5–6; Savovsky 1977, figs 5:3; 61; Skripkin 1977, fig.3:10–17; Romanovskaya 1986, 79, fig.2:7; Bezuglov and Kopylov 1989, 176, fig.2:4–6; Ambroz 1989, 25, figs1:13; 14:20; Kuznetsov 1990, fig.1:14–16; Grosu 1990, fig.28:17
24. Aibabin 1990, 18, fig. 8:5
25. Shkorpil 1907, 14, fig.5; Shkorpil 1910b, 31–4, fig. 4:5, 12; Solomonik 1959, 132–4, fig 76
26. OIAK 1890, 34,130, fig. 18; Anokhin 1977, 154 no.280 27; Babenchikov 1963, pl. XV:4
28. Ambroz 1989, 2, 25–8; Aibabin 1990, fig.2:1–2
29. Vysotskaya 1972, fig. 43; Gushchina 1974, fig. III:10.194; Skripkin 1977, fig.4:19–20; Gudkova and Fokeev 1984, fig. 14:13–14; Maksimenko and Bezuglov 1987, 190, fig. 2:22; Shepko 1987, 172, figs 2:13,15; 9:3–4; Bezuglov 1988, 112–3, fig.2:21, 48; Ambroz 1989, figs 1:1, 10–12, 21, 24, 26; 2:4–7; Abramova 1990, fig. 3:3–7, 9–11; Grosu 1990, pl. 4, figs 2:4; 19:1–2; 26:11: 28:3, 6; Aibabin 1990, 27, fig. 22:1–2
30. Aibabin 1990, 27–8, figs 2:10; 22:3–4
31. Ashik 1849, part 3, 72, fig. 209; Reinach 1892, 40–1, 43; Shkorpil 1910b, 33, fig. 13; Rostovtzeff 1923a, 115–25; Rostowzew 1931, 221–4
32. Belinsky and Boiko 1991, 87–90, figs 22:1–4; 23:1–4; 26; 27
33. Betrozov 1987, 17–8, fig. V:1–2; VIII:1–6
34. Ambroz 1992, pl. I:5
35. Rostovtzeff 1923a, pl. IV
36. Ambroz 1992, pl. I:6
37. Romanovskaya 1986, 77, fig. 2:1
38. Gushchina 1966, 74, fig. 1:6; Savovsky 1977, 65–6, fig. 5:2; Bezuglov and Zakharov 1989, 44, 55, figs 2:1; 4:2
39. Chrapunov 1995, 182–4, nos 28, 29, 32–5.
40. Gushchina 1974, fig. 4:4
41. Ambroz 1989, 25–6; Kuznetsov 1993, 92
42. Kazanski and Legoux 1988, 13–14, fig. 9:44; Kazanski 1995, 191–3
43. Ambroz 1989, 23–7; Ambroz 1992, 8–10
44. Bespalyi 1992, 180–1, 190, figs 4–6
45. Shkorpil 1910b, 33, fig. 15; Beck *et al.* 1988, fig 1:28
46. Kuznetsov 1990, fig. 1:7–8
47. Runich 1976, fig. 4:3; Ambroz 1989, 77
48. Guguev and Bezuglov 1990, 172–3, fig. 4
49. Zasetskaya 1975, 55, fig. 40; Runich 1976, fig. 3:12; Gening 1976, fig. 32:6; Subbotin and Dzigovsky 1990, fig. 22:179; Ambroz 1989, fig. 2:30
50. Damm 1988, 101–2, figs 31–2; 35–6; 66; Aibabin 1990, 28, fig. 23:3,5
51. Zasetskaya 1993, 35–6

52. Zasetskaya 1993, 95–8
53. Zasetskaya 1993, 96, cat. 233–4, 261 a, b; Aibabin 1990, 28, figs 2:26;22:8–11,16,17,18
54. Sorokina 1971, 86–7,89, fig.1:2,6; Aibabin 1990, 13, figs 2:36, 40; 3:4, 6
55 Barkóczi and Salamon 1968, 39, figs 2:1–3; 3:3; 4:1; 6:2; 7: 1, 2; Böhme 1974, 137, 150, 315–16; pl. 122: 15
56. Zasetskaya 1993, 96, cat. 260–5
57. Zasetskaya 1993, 96, cat. 236
58. Zasetskaya 1993, 96
59. Sorokina 1971, 87, fig. 1:3
60. Aibabin 1990, 13, fig. 3:9
61. Zasetskaya 1993, 96, cat. 243, 245
62. Zasetskaya 1993, 96, cat. 219
63. Ambroz 1992, 65, pl. 2:12; Zasetskaya 1993, 96, cat. 222
64 Zasetskaya 1993, 96, cat. 220, 221, 225
65. Zasetskaya 1993, 96, cat. 223; Aibabin 1990, 28, fig. 23:10
66. Zasetskaya 1993, 96, cat. 231a
67. Zasetskaya 1993, 96, cat. 231b; Aibabin 1990, 28, figs 2:48; 22:12
68. Zasetskaya 1993, 96, cat. 232
69. Zasetskaya 1993, 96, cat. 230
70. Sorokina 1971, fig. 4:4
71 Aibabin 1990, 18, fig. 2:42
72. Tejral 1988, 295, figs 16:3, 4; 27:5; 29:5
73. Zasetskaya 1993, 97, cat. 288
74. Zasetskaya 1993, 97, cat. 291
75. Aibabin 1990, 28, figs 2:48; 22:12; Zasetskaya 1993, 97, cat. 292
76 Aibabin 1990, 29, fig. 1:4; Zasetskaya 1993, 97, cat. 289–90
77. Zasetskaya 1993, 97, cat. 293
78. Zasetskaya 1993, 97, cat. 295–6
79. Zasetskaya 1993, 97, cat. 300
80. Aibabin 1990, 28, figs 2:47; 23:1–2
81. Zasetskaya 1993, 97–8, cat. 303
82. Zasetskaya 1993, 97, cat. 278–80, 283
83. Zasetskaya 1993, 97, cat. 286; Aibabin 1990, 51. figs 2:49; 47:18
84. Zasetskaya 1993, 97, cat. 284.
85. Csallány 1961, 121, 234, pls CCXV:11, CCXVII:3, CCXVIII:6
86. Tejral 1988, 295, figs 27:7; 35:3
87. Werner 1960, 177–8; Ambroz 1982, 107
88. Tejral 1988, 295, figs 9:4; 27:8–9; 28:14; 27–8; 3
89. Werner 1959, 423–7, 432 note 27; Werner 1961b, 28–9, nos 100–3; Annibaldi and Werner 1963, 368
90. Tejral 1988, 267–86, 295
91. Bierbrauer 1992, 264, 274–5
92. Zasetskaya 1993, 96, cat. 220, 222–3.
93. Damm 1988, 132–3, figs 91–2
94. Bierbrauer 1975, pl. XXXII:4
95. Zasetskaya 1993, 96, cat. 243
96. Zasetskaya 1975, 57 no. 43; Damm 1988, 190–1, figs 204–5; Zasetskaya 1993, 63, cat.138
97. Aibabin 1990, fig. 47:2
98. Minaeva 1956, 246, fig. 8:3; Werner 1961b, 40, pl. 39:202; Damm 1988, 140–1, figs 110–11
99. Annibaldi and Werner 1963, 371, fig. 44:6,7
100. Csallány 1961, 329, pl. CCIV:12; Theodorescu 1976, fig. 91; Kiss 1983, fig. 5:1, 2, 6, 7.
101. Dalton 1924a, pl. XXXVII:13
102. Werner 1961b , 72, pl. 37:172
103. Damm 1988, 125, fig. 72
104. Bierbrauer 1975, 165, pl. LXXVIII:6, 7
105. Repnikov 1907, pl. I:13, 17, 19
106. Ajbabin 1995b, figs 73, 78
107. Aibabin 1990, 58, fig. 2:60
108. Werner 1961b, 48. Vinski 1957, 158–60; Ambroz 1966, 35, 143
109. Aibabin 1990, 26–7; figs 2:64, 10:7, 13
110. Ambroz 1968, 17–20; Veimarn and Ambroz 1980, 249–61
111. Veimarn and Ambroz 1980, 261
112. Aibabin 1990, 35, figs 2:166, 177, 178; 36
113. Götze 1907, 2, 3, 9, fig. 2:8; Csallány 1961, pls VIII:10; XXVII:9; L:13; LXXIX:16; CXXXIV:2; CCLIX:2; Kovačević 1960, figs 26, 31, 90, 95; Vinski 1978, pl.14:1, 2; Bierbrauer 1975, pls XXXIX; 8, LII:1; LXXIII:3; Werner 1961b, 31–3; Aibabin 1990, 20–1
114. Aibabin 1990, 20, figs 2:72; 14:11
115. Aibabin 1990, 20, figs 2:72; 14:13
116. Aibabin 1990, 31, fig. 2:105
117. Kühn 1965, 92
118. Aibabin 1990, 21, figs 2:8; 15:2–3; 32:1, pl. II
119. Kühn 1940, pl. 62:1–3
120. Vinski 1972–3, pl. Xl:60; Vinski 1978,p.40, pl. X:1, 12
121. Aibabin 1979, 212–14
122 Ambroz 1992
123. Aibabin 1990, 16, 21, figs 5:11; 15:3
124. Hayes 1972, 335, figs 68:28; 69: 37
125. Hayes 1972, 335; Abadie-Reynal and Sodini 1992, 23, fig. 7:CF 105–6
126. Robinson 1959, 116, pls 33:M:350; 71:M350
127. Aibabin 1990, 21, fig. 2:88, pl. II
128. Ambroz 1988, 5, 7, fig. 1:2
129. Aibabin 1990, 33
130. Ambroz 1971, 114, pl. II:4
131. Ambroz 1988, 7
132. Aibabin 1990, 19, 33–4, figs 2:90–1; 30:2
133. Aibabin 1990, 19, 33–4,62, figs 2:80, 91, 107; 32:2; 33:2, pl. XI
134. Aibabin 1990, 33–4, 62, figs 2:136,166: 33:1: 34
135. Aibabin 1982, 186–7, fig. 10:1–3, 5, 10
136. Aibabin 1990, 34, 62, fig. 54
137. Aibabin 1990, 21, fig. 2:88, 136
138. Csallány 1961, pl. CCVIII:5, 6; Bierbrauer 1975, 89 215, 217, 220, 240, pls XLII:1, 2; LXXIV:7; Pilet 1995, 328, fig. 2:6
139. Vinski 1978, 40, pl. II:3
140. Aibabin 1990, 21, fig. 15:6
141. Kühn 1940, 100, pls 63–5
142. Werner 1961b, 29–30
143. Ambroz 1992
144. Aibabin 1990, 31, fig. 2:105
145. Aibabin 1990, 21–2, 38, 61, figs 2:75, 125, 128–9, 138,140; 15: 5,6; 39:6; 50:16, 18, 28–9, 39, 40
146. Aibabin 1990, 33, fig.35; Aibabin 1993b, 165, fig. 1:1
147. Vinski 1978, figs 2, 3
148. Rusu 1959, fig. 2:3
149. Gomolka-Fuchs 1993, 358, fig. 4:1
150. Aibabin 1993b, fig. 1:1
151. Ambroz 1968, 16–17; Vinski 1968, 332–5
152. Csallány 1961, 355, 358
153. Aibabin 1990, 34, figs 2:112, 119–21, 128, 138, 140; 12:3; 26:1; 50:16, 18, 28, 39, 40
154. Aibabin 1990, 34, fig. 26:4
155. Bierbrauer 1975, 143–5, 150–8
156. Vinski 1968, 339
157. Procopius, trans. Dewing, 1940, III:VII, 12–13
158. Aibabin 1990, 37, fig. 37:2
159. Salin 1904, fig. 300; Ambroz 1970, 71; Aibabin 1990, 37
160. Aibabin 1990, 36–7, fig. 37:17; Kazanski 1994, 155–6, fig. 15:2–7
161. Aibabin 1990, 37, figs 2:70; 38: 23; 39:2
162. Dmitriev 1982, 104, 106, fig 5:12
163. Aibabin 1990, 37, figs 2:70, 71, 74, 75; 39:5
164. Aibabin 1990, 43, figs 2:122; 42:6–7
165. Aibabin 1993b, 168
166. Malalas 1986, 250–57, fig. 432(?)
167. Fettich 1951b, pl. XLVI:1–7
168. Aibabin 1985, 198–9, fig. 8:1–2, 23, 29–31; Aibabin 1991b, fig. 2:11–12; Bobrinsky 1914, figs 29, 46, 48, 52, 54
169. László 1955, 255, 278–85, pls XXXV:1–18, LVII:2–4
170. Werner 1986, pls 14; 15; 19:1, 3; 20:1
171. Uvarova 1900, 240, pl. LXIV:6; Artamonov 1962, 129
172. Aibabin 1985, 200
173. Kondakov 1896, 200–2, figs 115–6
174. Akhmerov 1951, fig. 36
175. *Archéologie de la Mer Noire* 1997, 85–7, no. 142
176. Brown 1984, 10–11, pl. 9
177. Ross 1965, pls X:B; XII; Aibabin 1991, 32, fig. 3:12
178. Sedova 1981, 94, 96–7, fig. 37:4, 5a, 12, 13
179. Aibabin 1993a, 126, fig. 12:2, 7
180. Talis 1990, 85, 87, fig. II
181. Talis 1990, 87–8
182. Dalton 1924a, b

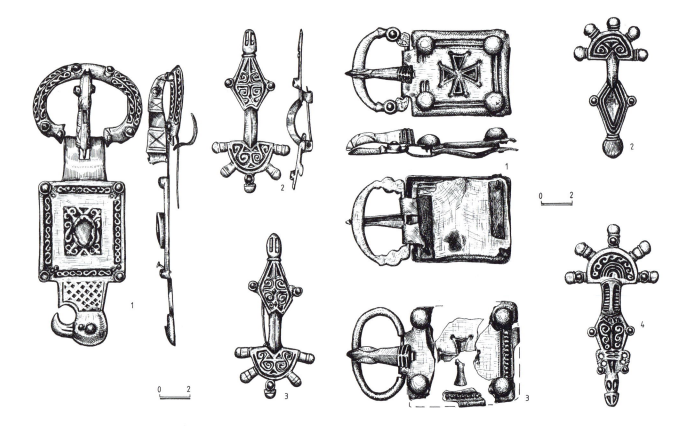

Figure 1 Buckle (1) and brooches from Luchistoe from skeleton 12 in vault 54.

Figure 2 Buckles (1, 3) and brooches (2, 4) from Luchistoe from vault 77.

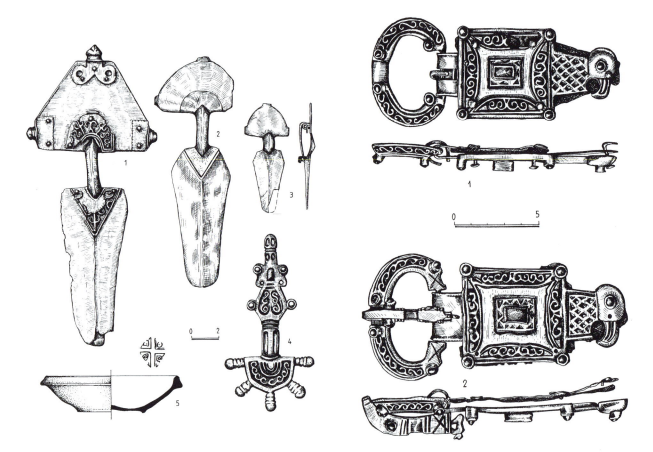

Figure 3 1, 2 – brooches from Luchistoe from vault 10;   3 – brooch from Eski-Kermen from grave 315;   4 – brooch from Kerch from vault 152/1904;
5 – red lacquered bowl from Kerch grave 19/1904.

Figure 4 1, 2 – Buckles from Luchistoe from vault 42.

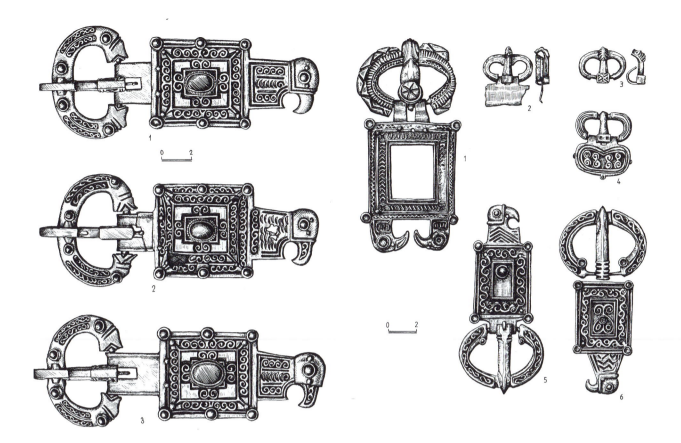

Figure 5 1-3 – Buckles from Luchistoe from vault 10.

Figure 6 Buckles: 1 – from Kerch from vault 163/1904;   2 – from Skalistoe from grave 447a;   3 – from Chersonesus from vault 62/1909;   4 – Berthier-Delagarde collection cat. no. 74;   5 – from Kerch from grave 1/1905; 6 – from Kerch from a vault 152/1904.

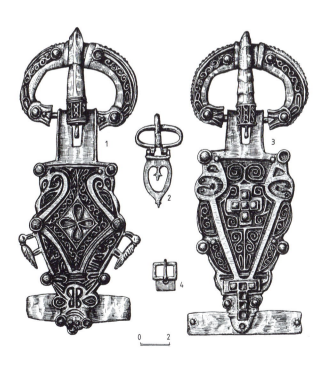

Figure 7 Buckles: 1–2 from Skalistoe from vault 288;   3 – from Skalistoe from vault 321;   4 – from Aromat from vault 1.

Crimean Metalwork:
Analysis and Technical Examination

Susan La Niece and Michael Cowell

Compositional analysis

Techniques

Two analytical techniques were used in the investigation of the jewellery: energy dispersive X-ray fluorescence (XRF) and X-ray diffraction (XRD). X-ray fluorescence (XRF) was used to determine the metal composition of the artefacts and, since many of the artefacts are composite, in some cases the individual components were analysed to establish their integrity. X-ray diffraction analysis was used to identify the inlay materials.

The instrument used for XRF analysis was a modified Link Analytical 290 spectrometer incorporating a molybdenum target X-ray tube operated at 45kV which analyses an area about 1.5 mm in diameter on the artefact.[1] XRF is essentially a surface method since, due to the low penetration of X-rays, the analysed depth rarely exceeds 100 μm (0.1 mm). Hence, to obtain an accurate analysis of an artefact, the exposed surface must be representative of the bulk composition. The surface compositions of most ancient artefacts have usually been altered by corrosion processes, either through leaching of less noble metals (e.g. copper, leading to an apparent *surface enrichment* of the more noble metals, such as silver and gold) or a build-up of corrosion products. Consequently the surfaces are not representative of the bulk. These problems can be overcome by preparing the surface, for example by abrasion, to expose a representative surface, but this was not generally possible with these artefacts. Those analyses carried out with no surface preparation (i.e. non-destructively) are therefore at best semiquantitative (i.e. approximate) or only qualitative.

For the gold jewellery, where corrosion deposits are usually absent, there will be some alteration of the surface composition so that only semiquantitative analysis is possible. The non-destructive analysis results are likely to show an overestimation of the gold and possibly the silver contents and a corresponding under-estimation of the copper. The precision (reproducibility) of these analyses is about ±1-2% relative for the major component (gold) and about ±5-20% relative for silver and copper; the accuracy cannot be defined because of the uncertain surface enrichment effects. In the case of artefacts made of silver or copper-based alloys, the surface alteration may be more extensive so that only a qualitative analysis was justifiable. Thus, only the alloy type was recorded with a note of any traces of other metals. The alloy terminology is as follows:

brass	alloy of copper with zinc.
bronze (or tin bronze)	alloy of copper with tin.
leaded bronze	alloy of copper with tin and lead.
gunmetal	alloy of copper with tin and zinc.
leaded gunmetal	alloy of copper with tin, zinc and lead.

For the limited number of artefacts where a small area could be abraded, the analytical precision is about ±1–2% for the major components (greater than 50%), about ±5–10% for the minor components (5–50%) and ±10–50% for the remaining trace components. The accuracies are expected to be similar.

X-ray diffraction was used to identify the inlay materials where microscopic examination was not conclusive. The technique determines the mineralogy, or the chemical structure of compounds.

Results and discussion of analyses

The fully quantitative, semi-quantitative and qualitative analyses are listed respectively in **Tables 1–3**.

Gold-based alloy artefacts

These artefacts are gold-silver-copper ternary alloys with gold contents generally in excess of 75% and covering a wide range of compositions. The silver content is usually higher than that of the copper which is typical of early gold alloys; some of the backing panels of earrings appear to be rich in copper but this may be due to contamination from a copper-rich solder. Although the artefacts as a whole have a wide range in composition, the components of individual artefacts tend to have similar compositions, as noted in the individual catalogue entries. An exception to this is one of the pendants (**cat. no. 105**) where the composition of the small pyramid component is quite different from that of the main part of the artefact.

The composition of this gold metalwork is not particularly distinctive by comparison with ancient goldwork in general. Most of the gold items which have been analysed are within the range of composition of Late-Roman (e.g. 4th–5th centuries AD) and Byzantine (post-5th century AD) gold coinage and could in theory have used coins for their raw material.[2] However, these analyses can only indicate this as a possibility and cannot prove such a connection.

Silver-based alloy artefacts

Only a limited number of silver items were analysed quantitatively; these are similar in composition being base silver-copper alloys (50–75% silver) with small amounts of lead, zinc, tin and gold. The qualitative analyses are generally consistent with this. This type of alloy is similar to items of jewellery analysed from the Martynivka (Martynovka) hoard.[3] The gold in the alloy is probably derived from the ore from which the silver was extracted and the lead is derived both from the ore type (usually silver-rich galena, lead sulphide) and the method of refining (cupellation). The zinc and tin are probably derived from the use of brass or bronze to alloy with the silver rather than pure copper.

Copper-based alloy artefacts

Only two of the copper-based artefacts were analysed quantitatively. Combined with the qualitative analyses these cover a wide range of alloy types, from almost pure copper to brass, bronze and more complex alloys such as gunmetals (copper-tin-zinc). These are all typical of the period. The metal used for particular components shows that the properties of the alloys were understood; copper was used for backing sheets and rivets, brass may have been used in some jewellery items for its golden colour (for example brooch, **cat. no. 22**). The apparent use of brass and bronze to alloy with the silver (as noted above) is an indication of the wider use of such alloys.

Mercury gilding

Several copper-based and silver-based articles are plated with gold using the technique of mercury or fire-gilding. This was carried out by applying an amalgam of mercury and gold to the surface of the artefact and heating to above 350°C to drive off the mercury, leaving a thin plating of gold. The surface then had to be burnished. This method may be revealed by the detection by XRF of small amounts of mercury which remain in the plating. This technique of gilding was widely used from the Roman period onwards.[4]

Platinum group element (PGE) inclusions

A small number of the gold artefacts (e.g. **cat. nos 1, 11 and 105**) have observable white metal inclusions on the surface. These are platinum group element (PGE) grains, usually alloys of osmium, iridium and ruthenium, which have a high density and melting point;[5] they are not generally dissolved in the gold alloy when this is simply melted for casting although they may be attacked by certain refining operations.[6] The presence of such inclusions is an indication that the gold has originated from an alluvial source rather than mined gold, but as the inclusions on an individual artefact have been found to range widely in composition, in general they cannot be used to locate the gold to a particular source.

Summary of the Technical Examination

Most of the more complex pieces of jewellery were examined microscopically and details of construction of individual items are included in their catalogue entries. Some features are common to many of the pieces and there are a small number of items of jewellery which stand out by reason of manufacturing techniques or materials used. Both these aspects are discussed here.

Restoration

A problem which should be mentioned straight away is the difficulty in establishing how much the pieces were altered or embellished by restoration after excavation, but before entering the British Museum's collection. Some features, such as modern adhesives, are easily recognised, but the use of beeswax or gypsum (plaster of Paris) as adhesives or for reinforcement could be ancient or modern. A specific example of the problem of attributing original workmanship is a gilt-silver buckle (**cat. no. 75**) with a triangular insert of clear glass with three blue blobs. This type of glass decoration was used for vessels during the 4th and 5th centuries[7] and the curvature of the fragment does suggest that it could be re-used vessel glass. Re-use of Roman materials such as glass and intaglio gems was common in the centuries after the collapse of the Roman Empire, but the long edges of this fragment of glass are very smooth and straight, as if cut by a powered cutting-wheel, suggesting the glass may be a modern restoration. A number of the gemstones do not fit their settings, but is this evidence that they are replacements or is it simply poor workmanship? Some pieces may have been in use over long periods, with repairs and embellishments, becoming family heirlooms before they were finally lost or buried. Others acquired the repairs and embellishments after they were taken out of the ground. Without full excavation records, which are not available for this collection, all such information is lost. Where there are obvious doubts about the antiquity of a decorative feature a comment has been inserted in the catalogue entry, but it cannot be assumed that everything else described is an original feature.

A number of pieces show evidence of extensive wear, particularly on the suspension loops of earrings, but sadly there are others which have been so ferociously chemically stripped of their corrosion products (before acquisition by the British Museum) that all evidence of tool marks or wear has been completely obliterated.

Construction Techniques

Most of the items of jewellery in this catalogue are composite: they are made of several components, sometimes of different materials. Joining methods include soldering as well as mechanical joints such as rivets and crimping.

The majority of the cast objects are silver or copper alloys. The techniques employed in the manufacture of the gold jewellery are mostly based on sheet metalwork and wire and, not surprisingly, the shapes of the jewellery were particularly suited to this approach. Where three-dimensional shapes in gold are used, they are hollow. This is for reasons of economy and, in the case of earrings, probably for lightness. For example, the large, hollow bead of gold earring **cat. no. 8** is filled with sulphur. Molten sulphur was commonly used in Hellenistic and Roman hollow gold jewellery and there was continuity of this technique into later periods. The molten sulphur was poured in after all soldering was completed and, when set, it provided support for the thin gold without adding noticeably to the weight.[8]

Wire and granulation

Wire is a common decorative feature, particularly of the gold jewellery. No evidence for drawn wire was found. The simplest forms were the relatively thick, hammered wires used for earring suspension loops. Twisted, square-sectioned wire was used decoratively (e.g. **cat. no. 3**; **Pl. 65**). Round wire was often made by a combination of tightly twisting a thin strip of metal, then rolling it between two blocks of wood or other flat, hard material to smooth the surface.[9] The spiral seam typical of twisted wire can often be seen (e.g. **cat. no. 1**; **Pl. 66**). The commonest form of decorative wire found in this collection is beaded wire. It was made by rolling a round wire under an edged tool and repeating this at regular intervals along the length of the wire. The wire was constricted under the tool and the metal bulged out each side. A tool with two or more edges would be more efficient than a single blade. The regularity of the spacing and pressure of the beading tool determined the evenness of the finished wire, which was of very variable standard (compare the beading on **cat. nos 29D and 13** in **Pls 67 and 68**). Beaded wire was soldered around the edge of gem settings or the complete object as a collar or frame. An interesting variation on this is seen on a gilt-silver brooch (**cat. no. 15; Pl. 69** and on two mounted gems (**cat. no 29G–H; Pl. 70**). In these and other examples the frame is made up of a border of granules. Granulation was used decoratively on a number of pieces, mostly gold jewellery (see **Pl. 66**). The granulation and the wire-work all have their origins in antiquity.

Gems and glass
The identification of inlay and backing materials was carried out initially by optical microscopy with up to x50 magnification, and, where necessary, micro-samples were taken for X-ray diffraction analysis using a Debye-Scherrer powder diffraction camera.[10] It was found that the range of inlay materials was limited. The commonest gem material is garnet. Coloured glass, especially green, blue and brown, is found on many items. Enamel is rare (**cat. no. 104**) though this may reflect its fragility rather than lack of use. No niello inlays were found and the only example of faience (a pendant, **cat. no. 9**) is of doubtful origin. Carnelian, which is a variety of microquartz ranging in colour from red to orange, was used for cabochon gem settings (**cat. nos 29I, J, K, 32, 35–37 and 41–43**) and the only intaglio is a carnelian (**cat. no. 108**). **Catalogue no. 83** is a chalcedony ball in a silver sling. This is an opaque, whitish microquartz (the nomenclature used here for the quartz gem materials follows that of Sax).[11] Other gems such as amethyst (**cat. no. 39**) and agate (**cat. no. 138**) may not be original to this assemblage. One interesting inlay material is the square of white cristobalite (SiO_2) in the centre of the bezel of an East Germanic gold and garnet ring (**cat. no. 13**). Cristobalite is a soft, white mineral which is occasionally found as an inlay in Merovingian[12] and Anglo-Saxon garnet jewellery.[13]

Garnets were used, both flat cut and cabochon. The thickness of the flat cut garnets is very variable, though this is difficult to quantify with the garnets *in situ*. There is also considerable variability in the quality of finish of the edges. The finely drilled, circular grooves to take gold inlay, in the garnets of **cat. no. 24A**, are in marked contrast to the poor shaping of their edges which suggest re-use (**Pl. 71**). Many cloisonné garnets have one or more rough edges, suggesting re-use of stones. Well-finished, bevelled edges on well-fitting stones are not common in this assemblage.

Some, but by no means all, cloisonné inlays have foils behind them to improve the reflecting quality of the stones and also to wedge the gems into their settings. Where gold foils are found in this collection they are usually smooth and unpatterned (for example **cat. nos 4, 5, 12, 25, 26, 29A, 29E, 29F, and 70**). Gold foils were only used in the gold jewellery. Gilt-silver foils do not survive well, but were identified under both flat and cabochon garnets on the gold necklace pendants of **cat. no. 9**. On several of the items traces of silver foils were identified, both patterned (e.g. **cat. no. 24**) and plain (e.g. **cat. no. 23**). A red glass inlay on a strap-end (**cat. no. 90**), is backed by a metallic tin foil.

Cloisonnés in this type of jewellery often contained a backing paste which was soft when the stones were being set, allowing the jeweller to level the surfaces of all the stones, whatever their thickness. Access for analysis to the backing pastes behind these gems was only possible in a few cases, for example, the white paste underneath the garnets and foils of the bird-headed mounts (**cat. no. 24**) was identified as calcite ($CaCO_3$), as was the paste under the clear glass cabochons of buckle, **cat. no. 82**. Calcite occurs geologically as chalk, limestone and marble. Backing pastes for gemstones are made from finely crushed calcite, perhaps mixed with an organic binder like beeswax, though no binder could be identified in these pastes.[14]

Coloured glass was common, particularly green, and glass was also used to imitate garnet. An interesting example of this is seen on two belt suspension mounts (**cat. no. 91**) and a strap-end (**cat. no. 90**) which have brownish glass inlays with a layer of red ochre behind them to make the colour more like garnet. The strap-end also has one red glass inlay, probably coloured by manganese. There was no ochre behind this, but it has a foil of metallic tin, as mentioned above. Base metal foils and the use of coloured backings to improve translucent gems rarely survive burial, but there is no reason to doubt their antiquity on these pieces.

Conclusions
The alloys used for the jewellery are typical of the period when compared with Late-Roman and Byzantine artefacts and the alloy types are generally suitable for the methods of manufacture involved. The repertoire of decorative and manufacturing techniques seen on the objects in this collection is not great, but there is considerable variation in the quality of execution. The evidence for re-use of garnets is widespread, and the poor quality and quantity of materials used suggest that economy was an important consideration in the manufacture of most of the pieces. Nevertheless there is obvious continuity in jewellery-making traditions from the classical world.

Acknowledgements
We would like to thank our colleagues Paul Craddock, Ian Freestone and Nigel Meeks for their helpful comments.

Notes
1   Cowell 1998
2   Morrisson *et al.* 1985
3   Pekarskaja and Kidd 1994
4   Oddy 1993
5   Meeks and Tite 1980
6   Bowditch 1973
7   Sazanov 1995
8   Ogden 1982, 40
9   Whitfield 1990; Oddy 1977
10 Azaroff and Buerger 1958
11 Sax 1996, 63–72
12 Arrhenius 1985, 38
13 La Niece 1988
14 Arrhenius 1971, 78–97

Table 1 Semi-quantitative X-ray Fluorescence analyses

Cat. no.	Description	Part	%Au	%Ag	%Cu	Comments
1	Earring	Back sheet	75	22	3	
2	Earring	Backing sheet	91	4	5.4	
2		Loop	91	7	2.0	
3	Earring	Body	88	10	2.0	
3		Twisted wire	88	10	1.3	
4	Earring	Back-plate	93	6	1	
5	Earring	Cell side	91	8	1	
5		Granulation area	90	7	3	May include solder
6	Earring	Hoop	78	19	3	
7	Earring (Inv. no. 64)	Cell side	93	5	2	
7	Earring (Inv. no. 65)	Cell side	62	32	6	Difference between pair
8	Earring	Cell side	86	9	5	
9	Necklace	Sheet around pendants	79	10	11	
9		Spacers	85	11	4	
10	Pendant	Base-plate	90	8	2	
11	Pendant	Base-plate main part	90	8	2	
11		Base-plate addition	90	8	2	
12	Finger-ring	Sheet around cell	83	14	3	
13	Finger-ring	Sheet around cells	85	11	4	
13		Hoop	84	11	5	
14	Brooch	Back hinge	64	32	3	
14		Back catch-plate	64	33	3	
15	Brooch	Back sheet, ungilded	1	68	32	May be contaminated by gilding
23	Mounts	Cell side	99	0.7	0.2	
24	Mount	Bird: gold strip	86	11	3	
26	Strap-attachment	Body, front	79	19	3	
28	Stud	Beaded rim	81	18	2	May include solder
29A	Stud	Cell side	86	12	2	
29B	Stud	Back of cell	74	22	3	
29C	Stud	Back of cell	78	19	3	
29D	Stud	Back of cell	89	10	1	
29E	Stud	Back of cell	79	18	3	
29F	Stud	Back of cell	78	19	3	
29G	Stud	Back of cell	71	25	4	
29H	Stud	Back of cell	40	51	9	Silver solder or gilded ?
29I	Stud	Back of cell	95	1	4	
29J	Stud	Back of cell	94	1	5	
29K	Stud	Back of cell	96	1	3	
70	Buckle	Loop	89	9	2	
70		Side of cell	88	9	2	
71	Buckle-tongue	Body	92	7	1	
72	Buckle	Cell side	84	12	4	
84	Earring	Body	95	4	2	
85	Earring	Body	90	8	2	
86	Pendant	Body	89	7	5	
87	Kolt	Body	97	1	2	
100	Brooch	Body	82	15	2.9	
101	Brooch	Body	91	7	2.2	
102	Brooch	Body	88	10	1.5	
103	Brooch	Body	66	30	3.9	
104	Pendant	Body	83	13	3.9	
104		Loop	81	14	5.0	
105	Pendant	Pyramid	97	3	0.7	
105		Large ring	73	23	4.4	
105		Loop	69	24	7.2	
106	Earring	Body	72	24	4.1	
106		Bead	74	23	2.9	
106		Suspension loop	76	21	2.8	
107	Earring	Back-plate	83	14	2.3	
107		Body	84	14	1.7	
108	Earring	Body	76	19	5.0	
108		Wire hook	76	22	3.0	
109	Earring	Back sheet	92	6	2.0	
109		Twisted wire	95	4	0.8	
109		Wire hook	93	6	1.0	
110	Pendant/Earring	Back-plate	95	4	0.7	
110		Body	93	6	0.7	
111	Earring	Body, side	95	4	1.2	
111		Backing plate	93	5	1.5	
111		Backing plate	94	5	0.8	Abraded
111		Loop	93	7	0.4	

Note: The majority of analyses are on the unabraded surface and are therefore approximate. There may be some bias in the results due to surface enrichment.

Table 2   Quantitative X-ray Fluorescence analyses, on abraded surfaces

Cat. no.	Description	Ag	Cu	Pb	Zn	Sn	Au
19	Brooch (Inv. no. 39)	69	23	3	1	1	3
19	Brooch (Inv. no. 40)	61	32	2	1	2	2
20	Brooch (Inv. no. 41)	58	38	1	2	<0.1	1
20	Brooch (Inv. no. 42)	56	41	0.5	1	<0.1	1
21	Brooch (Inv. no. 43)	57	35	2	3	2	1
21	Brooch (Inv. no. 44)	58	37	0.5	3	0.5	1
22	Brooch	<0.1	81	2	16	0.5	<0.1
44	Mount	75	23	<0.1	0.5	<0.1	0.5
57	Buckle	<0.1	99	0.1	<0.1	0.5	<0.1
80	Buckle	64	27	2	3	2	2
82	Mount	46	46	2	3	1	0.5

The precision of major elements (e.g. Ag, Cu) is 1-2%, others ± 10-25%. The accuracy is similar.

Table3   Silver and copper-based artefacts: Qualitative X-ray fluorescence analyses

Cat. no.	Description	Part	Analysis
16	Brooch	Body	Silver-copper, traces of lead, zinc, gold
17	Armlet	Body	Silver-copper alloy with traces of zinc, tin
18	Armlet	Body	Silver-copper alloy with traces of zinc
19	Brooch (Inv. no. 39)	Body	Base silver-copper, traces of lead, zinc, tin, gold
19	(Inv. no. 40)	Body	Base silver-copper, traces of lead, zinc, tin, gold
20	Brooch (Inv. no. 41)	Body	Base silver-copper, traces of lead, gold
20	Brooch (Inv. no. 42)	Body	Base silver-copper, traces of lead, gold
21	Brooch (Inv. no. 43)	Body	Base silver-copper, traces of lead, zinc, tin, gold
21	Brooch (Inv. no. 44)	Body	Base silver-copper, traces of lead, zinc, tin, gold
22	Brooch	Body (abraded)	Brass with trace of lead
27	Mount	Side panel	Gilded copper
27		Back	Copper with traces of zinc and tin
30	Stud (Inv. no. 99)	Base	Brass
30		Collar	Mercury gilded brass
30	Stud (Inv. no. 100)	Body	Gilded copper
31	Mount	Back-plate	Base silver-copper, traces of zinc and tin
31		Tongue backing	Copper
31		Rivet on tongue	Copper
32	Mount	Back-plate	Copper with traces of lead
32		Front sheet	Mercury gilded silver
32		Domed rivets	Silver-copper alloy, traces of gold
33	Mount	Back-plate	Copper
33		Front sheet	Gilded silver (mercury not detected by XRF)
33		Rivet	Silver
34	Mount	Back-plate	Copper
34		Front sheet	Mercury gilded silver
34		Rivet	Silver
34		Silver sheet	Silver-copper alloy, traces of gold and lead
35	Mount	Back-plate	Copper
35		Rivet	Silver-copper alloy
36	Mount	Back-plate	Copper
36		Rivet	Silver-copper alloy
37	Mount	Back-plate	Copper with traces of tin
38	Mount	Silver sheet	Silver-copper alloy, traces of lead and gold
39	Mount	Silver sheet	Silver-copper alloy, traces of lead and gold
40	Mount	Back-plate	Silver-copper alloy, traces of zinc
40		Rivet	Base silver-copper alloy with zinc
41	Mount	Cell at back	Base silver-copper alloy, traces of lead, zinc, tin
41		Outer base-plate	Base silver-copper, traces of zinc and tin
41		Backing plate	Copper with traces of tin
42	Mount	Inner base-plate	Tin bronze with traces of arsenic
42		Outer back-plate	Base silver-copper, traces of zinc and lead
42		Side joint solder	Tin-lead solder
43	Mount	Underlying base	copper with traces of tin
43		Front sheet	Silver-copper alloy, traces of lead and tin
44	Mount	Front sheet	Silver-copper alloy, traces of zinc and gold
44		Back sheet	Base silver-copper alloy, traces of zinc and gold
45	Buckle	Rivet-head	Gold-silver alloy
45		Loop	Silver-copper alloy, trace of lead and gold
46	Buckle	Rivet-head	Silver-copper alloy, trace of gold
46		Loop	Silver-copper alloy, trace of gold
47	Buckle	Loop	Copper
48	Buckle	Tongue	Silver-copper alloy
48		Loop	Silver-copper alloy
49	Buckle	Body	Brass with trace of tin
49		Tongue	Brass with trace of tin
50	Buckle loop (Inv. no. 138)	Body	Base silver-copper, traces of gold, zinc

Cat. no.	Description	Part	Analysis
50	Buckle loop (Inv. no. 139)	Body	Silver-copper alloy
51	Buckle	Loop	Silver-copper alloy
52	Buckle	Loop	Silver-copper alloy
53	Buckle (Inv. no. 140)	Loop	Silver-copper alloy with gold
53	Buckle (Inv. no. 141)	Loop	Silver-copper alloy with gold
53	Buckle (Inv. no. 141)	Loop attachment	Silver-copper alloy with gold
54	Buckle	Body	Tin bronze
55	Buckle	Body	Tin bronze
56	Buckle	Loop	Copper with trace of tin
57	Buckle	Body	Copper
58	Buckle	Body	Copper
59	Buckle	Loop	Tin bronze
60	Strap-distributor (Inv. no. 122)	Attachment	Silver-copper alloy, traces of lead and gold
60		Ring	Leaded bronze, traces of zinc
60	Strap-distributor (Inv. no. 127)	Attachment	Base silver-copper alloy, traces of tin and gold
61	Strap attachment	Body	Bronze
62	Strap attachment	Body	Brass with trace of tin
63	Mount	Body metal strip	Silver-copper alloy, traces of lead, tin, gold
64	Mount	Body metal strip	Silver-copper alloy, traces of lead, zinc, tin
65	Mount	Body	Silver-copper alloy, traces of lead, tin
66	Mount	Backing sheet	Base silver-copper alloy, traces of lead, tin
67	Mount	Backing sheet	Silver-copper alloy, traces of lead, gold
68	Mount	Sheet strip	Base silver-copper alloy, traces of lead, tin
69	Mount	Sheet strip	Base silver-copper alloy, traces of tin, lead
73	Buckle	Plate	Silver
74	Buckle	Loop front hinge	Base silver-copper, traces of lead, tin
75	Buckle	Front-plate	Mercury gilded silver
75		Back-plate	Base silver-copper alloy, traces of zinc
75		Tongue	Base silver-copper alloy, traces of zinc
76	Buckle	Body	Copper with traces of lead
76		Loop	Leaded gunmetal
77	Buckle	Body, side	Brass
77		Tongue	Brass
78	Buckle	Body	Brass
78		Loop	Brass
79	Buckle	Tongue	Brass with some tin
79		Loop	Mercury gilded silver
80	Buckle	Body	Base silver-copper with zinc, lead and tin
80		Rivet	Brass
81	Buckle	Body	Base silver-copper alloy, traces of tin, lead and zinc
81		Tongue	Gilded silver-copper, traces of tin and lead
81		Garnet setting base	Copper with traces of zinc
81		Folded flap	Copper
83	Sword fitting	Sling	Silver-copper alloy, traces of lead, tin and gold
88	Buckle	Plate	Leaded gunmetal
88		Tongue	Brass
89	Buckle	Body	Leaded gunmetal
90	Strap-end	Body	Base silver-copper, traces of gold
91	Belt mount (Inv. no. 36)	Body	Silver-copper, traces of gold and lead
91	Belt mount (Inv. no. 37)	Body	Silver-copper, traces of gold, lead and zinc
92	Belt mount (Inv. no. 34)	Body	Silver-copper, traces of gold, lead and zinc
92	Belt mount (Inv. no. 35)	Body	Silver-copper, traces of gold, lead and zinc
92		Pin	Copper
114	Buckle-plate	Body	Brass
115	Belt mount	Body	Leaded gunmetal
117	Earring	Body	Silver-copper alloy
118	Brooch	Body	Base silver-copper alloy, traces of lead and tin
118		Pin	Base silver-copper alloy, traces of lead and tin
131	Earring (Inv. no. 114)	Hoop	Silver-copper alloy, trace of lead
131		Sphere	Silver-copper alloy, trace of lead
131	Earring (Inv. no. 115)	Large sphere	Silver-copper alloy
132	Earring (Inv. no. 96)	Body surface	Mercury gilded (includes silver) on copper
132	Earring (Inv. no. 97)	Body surface	Mercury gilded (includes silver) on copper
132		Sample of interior	Silver and copper detected
133	Armlet (Inv. no. 117)	Body	Silver-copper alloy, traces of lead and gold
133	Armlet (Inv. no. 118)	Body	Silver-copper alloy trace of gold
135	Ring	Body	Silver-copper alloy, traces of gold
136	Mount	Front	Silver-copper alloy, trace of gold
136		Backing sheet	Copper with trace of tin
137	Mount (Inv. no. 146)	Body	Silver-copper alloy, traces of tin and lead
137	Mount (Inv. no. 147)	Body	Silver-copper alloy
137	Mount (Inv. no. 148)	Body	Silver-copper alloy, traces of gold

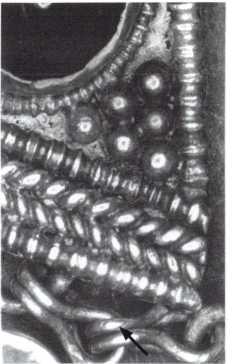

Plate 65 Detail of twisted square-sectioned gold wire, bordering garnet earring GR 1981,9-5,4 (**cat. no. 3**).

Plate 66 Detail of earring pendant P&E 1923,7-16,11 (**cat. no. 1**) showing several examples of filligree. The loop-on-loop chain has a spiral crease (**arrowed**) typical of wire made by twisting. The border is made up of beaded wire, granulation and a 'false-plait' all soldered to the base plate. The false-plait is formed from two pairs of wires, twisted like rope and laid side by side with opposite direction of twist.

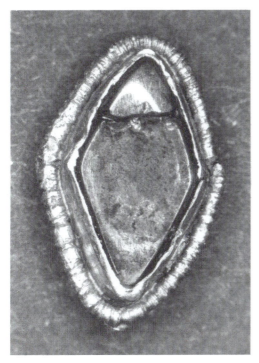

Plate 68 Detail of the hoop of ring P&E 1923,7-16,15 (**cat. no. 13**). It is decorated with a false-plait, bordered with beaded wire and shows evidence of wear.

Plate67 Garnet stud with beaded-wire border, P&E 1923,7-16,32 (**cat. no. 29D**).

Plate 69 Detail of the border of gilt silver and garnet brooch, P&E 1923,7-16,73 (**cat. no. 15**). The border is made up of silver granules soldered to the base-plate before gilding.

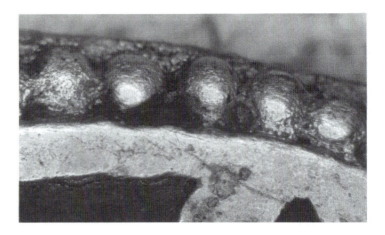

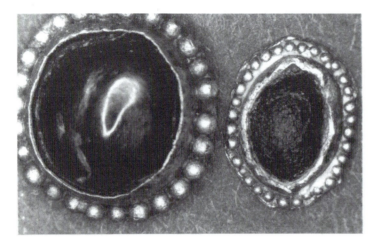

Plate 70 Cabochon garnet stud and a smaller stud of green glass P&E 1923,7-16,32 (**cat. no. 29 G–H**). Their borders are made up of individual granules soldered onto the base-plate.

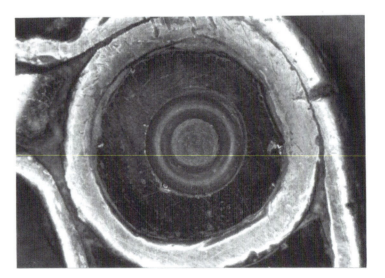

Plate 71 Detail of a garnet bird-head mount, P&E 1923,7-16,12 (**cat. no. 24A**). This circular garnet has been recut – note the straight edge on the right. The ring in the centre once held a gold inlay.

Glossary

Agate — A banded variety of microcrystalline quartz.

Amethyst — A purple variety of macrocrystalline quartz.

Beaded wire — Ornamental wire imitating rows of grains, produced by rolling a round section wire under either a single-edged, or a multiple-edged, tool, or by using a matching pair of swage blocks (organarium).

Brass — A golden-coloured alloy of copper with zinc.

Bronze — An alloy of copper with tin.

Buckle — Component parts see **Fig. 1 a, b, c**

Burnishing — Polishing a metal surface with a hard, smooth tool, usually of stone.

Cabochon — A stone with a convex surface and usually a flat base.

Carnelian — A variety of microcrystalline quartz ranging in colour from red to orange.

Chalcedony — A variety of microcrystalline quartz, usually of pale colour.

Chasing — A technique of metal decoration. A blunt tool known as a tracer or chasing tool is hammered into the metal while being moved across the surface in a smooth, continuous sequence. Chasing produces a groove by displacing the metal, not removing it (unlike engraving – see below).

Chip-carving — A style of decoration of sharply angled facets, also called 'kerbschnitt'. It is believed to have had its origin in the carving of softer materials such as wood and bone, and was done with metal chisels on bronze. The same name is also applied to cast metalwork for which the wax models were carved in this style.

Cloison — A strip of metal soldered to a base forming a cell and enclosing a stone (or enamel) of the same shape.

Cloisonné — A technique of stone setting (or enamelling) in which the stones are contained in cloisons. Most commonly used for flat pieces of stone.

Drawn wire — Method of wire production, that is pulling of a rod of metal through successively smaller holes in a draw-plate, thus making it longer and thinner. During the process the wire has to be annealed to restore its ductility.

Earring — Component parts see **Fig. 2 a-e**

Engraving — A technique of metal decoration. A sharp tool known as a graver is used to remove a sliver of metal and produce a groove. The graver is pushed into the metal by hand, not with a hammer (see chasing above).

Faience — A fired ceramic of ground quartz with an alkaline glaze, usually blue or green.

Filigree — Decoration with fine wire, normally of gold or silver, but also other metals.

Granulation — The decoration of a surface with tiny, spherical grains of metal.

Gunmetal — An alloy of copper with tin and zinc.

Hammered wire — Wire that is produced by hammering a strip or rod of metal into shape. Hammered wires are characterised by their slightly irregular cross-section.

Leaded bronze — An alloy of copper with tin and lead.

Leaded gunmetal — An alloy of copper with tin, zinc and lead.

Mercury gilding — Also known as fire-gilding. A method of plating gold onto silver- or copper-based objects by applying an amalgam of mercury and gold to a well-prepared surface, heating to drive off the free mercury, and then burnishing the plating.

Organarium — A tool for making beaded wire in which the wire is compressed between two dies or swage blocks.

Platinum group element (PGE) inclusions — Very small (only the largest are visible to the naked eye) white metallic inclusions in gold. These are usually alloys of osmium, iridium and ruthenium (rarely platinum). They are indicative of gold from an alluvial source, rather than mined gold.

Punching — Indenting an object, or impressing a shape or pattern on it by using a punch and a hammer.

Repoussé — Decorating sheet metal in relief from the back. In the process there is no loss of metal, as it is stretched locally and the surface remains continuous, though it may be cut through later. Often combined with chasing.

Swage blocks — A perforated or grooved block of metal which is used to shape rod or wire.

Twisted wire — Round-section wire was manufactured by tightly twisting strips or square sectioned rods of metal then rolling them between flat surfaces to produce a regular round-section wire. Wires made by this method are recognisable by the spiral crease left by the twisting (**arrowed in Pl. 66 above**).

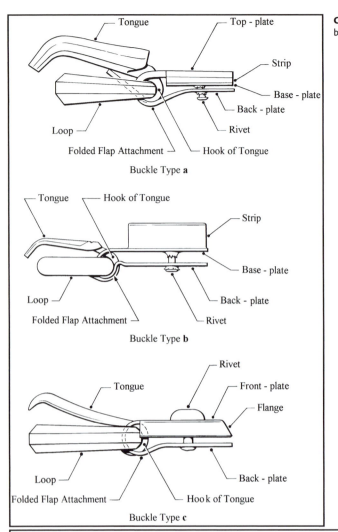

Glossary Figure 1 Identification of buckle components

Tongue

Top - plate

Strip

Base - plate

Back - plate

Rivet

Loop

Folded Flap Attachment

Hook of Tongue

Buckle Type **a**

Tongue

Hook of Tongue

Strip

Base - plate

Back - plate

Rivet

Loop

Folded Flap Attachment

Buckle Type **b**

Rivet

Tongue

Front - plate

Flange

Loop

Back - plate

Folded Flap Attachment

Hook of Tongue

Buckle Type **c**

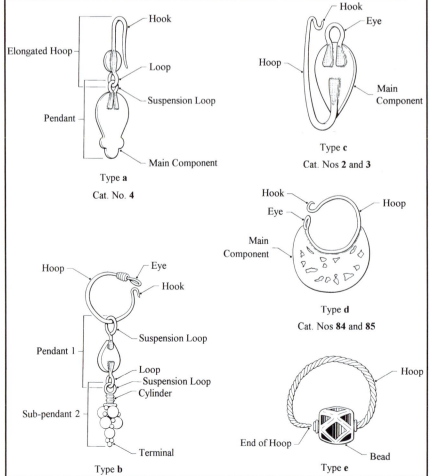

Glossary Figure 2 Identification of earring components

Elongated Hoop

Hook

Loop

Suspension Loop

Pendant

Main Component

Type **a**

Cat. No. **4**

Hook

Eye

Hoop

Main Component

Type **c**

Cat. Nos **2** and **3**

Hook

Eye

Hoop

Main Component

Type **d**

Cat. Nos **84** and **85**

Hoop

Eye

Hook

Suspension Loop

Loop

Suspension Loop

Cylinder

Pendant 1

Sub-pendant 2

Terminal

Type **b**

Hoop

End of Hoop

Bead

Type **e**

Bibliography
Andrási, Aibabin, La Niece and Cowell

Abbreviations

Act. Arch. Hung.	Acta Archaeologica Academiae Scientiarum Hungaricae (Budapest)
ADSV	ADSV – Antiquity and Middle Ages
AE	Archaeologiai Ertesítő (Budapest)
AP AN Ukraini	Arkheolohichni Pam'yatki Ukraini
Arch. Hung.	Archaeologia Hungarica (Budapest)
Arkh. Sbornik	Arkheologichesky Sbornik (St Petersburg)
Arkh. SSSR	Arkheologiya SSSR - Akademiya Nauk SSSR (Moscow)
Bayer. Vorgeschbl.	Bayerische Vorgeschichtsblätter (Munich)
Bayr. AW	Bayerische Akademie der Wissenschaften Philosophisch - historische Klasse (Munich)
Bonn Jbb	Bonner Jahrbücher des Rheinischen Landesmuseums in Bonn
BRGK	Bericht der Römisch-Germanischen Kommission (Mainz)
Comptes Rendus	Comptes Rendus de la Commission Impériale Archéologique (St Petersburg)
FA	Folia Archaeologica (Budapest)
Germania	Anzeiger der Römisch-Germanischen Kommission des Deutschen Archäologischen Instituts. (Mainz)
GHA	Germanen, Hunnen und Awaren. Schätze der Völkerwanderungszeit. Verlag des Germanischen Nationalmuseum. (Nuremburg 1987)
IAK	Izvestiya Imperatorskoi Arkheologicheskoi Komissii (St Petersburg)
IGAIMK	Izvestiya Gosudarstvennoi Akademii Istorii Material'noi Kul'tury (St Petersburg)
IPEK	Jahrbuch für Römisch-Germanischen Zentralmuseums (Mainz)
JPME	A Janus Pannonius Múzeum Evkönyve (Pécs)
JRGZM	Jahrbuch des Römisch-Germanischen Zentralmuseums (Mainz)
Klio	Klio. Beiträge zur alten Geschichte (Berlin)
KSIA	Kratkie Soobshcheniya Instituta Arkheologii Akademiya Nauk SSSR (Moscow)
KSIIMK	Kratkie Soobshcheniya Instituta Istorii Material'noi Kul'tury
MAIET	Materiali po Arkheologii Istorii i Etnografii Tavrii (Simferopol)
MAK	Materiali po Arkheologii Kavkaza (Moscow)
MAR	Materiali po Arkheologii Rossii (St Petersburg)
MIA	Materiali i Issledovaniya po Arkheologii SSSR (Moscow)
Otch. Imp. Arkh. Kom. (OIAK)	Otchet' Imperatorskoi Arkheologicheskoi Komissii (St Petersburg)
SA	Sovetskaya Arkheologiya (Moscow)
VDI	Vestnik Drevnei Istorii
Vjesnik	Vjesnik za Arheologiju i Historiju Dalmatinsku (Split)
VMMK	A Veszprém Megyei Múzeumok Közleményei (Veszprém)
VV	Vizantiiskii Vremennik (St Petersburg)
ZOOID	Zapiski Odesskogo Obshchestva Istorii i Drevnostei (Odessa)

Abadie-Reynal C. and Sodini J.P. 1992, *La céramique paléochrétienne de Thasos*. Etudes Thasiennes, XIII, Paris.

Åberg N. 1919, *Ostpreußen in der Völkerwanderungszeit*. Uppsala/ Leipzig.

Abramova M.P. 1990, Zapadnye raiony Tsentralnogo Predkavkazya vo II–III vv. n.e. *KSIA* 197.

Afanas'ev G.E. 1979, Novye nakhodki v Mokroi balke bliz Kislovodska. *SA* 1979 - 3, 171–85.

Afanas'ev G.E. 1980, *Pryazhki katakombnogo mogil'nika Mokraya Balka u g. Kislovodska. Severny Kavkaz v drevnosti i v Srednie veka.* Moscow, 141–52.

Ahrweiler H. 1971, Les relations entre les Byzantins et les Russes au IXe siècle. *Bulletin d'Information et de Coordination de l'Association International des Etudes Byzantines*, 5, 44–70.

Aibabin A.I. 1977, Saltovskie poyasnie nabory iz Kryma. *SA* - N1, 225–39.

Aibabin A.I. 1979, Pogrebeniya vtoroi poloviny V-pervoi poloviny VI v. v Krymu. *KSIA* 158, 22–34.

Aibabin A.I. 1982, *Pogrebeniya kontsa VII - pervoi poloviny VIII vv. v Krymu*. In: *Drevnosti epokhi velikogo pereseleniya narodov V–VIII vekov*, Moscow, 165–92.

Aibabin A.I. 1984, Problemy khronologii mogil'nikov Kryma Pozdnerimskogo perioda. *SA* 1984 - 1, 104–22.

Aibabin A.I. 1985, Pogrebenie khazarskogo voina. *SA* 1985 - 3, 191–205.

Aibabin A.I. 1987, *Etnicheskaya prinadlezhnost mogil'nikov Kryma IV-pervoi poloviny VII vv. n.e. Materialy k etnicheskoi istorii Kryma*. Kiev, 164–99.

Aibabin A.I. 1990, Khronologiya mogil'nikov Kryma Pozdnerimskogo i rannesrednevekovogo vremeni. *MAIET*. I, 3–86.

Aibabin A.I. 1991, Osnovnye etapy istorii gorodishcha Eski-Kermen. *MAIET*. II, 43–51.

Aibabin A.I. 1991b, *Kelegeiskoe pogrebenie voennogo vozhdya. Problemi na prablgarskata istoriya i kul'tura*. 2. Sofia, 28–35.

Aibabin A. 1993, La fabrication des garnitures de ceintures et des fibules à Chersonèse au Bosphore Cimmérien et dans la Gothie de Crimée aux VIe–VIIIe siècles. In: *Outils et ateliers d'orfèvres des temps anciens*. Antiquités Nationales, Mémoire 2, 163–70.

Aibabin A.I. 1993a, Mogil'niki VIII-nachala X vv. v Krymu. *MAIET*. III, 121–33.

Aibabin 1993b, Pogrebeniya kochevnicheskoi znati v Krymu kontsa IV–VI vv. *MAIET*. III, 206–10.

Aibabin A. 1994, Kompleksy s bol'shimi dvuplastinchatymi fibulami iz Luchistogo. *MAIET*. IV, 132–72.

Ajbabin A. (Aibabin) 1995a, Les tombes de chefs nomades en Crimée de la fin du IVe siècle au VIe siècle. In: F. Vallet and M. Kazanski (eds), *La Noblesse Romaine et les Chefs Barbares du IIIe au VII siècle*. Paris, 207–16.

Ajbabin A.I. (Aibabin) 1995b, Gli Alani, i Goti e gli Unni. In: *Dal Mille al Mille. Tesore e popoli dal Mer Nero*. Exhibition catalogue, Milan, 156–70.

Aibabine A. (Aibabin) 1996, *Population de Crimée au milieu du IIIe et au IVe siècle. L'identité des populations archéologiques*. XVIe rencontres Internationales d'archéologie et d'histoire d'Antibes, Valbonne, 13–40.

Aibabin A.I. and Chajredinova E.A. 1995, Necropoli di Luchistoe. In: *Dal Mille al Mille. Tesore e popoli dal Mer Nero*. Exhibition catalogue. Milan, 189–94.

Akhmerov R.B. 1951, Ufimskie pogrebeniya VI–VIII vekov nashei ery. *KSIIMK*, XL, 125–37.

Alföldi A. 1932, *Leletek a hun korszakból és etnikai szétválasztásuk - Funde aus der Hunnenzeit und ihre ethnische Sonderung*. Arch. Hung. IX.

Alföldi M.R. *et al.* 1957, *Intercisa II. (Dunapentele). Geschichte der Stadt in der Römerzeit*. Arch. Hung. XXXVI.

Ambroz A.K. 1966, Fibuly yuga Evropeiskoi chasti SSSR II–IV vv. n.e. *Svod Arkheologicheskikh Istochnikov.* Moscow, D1.30.

Ambroz A.K. 1968, Dunaiskie elementy v rannesrednevekovoi kul'ture Kryma (VI–VII vv.). *KSIA* 113, 10–23.

Ambroz A.K. 1970, Yuzhnie khudozhestvennie svyazi naseleniya Verkhnego Podneprov'ya v VI v. *MIA*, 70–7.

Ambroz A.K. 1971, Problemy rannesrednevekovoi khronologii Vostochnoi Evropy, 1. *SA* 1971 - 2, 96–123.

Ambroz A.K. 1973: Review of 1. Erdélyi *et al.*, 1969, Das Gräberfeld von Nevolino. (Budapest). *SA* 1973 - 2, 288–98.

Ambroz A.K. 1974, *Khronologiya rannesrednevekovykh drevnostei Vostochnoi Evropy V–IX vv.* Doctoral dissertation. Nauchnyi arkhiv Instituta Arkheologii AN SSSR, R.2 no. 24 41.

Ambroz A.K. 1981, *Vostochnoevropeiskie i sredneaziatskie stepi V - pervoi poloviny VIII v. Stepi Evrazii v epokhu srednevekovya.* Arkheologiya SSR. Moscow, 10–22.

Ambroz A.K. 1982, *O dvukhplastinchatykh fibulakh s nakladkami. Analogii k state A.V. Dmitrieva. Drevnosti epokhi Velikogo pereseleniya narodov (V–VIII vv.).* Moscow, 107–21.

Ambroz A.K. 1985, K itogam diskussii po arkheologii gunnskoi epokhi v stepyakh vostochnoi Evropy. *SA* 1985 - 3, 293–303.

Ambroz A.K. 1988, *Osnovy pereodizatsii yuzhnokrymskikh mogil'nikov tipa Suuk-Su. Drevnosti Slavyan i Rusi.* Moscow, 5–12.

Ambroz A.K. 1989, *Khronologiya drevnostei Severnogo Kavkaza V–VII vv.* Moscow.

Ambroz A.K. 1992, Bospor. Khronologiya rannesrednevekoykh drevnostei. *Bosporskii Sbornik.* 1 6–95.

Ambroz A.K. 1995, Yugo-Zapadnyi Krym. Mogil'niki IV–VII vv. *MAIET.* 4, 31–88.

Ament H. 1970, *Fränkische Adelsgräber von Flonheim in Rheinhessen.* Germanische Denkmäler der Völkerwanderungszeit. Serie B. Die Fränkischen Altertümer des Rheinlandes Bd. 5, Berlin.

Ammianus Marcellinus. 1972. Cambridge/London.

Andrews C. 1994, *Amulets of Ancient Egypt.* London.

Anna Comnena 1965, *Aleksiada,* (trans. Y.N. Lyubarskogo). Moscow.

Annibaldi G. and Werner J. 1963, Ostgotische Grabfunde aus Acquasanta. *Germania* 41, 356–73.

Anokhin V.A. 1977, *Monetnoe delo Khersonesa.* Kiev.

Archéologie de la Mer Noire 1997. *La Crimée à l'époque des Grandes Invasions IVe–VIII siècles.* Musée de Normandie, Caen.

Arrhenius B. 1971, *Granatschmuck und Gemmen aus nordischen Funden des frühen Mittelalters.* Stockholm.

Arrhenius B. 1985, *Merovingian Garnet Jewellery.* (Stockholm).

Artamonov M.I. 1962, *Istoriya Khazar.* St Petersburg [Leningrad].

Ashik A. 1849, *Bosporskoe tsarstvo.* Part 3. Odessa.

Azaroff and Buerger 1958, *The powder method in X-ray crystallography.* New York.

Babenchikov V.P. 1963, Chornorichensky mogil'nik. *Arkheologichni Pamiyatki URSR.* (Kiev) XII, 90–123.

Bakay K. 1978, Bestattung eines vornehmen Kriegers vom 5. Jahrhundert in Lengyeltóti. (Komitat Somogy. Kreis Marcali). *Act. Arch. Hung.* 30, 149–72.

Bálint Cs. 1978, Vestiges archéologiques des Sassanides. *Act. Arch. Hung.* 30, 173–212.

Bálint Cs. 1992, Kontakte zwischen Iran, Byzanz und der Steppe. Der Gürtel im frühmittelalterlichen Transkaukasus und das Grab von Üč Tepe (Sovj Azerbaidzhan). In: F. Daim, *Awarenforschungen,* vol. I, Vienna, 309–496.

Bálint Cs. 1995, *Kelet, a korai avarok és Bizánc kapcsolatai. (Régészeti tanulmányok).* Szeged.

Baranov I.A. 1975, Rannesrednevekovaya pryazhka iz Yalty. *SA* 1975 - 1, 271–5.

Baranov I.A. 1990, *Tavrika v epokhu rannego srednevekovya.* Kiev.

Barkóczi L. and Salamon A. 1968, Glasfunde von dem Ende IV. und Anfang des V. Jhs. in Ungarn. *AE*, 95.

Baur P.V.C. *et al.* 1933, *The Excavations at Dura-Europos. Preliminary Report of the Fourth Season of Work.* New Haven.

Beck F., Kazanski M. and Vallet F. 1988, La riche tombe de Kertch du Musée des Antiquités Nationales. *Antiquités Nationales* 20, 63 et seqq.

Belinsky I.V. and Boiko A.L. 1991, Tainik pozdnesarmatskogo vremeni kurgana 2 mogil'nika 'Aerodrom-I'. *Istoriko-arkheologicheskie issledovaniya v g. Azove i na Nezhnem Donu v 1990 godu.* Issue 10. (Azov), 85–96.

Beninger E. 1929, Germanengräber von Laa an der Thaya (NÖ). *Eiszeit und Urgeschichte* 6, 143–55.

Berkhin I.P. [Zasetskaya] 1961, O trekh nakhodkakh pozdnesarmatskogo vremeni v Nizhnem Povolzhe. *Arkheologicheskii Sbornik* 2 (St Petersburg [Leningrad]), 141–53.

Bespalyi E.I. 1992, Kurgan sarmatskogo vremeni u g. Azova. *SA* 1992 - 1, 175–91.

Betrozov R.Z. 1980, Zakhoronenie vozhdya gunnskogo vremeni u sel. Kishpek v Kabardino Balkarii. *Severny Kavkaz v drevnosti v srednie veka* (Moscow), 113–22.

Betrozov R.Zh. 1987, Kurgany gunnskogo vremeni u seleniya Kishpek. In: *Arkheologicheskie issledovaniya na novostroikakh Kabardino-Balkarii v 1972–1979 gg.* vol. 3. Nalchik, 11–39.

Bezuglov S.I. 1988, Pozdnesarmatskoe pogrebenie znatnogo voina v stepnom Podone. *SA* 1988 - 4.

Bezuglov S.I. and Kopylov V.P. 1989, Katakombnye pogrebeniya III–IV vv. na Nizhnem Donu. *SA* 1989 - 3, 171–83.

Bezuglov S. and Zakharov A. 1989, Bogatoe pogrebenie pozdnerimskogo vremeni bliz Tanaisa. *Izvestiya Rostovskogo Muzeya Kraevedeniy.* 6. Rostov-on-Don, 42–66.

Bich O.I. 1959, Pervye raskopki nekropolya Pantikapea. *MIA* 69.2–3, 296–321.

Bichir G.H. 1977, Les Sarmates au Bas-Danube. *Dacia* XXI (Bucharest), 167–97.

Bierbrauer V. 1975, *Die ostgotischen Grab- und Schatzfunde in Italien.* Centro Italiano di Studi sull'Alto Medioevo. Studi Medievali VII, Spoleto.

Bierbrauer V. 1992, Historische Überlieferung und archäologischer Befund. Ostgermanische Einwanderung unter Odoaker und Theoderich nach Italien. Aussagemöglichkeiten und Grenzen der Archäologie. In K. Godłowski (ed.), *Probleme der relativen und absoluten Chronologie ab Latènezeit bis zum Frühmittelalter.* Krakow, 263–77.

Bierbrauer V. *et al.* 1993, Die Dame von Ficarolo. *Archeologia Medievale* 20. 303–32

Blockley R.C. (ed.) 1985, *Historia. The History of Menander the Guardsman.* Liverpool.

Bobrinsky A.A. 1914, Pereshchepinsky klad. *MAR* 34, 110–20 .

Böhme H.W. 1974, *Germanische Grabfunde des 4. bis 5. Jahrhunderts zwischen Unterer Elbe und Loire. Studien zur Chronologie und Bevölkerungsgeschichte.* 2 vols. Münchner Beiträge zur Vor- und Frühgeschichte 19, Munich.

Bóna I. 1968, A bakodpusztai germán királynő. Die germanische Königin von Bakodpuszta. In: *A népek országútján. (Auf der Landstraße der Völker).* Budapest.

Bóna I. 1971, A népvándorlás kora Fejér megyében. *Fejér megye története az őskortól a honfoglalásig* 5, (Székesfehérvár), 221–314 .

Bóna I. 1974, *A középkor hajnala. A gepidák és a longobárdok a Kárpát-medencében.* Budapest.

Bóna I. 1976, *The Dawn of the Dark Ages. The Gepids and the Lombards in the Carpathian Basin.* Budapest.

Bóna I. 1986a, Daciától Erdőelvéig. A népvándorlás kora Erdélyben (271–896). In: *Erdély története,* vol.I. Budapest, 107–234.

Bóna I. 1986b, Ein gepidisches Fürstengrab aus dem 6. Jahrhundert in Tiszaszőlős. In: Über die völkerwanderungszeitlichen Fälschungen des Goldschatzes von Moigrad. A mojgrádi kincs hamis népvándorláskori aranyairól. *VMMK* 18, 95–113.

Bóna I. 1991, *Das Hunnenreich* (Budapest-Stuttgart).

Bóna I. 1993, *A hunok és nagykirályaik.* Budapest.

Borodin O.R. 1991, *Rimskii papa Martin I i ego pisma iz Kryma. Prichernomor'e v srednie veka.* Moscow, 173–90.

Bowditch D.C. 1973, A comparative study of three analytical procedures for the collection and determination of gold and platinoids in precious metal bearing ores. *Bulletin of the Australian Mining Development Laboratories* 15, 71–87.

Brentjes B. 1954, Zur Typologie, Datierung und Ableitung der Zikadenfibeln. *Wissenschaftliche Zeitschrift der Martin-Luther-Universität Halle-Wittenberg,* III. Halle. 901–3 .

Bromberg A.R. 1991, *Gold of Greece. Jewelry and Ornaments from the Benaki Museum.* Exhibition catalogue, Dallas Museum of Art, Dallas.

Brown K. 1984, *The Gold Breast Chain from the Early Byzantine period in the Römisch-Germanisches Zentralmuseum.* Mainz.

Brun F. 1880, *Chernomor'e,* Pt 2. Odessa.

Chadour A.B. 1994, *Ringe. Rings. Die Alice und Louis Koch Sammlung. Vierzig Jahrhunderte durch vier Generationen gesehen. The Alice and Louis Koch Collection. Forty Centuries Seen by Four Generations,* vol.1. Leeds.

Cherepanova E.N. 1966, Arkhiv O. L. Bert'e-Delagarda. *Arkhiv Ukraini* 6, 78–81.

Cherepanova E.N. 1968, *Arkheologicheskie Issledovaniya Srednevekovogo Kryma,* 205–12.

Chichikova M. 1980, Forschungen in Novae (Moesia Inferior). *Klio* 62 - 1, 55–66.

Chichurov I.S. 1980, *Vizantiiskie istoricheskie sochineniya: 'Khronografiya' Feofana, 'Breviarii' Nikifora.* Moscow.

Chrapunov I.N. 1995, Necropoli di Druznoe, distretto di Simferopol'. In: *Dal Mille al Mille. Tesore e popoli dal Mar Nero.* Exhibition catalogue, Milan, 180–6.

Coche de la Ferté E. 1962, *Antique Jewellery from the second to the eighth century.* Bern.

Collection of M.P. Botkine 1911. St Petersburg.

Constantine Porphyrogenitus 1989, *Ob upravlenii gosudarstvom [De Administrando Imperii].* Moscow.

Cowell M.R. 1998, Coin analysis by energy dispersive x-ray fluorescence spectrometry. In: W.A. Oddy and M.R. Cowell (eds), *Metallurgy in Numismatics* IV. Royal Numismatic Society, London, 448–60.

Csallány D. 1954a, A bizánci fémművesség emlékei. Antik Tanulmányok. *Studia Antiqua* I, 101–28.

Csallány D. 1954b, Pamyatniki vizantinskogo metalloobrabaty – vayunskogo iskusstva I. *Acta Antiqua.* (Budapest) II, 311–48.

Csallány D. 1961, *Archäologische Denkmäler der Gepiden im Mitteldonaubecken (454–568 u.Z.)* Arch. Hung. XXXVIII.

Cs. Dax M. 1980, Keleti germán női sírok Kapolcson. *VMMK* 15, 97–106.

Dalton O.M. 1924a, Sarmatian ornaments from Kerch in the British Museum, compared with Anglo-Saxon and Merovingian ornaments in the same collection. *Antiquaries Journal* IV, 259–62.

Dalton O.M. 1924b, The Sarmatian origin of Anglo-Saxon jewellery. *Illustrated London News* no. 268, 268–71.

Dalton O.M. 1924c, A gold pectoral cross and an amuletic bracelet of the sixth century. In: *Mélanges offerts à M. Gustave Schlumberger.* Paris, pt 4, 386–90.

Damm I.G. 1988, Goldschmiedearbeiten der Völkerwanderungszeit aus dem Nördlichen Schwarzmeergebiet. Katalog der Sammlung Diergardt 2. *Kölner Jahrbuch für Vor- und Frühgeschichte* 21, 65–210.

Davidson P.F. and Oliver, Jr A. 1984, *Ancient Greek and Roman Gold Jewelry in the Brooklyn Museum.* Brooklyn, New York.

De Baye Baron J. 1888, Les bijoux gothiques de Kertsch. *Revue Archéologique* 47, 2–3.

De Baye Baron J. 1891, *De l'art des Goths. Communication faite au Congrès Historique et Archéologique de Liège.* Paris.

De Baye Baron J. 1892, La bijouterie des Goths en Russie. *Mémoires de la Société nationale des Antiquaires de France* 51, 1–16.

De Baye Baron J. 1908, Les tombeaux des Goths en Crimée. *Mémoires de la Société nationale des Antiquaires de France* 67, 72–114.

Demirjian T. 1991, *Treasures of the Dark Ages in Europe.* Ariadne Galleries Exhibition catalogue, New York.

Deopik V.B. 1963, Klassifikatsiya i khronologiya alanskikh ukrasheny VI–IX vv. *MIA* 114, 122–47.

Deppert-Lippitz B. 1985, Griechischer Goldschmuck. In: *Kulturgeschichte der antiken Welt.* Bd 27, Mainz am Rhein.

De Ridder A. 1924, *Catalogue Sommaire des Bijoux Antiques.* Paris.

Diaconu G. 1971, Über die Fibel mit umgeschlagenem fuss in Dazie. *Dacia,* XV (Bucarest), 239–67.

Diner J. 1890, *Sammlung Géza v. Kárász. Catalog der Kunstgegenstände und Antiquitäten von J. Diner.* Budapest.

Dmitriev A.V. 1982, *Rannesrednevekovie fibuly iz mogil'nika na r. Dyurso. Drevnosti epokhi Velikogo pereseleniya narodov V–VIII vv.* Moscow, 69–107.

Dombay J. 1956, Der gotische Grabfund von Domolospuszta. Der Fundort und die Umstände des Fundes. *JPMÉ,* 104–30.

Dombrovsky O.I. 1974, *Srednevekovye poseleniya i 'isary' Krymskogo Yuzhnoberezhya. Feodalnaya Tavrika.* Kiev, 5–56.

Dorotheum 1996, *Ausgrabungen. Auktion am 19. Oktober 1996* (Vienna).

Entwistle C. 1994, Gold and garnet pectoral cross, and gold openwork earrings; cat. nos 100–2 in: D. Buckton (ed.): *Byzantium. Treasures of Byzantine Art and Culture from British Collections.* Exhibition catalogue, London.

Erdélyi I. 1982, Novy mogil'nik V v. v Keszthely-Fenékpuszta. In: A.K. Ambroz and I. Erdélyi, *Drevnosti epokhi velikogo pereseleniya narodov V–VIII vekov.* Moscow, 64–8.

Fëdorov Y.A. and Fëdorov G.S. 1970, K voprosu o yuzhnoi granitse Khazarii. *Vestnik Moskovskogo gosudarstvennogo universiteta.* Seriya istoriya. N3. Moscow.

Fettich N. 1932, *A szilágysomlyói második kincs. Der zweite Schatz von Szilágysomlyó.* Arch. Hung. VIII.

Fettich N. 1951, *Régészeti tanulmányok a késői hun fémművesség történetéhez.* Arch. Hung. XXXI.

Fettich N. 1951b, *Archäologische Studien zur Geschichte der späthunnischen Metallkunst.* Arch. Hung. XXXI.

Fettich N. 1953, *A Szeged - Nagyszéksósi hun fejedelmi sírlelet.* Arch. Hung. XXXII.

Firsov L.V. 1979, O polozhenii strany Dori v Tavrike. *VV. 40,* 104–13.

Fitz 1985–6, Eine Karolingerzeitliche Scheibenfibel mit Tierdarstellung vom Oberleisberg. Römisches Österreich. *Jahresschrift der Österreichischen Gesellschaft für Archäologie.* 13/14. 21–76.

Gadlo A.V. 1968, Rannesrednevekovoe selishche na beregu Kerchenskogo proliva. *KSIA.* N113, 78–84.

Gadlo A.V. 1968a, Problema Priazovskoi Rusi i sovremennye arkheologicheskie dannye o Yuzhnom Priazovie. VIII–X vv. *Vestnik Leningradskogo gosudarstvennogo universiteta.* St Petersburg [Leningrad]. N14, 55–65.

Gadlo A.V. 1979, *Etnicheskaya Istoriya Severnogo Kavkaza IV–X vv.* St Petersburg [Leningrad].

Gadlo A.V. 1980, *K istorii Vostochnoi Tavriki VIII–IX vv. Antichnye traditsii i srednie veka.* Sverdlovsk, 130–45.

Garam E. and Kiss A. 1992, *Népvándorlás kori aranykincsek a Magyar Nemzeti Múzeumban.* Budapest. (See also English trans. L. Boros, *Gold Finds of the Migration Period in the Hungarian National Museum*).

Garkavi A.Y. 1891, Krymskii poluostrov do mongolskogo nashestviya v arabskoi literature. *Trudy* IV Arkheologicheskogo s'ezda. Kazan.

Gening V.F. 1976, Turaevskii mogil'nik V v. n. e. *Iz arkheologii Volgo-Kam'ya.* Kazan, 55–108.

Gening V.F. 1979, Khronologiya poyasnoi garnitury I tisyacheletiya n.e. (po materialam mogil'nikov Prikam'ya). *KSIA* 158, 96–106.

Gertzen A.G. 1990, Krepostnoi ansambl Mangupa. *MAIET.* 1, 87–166.

Gertzen A.G. and Mogarichev Y.M. 1992, *Eshche raz o date poyavleniya kreposti na plato Chufut-Kale. Problemy istorii "peshchernykh gorodov" v Krymu.* Simferopol.

GHA 1987. Germanen, Hunnen und Awaren. Schätze der Völkerwanderungszeit. Verlag des Germanischen Nationalmuseum. Nuremburg.

Giesler-Müller U. 1992, *Das frühmittelalterliche Gräberfeld von Basel-Kleinhüningen.* Basler Beiträge zur Ur- und Frühgeschichte, vol. 11B; Derendingen-Solothurn.

Ginters W. 1928, *Das Schwert der Skythen und Sarmaten in Südrussland.* Berlin.

Golb N. and Pritsak O. 1982, *Khazarian Hebrew Documents of the Tenth Century.* Ithaca/London.

Golden P. 1980, *Khazar Studies,* vol. 1. Budapest.

Goldina R.D. and Vodolago N.V. 1990, *Mogil'niki Nevolinskoi Kultury v Priural'e. Izdatel'stvo Irkutskogo Universiteta,* Irkutsk.

Gomolka G. 1966, Katalog der Kleinfunde. *Klio* 47, 291–356.

Gomolka-Fuchs G. 1993, Ostgermanische Foederaten im spätrömischen Heer. Hinweise in der materiellen Kultur auf die ethnische Zusammensetzung der Bevölkerung vom 4.–6. Jahrhundert in Nordbulgarien. In: *L'armée romaine et les barbares du IIIe au VII siècle.* Paris.

Goryunov E.A. and Kazanski M.M. 1983, *K izucheniyu rannesrednevekovykh drevnostei Nizhnego Podunav'ya. Slavyane na Dnestre i Dunae.* Kiev, 191–205.

Götze A. 1907, *Gotische Schnallen.* Berlin, 1–35.

Götze A. 1913, *Gotische Schnallen. Germanische Funde aus der Völkerwanderungszeit.* Berlin.

Götze A. 1915, *Frühgermanische Kunst. Sonderausstellung ostgotischer Alterthümer der Völkerwanderungszeit aus Südrußland.* Königliche Museen zu Berlin, Berlin.

Greifenhagen A. 1975, *Schmuckarbeiten in Edelmetall.* I, II. Berlin.

Grosu V.I. 1990, *Khronologiya pamyatnikov sarmatskoi kultury Dnestrovsko-Prutskogo mezhdurechya.* Chişinău [Kishinev].

Gudkova A.V. and Fokeev M.M. 1984, *Zemledel'tsy i kochevniki v nizovyakh Dunaya I–IV vv. n.e.* Kiev.

Guguev V.K. and Bezuglov S.I. 1990, Vsadnicheskoe pogrebenie pervykh vekov nashei ery iz kurgannogo nekropolya Kobyakova gorodishcha na Donu. *SA* 1990 - 2, 164–75.

Gumilev L.N. 1960, *Khunnu.* Moscow.

Gushchina I.I. 1966, Pamyatnik pozdnesarmatskoi kultury v Podneprove. *Trudy GIM.* (Moscow) issue 40, 74–9.

Gushchina I.I. 1974, *Naselenie sarmatskogo vremeni v doline reki Belbek v Krymu (po materialam mogil'nikov). Arkheologicheskie issledovaniya na Yuge Vostochnoi Evropy.* (Moscow), 32–64, 127–45.

Hatt J.-J. 1965, Une tombe barbare du Ve siècle à Hochfelden (Bas-Rhin). *Gallia Préhistoire* 23, 250–6.

Hayes J.W. 1972, *Late Roman Pottery.* London.

Hoffmann H. and von Claer V. 1968, *Antiker Gold- und Silberschmuck. Katalog mit Untersuchung der Objecte auf technischer Grundlage.* Museum für Kunst und Gewerbe, Hamburg, Mainz.

Hoffmann H. and Davidson P.F. 1965, *Greek Gold.* Mainz.

Horedt K. 1979, Die Polyederohrringe des 5.–6. Jahrh. u. Z. aus der S.R. Rumänien. *Zeitschrift für Archaologie* 13. Berlin, 241–50.

Horedt K. and Protase D. 1970, Ein völkerwanderungszeitlicher Schatzfund aus Cluj - Someşeni (Siebenbürgen). *Germania* 48, 85–98.

I Goti 1994. Exhibition catalogue, Milan.

Imola dall'età tardo romana all'alto medioevo, lo scavo di Villa Clelia 1979. Exhibition catalogue, Imola.

Jordanes 1882, *Romana et Getica.* (Recensuit T. Mommsen; Monumenta Germaniae Historica, vol. V). Berlin.

Jordanes 1960, *O proiskhozhdenii i deyaniyakh getov. [De origine actibusque Getarum.]* (Trans. and commentary, E.Ch. Skrzhinskoi). Moscow.

Kalmár J. 1943, Népvándorláskori akasztóhorgok és veretek. Metallhaken und Beschläge der ungarländischen Völkerwanderungszeit. *AE.* 149–59 .

Kargopol'tsev C.Y. and Bazhan I.A. 1993, K voprosu ob evolyutsii trekhrogikh pel'tovidnukh lunnits v Evrope (III–IV vv.). *Peterburgsky arkheologichesky vestnik/ Petersburg Archaeological Herald* 7, 113–22.

Kazanski M. 1989, La diffusion de la mode danubienne en Gaule (fin du IVe siècle – debut du VIe siècle), essai d'interprétation historique. *Antiquités Nationales* 21. St. Germain-en-Laye.

Kazanski M. 1994, Les plaques-boucles méditerranéennes des Ve–VIe siècles. *Archéologie Médiévale* XXIV, 137–98.

Kazanski M. 1995, Les tombes des chefs alano-sarmates au IVe siècle dans les steppes pontiques. In: F. Vallet and M. Kazanski (eds), *La Noblesse Romaine et les Chefs Barbares du IIIe au VII siècle.* Paris, 189–205.

Kazanski M. and Legoux R. 1988, Contribution à l'étude des témoignages archéologiques des Goths en Europe orientale à l'époque des Grandes Migrations: la chronologie de la culture de Černjahov récente. *Archéologie Médiévale* 18, 7–53.

Keller E. 1967, Bemerkungen zum Grabfund von Untersiebenbrunn. *Germania* 45, 109–20.

Kepeska L. 1995, *Zadna Reka-Gruajte. The medieval Necropolis.* Prilep.

Kharuzin A.N. 1890, Drevnie mogily Gurzufa i Gugusha. *Izvestiya Imperatorskogo Moskovskogo Obshchestva Lyubitelei Estestvoznaniya, Antropologii i Etnografii* LXIV, (Moscow), 1–102.

Khazanov A.M. 1971, *Ocherki Voennogo Dela Sarmatov.* Akademiya Nauk SSR. Institut Etnografii Moskva. Moscow.

Khvolson D. 1869, *Izvestiya o Khazarakh, Burtasakh, Mad'yarakh, Slavyanakh i Russakh Abu-Ali Akhmeda ben Omar Ibn-Dasta...* St Petersburg.

Kirpichnikov A.A. 1973, Snaryazhenie vsadnika i verkhovogo konya na Rusi IX–XIII vv. *Svod Arkheologicheskikh Istochnikov* E1–36. Moscow.

Kiss A. 1983, Die Skiren im Karpatenbecken, Ihre Wohnsitze und Ihre Materielle Hinterlassenschaft. *Act. Arch. Hung.* 35, 95–131.

Kiss A. 1984, Über eine Silbervergoldete gepidische Schnalle aus dem 5. Jahrhundert von Ungarn. *FA XXXV*, 57–76.

Klumbach H. 1973, *Spätrömische Gardehelme.* Bayerische Akademie der Wissenschaften; Römisch- Germanisches Zentralmuseum Mainz, Munich.

Kondakov N.P. 1896, *Russkie klady.* St Petersburg.

Kondakov N., Tolstoi J. and Reinach S. 1891, *Antiquités de la Russie Méridionale,* Paris.

Korzukhina G.F. 1954, *Russkie klady.* Moscow/St Petersburg [Leningrad].

Kovačević J. 1960, *Varvarska kolonizacija jurnoslovenskih oblasti.* Novi Sad.

Kovalevskaya V.B. 1979, *Poyasnuye nabory Evrazii 4–9 v. Pryazhki. Arkh. SSSR* E 1–2.

Kovalevskaya V.B. 1993, *Novoe v srednevekovoi arkheologii Evrazii. Istoriko - kul'turnaya Assotsiatsiya 'Artefakt'.* Samara.

Kovpanenko G.T. 1980, *Sarmatskoe pogrebenie v Sokolovoi mogile.* *Skifiya i Kavkaz.* Kiev.

Kropotkin V.V. 1958, Iz istorii srednevekovogo Kryma. *SA XXVIII*, 198–218.

Kropotkin V.V. 1965, Mogil'nik Chufu - Kale v Krymu. *KSIA* 100, 108–15.

Kropotkin V.V. and Shelov D.B. 1971, Pamyati A.L. Bert'e-Delagarda. *SA,* 1971 - 1, 140–2.

Kubitschek W. 1911, Grabfunde in Untersiebenbrunn (auf dem Marchfeld). *Jahrbuch für Altertumskunde* 5 (Vienna) 32–74.

Kühn H. 1935a, *Die Vorgeschichtliche Kunst Deutschlands.* Berlin.

Kühn H. 1935b, Die Zikadenfibeln der Völkerwanderungszeit. *IPEK* 10, 85–106.

Kühn H. 1940, *Die germanischen Bügelfibeln der Völkerwanderungszeit in der Rheinprovinz,* 2 vols. Bonn.

Kühn H. 1965, *Die germanischen Bügelfibeln der Völkerwanderungszeit in der Rheinprovinz,* 2 vols. Graz, vol. 1, 92–100.

Kühn H. 1974, *Die germanischen Bügelfibeln der Völkerwanderungszeit in Süddeutschland,* vol. II. Graz.

Kulakovsky Y.A. 1881, Kerchenskaya khristianskaya katakomba 491g. *MAR* 6. St Petersburg.

Kulakovsky Y.A. 1896, K istorii Bospora Kimmeriiskogo v kontse VI v. *VV.* 3.

Kulakovsky Y.A. 1898, Khristianstvo u Alan'. *VV.* 5. St Petersburg.

Kulakovsky Y.A. 1899, *Alany po svedeniyam klassicheskikh i vizantiiskikh pisatelei.* Kiev.

Kuznetsov V.A. 1984, *Ocherki istorii alan.* Ordzhonikidze.

Kuznetsov V.A. 1990, Pogrebeniya III v. iz Kislovodska. *SA,* 1990 - 2, 251–6.

Kuznetsov V.A. 1993, *Alano-osetinskie etyudy.* Vladikavkaz.

La Niece S. 1988, White inlays in Anglo Saxon jewellery. In: E.O. Slater and J.O. Tate (eds), *Science and Archaeology (Glasgow) 1987.* BAR British Series 196, 235–45.

László Gy. 1955, *Etudes archéologiques sur l'histoire de la société des Avars.* Arch. Hung. 34.

Latyshev V.V. 1893, *Izvestiya drevnikh pisatelei grecheskikh i latinskikh o Skifii i Kavkaze,* Pt 2, 1. St Petersburg.

Latyshev V.V. 1894, *Etyudy po vizantiiskoi epigrafike.* VV. 1, 657–72.

Levashova V.P. 1967, Braslety. in: Ocherki po istorii ruskoi derevn X–XIII vv. *Trudy Gosudarstvennogo Istoricheskogo Muzeya* (Moscow) 43.

Loboda I.I. 1976, Novye rannesrednevekovye mogil'niki v Yugo-Zapadnom Krymu. *SA,* 1976 - 2, 135–47.

Macpherson D. 1857, *Antiquities of Kerch.* London.

Madyda-Legutko R. 1978, The buckles with imprint ornamentation. *Wiadomości Archeologiczne,* (Warsaw) XLIII.

Magomedov B.V. 1979, *Kaborga IV (raskopki 1973–74 gg.). Mogil'niki Chernyakhovskoi kul'tury.* Nauka, Moscow, 24–111.

Makarova T.I. 1965, Srednevekovyi Korchev (po raskopkam 1963 g. v Kerchi). *KSIA* N104, 70–6.

Makarova T.I. 1982, Arkheologicheskie dannye dlya datirovki tserkvi Ioanna Predtechi v Kerchi. *SA,* 1982 - 4, 91–106.

Makarova T.I. 1986, *Chernevoe delo drevnei Rusi* (Moscow).

Maksimenko V.E. and Bezuglov S.I. 1987, Pozdnesarmatskie pogrebeniya v kurgakh na reke Bystroi. *SA,* 1987 - 1, 183–92.

Maksimova M.I. 1979, *Artyukhovski kurgan.* St Petersburg [Leningrad].

The Chronicle of John Malalas. 1986. Melbourne.

Marin J.-Y. 1990, *Les influences Danubiennes dans l'Ouest de l'Europe au Ve siècle.* Exhibition catalogue, Caen.

Markevich A.I. 1928, K sud'bam kollektsii drevnosti i stariny A.L. Bert'e-Delagarda, *Izv. Tav. Uch. Arkh. Kom.* 59, 144–5.

Marshall F.H. 1911, *Catalogue of the Jewellery, Greek, Etruscan and Roman in the Departments of Antiquities, British Museum.* London.

Martin F.R. 1897, Fibulor och söljor från Kertch. *KVHAA Månadsbladet,* 32 (Stockholm 1894), 1–27 .

Martin M. 1991, Zur frühmittelalterlichen Gürteltracht der Frau in der Burgundia, Francia und Aquitania. In: *L'Art des Invasions en Hongrie et en Wallonie.* Actes du colloque tenu au Musée Royal de Mariemont du 9 au 11 avril 1979. Morlanwelz, 31–84.

Mashov S. 1976, Rannosrednovekovni fibuli ot Avgusta pri c. Khrlets, *Vrachanski okrg. Arkheologiya* (Sofia) XVIII. I, 35–9 .

Matsulevich L.A. 1926, *Serebryanaya chasha iz Kerchi* (St Petersburg).

Matsulevich L.A. 1933, K voprosu o stadial'nosti v gotskikh nadstroechnykh yavleniyakh. *IGAIMK,* 100, 577–97.

Medvedev A.N. 1981, Sarmatskoe pogrebenie bliz Voronezha. *SA,* 1981 - 4, 253–60.

Meeks N.D. and Tite M.S. 1980, The analysis of platinum group element inclusions in ancient gold antiquities. *Journal of Archaeological Science,* 7, 267–75.

Menghin W. 1994/95, Schwerter des Goldgriffspathenhorizonts im Museum für Vor- und Frühgeschichte. *Acta Praehistorica et Archaeologica* (Berlin), 26/27, 140–91.

Mészáros Gy. 1970, A regölyi népvándorláskori fejedelmi sír. Das Fürstengrab von Regöly aus der Frühvölkerwanderungszeit. *AE,* 97, 66–92.

Minaeva T.M. 1927, Pogrebenie s sozhzheniem bliz gor. Pokrovska. *Uchenie Zapiski Saratovskogo Gos. Uni.,* IV, 3, 91–123.

Minaeva T.A. 1956, Mogil'nik Baital-Chapkan v Cherkesii. *SA,* XXVI, 291–6.

Moosbrugger-Leu R. 1971, *Die Schweiz zur Merowingerzeit,* vols A and B. Bern.

Morrisson C., Brenot C., Barrandon J.-N., Callu J.-P., Poirier J. And Halleux R. 1985, *L'Or Monnayé: Purification et altérations de Rome à Byzance.* C.N.R.S., Orléans.

Mosin V. 1931, Les Khazares et les Byzantins. *Byzantion.* Brussels, 6.

Moss H.St.L.B. 1935, *The Birth of the Middle Ages.* Oxford, 395–814.

Mrkobrad D. 1980, *Arheološki nalazi seoba naroda u Yugoslaviji.* Fontes Archaeologiae Iugoslaviae III. Monografije – 6; Belgrade.

Nesbitt J. and Oikonomides N. 1991, *Catalogue of Byzantine Seals at Dumbarton Oaks and in the Fogg Museum of Art,* vol. 1. Washington.

Novoseltsev A.P. 1990, *Khazarskoe gosudarstvo i ego rol v istorii Vostochnoi Evropy i Kavkaza.* Moscow.

Novotný B. 1976, *Šarovce.* Bratislava.

Obolensky D. 1964, *The Principles and Methods of Byzantine Diplomacy.* Actes du XIIe congrès international d'études byzantines. I; Belgrade.

Obolensky D. 1966, *The Empire and its Northern Neighbours.* Cambridge Medieval History, vol. IV, pt. 1; Cambridge.

Oddy A. 1977, The production of gold wire in antiquity. *Gold Bulletin* (Marshalltown) 10/3, 79–87.

Oddy A. 1993, Gilding of metals in the Old World. In: S. La Niece and P. Craddock (eds), *Metal Plating and Patination.* London, 171–81.

Oddy A. and La Niece S. 1986, Byzantine Gold Coins and Jewellery. *Gold Bulletin* (Marshalltown) 19/1, 19–28.

Ogden J. 1982, *Jewellery of the Ancient World.* London.

Ogden J. 1991, Classical gold wire: some aspects of its manufacture and use. *Jewellery Studies* 5, 95–105.

Otch. Imp. Arkh. Kom. (St Petersburg 1890).

Otch. Imp. Arkh. Kom. za 1890. (St Petersburg 1893).

Otch. Imp. Arkh. Kom. za 1891. (St Petersburg 1893).

Otch. Imp. Arkh. Kom. za 1901. (St Petersburg 1903).

Otch. Imp. Arkh. Kom. za 1903. (St Petersburg 1906).

Otch. Imp. Arkh. Kom. za 1905. (St Petersburg 1908).

Otch. Imp. Arkh. Kom. za 1909–1910 (St Petersburg 1913).

Olkhovsky V.S. and Khrapunov I.N. 1990, *Krymskaya Skifiya.* Simferopol.

Ondřejová I. 1975, *Les Bijoux Antiques.* Prague.

Opaiţ A. 1991, O sapatura de salvare în oracul antic Ibida. *Studii si Cercetâri de Istorie Veche ci Archeologie* 42/1–2, 21–56 .

Pekarskaja L.V. and Kidd D. 1994, *Der Silberschatz von Martynovka (Ukraine) aus dem 6. und 7. Jahrhundert.* Innsbruck.

Photii Patriarchae Constantinopolitani, Epistolae et amphilogia, vol. 1. 1983. Bibliotheca scriptorum graecorum et romanorum Teubneriana; Leipzig.

Pilet C. 1995, Un centre de pouvoir: le domaine d'Airan, Calvados (IVe–IXe siècles). In: F. Vallet and M. Kazanski (eds), *La Noblesse Romaine et les Chefs Barbares du IIIe au VII siècle.* Paris, 327–33.

Pletněva S.A. 1974, Polovetskie kamennye izvayaniya. *Svod Arkheologicheskikh Istochnikov.* Moscow. E4–2.

Pletněva S.A. 1981, Pechenegi, Torki, Polovtsy. Arkheologiya SSSR. Stepi Evrazii v epokhu srednevekovya. Moscow, 62–75.

Pletněva S.A. 1982, *Kochevniki srednevekovya.* Moscow.

Pletněva S.A. 1990, Khazarskie problemy v arkheologii. *SA,* 1990 - 2, 77–91.

Pletněva S.A. 1990a, *Polovtsy.* (Moscow).

Pletněva S.A. 1991, Otnoshenie vostochnoevropeiskikh kochevnikov s Vizantiei i arkheologicheskie istochniki. *SA,* 1991 - 3, 98–107.

Pokrovsky M.V. 1936, Pashkovsky mogil'nik no.1. *SA,* 1936 - 1. 159–69.

Pósta B. 1905, *Régészeti tanulmányok az Oroszföldön. Archäologische Studien auf russische Boden* II. Budapest/Leipzig, 235–600.

Preda C. 1980, *Callatis Necropola romano-bizantini.* (Bucharest).

Prisciani Grammatici Caesariensis Institutionum Grammaticarum 1855. Ed. M. Hertz. Leipzig.

Procopius of Caesarea 1914, *De Bellis. History of the Wars,* book 1. (Trans. H.B. Dewing). Cambridge, Mass.

Procopius of Caesarea 1928, *History of the Wars,* vol. V, books VII and VIII. (Trans. H.B. Dewing). Cambridge, Mass.

Procopius of Caesarea 1940, *Buildings,* vol. VII. (Trans. H.B. Dewing). Cambridge, Mass .

Procopius of Caesarea 1962, *De Bellis.* Opera Omnia. Libri I–IV. Bibliotheca scriptorum graecorum et romanorum Teubneriana, vol. I. Leipzig.

Procopius of Caesarea 1964, *De Aedificiis.* Opera Omnia. Libri VI. Book III. Bibliotheca scriptorum graecorum et romanorum Teubneriana, Leipzig.

Pudovin V.K. 1961, Datirovka nizhnego sloya mogil'nika Suuk-Su (550–50 gg.) *SA,* 1961 - 1, 177–85.

Pudovin V.K. 1962, Tri bosporskie luchevye fibuly. *SA,* 1962 - 2, 142–8.

Pusztai R. 1966, A lébényi germán fejedelmi sír. Das germanische Fürstengrab von Lébény. *Arrabona* 8. (Győr) 99–118.

Pyankov A.V. 1997, Pryazhka V veka n.e. iz g. Krasnodara. *Istoriko-Arkheologicheski Almanakh* 3. Armavir, Moscow.

Quast D. 1993, *Die merowingerzeitlichen Grabfunde aus Gültlingen (Stadt Wildberg, Kreis Calw).* Stuttgart.

Rau P. 1927, Prähistorische Ausgrabungen auf der Steppenseite des deutschen Wolgagebietes im Jahre 1926. *Mitteilungen des Zentralmuseums der Aut. Soz. Räte-Republik der Wolgadeutschen,* 2. Pokrovsk.

Ravennatis Anonymi 1860, *Cosmographia et Guidonis Geographica.* Berlin.

Reinach S. 1892, *Antiquités du Bosphore Cimmérien.* (Paris).

Repnikov N.I. 1906, Nekotorie mogil'niki oblasti krymskikh gotov. *IAK,* 19, 1–80.

Repnikov N.I. 1906a, Raskopki v okrestnostyakh Gurzufa. *Izvestiya Tavricheskoi Uchenoi Arkhivnoi Komissii.* (Simferopol) 39, 106–10.

Repnikov N.I. 1907, Nekotorye mogil'niki oblasti krymskikh gotov. *ZOOID* XXVII, 101–48.

Rhode Island School of Design 1976. *Classical Jewelry.* Museum of Art, Rhode Island.

Rikman E.A. 1975, Pamyatniki Sarmatov i Plemen chernyakhovskoi kul'tury. *Arkheologicheskaya Karta Moldavskoi SSR,* 5. Chişinău [Kishinev].

Robinson H.S. 1959, *Pottery of the Roman Period. The Athenian Agora,* vol. V. Princeton.

Roes A. 1953a, A Travers les Collections Archéologiques de la Hollande. *Berichten van de Rijksdienst voor het Oudheidkundig Bodemonderzoek in Nederland,* V. Amersfoort, 65–9.

Romanchuk A.I. 1976, Raskopki selskogo poseleniya v nizovyakh reki Belbek. *Antichnaya drevnost i srednie veka.* (Sverdlovsk). 13, 9–26.

Romanovskaya M.A. 1986, Alanskoe pogrebenie iz Stavropolya. *KSIA.* 186, 77–80.

Ross M.C. 1965, *Catalogue of the Byzantine and Early Mediaeval Antiquities in the Dumbarton Oaks Collection,* vol. II. Washington.

Rostovtsev M.I. 1900, Rimskie garnizony na Tavricheskom poluostrove. *Zhurnal Ministerstva Narodnogo prosveshcheniya.* St Petersburg, 140–58.

Rostovtsev M.I. 1907, Novye latinskie nadpisi iz Khersonesa. *IAK,* 23.

Rostovtsev M.I. 1916, K istorii Khersonesa v epokhu rannei Rimskoi Imperii. *Sbornik statei v chest grafini P.S. Uvarovoi.* Moscow, 5–16.

Rostovtsev M.I. 1918, *Ellinstvo i iranstvo na Yuge Rossii.* St Petersburg.

Rostovtsev M.I. 1920, Rimskie garnizony na Tavricheskom poluostrove. *Zhurnal Ministerstva Narodnogo prosveshcheniya.* St Petersburg [Petrograd].

Rostovtzeff M.I. (Rostovtsev) 1922, *Iranians and Greeks in South Russia.* Oxford.

Rostovtsev M. 1923, Une trouvaille de l'époque gréco-sarmate de Kerch au Louvre et au Musée de Saint-Germain. *Monuments et Mémoires Fondation Eugène Piot,* XXVI. Paris, 145–61.

Rostovtsev M. 1930, La porte-épée des Iraniens et des Chinois. In: G. Millet, *L'Art Byzantin chez les Slavs, Les Balkans 1.* (Orient et Byzance IV). Paris, 337–46.

Rostowzew M. (Rostovtsev) 1931, *Skythien und der Bosporus.* Berlin.

Rostovtzeff M.I. (Rostovtsev) 1936, The Sarmatae and the Parthians. *Cambridge Ancient History,* vol. 11.

Roth H. 1979, *Kunst der Völkerwanderungszeit.* Propyläen Kunstgeschichte. Supplementband IV, Oldenburg.

Rudakov V.E. 1981, *Bakla-malyi gorodskoi tsentr yugo-zapadnogo Kryma. Antichnyi i srednevekovyi gorod.* Sverdlovsk.

Rudolph W. and Rudolph E. 1973, *Ancient Jewelry from the Collection of*

Burton Y. Berry. Bloomington.

Runich A.P. 1976, Zakhoronenie vozhdya epokhi rannego srednevekov'ya iz Kislovodskoi kotloviny. *SA,* 1976 - 3, 256–66.

Rupp H. 1937, *Die Herkunft der Zelleneinlage und die Almandin Scheibenfibeln im Rheinland.* Rheinische Forschungen zur Vorgeschichte. II, Bonn.

Ruseva-Slokoska L. 1991, *Roman Jewellery.* Sofia .

Rusu M. 1959, Pontische Gürtelschnallen mit Adlerkopf.(VI–VII Jh. u. Z.). *Dacia,* III (Bucharest), 485–523.

Rybakov B.A. 1953, Drevnie Rusy. *SA,* XVII, 23–104.

Ryndina N.V. 1963, Tekhnologiya proizvodstva novgorodskikh yuvelirov X–XV vv. *MIA,* 117.

Sakhanev V.V. 1914, Raskopki na Severnom Kavkaze v 1911–1912 gg. *IAK* 56, 75–219.

Salamon A. and Barkóczi L. 1971, Bestattungen von Csákvár aus dem Ende des 4. und dem Anfang des 5. Jahrhunderts. *Alba Regia,* 11. (Székesfehérvár). 35–77.

Sale Cat. 1924, *Objets d'Art Antiques, Trouvés en Crimée.* L'Hôtel Drouot, Paris, 13–14 June 1924.

Sale Cat. 1987, *Antiquités et Objects d'Art. Collection de Martine, Comtesse de Béhague provenant de la Succession du Marquis de Ganay,* Sotheby's Monaco, 5 December 1987.

Salin B. 1904, *Die Altgermanische Thierornamentik.* (Stockholm).

Salin E. and France-Lanord A. 1956, Sur le trésor barbare de Pouan. *Gallia Préhistoire* 14, 65–75.

Savovsky I.P. 1977, Novi sarmatski pokhovannya na zaporozhzhi. *Arkheologiya* (Kiev) 23, 61–71.

Sax M. 1996, The recognition and nomenclature of quartz materials with specific reference to engraved gemstones. *Jewellery Studies* 7, 73–7.

Sazanov A. 1995, Verres à décor de pastilles bleues provenant des fouilles de la Mer Noire. In: D. Foy (ed.), *Le Verre de l'antiquité tardive et du haut moyen âge.* Musée archéologique départemental du Val d'Oise, 331–44.

Schlunk H. and Hauschild T. 1978, *Die Denkmäler der frühchristlicher und westgotischen Zeit.* Mainz am Rhein.

Sedova M.V. 1981, *Yuvelirnye izdeliya drevnego Novgoroda (X–XV vv.).* Moscow.

Seger E. 1912, Grabfunde der Völkerwanderungszeit aus Südrussland. *Schlesiens Vorzeit in Bild und Schrift.* Wrocław [Breslau] VI, 47–9.

Seipel W. (ed.) 1993, *Gold aus Kiew.* Exhibition catalogue, Vienna.

Shandrovskaya V.C. 1995, *Tamozhennaya sluzhba v Sugdee VII–X vv. Vizantiya i srednevekovyi Krym.* Simferopol.

Shepko L.G. 1987, Pozdnesarmatskie kurgany v Severnom Priazov'e. *SA,* 1987 - 4, 158–73.

Shkorpil V.V. 1907, Otchet o raskopkakh v Kerchi v 1904g. *IAK* 25, 1–66.

Shkorpil V.V. 1910a, Otchet o raskopkakh v g. Kerchi i na Tamanskom poluostrove v 1907 g. *IAK* 35, 12–47 .

Shkorpil V.V. 1910b, Zametka a rel'efe na pamyatnike s nadpis'yu Yevpateriya. *IAK* 37, 23–35.

Shkorpil V.V. 1911, Bosporskie nadpisi, naidennye v 1910g. *IAK* 40, 92–114.

Shtern É.R. 1897, K voprosu o proiskhozhdenii 'Gotskogo stilya' predmetov yuvelirnogo iskusstva. *ZOOID* 20, 1–15.

Sidorenko V.A. 1991, 'Goty' oblasti Dori Prokopiya Kesariiskogo i "dlinnye steny" v Krymu. *MAIET* 1991 - II, 105–18.

Silantyeva L.F. 1976, *Trudy Gosudarstvennogo Ermitazha* 17.

Simonenko A.V. 1993, *Sarmaty Tavrii.* Kiev.

Simonenko A.V. and Lobai B.I. 1991, *Sarmaty Severo-Zapadnogo Prichernomorya v I n.e.* Kiev.

Skripkin A.S. 1977, Fibuly Nizhnego Povolzh'ya. *SA,* 1977 - 2. 100–20.

Smith R.A. 1923, *A Guide to the Anglo-Saxon and Foreign Teutonic Antiquities in the Department of British and Mediaeval Antiquities, British Museum.* London.

Solomonik E.I. 1959, *Sarmatskie znaki severnogo Prichernomor'ya.* Kiev.

Sorokina N.P. 1971, O steklyannykh sosudakh s kaplyami sinego stekla iz Prichernomorya. *SA,* 1971 - 4, 85–101.

Spitsin A.A. 1902, Drevnosti Kamskoi Chudi po Kollektsii Teploukhovukh'. *MAR,* 26.

Spitsin A.A. 1905, Veshchi s inkrustatsiei iz Kerchenskikh katakomb 1904 g. *IAK,* 17, 115–26.

Stefanelli L.P.B. and Pettinau B. 1992, *L'oro dei Romani. Gioielli di età Imperiale.* Rome.

Subbotin L.V. and Dzigovsky A.N. 1990, *Sarmatskie drevnosti Dnestrovsko-Dunaiskogo mezhdurechya.* Part 3. (Kiev).

Sulimirski T. 1970, *The Sarmatians.* London.

Tackenberg K. 1928/29, Germanische Funde in Bulgarien. *Izvestiya na Blgarskiya Archeologichesky Institut,* V. Sofia.

Tait G.H. (ed.) 1976, *Jewellery through 7000 Years.* London.

Tait G.H. (ed.) 1986, *Seven Thousand Years of Jewellery.* London.

Talis D.L. 1990, *Klad iz raskopok Baklinskogo gorodishcha. Problemy arkheologii Evrazii.* Moscow.

Tatić-Burić M. 1958, Gotski grob iz Ostruzhnitse. *Zbornik Radova Narodnogo Muzea.* 1956/57 (Belgrade) 164–8.

Tejral J. 1973, *Mähren im 5. Jahrhundert.* Prague.

Tejral J. 1985, Naše země a římské Podunají na počatku doby stohování národů. *Památky Archeologické.* LXXVI - 2 (Prague) 308–97.

Tejral J. 1987, Zur Chronologie und Deutung der südöstlichen Kulturelement in der frühen Völkerwanderungszeit Mitteleuropas. Die Völkerwanderungszeit im Karpatenbecken. *Anzeiger des Germanischen Nationalmuseums* (Nuremburg) 11–46.

Tejral J. 1988, Zur Chronologie der frühen Völkerwanderungszeit im mittleren Donauraum. *Archaeologia Austriaca* 72 (Vienna) 223–304.

Tenishcheva M.K. 1930, *Emal i inkrustatsiya.* Seminarium Kondakovianum,; Prague.

Theodorescu R. 1976, *Un mileniu de artă la Dunărea de Jos.* Bucharest.

Thompson E.A. 1948, *A History of Attila and the Huns.* Oxford.

Tizingauzen V.G. 1884, *Sbornik materialov, otnosyashchikhsya k istorii Zolotoi Ordy. I. Izvlecheniya iz sochinenii arabskikh.* St Petersburg.

Tóth E.H. and Horváth A. 1992, *Kunbábony. Das Grab eines Awarenkhagans.* Kecskemét.

Treadgold W. 1988, *The Byzantine Revival 780-842.* Stanford.

Trousdale W. 1969, A possible Roman jade from China. *Oriental Art,* new ser. XV, 58–64.

Trousdale W. 1975, *The Long Sword and Scabbard Slide in Asia.* (Smithsonian Contributions to Anthropology, no. 17; Washington).

Tsvetaeva G.A. 1979, *Bospor i Rim.* Moscow.

Uvarova P.S. 1900, Mogil'niki Severnogo Kavkaza. *MAK,* VIII.

Vágó E.B. and Bóna I. 1976, *Der spätrömische Südostfriedhof. Die Gräberfelder von Intercisa I.* Budapest.

Vasilevsky V.G. 1912, Zhitie Ioanna Gotskogo. *Trudy,* II.2. St Petersburg.

Vasilevsky V.G. 1915, Zhitie Stefana Surozhskogo. *Trudy,* 2.1. St Petersburg.

Vasiliev A.A. 1936, *The Goths in the Crimea.* Cambridge, Mass.

Veimarn E.V. 1963, Arkheologichni roboty v raioni Inkermana. *Arkheologichni pamyatki Ukrainy,* XIII (Kiev) 15–89.

Veimarn E.V. 1979, Skalistinsky sklep 420. *KSIA* 158, 34–7.

Veimarn E.V. and Aibabin A.I. 1993, *Skalistinsky mogil'nik.* Kiev.

Veimarn E.V. and Ambroz A.K. 1980, Bol'shaya pryazhka iz skalistinskogo mogil'nika (sklep 288). *SA,* 1980 - 3, 247–62.

Vernadsky G. 1941, Byzantium and Southern Russia. *Byzantion.* 15. (Boston).

Vickers M. 1979, *Scythian Treasures in Oxford.* Oxford.

Vinogradov V.B. and Petrenko V.A. 1974, Mogil'nik sarmatskoi epokhu na gore Lekhkch-Kort. *SA,* 1974 - 1, 171–80.

Vinski Z. 1957, Zikadenschmuck aus Jugoslavien. *JRGZM* 4, 136–60.

Vinski Z. 1967, Kasnoantički starosjedioci u Salonitanskoj regiji prema arheološkoj ostavstini predslavenskog supstrata. *Vjesnik* LXIX, 5–86.

Vinski Z. 1968, Adlerschnallenfunde in Jugoslavien. In: K. Jażdżewski (ed.), *Liber Iosepho Kostrzewski octogenario a veneratoribus dicatus.* Warszaw, 314–25.

Vinski Z. 1972/73, Orovasenim fibulama Ostrogoti i Tirinzana povodom rijetkog tiriskog nalaza u Saloni. *Vjesnik arheološkoga muzeja u Zagrebu,* VI–VII. Zagreb.

Vinski Z. 1978, Vinski, Archäologische Spuren ostgotischer Anwesenheit im heutigen Bereich Jugoslawiens. In: *Problemi seobe naroda u Karpatskoj kotlini.* Novi Sad, 35–42.

Von Freeden, U. 1979, Untersuchungen zu merowingerzeitlichen Ohrringen bei den Alamannen. *BRGK* 60, 231–441 .

Voronov Yu.N. 1975, *Taina Tsebel'dinskoi doliny.* Moscow.

Voronov Yu.N. and Yushin V.A. 1973, Novye pamyatniki Tsebel'dinskoi kul'tury v Abkhazii. *SA,* 1973 - 1, 171–91.

Vysotskaya T.N. 1972, *Pozdnie skify v Yugo-Zapadnom Krymu.* Kiev.

Werner J. 1950, Slawische Bügelfibeln des 7. Jahrhunderts. In: G. Behrens (ed.), *Reinecke Festschrift, zum 75. Geburtstag von Paul Reinecke am 25. September 1947.* Mainz, 150–72.

Werner J. 1955, Byzantinische Gürtelschnallen des 6. und 7. Jahrhunderts aus der Sammlung Diergardt. *Kölner Jahrbuch für Vor- und Frühgeschichte.* Cologne, 36–43.

Werner J. 1956, *Beiträge zur Archäologie des Attila-Reiches.* (BayrAW. Abh., NF 38a) Munich.

Werner J. 1959, Studien zu Grabfunden des V. Jahrhunderts aus der Slowakei und der Karpatenukraine. *Slovenská Archeológia* (Bratislava) 7, 422–38.

Werner J. 1960, Die frühgeschichtlichen Grabfunde vom Spielberg und von Fürst. *Bayer. Vorgeschbl.*, 25.

Werner J. 1961a, Ostgotische Bügelfibeln aus bajuwarischen Reihengräbern. *Bayer. Vorgeschbl.*, 26, 68–75.

Werner J. 1961b, *Katalog der Sammlung Diergardt. (Völkerwanderungszeitlicher Schmuck) I. Die Fibeln.* Berlin.

Werner J. 1974a, Archäologische Bemerkungen zu den dendrochronologischen Befund von Oberflacht. *Fundberichte aus Baden-Württemberg*, I (Stuttgart) 650–7.

Werner J. 1974b, Nomadische Gürtel bei Persern, Byzantinern und Langobarden, in: *La Civiltà dei Longobardi in Europa.* Accademia Nazionale dei Lincei, no. 189; Rome, 109–40.

Werner J. 1980, Der goldene Armring des Frankenkönigs Childerich und die germanischen Handgelenkringe der jüngeren Kaiserzeit. *Frühmittelalterliche Studien* 14, 1–41.

Werner J. 1984, *Der Grabfund von Malaja Pereščepina und Kuvrat, Kagan der Bulgaren.* Munich.

Werner J. 1986, *Der Schatzfund von Vrap in Albanien.* Vienna.

Werner J. 1988, Dančeny und Brangstrup, Untersuchungen zur Černjachov-Kultur zwischen Sereth und Dnestr und zu den 'Reichtumszentren' auf Fünen. *Bonn Jbb.* 188, 241–86.

Whitfield N. 1990, Round wire in the early Middle Ages. *Jewellery Studies* 4, 13–28.

Rubruk Gil'om [William of Rubruck] 1957, *Puteshestvie v Vostochnye strany [Journey to the Eastern Parts of the World].* Moscow.

Williams D. and Ogden J. 1994, *Greek Gold.* Exhibition catalogue, London.

Wolfram H. 1990, *Histoire des Goths.* Paris.

Yakobson A.L. 1954, Razvedochnye raskopki srednevekovogo poseleniya Gorzuvity. *KSIIMK* 53, 109–20.

Yakobson A.L. 1959, Rannesrednevekovy Khersones. *MIA*, 63.

Yakobson A.L. 1964, *Srednevekovyi Krym.* Moscow/St Petersburg.

Yakobson A.L. 1970, Rannesrednevekovye selskie poseleniya Yugo-Zapadnoi Tavriki. *MIA*, 168.

Yakobson A.L. 1979, *Keramika i keramicheskoe proizvodstvo srednevekovoi Tavriki.* St Petersburg.

Yanushevich E.V. 1976, *Kulturnye rasteniya Yugo-Zapada SSSR po paleobotanicheskim issledovaniyam.* Chişinău [Kishinev].

Yetts W.P. 1926, A Chinese scabbard-jade, *Burlington Magazine* 49, 197–201.

Zasetskaya I.P. 1968, O khronologii pogrebenii epokhi pereseleniya narodov Nizhnego Povolzhya. *SA*, 1968 - 2, 60–2.

Zasetskaya I.P. 1975, *Zolotye ukrasheniya gunnskoi epokhi. Po materialam osoboi kladovoi Gosudarstvennogo Ermitazha.* St Petersburg [Leningrad].

Zasetskaya I.P. 1978, O khronologii i kulturnoi prinadlezhnosti pamyatnikov yuzhnorusskikh stepei i Kazakhstana. *SA*, 1978 - 1, 54–69.

Zasetskaya I.P. 1979, Bosporskiye sklepi gunnskoi epokhi kak khronologicheskiy etalon dlya datirovki pamyatnikov Vostochnoevropeiskikh stepei. *KSIA* 158, 5–17.

Zasetskaya I.P. 1982, *Klassifikatsiya polikhromnykh izdelei gunnskoi epokhi. Drevnosti epokhi velikogo pereseleniya narodov V–VIII vv.* Moscow, 14–30.

Zasetskaya I.P. 1986, Nekotorie itogi izucheniya khronologii pamyatnikov gunnskoi epokhi v yuzhnorusskikh stepyakh. *Arkh. Sbornik* 27, 79–91.

Zasetskaya I.P. 1990, Otnositel'naya khronologiya sklepov pozdneantichnogo i rannesrednevekogo Bosporskogo nekropolya (konets IV - nachalo VII. v.). *Arkh. Sbornik* 30, 97–106.

Zasetskaya I.P. 1993, Materialy bosporskogo nekropolya vtoroi poloviny IV - pervoi poloviny V vv. n. e. *MAIET* III, 23–105.

Zasetskaya I.P. 1994, *Kul'tura kochevnikov Yuzhnorusskikh stepei v Gunnskoi epokhi (Konets IV–V vv.). Nomadic Culture of the South Russian Steppelands: The End of the Fourth and the Fifth Centuries* AD. St Petersburg.

Zonaras Ioannes 1884, *Annales.* Corpus Scriptorum Historiae Byzantinae. vol. 2, Bonn.

Zosimus 1982, *New History.* (Trans. with commentary R.T. Ridley) Canberra.

Zubar V.M. and Ryzhov S.G. 1976, Raskopki nekropolya Khersonesa. *Arkheologicheskie Otkrytiya*, 1975 goda (1976) 327–8.

Zubar V.M., Savelya O.Y. and Sarnovsky T. 1997, *Novye epigraficheskie pamyatniki iz okrestnostei Khersonesa Tavricheskogo. Khersones v antichnom mire. Tezisy dokladov mezhdunarodnoi konferentsii.* Sevastopol.

Zuckerman C. 1991, The early Byzantine strongholds in Eastern Pontus. *Travaux et Mémoires* 11, 527–53.

Zuckerman C. 1995, On the date of the Khazars' conversion to Judaism and the chronology of the kings of the Rus Oleg and Igor. *Revue des Etudes Byzantines*, 53, 237–70.

Zukerman K. [Zuckerman] 1997, K voprosu o rannei istorii femy Khersona. *Bakhchisaraiskii istoriko-arkheologicheskii sbornik*, 1 (Simferopol) 210–22.

Zuckerman C. 1997b, Les Hongrois au pays de Lébédia. Une nouvelle puissance aux confins de Byzance et de la Khazarie *c.* 836–*c.* 889. In: *Byzantium at War.* Athens, 51–74.

List of Place-names Mentioned in the Catalogue

Alt-Weimar, Russia
'An Kache (Sourcil Blanc)' possibly related to the river Kacha in the Krym (Crimea), Ukraine, or alternatively the French transliteration of a Turkic name meaning 'White Brow' ('Sourcil Blanc' in French).
Aquileia, Italy
Aromat, Krym (Crimea), Ukraine
Artek, Krym (Crimea), Ukraine
Ascoli-Piceno, Italy
Atzgersdorf, Austria
Bácsordas, see Karavukovo
Baital-Chapkan, south Russia
Bakodpuszta, see Dunapataj-Bödpuszta
Balka, Ukraine
Bartimska, Russia
Basel-Kleinhüningen, Switzerland
Beja, Portugal
Beograd-Čukarica, Yugoslavia
Berkasovo, Yugoslavia
Berlin, Germany
Bócsa, Hungary
Borkovskaya, Russia
Borovoe, Kazakhstan
Brodovsk (Ural region), Russia
Budapest, Hungary
Budeşti, Romania
Bylym, see Kudnietov
Callatis (Mangalia), Romania
Cebelda, Georgia
Chorna/Chernaya Rechka, Krym (Crimea), Ukraine
Cherson (Khersones, Chersonesus, Korsun), Ukraine
Chufut-Kale, Krym (Crimea), Ukraine
Cluj-Someşeni (Kolozsvár-Szamosfalva), Romania
Cologne (Köln), Germany
Constantinople (Istanbul), Turkey
Desana, Italy
Demidovka, Ukraine
Dnipropetrovsk, Ukraine
Domolospuszta, Hungary
Dubravica, Yugoslavia
Dunapataj-Bödpuszta ('Bakodpuszta'), Hungary
Dunaújváros (Intercisa), Hungary
Dura Europus (Qalat es Sālihīya), Syria
'Ecaterinos tertre' ('tertre' is French for 'mound' or 'barrow')
'Eltine' (Eltigen, Heroyivske/Geroyevskoye) near Kerch, Krym (Crimea), Ukraine
Er Rastan, Syria
Eski-Kermen, Krym (Crimea), Ukraine
Ficarolo, Italy
Flonheim, Germany
Fundătura (Kisjenő), Romania
Gáva, Hungary
Grocka, Yugoslavia
Gurzuf, see Hurzuf
Gültlingen, Germany

Hamburg, Germany
Harlec, Bulgaria
Herpes, France
Hessen, Germany
Hochfelden, France
Höckricht, see Jędrzychowice
Hurzuf, Krym (Crimea), Ukraine
Iatrus (Krivina), Bulgaria
Ibida, Romania
Imola, Italy
Intercisa, see Dunaújváros
Jędrzychowice (Höckricht), Poland
Kabardino-Balkaria, south Russia
Kaibal, Russia
Kalna, Slovakia
Kapolcs, Hungary
Karavukovo (Bácsordas), Yugoslavia
Kassel, Germany
Kerch, Krym (Crimea), Ukraine
Keszthely-Fenékpuszta, Hungary
Kishpek, south Russia
Kislovodsk, south Russia
Kolozsvár-Szamosfalva, see Cluj-Someşeni
Kovin (Kubin), Yugoslavia
Krasnodar, south Russia
Krivina, see Iatrus
Kuban, south Russia
Kudnietov (Bylym),south Russia
Kumbulta, south Russia
Kunbábony, Hungary
Laa an der Thaya, Austria
Landriano, Italy
Lébény, Hungary
Lizgor, south Russia
Lörrach, Germany
Lucerne (Luzern), Switzerland
Luchyste/Luchistoye, Krym (Crimea), Ukraine
Mahlberg, Germany
Maikop, south Russia
Makhchesk, south Russia
Mala Pereshchepina, Ukraine
Marosszentanna, see Sîntana de Mureş
Mengen, Germany
Mersin, Turkey
Mezőszilas, Hungary
Mikelaka, Romania
Miszla, Hungary
Mokraya Balka, south Russia
Monaco
Muslyumovo, Russia
Nagyvárad, see Oradea
Nevolino, Russia
New York, USA
Nikopol, Ukraine
Nocera Umbra, Italy
Novae (near Svishtov), Bulgaria
Novi Banovci, Yugoslavia
Novogrigorevka, Ukraine
Nymphaion (Crimea, Ukraine)
Odessa, Ukraine

Olbia (near Mikolayiv), Ukraine
Oradea (Nagyvárad), Romania
Oxford, Great Britain
Palaiokastro, Greece
Pashkovska, south Russia
Pécsüszög, Hungary
Pfersee (near Augsburg), Germany
Pforzheim, Germany
Pilismarót, Hungary
Pokrovsk, Voshkhod, Russia
Portove/Portovoye (Razhdol'noye), Krym (Crimea), Ukraine
Pouan, France
Razhdol'noye, see Portovoye
Regöly, Hungary
Sahlenburg, Germany
St Petersburg (formerly Petrograd and Leningrad), Russia
Saône-et-Loire, France
Šarovce, Slovakia
Schinna, Germany
Schwarzrheindorf, Germany
Segesvár, see Sigişoara
Shipovo on Derkul, Ukraine
Sigişoara (Segesvár), Romania
Simferopol, Ukraine
Şimleul Silvaniei (Szilágysomlyó), Romania
Sîntana de Mureş (Marosszentanna), Romania
Sirmia, former Yugoslavia
Sirmium, former Yugoslavia
Skalyste/Skalistoye, Krym (Crimea), Ukraine
Sladovsky, Russia
Slivka, Bulgaria
Soponya, Hungary
Spas Pereksha, Ukraine
Strachotín, Czech Republic
Suuk-Su, Krym (Crimea), Ukraine
Szeged, Hungary
Szeged-Nagyszéksós, Hungary
Szilágysomlyó, see Şimleul Silvaniei
Taman, south Russia
'Tertre Coul Obas' (Kuloba), Krym (Crimea), Ukraine ('tertre' is French for 'mound' or 'barrow')
Timoshevskaya-Staintsa (Kuban region), south Russia
Tîrgşor, Romania
Tiszafüred, Hungary
Tortona, Hungary
Turaevo (Kama region), Russia
Untersiebenbrunn, Austria
Valea Strîmbă (Tekerőpatak), Romania
Vasilevka, Ukraine
Verkhnaya Rutka, Ossetia
Verkh-Sainska, Russia
Vienna (Wien), Austria
Wachendorf, Germany
Wien, see Vienna
Wolfsheim, Germany
Yalta, Krym (Crimea), Ukraine
Zmajevo, Yugoslav

Concordance of Catalogue and Registration Numbers

Cat. no.	Reg. no.	Cat. no.	Reg. no.	Cat. no.	Reg. no.
1	1923,7-16,11	51	1923,7-16,143 and 144	102	GR 1981.9-5.6
2	GR 1981.9-5.12	52	1923,7-16,142	102	1923,7-16,50
2	1923,7-16,69	53	1923,7-16,140 and 141	103	GR 1981.9-5.9
3	GR 1981.9-5.4 and 5	54	1923,7-16,133	103	1923,7-16,61
	1923,7-16,48 and 49	55	1923,7-16,132	104	GR 1981.9-5.7
4	1923,7-16,6	56	1923,7-16,136	104	1923,7-16,51
5	1923,7-16,9 and 10	57	1923,7-16,134	105	GR 1981.9-5.8
6	1923,7-16,30 and 31	58	1923,7-16,135	105	1923,7-16,56
7	1923,7-16,64 and 65	59	1923,7-16,137	106	GR 1981.9-5.16
8	1923,7-16,92	60	1923,7-16,122 and 127	106	1923,7-16,109
9	1923,7-16,8	61	1923,7-16,129	107	GR 1981.9-5.14 and 15
10	1923,7-16,54	62	1923,7-16,128	107	1923,7-16,90 and 91
11	1923,7-16,55	63	1923,7-16,105	108	GR 1981.9-5.3
12	1923,7-16,14	64	1923,7-16,106	108	1923,7-16,5
13	1923,7-16,15	65	1923,7-16,107	109	GR 1981.9-5.10 and 11
14	1923,7-6,59	66	1923,7-16,103	109	1923,7-16,62 and 63
15	1923,7-16,73	67	1923,7-16,104	110	GR 1981.9-5.13
16	1923,7-16,57	68	1923,7-16,102	110	1923,7-16,74
17	1923,7-16,119	69	1923,7-16,101	111	1923,7-16,13
18	1923,7-16,120	70	1923,7-16,29	112	1923,7-16,84
19	1923,7-16,39 and 40	71	1923,7-16,4	113	1923,7-16,83
20	1923,7-16,41 and 42	72	1923,7-16,58	114	1923,7-16,85
21	1923,7-16,43 and 44	73	1923,7-16,52	115	1923,7-16,86
22	1923,7-16,87	74	1923,7-16,47	116	1923,7-16,88
23	1923,7-16,110 and 111	75	1923,7-16,46	117	1923,7-16,116
24	1923,7-16,12	76	1923,7-16,112	118	1923,7-16,121
25	1923,7-16,12	77	1923,7-16,45	119	GR 1969.11-1.1
26	1923,7-16,108a	78	1923,7-16,60	119	1923,7-16,38
27	1923,7-16,98	79	1923,7-16,47b	120	GR 1969.11-1.2
28	1923,7-16,108b	80	1923,7-16,53	120	1923,7-16,75
29	1923,7-16,32	81	1923,7-16,113	121	GR 1969.11-1.3
30	1923,7-16,99 and 100	82	1923,7-16,71	121	1923,7-16,76
31	1923,7-16,16	83	1923,7-16,149	122	GR 1969.11-1.4
32	1923,7-16,20	84	1923,7-16,67	122	1923,7-16,77
33	1923,7-16,21	85	1923,7-16,68	123	GR 1969.11-1.5
34	1923,7-16,22	86	1923,7-16,66	123	1923,7-16,78
35	1923,7-16,23	87	1923,7-16,7	124	GR 1969.11-1.6
36	1923,7-16,24	88	1923,7-16,82	124	1923,7-16,79
37	1923,7-16,25	89	1923.7-16,81	125	GR 1969.11-1.7
38	1923,7-16,27	90	1923,7-16,33	125	1923,7-16,80
39	1923,7-16,28	91	1923,7-16,36 and 37	126	1923,7-16,93
40	1923,7-16,26	92	1923,7-16,34 and 35	127	1923,7-16,1
41	1923,7-16,18	93	GR 1924.5-2.1	128	1923,7-16,95
42	1923,7-16,17	94	GR 1924.5-2.2	129	1923,7-16,89
43	1923,7-16,19	95	GR 1924.5-2.3	130	1923,7-16,94
44	1923,7-16,123	96	GR 1924.5-2.4	131	1923,7-16,114 and 115
45	1923,7-16,125	97	GR 1924.5-2.5	132	1923,7-16,96 and 97
46	1923,7-16,126	98	GR 1924.5-2.6	133	1923,7-16,117 and 118
47	1923,7-16,124	99	GR 1924.5-2.7	134	1923,7-16,70
48	1923,7-16,131	100	GR 1981.9-5.1	135	1923,7-16,72
49	1923,7-16,130	100	1923,7-16,2	136	1923,7-16,145
50	1923,7-16,138 and 139	101	GR 1981.9-5.2	137	1923,7-16,146 to 148
		101	1923,7-16,3	138	1923,7-16,150

Colour Plate 1 Catalogue nos 84, 85, 86, 7, 6, 26, 72, 9, 15, 23, 8

Colour Plate 2 Catalogue nos 2, 1, 5, 92, 87

Colour Plate 3 Catalogue nos 10, 4, 11, 3, 29B

Colour Plate 4 Catalogue nos 24a,b,c, 70, 14, 25